by Anna Banti

Artemisia

Translated and with
an afterword
by Shirley D'Ardia
Caracciolo

University of Nebraska Press
Lincoln

First Bison Book printing: 1995
Most recent printing indicated
by the last digit below:
10 9 8 7 6 5 4 3 2 1

Originally published as *Artemisia*
© 1953 by Anna Banti

⊛ The paper in this book meets the
minimum requirements
of American National Standard for
Information Sciences –
Permanence of Paper for Printed
Library Materials,
ANSI Z39.48-1984.

Library of Congress
Cataloging in Publication Data
Banti, Anna.
[Artemisia. English]
Artemisia / by Anna Banti;
translated and with an afterword
by Shirley D'Ardia Caracciolo.
p.   cm. –
(European woman writers series)
ISBN 0-8032-1203-8
(alkaline paper)
ISBN 0-8032-6119-5 pa.
1. Gentileschi, Artemisia,
b. 1597 or 8 – Fiction.
I. Title.   II. Series.
PQ4827.O635A913   1988
853'.912 – dc19   88-6498   CIP

Contents

To the reader

Anna Banti

Another convergence and alliance of past and present, another instance of historical-literary symbiosis, an attempt at infusing into the polluted swamp of contemporary literature the pure spring waters of our language as it once was: such were the ambitions of the story which, under the title "Artemisia," had reached its final pages in the spring of 1944. That summer, due to events of war which were unfortunately in no way exceptional, the manuscript was destroyed.

To justify the heartbroken obstinacy with which my memory never tired, during subsequent years, of remaining true to a character of whom it was perhaps too fond, is what these new pages should, at least, succeed in doing. But because this time the aim of the narrative was to preserve only the commemorative form of the unfinished story and because the writing of it became bound up, instinctively, with personal emotions too imperious to be ignored or betrayed, I think that the reader is owed a little information about the life of Artemisia Gentileschi, one of the most talented female artists, and one of the few, recorded by history. She was born in Rome in 1598 to a family of Pisan origin. Daughter of Orazio, an excellent painter. Her honor and her love violated on the threshold of womanhood. The reviled victim in a public rape trial. She established an art school in Naples. And bravely set off, in or about the year 1638, for heretical England. One of the first women to uphold, in her speech and in her work, the right to do congenial work and the equality of spirit between the sexes. Biographies do not indicate the year of her death.

Artemisia

∽

"Do not cry." In the silence that separates each of my sobs this voice conjures up the image of a young girl who has been running uphill and who wishes to deliver an urgent message as quickly as possible. I do not raise my head. "Do not cry": the suddenness of these three syllables bounces back now like a hailstone, a harbinger, in the heat of summer, of high, cold skies. I do not raise my head; there is no one beside me.

Few things exist for me in the white, troubled dawn of this August day as I sit on the gravel of a path in the Boboli gardens, wearing, as in a dream, only a nightdress. From the waist up I am racked with sobs; I cannot help it, in all honesty, and my head is bent on my knees. Beneath me, amidst the pebbles, are my bare, gray feet; above me, like the waves over someone who is drowning, are the muffled sounds of people going up and down the slope I have just descended, people who have no time for a woman huddled up in tears. People who at four o'clock in the morning are pushing forward like frightened sheep to have a look at their city in ruins, to see for themselves the reality of the terrors of this night during which the German mines one after the other shook the earth's crust. Without being aware of it, I am crying for what each one of them is about to see from the vantage point of Forte di Belvedere and my sobs continue to boil over, senselessly, revealing in flashes, like crazy motes in the eye, the bridge of Santa Trinita, golden turrets, a small, flowered cup I drank from as a child. And once more, as I stop for an instant and in my disarray take stock of the fact that I shall nonetheless have to stand up, I am touched briefly by the sound of that "Do not cry," as by a receding wave. I finally raise my head, but already it is only a memory and as such I pay it heed. I stop crying, stunned at the realization of my most grievous loss.

Under the rubble of my house I have lost Artemisia, my companion from three centuries ago who lay breathing gently on the hundred pages I had written. At the same time as I recognize her voice, hordes of swirling images pour out from hidden wounds in my mind; images, at first, of a disillusioned and despairing Artemisia before she died, in spasms, like a dog that has been run over. Images, all of them crystal clear and sharp, sparkling under a May sun. Artemisia as a child, skipping among the artichokes in the monks' garden on Pincio hill, a stone's throw from her house; Artemisia as a young girl, shut in her room, holding her handkerchief over her mouth to stifle her sobs; and hot-tempered, her hand raised in anger, calling down curses with knitted brow; and a young beauty, with bent head and a faint smile on her lips, all dressed up in a slightly severe gown, on these paths, on these very paths; the Grand Duchess will be passing any moment. I begin to talk to her, without crying, beneath the ashes of the explosions: And what about the window on Borgo San Jacopo that you looked out of onto the Arno? The portrait of your friend the singer who is buried in Santa Felicita? I cannot reach her any more; or else she has grown too small, even become a babe in arms, along with the babies of the refugees who have begun once more to cry from hunger under the colonnade. The images continue to flow with a mechanical, ironical ease, secreted by this shattered world like ants from an anthill: I cannot stop them nor recognize those which oppress me most. The can of milk to be distributed in two hours' time at the welfare center, the faces of the complaining women, each one with her instant expression of disgruntlement and dejection, the two whining beggars, the epileptic looking for his unobtainable medication, the angina patient suffering an attack, the tubercular street singer, the five cunning children getting double rations. By some miracle, Angelica, the little paralytic, brings up the rear of the procession. I remember her pale blue eyes, spellbound but faithless, and how her mother the peddler says of her "That one's so religious." Those eyes tempted me with another story at a time when I did not know that I would lose Artemisia; and as I wonder whether Angelica was very frightened or not, I see at the height where her head would be, and more clearly than has ever happened before, the small, green-tinged face of a neglected child with eyes bordering on gray and dull blond hair, delicate features expressing pride and ill-treatment: Artemisia at ten years of age. In order to further reproach me and make me regret her loss, she lowers her eyelids, as though to let me know that she is thinking about something and that she will never tell me what it is. But I can guess: "Cecilia, are you thinking about Cecilia Nari?" I can feel her, with a young girl's despair, gripping my knees. I have still not got up onto my feet and now my sobs are for myself and her alone; for her born in 1598, old in death, the death that is all around us, and now buried in my fragile memory. I had presented her with a friend; I must reassure her even though I do not believe, as happens with adults, that I can give her friend back to her. And in the sympathy I feel for her I find an excuse for myself, an excuse beyond my control, an excuse born of today. Angelica has Cecilia's eyes, Cecilia's illness; that is why I hold her dear. I recall, I recall very clearly just what happened.

Cecilia Nari, the daughter of gentlefolk who had a palazzo on Via Paolina and Artemisia Gentileschi, the oldest child of Orazio, a Pisan artist living in Rome, had become friends. The window of the large attic where Cecilia's room is situated projects out over the steep escarpment that Artemisia reaches by jumping down from Trinità dei Monti where she lives in a wretched little house that belongs, in fact, to the Naris. Artemisia stands on the small mound at the edge of the escarpment and is not afraid to stretch her arm across the ravine to reach the stone window ledge on which the sickly young girl places something for her to eat every day. Cecilia smiles—she smiles like Angelica—and enjoys the fear of imagining that Artemisia might fall, while the latter shows off, dancing and jumping, sticking first her right leg and then her left out over the ravine. "Did you see that?" Suddenly she crouches down on the stones and rough grass and eats the cake or biscuits, never taking her eyes off Cecilia and making small mute signs of greeting, like someone going off in a boat. When she has finished, the conversation begins. "My mother has gone out," says Cecilia in a sharp, shrill voice, her small bony chest heaving, and it is not unlike the shrill sounds the swallow makes as it dives in to find its nest under the eaves. Artemisia listens very attentively, but her head sways and she carries on chewing as though thinking of something quite different. "She has gone out in the carriage," Cecilia continues, "to the festival of the Pace." Numerous are the feast days in Rome and

6

equally numerous for the two girls are the occasions when together they can savor the pleasure of their lonely freedom, a sense of adventure tinged with melancholy. Cecilia cannot go out, and who is there to take Artemisia for a walk? These are the days when even the servants and the nuns rush off to the illuminations and festivities, and Palazzo Nari, empty from top to bottom, means as much to the small prisoner as the whole of the Pincio hillside in its rusticity and dust does to the other girl, who is free to wander. The silence rises from the blades of grass straight up to the cloudless sky; the creaking of Cecilia's armchair barely impinges on it at all. "How many carriages do you have then?" Artemisia asks aggressively, but her eyes are elsewhere as she grips between thumb and middle finger the legs of a grasshopper she has captured by stealth. Cecilia shrugs her shoulders, two small cartilaginous wings: "How should I know? maybe twelve, thirteen. . . . " "And can't you walk today either?" As a young child Artemisia was quite cruel, and now she makes as if to throw the grasshopper at the other girl's head: her face puckers, feigning such a fierce expression of concentration and satisfaction that it alone is enough to justify Cecilia's howl of fright. "Don't, don't." "You're so silly," says Artemisia, suddenly grown cheerful and full of affection. She gets to her feet, throws the insect into the ravine, and pushes up onto her shoulders the sleeves of her simple dress made of coarse material. "Now I'll jump over and pay you a visit." Another shriek from the invalid as Artemisia steps back as though to take a leap. Then, in a heap of limbs and clothes on the ground, she laughs. Thus the hours pass.

Rarely does Cecilia ask a question, for few give her a reply: even her nursemaid barely interrupts what she is doing to exclaim, "If only Our Blessed Lady would take her." But she knows that Artemisia's father paints saints such as her aunt, the nun, in fact even bigger. "This tall, this wide," demonstrates Artemisia, spreading her arms and legs as wide as she can, standing on the mound. "Now he's doing a Saint Sebastian, completely naked, with the arrows and the wounds and the blood running down. Yes, real blood," she specifies shamelessly, spurred on by the amazement in the blue eyes, "whoever's modeling for Saint Sebastian has to put up with being hurt." When she talks of her father, of his painting, of his successes, with a mixture of innocent invention and plain truth, Artemisia in her haste swallows both the sounds and the meanings of words. "There's the executioner with his mouth open, his teeth clenched, his sword in his hand, you can feel the draught caused by the blow. There's Magdalene, who's really Caterina, the washerwoman's daughter, she's lovely, with blond hair, she gets tired of kneeling, daddy won't let her talk to us. I'm the angel with wings." "Wings, what wings?" asks Cecilia, overcome with wonder. "Real wings made of feathers, Vincenzo in the convent sewed them. In fact, one of these days I'll fly with them." As always, when the inventing has become outrageous Artemisia hardens her expression and looks from side to side in imitation of a woman who has a lot to do, confident of what she does and says. Cecilia makes no reply to this, but her eyes become lifeless crystals, as devoid of expression as though closed. She has visibly gone off into an impenetrable, nocturnal world of her own and Artemisia can see her making certain twitching movements, the uneasy gestures of an abandoned girl attempting to keep herself company with her own limbs. The silence that had risen from the earth to the sky, to the earth returns shatteringly and glides into the ravine that begins underneath the girls' eyes and ends behind Palazzo Nari in a ditch full of broken crockery, rags, dead rats, filthy water. Face to face, it seems as though the two friends no longer know one another, as though life, or death, has already separated them; then a murmuring is heard, it is Artemisia thinking aloud as she does when, after running, she stops alone among the bushes on the hill. "Monica wants her woollen blanket back, and Cecco is cold." Or else, "One more Christmas, one more Easter, then I'll be twelve and can get married." Or, in a sing-song voice, "Daddy's better than all of them, even uncle Cosimo who is a Vatican official said so. Now he's paintin' for the monks."*

To have remembered that at the age of ten Artemisia used to say, "Now he's paintin' for the monks," truncating the flow of her inherited Tuscan speech with a harsh borrowed accent, seems to me a measure of success, evidence of my belief in her story. I continue with my recollections. The sun is already casting long shadows, it is nearly six in the evening. Outside, everything is still bright, but in the attic the shadows are advancing every minute. Ersilia the nursemaid comes in puffing from the heat of the festivities, sweating in her best bodice, impatient and concerned, in her hand a cup with an herbal tea, on her lips complaints: "Jesus, Mary and Joseph, saints above, just look at who's alive while fathers of families die." She does not embrace her charge, but from under her taffeta apron she digs out sweets from the fair, almond cakes, hard cookies and a holy medal. She seems unaware of Artemisia; nonetheless she puts the sweets on the window ledge. I can see the effort of the trembling gesture with which Cecilia pushes them towards her friend, the shiny skin of her small hand. I do not know how Artemisia takes them. And I can see too the movement of unspoken, almost austere fatigue with which she lowers her bruised eyelids with their sparse lashes over the pale blue eyes, and the way her small shoulders sink back into the cushion as her mouth pouts childishly and then curls in an adult grimace of contempt, the innocent expression of pain borne too long.

Perhaps it was due to this grimace, rendered more fastidious and arrogant by the breath of youth, that a year later Artemisia secretly said goodbye to Cecilia, for in that spring she had become a woman and bound her waist tightly be-

*This is a regional English accent which, although it conveys the idea of the abbreviation of words, is probably meaningless to American readers, and would therefore need a regional American equivalent which I am unable to provide.

neath her small breasts, in the fashion of the other girls in her neighborhood. Now she had to go by another route to reach Cecilia's high window. Once more Orazio Gentileschi had moved house, a restless man left without a wife (he had had three in ten years, and the last one, a redhead, had run off with Monsignor's cook) and with all those children. He lived now in Via della Croce in a state of extreme touchiness over that daughter of his who was growing up and whom he wanted to enter the convent, and woe to her if he found her roaming around the streets as she did as a child. He no longer had apprentices: he had dismissed the last one over six months ago, the English boy with the pale eyes and fair hair who every evening would stand at the door of the wretched house shouting, "Come on puss, come and eat, damn you!" When Orazio was out of the house he would ask the neighbors in a contemptuous way to keep an eye on his door to see that his daughter did not go out. Then he would come back late in the evening, and Artemisia and Francesco would have fallen asleep at the table, beside the plate of cold soup. But now Artemisia had discovered that she could go out if she joined the women and older girls as they went busily from church to monastery to the kitchens of the rich, and also that she could use the excuse of getting a candle or some oil for the lamp. Already there was gossip because every now and then she would separate from them and disappear for about an hour. They would see her set off along the road that ran between the fields and wink to one another, not knowing that she was going to see Cecilia.

But she went rarely and the last occasion was on an October day with the sun hanging in the sky like a golden medal and the air so transparent that the fragrance of the musk-scented oil that she secretly put in her hair rose up to Cecilia's nostrils. Anything could have happened during the summer to either of the two girls without the other knowing, so seldom had they seen one another. And Artemisia began to tell her that she too knew how to paint now; that her father, who frequented all the most important people, was teaching her; and even Agostino Tasso, gentleman and famous painter, was explaining perspective to her, so that they were all saying, even Cosimo the Vatican official who has become very rich . . . It was at this point that Cecilia's mouth, twisting in its customary reflex of pain, appeared to her friend as the elegant mouth of a bored lady. Two small feathery curls had grown behind Cecilia's ears, she was wearing a blue scapular round her neck and a plain gold band on the fourth finger of her right hand which, abandoned in her lap, had a distant, precious fragility, and for the first time Artemisia became aware of the wide gulf that inexorably separated her from that hand. Vexation, regret, bitterness and jealousy, and underneath it all an obscure feeling of incurable unworthiness, like a silent moan. "Very, very rich," she carried on, blinded by a caustic Tuscan anger, "and he sends me boxes of sweets and sherbets and Spanish wines and gold chains. . . . " The impetuosity of her inventions opened a treacherous crack through which the real Cosimo came on stage in person; the fat, white Vatican official, his hands eternally in the belt of his trousers; this vague uncle Cosimo, vague patron of artists in need, with his illegitimate offspring, his tarnished silverware and secondhand velvets. Her boast, "And he'll give me a dowry," retrieved from the memory of him whispering heavily into her unwary ear, collided with the blinding realization of an uneasiness that now licked at her feet like a dirty dog, and she could not articulate it. "Fresh mushrooms, small mushrooms," sang the tired, gentle voice of the usual peasant on the corner of Via Ferratina. Without saying a word, Cecilia arched her back with a sigh and her nursemaid came running over, all attentive and obsequious in her role as lady's maid. "Farewell, farewell," shouted Artemisia as she turned away, finding again the reckless agility of a young child as she leapt from stone to stone and disappeared. She was crying on the road between the vineyards as she careered down to the bottom, and the men dressing the vines watched her uncomprehendingly. She tore the dress she had mended for her visit to Cecilia and never wore it again.

In the courtyard of the Palazzo Pitti the human cicadas are screeching: already it is midday, it has been light for eight hours, the South Africans have been here for six and the women have been kissing them, as we could see from the broken windows of the Palatine gallery, our refuge. In the burning sun an overpowering nausea attacked those standing watching. With an unforgiveable lack of tolerance I banish Artemisia in her dismay and regret: I am ashamed of the persistence with which I have kept her here all morning in the midst of war. But I know that I will relapse into my madness, and already I can feel her grinding through clenched jaws, as though my own, "It's not true, Cosimo never laid a finger on me." She is obsessed with her departure from Cecilia, with what Cecilia must have thought, with what she must have heard; those malicious servants in the house, that nursemaid who would not look at me.

When I think of the destroyed manuscript, of the caution and discrimination with which I gave life to a protagonist now so real, I no longer know what I regret the most. I am shocked by the impetus with which I am carried beyond the limits my memory allows me, beyond the bounds of the story, and yet I have to swear that Cecilia Nari meant no ill when she curled her lips; it was the fault of the pain that had by then come to govern her behavior, that was increasingly demanding her attention. She died a year later. To be precise, in the year 1611, in the month of April. I specify this, half closing my eyes against the sun which is red under my eyelids, like the flames of the torches at her quiet funeral, which to tell the truth was not really all that quiet. The Naris ostentatiously displayed her release; the procession of unmarried girls in white and black, sky-blue and gray, stretched from Via Paolina to San Lorenzo. Friends made in childhood always remain children; Artemisia cannot take in the fact of Cecilia's death. "You didn't tell me." Then, beside the torches, she finds herself once more in the tomb of her shame, a red-hot tomb, and I begin anew to console her. "She knew nothing about it, she knew nothing of love, of desertion, of betrayal. The only story Ersilia ever told her was that of Genevieve. She thought you were a sort of Saint Barbara the warrior; from her windows you seemed as tall as the tower of Mount Trinità." In my improvised role of comforter, the words I had written and lost become priceless, as though they were a unique text, and my grief is made all the more acute as Artemisia, her confidence restored, regains her dignity. Having been driven out of the rational time-setting of her story, she now carries all her ages with her mysteriously, and I watch her go off with the same hard expression Diana had between the ages of eighteen and twenty when, forced to marry as an expedient, she rejected her husband and lived in solitude.

I come upon her once more on the lawn up at the Forte di Belvedere, where people are lying out on the grass at the risk of being machine-gunned. "I took no notice of what people were saying about me, the whole neighborhood of Santo Spirito and Sant'Onofrio. I walked tall, my eyes opened wide, not looking at anyone. I used to go out alone, in defiance." The movement of her lips as they curl is just like that of Cecilia's, by whom she was hurt. "By whom she was hurt." These words were written about halfway down one of the pages and a drop of water had smudged the line. So now Artemisia—and not only Artemisia—is succumbing to the force of memory. Silently she moans, like a Medusa among her snakes, and once again she is supine, crushed in a white sleep of dust, turning her head to one side like a woman in death searching for her last breath. Dusk has overtaken us; this time yesterday Florence and all her stones were solid, everything that they sheltered was intact. Down below in the city the last beams are caving in; there are reports of mysterious fires burning among the rubble.

13

Cursed night is upon us once more, but amid the terms of my lethargic sleep, striking terror on the floor of the palace, there intrudes another presence which demands to be dealt with at all costs. To avoid it I question her, not without a touch of malicious irony: "When are you going to stop regretting everything? Do you even regret Serafino Spada, whose name I invented? He whose hand trembled, as he took down the minutes of the trial, when you were condemned to the rope torture? Did he really have freckles and yellow but kind eyes? Was he from Bergamo? Arrived in Rome in 1608? The year Palazzo Farnese was burnt? And from the square he watched the people who lived in the neighborhood of St. Peter's passing buckets of water to put out the fire?" In the dark, in the brutal roar of war, Artemisia's face, underneath my tightly closed eyelids, becomes inflamed like a hot-tempered woman's. I could reach out and touch it; in the middle of her forehead I can see the vertical line that she had from an early age and which deepened as she grew older. She begins to scream into my ear like a furious sleepwalker; she has the jarring voice and mangled accent of a lower-class girl from the Borgo, the wornout but inexhaustible means by which the destitute express and justify themselves. And what else has Artemisia done but justify herself, from the age of fourteen onwards?

"Agostino used to come every day, you see. He came in with that special air of his, sometimes dressed as a Turk, sometimes as a dandy, with a chain hanging on his chest. He was great at playing Rugantino;* he made us children laugh, which was pretty kind of him, since he considered himself so highly. Daddy was painting and not saying anything. Agostino stopped to look at what I was drawing on that little board and he says, 'D'ya wanna learn about perspective?' We were living in the Santa Croce district. There

*A Roman mask character.

were two entrances, with people coming and going all the time. I did the cooking, even the cleaning, and I minded the children, see? They were still little, Francesco ten and Marco not yet in trousers. Beams on the ceiling, cold in winter, hot in summer. I couldn't open the window, someone would always make rude signs at me; that's what Rome was like. There was the guy dressed in a long cloak with the blond beard, red in the face as if he was always too hot; Pasquino the flunky, impudent and bare-chested, and Luca the tailor, who secretly sent me the green wool cloak; they all wanted to come in, it was no good keeping the doors closed. Daddy wanted to put me with the nuns, and then Cosimo the official would come with his carriage and take everyone off to the inn. Agostino used to sit beside me. I would cry, and laugh, I wanted to get married. My neighbor Tuzia used to come down to get water or firewood, she would hang around me the whole day, talking all the time. She'd say, 'Let's make a pie, I'll put honey in it.' She would make the dough so that I didn't ruin my hands, she'd bring the baby for me to do a portrait of him. She said it wasn't right for me to be in the house with all those men coming to buy paintings, gentlemen and merchants. 'Those types want to ruin you, but just you listen to me who could be your mother; there's Agostino there, he's dying for you. Cosimo told me so. Go on, ask him if he won't marry you. But be careful of Cosimo too. Keep him as a friend. He's the type who'd chase after you; he's got more women than Mohammed.' She cut up the pie, gave some to the children, bit into a slice: 'You'll have a baby too before the year's out. Marry Agostino, you goose, he can afford to have you going around in a carriage far better than Cosimo can.' Agostino would appear from goodness knows where. He would take me into the room for my lesson. Tuzia came behind us and closed the door. . . . I was fourteen years old."

"Fourteen years old," she goes on to stress in a tearful voice, with the last light of day, now a different Artemisia, a wronged and dignified young woman. It does not matter to

15

her that I am getting over my distress at having lost her. She vaunts the fact that she exists independently of me and she all but takes it upon herself to walk one step ahead of me when the sunny path along which I am walking turns a corner into the shade. Paths hedged with box and clipped holmoak, sufficiently wide to allow two women in stiff skirts to pass in comfort. Her language is soft, modulated, drawn from all sorts of experiences, experiences of telling an everlasting story which, from being painful, can turn into pathetic boasting for the benefit of a friend. "Fourteen years old! I tried to defend myself, but to no avail. He had promised to marry me, he promised it right up to the end, the traitor, to thwart me of my revenge. He'd given me a ring with a turquoise: 'With this ring I am married to you," he'd say. I underwent torture in front of him, his face turned gray and he did not utter a sound." These the confidences she embellished for the sake of her friend the singer, Arcangela Paladini, a pale-skinned brunette with a sharp nose who just a moment ago had come out of the old Duchess's bedroom. The two artists stroll along like ladies of rank, and the rhythm of their steps is accompanied by the jangling of their inexpensive necklaces; in silence they wonder how to proceed with their theatrical friendship in a dignified manner. But Arcangela's shadow is fragile and the refugees in the courtyard are shouting in ill temper; nothing simpler than for me to take Arcangela's place and once more force Artemisia into the harsh sincerity of the present. Unsteadily she follows the troubled remembrance of what I had written, of what I had tried to guess or sacrifice to the accuracy of her story. She bursts out with her exaggerated cry, so dramatic in such a young mouth: "So this is the ring you gave me, these the promises you made!" Serafino Spada, the Court clerk's young assistant, writes with his eyes half closed, deeply alarmed. Artemisia confesses to me: "He was ugly, Agostino was, thickset and sallow, and his face had turned deathly pale with fright. I didn't like him. I had never liked him. And, for greater effect, I threw the ring, I don't know how, at the judge. He was a fat, middle-aged man with a wart on his forehead and a nasal accent. He lived in the Giubbonari; his wife was called Orinzia. He ducked to one side when he saw me throw the ring; his eyes opened wide and the corners of his mouth drooped down. I thought he was going to make a scene but he didn't say anything, he thought all women were the same, all of them. . . . "

Now it is for my benefit alone that Artemisia recites her lesson; she wants to prove to me that she believes everything that I invented and she has become so docile that even the color of her hair changes, becomes almost black, and her complexion olive, such as I imagined her when I first read the accounts of her trial on the mold-spotted documents. I close my eyes and for the first time use 'tu' to her. "It's not important, Artemisia, it's not important that you remember what the judge thought of women; even if I wrote it, it wasn't true." With her head bent, her hair returns to its dull blond color, typical of an unhealthy child, smelling of sour sweat; but she insists. "Through the window of Corte Savella came blasts of heat, flies, the whining of the beggars quarreling in the street over the prisoners' leftover soup. Beside me, I could smell the stench of the two cops who still held in their hands the ropes and instruments of torture. One of them was compassionate; he had a watery eye. I was aware too, without looking at him, that Agostino's chin was trembling. I didn't care whether he married me or not, that he had, as they say, dishonored me. It was then that I told everything that had happened, everything in greatest detail. . . . " I must help her, though my fatigue is greater than hers. "It was not at the second but at the first examination that you recounted everything. Your father, who had made the charge in the heat of his anger, had left for Frascati: he did not want to see you. You were left in the hands of the neighbors, the whining Stiattesis, madam Tuzia the go-between, Cosimo the official; everyone was giving you different advice, but you wanted to do it your own way, as if in confession." She drinks in the words from my mouth, nodding her head in agreement. "We were alone in the room. Madam Tuzia was in the kitchen, busy at the chopping board. I said, 'I have a temperature, leave me alone.' He said, 'My temperature is higher than yours.' He took me by the hand, he wanted us to walk up and down the room; the door of my bedroom was open. He held me down on the bed by force, fighting tooth and nail, but I had spotted Francesco's knife on the coffer. I reached out and grabbed it, and used it with an upward motion, cutting the palm of my hand." The bewildered anatomical precision of Artemisia's interrogation as a young girl has no place here between us; the words that the midwives taught her after they examined her have passed across my memory like sparks, leaving sad ashes. Not even gentle Artemisia can remember them now. She rests her head on my shoulder, it weighs no more than a sparrow, and says in the voice of a convalescent, "Every time after that I used to bleed and Agostino would say that I had a weak constitution." Her grimace of contempt no longer serves a purpose either, her wide eyes take on a faraway expression, devoid of rancor, and they are the eyes of an innocent who will never be convinced by life's secret.

Through Artemisia I have come to realize all the forms, all the different ways in which the grief of a violated purity can express itself. I have gained this realization from Artemisia's mien of sacrifice and danger which is increased, along with everyone's regrets, by her regret at having in vain been brought back to life. Our paltry freedom is linked to the humble freedom of a virgin who, in the year sixteen hundred and eleven, has only the freedom of her own intact body, the eternal loss of which she cannot ever come to terms with. For the rest of her life she endeavored to replace it with another, higher and stronger, but her regret for that unique freedom never left her. I had thought, with my pages, to have alleviated it, but now it returns stronger than ever, similar to the movement of flotsam that appears and disappears on the wave on which it floats, seeming at times as though it must have been swallowed by the clear water.

Scorched a thousand times by the flames of her violation, a thousand times Artemisia steps back only to draw breath to throw herself once more at the fire. Thus was her wont then, thus does she behave with me today.

"Tell about the walk." She is the child pulling at the adult's sleeve, asking for her favorite story; she is the accused who never tires of calling on the sole witness in her favor. Once again she tries to step over the irreparable, to go against the current, to undo the event with an explanation; and she will not allow me to arrange her words. "You were pale after a whole winter spent indoors, and in the evening when your father left the door slightly ajar after his return from Monte Cavallo, Tuzia was there immediately, saying: 'This daughter of yours, Signor Orazio, really doesn't look well. I'm saying this for your own good, because the Observantine nuns want strong girls and the Mother Superior would send her straight back to you. I've always said: fresh air and prayer for good health.' Your father looked at you with a doubtful and weary expression and quickly said, 'Yes, Tuzia could take you for a walk if she wanted, early in the morning.' That summer morning the sun was veiled and pale; up above the cliffs of Trinità dei Monti you could see Cecilia Nari's window, closed. The sun came out as you turned into the San Giovanni road, a river of thick dust that rose up to the sky as the carriages rattled past. 'If only I had one of those for myself,' sighed Tuzia. She had brought the whole tribe with her, her hunchback daughter, the four boys, the baby who was crying, and even Francesco had wanted to come too, but he stayed at a distance, as though sulking. Past Santa Maria Maggiore there were two men standing at the foot of a holmoak, Agostino and Cosimo the official. 'Where are these ladies going so early in the morning?' said Cosimo, nudging Agostino's elbow, and then Francesco joined us. 'Your sister must be tired and there's the vineyard of a friend just here,' Agostino said to him as though he were an adult, but he shoved half a dozen sugared doughnuts into his arms. You carried on walking, leaving them all behind you. Tuzia was deep in talk, shouting and laughing; already you couldn't make out what she was saying. Then you heard her heavy breathing at your back: she was running up to you, chewing lozenges. 'D'you want one? They're sweet and they take your thirst away.' You did not reply, you walked on ahead, hurrying, you felt like crying, but you also felt a strange, shameful pride. Francesco too caught up with you, chewing his doughnuts. He too offered you some. Maybe Agostino and Cosimo had not moved, or maybe they were following you; you did not want to turn round."

Artemisia is not pleased: is the fact that she did not turn round supposed to be to her credit? She was expecting more, above all a logical, calm account, a carefully considered interpretation of her actions, the very thing that I can no longer give her, for she is too close to me. Having her follow me so closely means that she distorts the images and memories I have of her. Now it is she who tells me about the time she went to San Paolo, no longer a maiden, and yet every time it seemed to her that she was being violated.

"I went there by carriage. We lived in Santo Spirito at the time; the whole neighborhood knew about it and sometimes Agostino would say, half daring me, 'Why don't you give in to that fellow who wears the long cloak?' I thought he meant it, but then he would threaten to kill me. I got the idea into my head of going to San Paolo to have a look at father's altarpiece that I had never seen in position, and I felt in my heart that it would do me good. It was very windy but I wanted to go just the same; Tuzia was against it because of Agostino's threats. So I said, I'll go on my own; I thought then that after my disgrace I at least had the right to be as free as a man. Even the children got on my nerves when I thought about how they were born, but she came after me with all her brood, and I only had to see the way she tied her kerchief and blew her nose as soon as we were in the street to realize that we would not remain alone for long. There was a carriage stopped at the beginning of the street that ran alongside the river, totally covered in dust, and a man wrapped in a cloak standing with his hand on the door. I turned round to go back home because I had recognized Agostino's bowlegs, but the wind blew my hair right across my eyes and when I managed to open them again Agostino was there, signaling to me to get in and smiling as if it were all agreed. The carriage seemed as big as a cave; there was room for all of us, and inside was old man Stiattesi saying his rosary and sighing. 'So you want to go to San Paolo?' Agostino said as soon as he had closed the door, showing his rotten teeth. 'I'll take you there. Drive on, coachman!' My anger died down as I felt myself being bowled along; I grew calm and almost happy. I've always loved riding in coaches. He wanted to get out when we reached the open fields. Tuzia said her back was aching and the children would get lost in the ditches, the little devils. Only my Francesco wanted to get out with us but Agostino threatened him not to follow us. Francesco picked up a stone but then he dropped it quietly and watched us go off. The grass was spiky, the ground soft and I got my feet wet. The wind had dropped. I tried to imagine that I was wandering alone, lost; I closed my ears to the sound of Agostino's voice and foot-steps, but our shadows had already joined together. And so once again he did what he wanted. I was exhausted by the speed with which, at that time, I would change from being unwilling to giving in; and yet in the depths of my heart I never stopped struggling to the very end. That was the day Agostino gave me the ring with a solemn promise to marry me as soon as he got the certificates; and he said that his wife had been a loose woman and had surely died in Lucca. I said nothing, then all of a sudden I answered and it was as if someone were prompting me, with words that weren't mine. But that day, when we reached the church where the others were waiting for us, it seemed to me that I had changed forever. I felt like a young bride; I wasn't even ashamed. Tuzia pinched me connivingly, as was her wont, and my despair returned. I felt like hitting her. I had to go in, make the sign of the cross, look at my father's painting and listen to Agostino showing off: 'This part here isn't well drawn, there isn't enough light here, the color is too dark. In a loud voice Francesco said, 'I'm tired.'"

I am responsible for the silence that follows her agitated account of this episode, told with feverish haste and urgency. I decide that I will not let Artemisia speak again, nor will I speak for her again; in my present there is no longer any place for the past, or the future. But as I converse with the dust-stained living, her small, young voice stubbornly and fretfully repeats its question, "Don't I tell it right?" reminiscent of the inept manner of a silly, nosey woman; but Artemisia was a great woman. Just like an angry husband, I return to the attack: "As if you really believed what I had written! As if you really cared about what I have lost!" I find a clean stone on which to sit down. Another day of wartime is drawing to a close. I am tired and the avenues in the Boboli gardens are like one huge latrine. Around the meager fountain that was originally a plaything for the rich, ten women are fighting over the water, but I pay them no heed. I am a repentant bully trying to make amends, and Artemisia's third excursion is haunting me.

She received a message from Corte Savella, brought by a beggar covered in fake ulcers who climbed the stairs with a heavy tread. "Signora Artemisia is requested to come after six p.m., Signor Agostino wishes to talk to her." The man expressed himself with difficulty; he was a Sicilian, and when he reached the ground floor he slipped into the Stiattesis' one-room hovel and did not come out again. Later, old man Stiattesi came up the stairs, dragging his feet, his eyes watering, constantly grabbing first Artemisia's hand, then her arm, then her dress, in order to lend conviction to his argument and persuade her. "I cannot sleep or eat as long as this shameful situation is allowed to continue, you must both get married, as God commands. I'll go with you to Corte Savella, we'll tell Orazio we're going to the forty-hour devotions. Grazia will come too, she'll act as your mother, she's getting up from her bed specially." He kissed the floor, raised the crucifix to the sky, placed it on his chest.

It was already dark, Grazia, exhausted by her fever, could walk no further, and her husband told her to sit down on a step and wait for us; no one would bother her anyway because she was old. They passed Ponte Sisto, then, instead of heading for San Carlo, they turned left. "Don't tell anyone about this," the old man whispered, "don't tell Tuzia or Clementina that it was me who brought you. I'm the only one you can trust, you must keep it secret. Your father must never find out, for goodness sake, he has a terrible temper." The lamp in the guardroom had only just been lit because it was still flickering, and Stiattesi said, "Wait for me here," and he made his way to a table where two cops were playing cards with another man who had his back to her. When he turned round she saw it was Agostino. The old man doffed his cap to him, and stood bent over as if before a superior. They talked and talked. Every so often Agostino would move restlessly; he gave no sign that he was aware of Artemisia standing over by the door, he seemed to be in charge even in here. Finally the old man moved away from him and said in a loud voice, "Come forward, Signora Artemisia, your betrothed wishes to talk to you." His pedantic, oily voice provoked an outburst of coarse laughter from the dark corners of the room, and one of the soldiers, barring her way, pretended to bow to the young girl, then doubled up in scornful guffaws. One soldier was saying, "most noble lady," another was imitating a hen's cackle, a third trilled excessively, "My darling." By means of these impudent jeers the men revealed their invisible presence, inseparable from the stench of leather and sweat. "This is an honest proposal from a gentleman whose reputation is important to him," continued Stiattesi, looking round and at the same time smiling as if the jeering were no more than the racket made by children. "If you say that he wasn't the first, then the charges will be dropped, you'll get him out of jail and he'll marry you straight away. If it's true, you can make repentance; if it's a lie, offer it up for the souls in Purgatory. My advice is . . . "

Not a sound could be heard in the ensuing silence, but a deafening roar filled Artemisia's ears and all her senses, her blood turned to lead in her veins and her face was inflamed, if anyone bothered to notice, as though by a dark bruise. In the light of the lamp which, like a small bat, continually beat its shadow on the floor, Agostino is a dark shape looking at her, and it is impossible to attribute to him the character of a man, far less that of a friend or lover. Maybe he greeted her, maybe he said something, but now Cosimo Quorli the official bursts out, "Take courage, lovely maiden, you know how to write your name. Here is the paper and here is the bridegroom." And her salvation was due to the same instinct which, for a totally different reason, separated her from Cecilia: the impulse to turn around and flee. She was running through the night, the darkness was oppressive and heavy but not thick enough to drive out the memory of the red lantern and the confused sound of the voices of the policemen and prisoners, who were all taken by surprise at her flight. Maybe old Stiattesi was chasing her, but she knew how to run, thank God, without stumbling, and the road was smooth and trusting under her flying feet. She was not afraid of any unpleasant encounters, and when she realized that no one was pursuing her, her breathing immediately became slow and light once more, and she shouted to poor Grazia shivering on the step, as if it were broad daylight, "Come on, let's go." She was prepared to pick her up and carry her in her arms, she felt as strong as an ox. And everything went perfectly, as if by miracle: the streets were deserted, as were the front door and the stairs; no one saw her go up and close the door. Only those who have burnt with shame can call these trifles good luck. Tuzia was not there, Orazio had not come home. As quiet as a mouse, she slipped between the sheets without even a glance at her sleeping brothers, poor things. Her blood was swollen and distended, like a storm cloud; then it gradually liquefied and began to flow once more, pierced through with phrases and comments that were too quick, too desperately concise for a brain as young as hers: "If only the dark would last forever, no one would recognize me as a woman, such hell for me, woe to others"—to mention just a few of the many.

That night it did not occur to her to redeem the memory of her former innocence and dwell on it, unable to believe what had happened, convinced that the outrage gave her some right to compensation, perhaps even to the victory of the wronged. She did not have the strength to hate her violent, cowardly lover, the go-betweens, the false witnesses, Cosimo, Tuzia and all the apprentices, washerwomen, models, barbers, painters, the parasites: people who seemed to have scarcely noticed her ever since she was a child and who instead had followed her hour by hour, substituting her actions and movements with unrecognizable ones in the presence of the judge. Today she feels guilty, guilty as everyone wishes her to be, guilty right from the time she stole strawberries in the monks' garden and pale Cecilia saw her. If they are treating her like this, they must be right: a stain has always marked her out to the eyes of others. Tuzia was right when she replied to Orazio, "Look after her yourself, the little whore"; it is right that the women of the neighborhood, crouched like cats on the windowsills in the courtyard, should exchange gossip about her latest doings every day in loud voices, without the slightest consideration. Consequently, her attitude of weary indifference reveals the prospect of a lonely, resigned future as an outcast, which will at least be her kingdom, as are hers this darkness and this bed in which she is hidden and the sleep which no one can prevent her from feigning if a light were to try to interrupt it. There she will dwell, mistress of her own self-pity and forbidden thoughts, different from the pure but also from the corrupt. She will be able to make her own reckonings, like the beggar counting his few coins that everyone wants to find out about. Time will be her companion; she will fill it in her own fashion, with tears, indifference, fun, into which no one will be able to intrude and which will secretly feed her tattered pride. And, finally, turning over onto her right side to fall asleep properly, "They'll see just who Artemisia is," she says. Her pride, girlish and slightly arrogant, comes now to comfort her, a black, childlike angel, innocent and strong, that slowly returns to watch over her. It is not familiar with the humility, the softness, the cautious, touchy uncertainty of the female character; nothing holds the wind back from its wings. It can only be stopped by a feeling of affectionate awe if Artemisia Gentileschi thinks of her father. But Orazio's difficult love has been removed from her and its great value is as a sword that slays all weakness, the very image of which is enough to pierce through. She must wean herself from it if she does not want to die of grief.

Artemisia's third excursion has set me once more on a path that has neither purpose nor end, as the days change but not the things and events around me. Nor does this obstinate labor change, a labor not of the memory, but of the images that from the memory draw an imperceptible sustenance. She who consoled me, who grieved and was alive with me, passionately alive, obsesses me like a character who cannot be ignored, of great renown, a shining example: a character whose biography is manifest, year by year, and worth reviving, hour by hour, especially now when her story is silent. Not one page has been recovered from the ruins, but there is the memory of a sort of textbook, an illustrated manual. Agostino acquitted and released due to the scheming of Cosimo the official and the venal services of Giambattista Stiattesi; Orazio Gentileschi returned once more to an intellectual indifference slightly tinged with disgust; Artemisia condemned by her shortlived, scandalous fame to an unruly, besieged solitude: all facts of which I avail myself— and I am unsure if I ought to be ashamed or not—as a sort of second Punic War. It is not difficult to guess what the African elephants ate in Italy; it is not difficult to imagine how Artemisia passed the evenings in the summer of sixteen fifteen. She is now seventeen years old. They have not moved house, Orazio is not bothered about what the neighbors remember when he himself has forgotten, and he is not troubled by the fact that every day his daughter meets people who can point their finger at her. In May sixteen hundred and twelve Luca Ponti, tailor, witness for Agostino, said insolently to the judge, "You know, in Rome all we talk about among friends is f—ing and fighting." The custom has not changed and Artemisia, despite the heat, keeps the windowpanes closed even in the middle of the day, lest anyone see her. Her brothers are working, Marco in the leather trade, Giulio as an apprentice and Francesco as a stucco-worker; they have the freedom of adults and in the evening they have dinner in a tavern, in the open air. At that hour Artemisia's prison-like pallor is tinged with green, her hair hangs down her cheeks like skeins of dull silk. She sits and draws until it grows dark and then, without opening the window, lights the lamp. Her models, clothed dolls and small statues, come from the studio of her father who works, eats and sleeps away from home at Monte Cavallo. With the ribbons and silks from her meager young girl's trousseau she attires the models, then adds flowers, fruit, a skull. At times these prepared, silent scenes terrify her if she so much as relaxes her visual attention. When that happens she gets up, walks round the room, which in this case is really the kitchen, for the house has no living room. She halts in front of the window but does not open it, grows spellbound listening to the great clamor of voices in the courtyard whose every sound she recognizes. Clementina is beating the eggs for an omelette and asking the new tenant for some basil. On the balcony Lucia is calling all her friends together to suggest an outing that evening to Sant'Onofrio because it is cool there. Mastro Pasquale's sons, who have come back from work, are cursing and asking for water to wash in. And from the ground floor where the Stiattesis still live there rises up an unfamiliar song for two voices: "Tell me, my love, tell me what is . . . "—which, more than anything else, heightens her desire to lean out, to listen, to examine, to observe. But the sound of Tuzia's drawling voice—she has now moved from the first to the second floor ("I'll pass the chamber pot to you in a minute, it really stinks . . . ")—is enough to cause her hand, already on the latch, to fall once more down by her side. One more turn round the room, a few meaningless gestures, move the pot from the cupboard over to the sink, pour herself a glass of water, and once again the young girl is seated with her pencil-holder in her hand. The lamplight, steadily winning against the dusk, multiplies the play of shadows in the folds of the garments and rekindles her interest in the subject: a new sheet of white paper is christened.

Her brothers return home late at night, but Artemisia has still not allowed herself to open the window even now that no one can see her, and breathe in the fresh air. She is still drawing with a skilled concentration that almost belies the signs of tiredness, her narrowed eyes surrounded by dark shadows. Giulio and Marco fall straight into bed, but Francesco stays and wanders round the kitchen, stroking the cat, trimming the lamp and always finds a way to pause for a second at his sister's back; a second and no more, for he knows well that Artemisia does not like anyone to watch her while she is working. In the end he cannot resist the temptation of drawing up a stool and sitting down too, with a sheet of paper in front of him and a piece of charcoal in his hand. He makes do with a small corner of the table and the portion of the model that is visible from where he sits. His hand, grown stiff through manual labor, gradually relaxes, and the silence of the night seems to relax as well in that occupation which is like a conversation for the Gentileschi family. The real conversation gets under way with mono-syllables and brief phrases and then Francesco's drawing proceeds slowly and distractedly; his gaze frequently wan-ders away from the paper and the model to rest on Artemisia's hands, on her work. Now he is not afraid of irritating her if he follows the movements of her pencil and if, leaning towards her, he studies her drawing at length. Her thin hand, lightly freckled on the back, is so intense in its absorption that it counts for both of them, secret and open at the same time, so much so that in the end the boy freely encourages and praises her. Sometimes he makes a few suggestions to her: "More light on the right-hand side," or corrects a graceless fold on the model's clothes, observations of an infallible eye. The hours pass, finally Artemisia yawns, and Francesco turns his attention from the drawing to her face. He does not say "Stop now," but with his elbows on the table and his head on his hands, in an attitude suggestive of relaxation, he begins to tell her about Carlo Veneziano who has such a lovely use of coloring, about what Borgianni did in Spain, about the Frenchman Valentino who is as irascible as Caravaggio, about the paintings that Lord Giustiniani has commissioned, about the painters in demand in Madrid or requested by the King of France. "They have hung the painting by Antiveduto." "Baglioni's San Lorenzo is not liked." Without being aware of it, Artemisia has stopped working. She listens, she asks questions, she even smiles with those pale, chapped lips, she even jokes. It has been so long since she last went outside, since she last saw her father's friends, since she was present at their conversations. And often Francesco keeps till last the surprise, the spark of happiness: "In the studio of Angelo the sculptor, the painter from Modena said, 'I'd love to be able to paint like that young girl who lives in San Spirito, Gentileschi's daughter.'" It is not easy, even for Francesco, to decipher the emotions on Artemisia's face: she hides them by bending down to gather up her paper, to pick up her pencil which has fallen onto the floor, but the harmony of the gestures with which brother and sister tidy the table and extinguish the lamp is worth as much as a handclasp, a sign of gratitude. Before he disappears behind the green curtain that hides his straw pallet, the boy opens the window and the cold night air is like a gift that he leaves for Artemisia. Who pauses to breathe it in before going to bed and feels a little dizzy and almost dazed by the great, high, distant sky against which the big bell of Saint Peter's seems to strike. Up there the stars form their own patterns as though they had been sprinkled through a luminous pounce bag and were awaiting a giant paintbrush. With her hot palms against the cold marble, her knees on the stool, Artemisia lets her head drop onto the windowsill, with the impression that she is sailing on to meet her destiny.

And sometimes she dreams that there are footsteps climbing the stairs, stopping outside the door, that there is a key turning in the lock. She is not dreaming, it really is her father, Orazio, who tonight returns home, and now enters the kitchen. Such fear, and such suppressed happiness. In suspense, turned to stone, the young girl witnesses a sort of cataclysm taking place in her own thoughts which very quickly formulate the facile conclusions that Orazio must come to in finding her still up, late at night, at the window. An abyss opens at her feet, she the eternally guilty one; if her father opens his mouth she will not know what to say and will immediately plunge straight into it. It is only a moment, but long enough for her to despairingly adore those clothes dampened by the night breeze, the hand that has painted all day long, that has held a glass and broken bread, far from her eyes: the severe brow, the unintentionally withering glance that is immediately withdrawn towards inner, mysterious satisfactions. In silence Orazio performs tired, distracted actions and now she is trembling, quivering, and she begins to speak. The truth is simple, honest, but Artemisia is not able to sustain it, just as she cannot bear the silence, just as a cracked vase can no longer hold fresh water. To make herself worthy of his trust she is ready to invent some offense, another lover; more probable, it seems to her, than this innocent lingering beside an open window. Yet it is the truth that issues awkwardly from her lips: "I was just standing here, I was hot, I was almost asleep." But it is so faltering, so mumbled, that no one would recognize it as such. Orazio in fact does not reply, maybe he has not even heard, so bitterly sated is he with suspicion and contempt; a state that his daughter shrewdly perceives and would love to change, by crawling on the ground, to show him, as it were, the color of her own contrite blood, a pointless fantasy. And pointlessly she dreams in her imagination of kissing his right hand that now strikes the flint, of going up and resting against his fatherly chest. Meanwhile, cast loose in a crazy instinct of self-defense, her voice goes on and on repeating words that sound so like excuses and lies, and the tone it takes on is that of a silly, whining, untrustworthy woman caught red-handed. Now Orazio has lit his lamp, now he is moving off, cold and grim, towards his room. "Good night," he utters before he disappears: Artemisia is stunned, emptied even of despair as she stands beneath the empty sky. It is only much later, at dawn, that she is able to cry and fall asleep on her bed.

But one evening near the end of August Orazio returned home unexpectedly, at six o'clock, before the neighbors had eaten, and the air filled with chatter and banter on the other side of the closed window emphasized even more Artemisia's isolation in her lonely work as she sat at the table, unmindful of her appearance in an old dress, a cup of milk set beside her sheets of drawings. No matter how insidiously she might fabricate the conviction of being suspected and judged badly, this time Artemisia could not but appear innocent. Her subject was a gray pigeon's wing, patiently sewn together and glued, which she was using as the model for the wing of an angel, and she had draped the dummy in a remnant of blue brocade. The blue was reflected in the girl's light eyes which she raised towards her father as he came in: she appeared to him as absorbed and as pure as when he used to draw her as a child, when she would stand quietly watching him paint. At first no words were spoken, but in Orazio's eyes was the genial light that appeared whenever he discussed painting or was being shown pictures, the reflection of a longed-for, happy activity. It was years since his daughter had seen it and it was a ray of sun that relaxed her hand holding the pencil, illuminated the sheet of paper, released her mortified limbs. As he bent over her she saw the laughter lines at the corners of his eyes contract, the prelude to a smile, a sign of satisfaction; with the fleshy part of his thumb he delicately softened a rather hard charcoal line in the angel's garment. He stood up again and she too began to get to her feet, timid but no longer awkward. Orazio said "Carry on," and went into the bedroom. A minute later she heard him whistling as he washed.

That evening in the Gentileschi household there was soup and an omelette as in all the other houses in the neighborhood, and father and daughter ate together, sitting opposite one another. Orazio had opened the window, the swallows flew past it, and the din in the courtyard, even Tuzia's unfailing voice, remained external just as if the shutters were closed. As he poured himself a last glass of wine Orazio began to speak and Artemisia was so happy that the meaning of the words escaped her; all she heard was the sound of his voice. It was a low, quiet voice, almost listless, and never more so than when he knew he was delivering a piece of news, to be greeted with interest or amazement. "I've finished at Montecavallo, I don't want to work in Rome any more, I need to travel. For the time being we'll go to Florence, I've heard from the Grand Duke, the time is right. There will also be a trip to Pisa." Orazio empties his glass and gets up from the table, his lean back outlined against the pale light from the window. His daughter remains seated among the dishes that she will have to wash up, but she is speechless, torn between fear and hope. "We'll go?" Who did her father mean? Maybe he wants to bring Francesco with him, maybe all the brothers; she will stay behind in Rome on her own. And then Orazio turned round, looked at her for a moment, then stared intently at the sink: "If you want to come, I'll take you with me, and with me you can work. But first you'll have to get married."

I will never be able to be free of Artemisia again; she is a creditor, a stubborn, scrupulous conscience to which I grow accustomed as to sleeping on the ground. It is no longer our conversations that bind me, as in the early days, but a sort of contract legally drawn up between lawyer and client, and which I must honor. In the meantime I can let my thoughts wander, practise certain stratagems on a memory which, at this point, I am concealing. Orazio said, "You'll have to get married." But already I am dragging Artemisia on a walk through the Boboli gardens, battered and deserted after the departure of the refugees; and I compel her to move along with the remaining few, the unhappy proprietors of this large, polluted area, there to meet prostitutes and rough soldiers, there to be soaked by the autumn rain. The rhythm of her story had its own moral and meaning which perhaps have collapsed with my recent experiences. A moral and a meaning with which I trifle. Artemisia will have to be satisfied with what follows next: today, the group of her Florentine girlfriends, on the rough gravel of the steep main avenue, each one with her own name—Violante the widow, Giovanna Sorri, the two Torrigiani sisters-in-law, Caterina the spinster—each one with her high, stiff, lace collar that gets caught up in the short hairs on the nape of the neck. They are slightly out of breath because they are walking uphill hurriedly, and each is losing more dignity than she would like. Signorina Gentileschi accompanies them rather unwillingly, caught between being sociable and her own natural reserve: these ladies honor me, but they must realize who I am, a talented artist, not one of their usual little singers. When the harsh, massive structure of the palace comes into view at the next bend, the injustice of my decision leaves a bitter taste in my mouth and compels me to take up once more, like an object that has been lost, that golden Roman October in which Artemisia is bent over a chest stuffing in clothes, household goods, the things that mean most to her in the world: the rest she will throw into the Tiber, for she won't be coming back to Rome again. She must not make a noise, lest the Stiattesis hear and suspect something, for her husband is one of them. But if she stops to dwell on the fact that she is going away with her father, that the great Gentileschi is taking her with him, then these precautions seem ridiculous to her and as she goes about her chores she bangs her heels loudly. Papers, old ribbons, letters, yes, the four letters from Agostino that she had kept up until now; all out of the window, thrown to the wind, who cares who sees them? As she leans out, offering herself heedlessly to the clear air—she feels as though she is already in the carriage—she catches sight of the feet of Giambattista, sitting on his doorstep, his gouty feet seeking the sun, long and thin like those of his son Antonio who disappeared on their wedding day. The girl is not aware that she has grown absent-minded for a moment, a severe frown on her brow, her arms hanging loosely, her hair moving in the breeze, as though waiting, listening for something. "My kerchiefs." She shakes herself and runs off to look for them in her bedroom.

But she could not free herself of an insidious feeling of anxiety which trembled in her hands and her throat right up to the last, in that unnatural silence that Orazio maintained now that he had made his decision, almost as if they were going to stay at home as usual. One by one her brothers had left, Giulio to Velletri, Marco to his employer's, and Francesco had found a place for himself in Strada Pia in a convent where he had the use of a studio. He wanted to set up his own studio, he said, but as soon as he uttered the words they seemed to bore a hole in his thin chest. He was talking too much: the Gentileschis, when they are happy, do not speak. And the place was so nice, a real bit of luck, with the advantage of having the Pope at Monte Cavallo during the summer, and nearby the vineyards of the best gentry, and models from among the farm laborers, without spending a penny. He was trying hard to appear decisive and shrewd, in the manner of experienced artists, but he must have been accomplishing very little in Strada Pia at the moment for he was constantly to be seen in San Spirito, one day bringing her a fine paintbrush, another some special chalk, just in case she ever needed to do some sketching, because in Florence you can't get chalk like it; and even the concoction for heart trouble specially brewed by his nuns. He would sit down, let her serve him a cursory meal, and if she had things to do in her room he would remain sitting there with staring eyes. Finally even his sister would stop going to and fro; her luggage was packed, and she too sat down with staring, troubled eyes. It was a month now since Orazio had made any mention of the move: maybe he had forgotten the project or his invitation to her, nor was there any way to guess at his intentions because he did not keep his things in the house. There was not even a pencil lying around anymore, or a piece of canvas, only a couple of old broken stretchers hanging on a nail. The cat was mewing: at moments like this Artemisia's anxiety beat like a pulse. "In a month's time," Francesco would say then, "you'll be in Florence, all settled in. Be very careful how you choose the direction the windows face. The light in Florence is white and treacherous; it's much better on the ground floor rather than on the top floor." Because Francesco always knew all about things he had never seen and expedients of which he had no need.

On the twenty-second of October, at dawn, Artemisia set off. The truth does not lie in the date, but in the eternal constancy of the words that establish it. But a date is needed, as it was needed then to make a young girl's heart leap, a girl who had never been away from home and who there had suffered disgrace. The porters carried down the chests and a corner of the heaviest one chipped the wall on the stairs. The neighbors were astounded; Giambattista Stiattesi, unhonored father-in-law, raised his arms to the sky for many days afterwards. But in the meantime the young blond girl was leaving, seated between her father and a fat priest from the Romagna who was returning, he at once said, to Bologna. After a night spent sitting on a chair, fully dressed, the precarious immobility of those first minutes of the journey filled her with a dizzy feeling of eternity. Stablemen and postilions were moving round with lanterns as though it were still dark; flickering lights shone through the shuttered windows of inns. A beggar, stretched out on a stone bench, looked as though he were dead. A rider with a full, Spanish-style moustache made his mount rear up, terrifying a groom who had a limp. The bell in the church of Santa Maria del Popolo rang and for a moment Artemisia had the disastrously absurd idea of getting out of the carriage, going into the church, hearing mass. She was tired; maybe if she fell asleep she would be able to lean against her father's shoulder in a long, infinitely sweet slumber. But when the big carriage moved off ("Bon voyage" and "Good luck," two voices shouted almost simultaneously) her now closed eyes clearly saw Francesco, round-shouldered, with the keys in his hand, saying, "This winter." A memory of yesterday, already so far away.

I discover that one moonlit evening in Naples, overlooking the sea, Artemisia said, "I too have kept a written record of my first journey." She was speaking to Tommaso Guaragna whom she had known for only six hours. She was thirty-six years old, and she was lying. She was lying in a sort of good faith, lending to her memory the image of a sheet of white paper covered in attractive handwriting; and it was the least she could do, so strongly did she taste the flavor of the eels in Bologna and feel the hardness of the bed in San Quirico and hear the voice of the postilion saying, "From here to Radicofani it's downhill all the way." But the real truth of that week lay entirely in the vindication of her childhood, a childhood suspended but now being restored to her, so that the sights, the people, the surprises, even the fear, none of these mattered in comparison to the future that had been given back to her. Everything rested on the unutterable certainty that Orazio was beside her and that she could fall asleep and wake up a hundred times over and always see him there. She admired his relaxed bearing, neither that of an artisan nor a merchant, the way he entered into a conversation and withdrew from it again, his lordly expansiveness with money, the frankness of his humor and laughter. Faultless it seemed to her were his clothes made of fine cloth, of a slightly severe cut, and his thin beard speckled with gray. To be the daughter of this gentleman, to lightly place her hand on his sleeve, to talk only in monosyllables like a high-class young lady, this was enough to make her feel exonerated from every memory, from every obligation. The longer she stayed silent, the more absurd grew her hopes. Who could tell whether that whole marriage, arranged from one day to the next, was not just a pretense carried out for the purpose of atonement, a fiction that Orazio had put together in order to protect her from the dangers of being a disgraced maiden? All ready and waiting for her in Florence, perhaps, was a noble husband whom her father had secretly chosen for her. In the autumn she would go to their villa, one of those small castles with orchards of apple and other fruit trees; she would not meet her husband until everything was final, just like a well-brought-up young lady. She would forget her painting, look after her family instead. Artemisia puts these dreams aside and picks them up again like a lady with her embroidery at the fireside: for her the fireside is this carriage seat, her truest home since she was born. One of the wheels broke and they had to spend the night at Buonconvento. It was there that Orazio's face began to darken; on it his daughter read inflexible plans that had nothing in common with her incoherent dreams. He was in a hurry: why on earth was he in a hurry? And she began to feel alone once more.

The first autumnal wind is blowing, the first fine rain is falling. And in the rain they walk round Siena, Gentileschi and his daughter, he in front and she behind, slightly out of breath, clumsily holding up her skirts to keep them out of the mud. They were searching the churches for modern paintings, particularly works by one Rutilio, a young man of great promise, so everyone was saying. But Siena was full of stuffy, old-fashioned works and Orazio went back to the inn and started to drink out of annoyance and vexation. He drank too much, he quarrelled over the bill: bad signs. Then he found out that a carriage was leaving at one o'clock in the morning. He wanted to reserve a seat immediately and said to his daughter, "If you want to stay here and sleep, you can. I have to be in Florence by tomorrow evening." The good times were over. They crashed down the stony hills in a thick fog that hid the road. The door was broken; the freezing air blew in. Orazio sat in silence, his thoughts far away. And back into Artemisia's mind came the ungainly, makeshift husband she had married.

I was on my own (this commemoration often slips from the third person), I was on my own in Florence for most of the day. My room in the inn looked onto a small courtyard where there was no light, neither good nor bad. I did not dare unpack my painting materials. The landlady brought me my meals in the room. Father came back at night: I would hear him laughing as he took leave of his friends. He had begun to talk in the Tuscan dialect again. "You've plenty of time," he said, "to see the city." And one evening: "I've made a deal with Buonarroti, if you feel up to it you can paint the ceiling in one of his rooms. I'll leave you enough to eat; if you feel like working, go ahead, if not . . . " He began to swear like he did when the scandal was at its height: injustice is a wine that inebriates both judge and victim. I had experienced the taste of that wine. His inebriation aside, I realized that he was looking for an outlet for some cruel and arbitrary decision: that was how he always behaved. And a day later he said, "I'm going to my brother in Pisa, he wants to see me. I'd be ashamed to bring you, after what has happened. And I don't want to have to explain anything to anyone, is that clear?" He was getting angry again. Not a word from me, in my role of Lady of Sorrows. After the journey, I was having difficulty just living for myself.

And so I really was left on my own, under the watchful eye of an old woman who believed I was a widow. She lived on the far side of the Arno, opposite the "Sardegna"; there was a terrible smell, but the light, apart from being too cold, was good. She was a malicious old woman, and would try to drag me over to the window every time there was any sort of procession: there's so-and-so, there's that other one. She used to fly into a rage when I went over to the easel: "It's more than Madonnas that you need, what are you waiting for?" She wanted me to marry again, she asked about my dowry, she had faith in marriage brokers. But once she saw my first completed painting she quieted down, peevishly. She used to sleep all day, she took to not coming downstairs even with the waste, she didn't even cook for me. I took a certain pleasure in behaving like a widow—I dressed in black, I went to mass every day—except that widows like men and I hated them. At the market in Via Larga I would come across those friends of my father's whom I had glimpsed. I knew that they were talking about me; they stared at me a lot, they barely greeted me. And I greeted no one. When I thought about their filthy talk, I would go out of my mind in my obsession with being chaste: compared to me a nun was a harlot. I had finished the work for Buonarroti, but he hadn't paid me. I found my first client all by myself.

She was called Giovanna. I met her in church where she used to go to show off her trousseau: she was a country girl but she had married a courtier. She gave herself the airs of a lady of rank, had money and jewels, and ordered her greedy mother-in-law around with bribes of sweetmeats. She had a craving to appear gradiose, wanted to take me home in her carriage when I only lived a few steps away. She followed me up the stairs to pry around, even came into my bedroom. I felt like a wise matron, and let her do as she pleased. She sniffed the turpentine, got red and yellow paint on herself, and when she saw the painting of Lucretia that I was working on she said it looked like her, and I didn't contradict her. She wanted her portrait done immediately; she'd have had it on the same day if she could. I painted her with milky skin and the hands of a princess, in the background a brocade curtain and at her side a coffer, a pageboy and a small dog. I gave her a painting of Clorinda,* with a helmet on her head because they looked alike. She talked incessantly, always asking questions. It was not difficult to prepare cautious, mysterious answers for her, to excite her curiosity. I learned a lot from dealing with her.

She had some very inquisitive friends who were also interested. She brought them all to the house that I had found for myself, with a large, elaborate reception room on the ground floor, right beside the Arno: at night, I could hear the river as it flowed in eddies, and the silversmith's children used to catch small fish from the window of the warehouse next door. It was then that the young Grand Duchess sent for me; because she knew my father, she said. She received me in her garden, sipping continually on sorbets, she talked in Tuscan and then in German to her ladies-in-waiting. When she asked me if I painted, I replied very drily, "I dabble a little, your Excellency." She pretended she hadn't heard, then the chief physician brought her a phial containing the Grand Duke's urine which she held up to the light, playing the doctor. One by one, the ladies-in-waiting drew me aside with their silly, nosey questions. They asked me whether I painted standing up or sitting down, whether my confessor had not raised some objections to my profession. There were carriages and sedans outside my door the whole time. But men of those I received none.

This is a delicate moment: I carry Artemisia round with me in fragments. It matters little where I happen to be: today I am keeping her company on the heaps of rubble which it is enough to have seen just once. In this place there once existed, and since a few days ago no longer exists, the house in which I had so easily placed her and heard her confession:

*Clorinda, a warrior in Tasso's *Gerusalemme liberata*.

now she is obliged to help me find the house again and with it her activities. I do not spare her any of the suffering.

"They became close friends of mine, not only Giovanna, but also Caterina Macci the spinster, Violante Astorri the widow and the Torrigiani sisters-in-law. Women can only be friends in twos. I was well aware that they whispered about me when they were together, and yet they were constantly resorting to all sorts of subterfuge to be alone with me and open up their hearts to me in the strangest conversations. My constant silence and the danger they placed themselves in by confiding in me excited them. They were equally unaware of being either stupid or intelligent: they all begged me to teach them painting and drawing, but in secret. Giovanna insisted excessively, those small eyes of hers alight with the fire of ambition, while she bit her lips which were pale and narrow. She used to pour gifts into my lap: ribbons, combs, cheap kerchiefs, small cheeses, stale candied fruits, for she was also mean. She would haphazardly buy drawing paper and pencil-holders; she wanted to start immediately, without anyone knowing, and amaze them all in a month's time. Violante, the wiseacre, a flatterer who wants to be flattered, showed me certain schoolgirl daubs, certain holy saints, she who laughed at everything: she wanted praise, in her false humility. It was dangerous dealing with this cunning woman; I did not know what she was after. The Torrigianis always came together, to keep an eye on each other. Married to two brothers, they were engaged in a combat within the family that was masked by harmony, always competing in warmth and kindness. They talked about their husbands with sharp smiles, as though to defend them, poor things. They wanted to have lessons together, but if one of them had her back turned, the other would begin miming furious gestures that I was not able to interpret. Caterina was the only one who succeeded. She had such a sustained, intense way of pleading with me, with her fat, unhealthy face and her mute awkwardness, so surprising in the midst of all that chatter. She was the one who was free, a wealthy heiress, but everyone bossed her around: her nurse, her coachman, her godmother, her administrator. She wore sumptuous clothes in a graceless manner that was indicative of her lack of belief in happiness. She drew well right from the start, and she used to work for hours, as industrious as any workman, shut up in a small room behind my salon, praying that no one would catch her engaged in such activity. She would draw from imagination, without lifting the charcoal from the paper. I taught her very little, but the day that Giovanna discovered her she screamed as though she were being flayed alive, went as white as a sheet and started to tremble: there was no way of making her continue. In the end they all came, every day, and every day they got together. At that time I was painting Holofernes."

I feel that I have reached the truth, an inexpressible truth, as I form these words on Artemisia's lips. She must have uttered them at least once, with that Spanish haughtiness she acquired in her thirties in Naples. She would raise her strong chin, so typical of a stubborn blond, and with Tuscan rapidity dispatch those flowing syllables: Holofernes. Syllables which only today, now that they have been decanted from those foreign, very remote events, release the flavor of a strange smile, both shy and insolent at the same time, the very essence of her character and manner. "Do you, Signora Artemisia, feel disposed towards doing this large painting for her Excellency? An epic subject, suitable to your talent." Perhaps it was a sarcastic proposal, made by a scornful man to a proud woman. But in Artemisia's mind the whole thing was already prepared. Holofernes, Judith and Holofernes. His head wrapped up in a cloth. No, his head bare and bloody. And why not the rest of his body, his big, tyrant's body? I'll show these Tuscans that I know how to draw.

It is not possible that Artemisia did not say to her friends, "I have an important commission from the Grand Duchess." But they all knew already and seized any pretext, imperious, intrusive, foolish, to come and poke their noses in. They would find the artist dressed in a voluminous smock, her lank hair hanging loose, her face drawn with fatigue, standing or sitting on a high trestle in front of the large canvas. They would remain dumbfounded and inert in the presence of the unfamiliar gestures that Artemisia abandoned to their greed, forgetting to compose herself, to appear as she wanted them to see her: at times pathetic, almost crushed by her work; at others majestic, full of daring. They would not have known what to do if they had not noticed over by the window, sprawled on a blanket with his head hanging downwards and bare-chested, Anastasio the Greek giant, a common workman who two years before had amused Florence with his size and now earned his living without any longer causing anyone amazement. The women cast sidelong glances at his large body, moved a chair, leant forward, all with the excuse of getting closer to him. More than by the range of sizes of Artemisia's brushes and the color of the earths she tempered and mixed, more than by her use of the palette, a constant source of envy, they seemed to be attracted by the presence of that large, half-naked man, not servile although bound by servitude, but obedient to some necessity on a higher plane than ordinary custom. Giovanna would start to laugh: "Just look at the great big wig you've got on him. Where'd you find it, Artemisia?" The two Torrigianis would wrinkle their noses: "Oh Lord, what an awful smell." And Violante, the expert: "Get him to twist his hips so you can see the muscles better." Artemisia barely noticed these gibes; rarely did she reply. She who used to be so shy if her brother even looked at a drawing of hers, had grown accustomed to the remarks these women made and to their lack of discretion with an indifference that did not even surprise her. And sometimes, getting hurriedly to her feet and going resolutely over to the model to arrange him in a position more in keeping with her purpose, it would happen that she might trample the hem of a dress, or bump into a curved shoulder without apologizing, so little did their presence count for her. They

43

would stop their talking, not moving except to follow her with their eyes, with bated breath, and from those accidental contacts, from that feeling of expectancy would come the uneasy impression of a hidden ambush and a sort of reluctance to touch the man's flesh and his cheap rags. Meek and extremely docile, like all very good models, Anastasio let himself be moved about and positioned, but on a couple of occasions she happened to notice a strange stiffness in his limbs, and in his humble eyes a sort of uneasy shame. And twice she dismissed her model without an explanation.

After a while the five friends, although continuing their sort of seige, would chat among themselves with a lack of constraint that reassured her, sitting there on her trestle, for it was as though they had almost forgotten her presence. But not a day passed without the conversation, which was always on the recurring theme of domestic affairs, moving from matters of gloves and perfumes to rest on that of men, whether in the house or outside of it; and immediately their voices would grow animated. Often they might start at the top. The present Grand Duke, and the late one, God rest his soul; the foreign Princes and the native one, each man seen through sharp, wary eyes, not when out of doors, armed and on horseback, but sitting down within four walls, engaged in the acts of eating and drinking, and particularly in the act of anger, and all this would bring them back to their own homes. This one roars, that one curses, you should see Tommaso's eyes, Vieri's grim face. The agitated, repressed voices of the two Torrigianis could be heard above the others; they always ended by saying more than they meant to, and, having fired their arrows, were eager to protect themselves with the shield of conjugal love. But in the meantime each of them had named the other's husband, an insult or a favor which they exchanged by turns. Violante would let herself go, openly derisive, the freest of them all, unequalled when it came to giving examples of male brutality combined with stupidity, and of how easy it was to calm their suspicions and their anger: with cunning, with blandishments, with fear. And when they had all laughed, poor Caterina last of all, "Even the Orsini who killed his wife was afraid," cited Violante, her voice slightly shrill. Following on this mockery came tales of secret, legendary tortures evoking the ghosts of wives who had been cloistered or poisoned, who had disappeared without trace, ghosts who seemed to mingle with this group of living women, subtly goading them into ideas of revenge which, with the smell of the turpentine, made their nostrils flare. From time to time, very rapid, harsh glances were darted towards the model and passed beyond him, glittering. Then the women would turn their backs on him, make a show of suddenly and affectionately remembering the artist and her painting, crowding around to note its progress, to admire it in their own way: "The sheet looks like silk: was Holofernes a prince?" "Blood from the throat is darker than that." "Is that how you hold a dagger?" "I wouldn't be able to stick it in." "I would." "I'd love to try." "All that blood. . . . " They always came back to the blood that Artemisia was painting, a carnage woven, drop by drop, like embroidery on the white linen. The light was fading, twilight was descending over the Arno, a green twilight, and Artemisia stretched her arms as though she were alone. Her attention focused on the problems of the painting, which she could not communicate to the other women, she nonetheless shared with them a certain neglect of demeanor that was not justified by familiarity, but was rather the result of the snatches of their conversations she had picked up, absentmindedly yet with an obscure feeling of complicity. The foolish women did not realize whose was the truculent expression which Judith, on the canvas, had begun to reveal: earlier, while she was alone, Artemisia had looked in the mirror for the features of her heroine and she had been rewarded by a sneer, the motives for which now belonged to the remote past. Motives which were no more noble, no more pure, than those which Violante the widow cultivated and fostered around herself, the reasons for which she alone knew. Agostino, the dagger, the

45

pitiful scene in the fourposter bed had all found a means of expression, not with words or silent self-pity, but by a route that the mind ought to have defended and maintained inviolate.

This is why Artemisia feels she is guiltier than the Torrigianis or Violante: the gesture with which she dismisses Anastasio is brusque, evasive. Meanwhile, an immense feeling of pride swells her breast, the awful pride of a woman who has been avenged, in whom, despite her shame, there is also room for the satisfaction of the artist who has overcome all the problems of her art and speaks the language of her father, of the pure, of the chosen. But her father does not come back from Pisa, far away is the brother who is also a friend to her, and with those men in Via Larga, the garrulous Florentine painters, the pure language of mutual comprehension would be turned into a flirtatious, pandering servant. Only with herself, on the canvas, is she able to speak it, and she receives a response not only from the artist but also from the young Artemisia desperate to be justified, to be avenged, to be in command. To be in command at least over these women, to transmit to them her own rancor, is a great temptation and her easy success is still a victory of sorts. A lonely victory: with so many friends, and introduced as she was at Court, Artemisia still spends the long June evenings alone, on her balcony which almost touches the river, spellbound by the green water, by the bridges on which people stroll and chat, by the many church bells. She yawns, breathes, sighs. A year ago she did not dare open her window in Santo Spirito; today, behind Judith and Holofernes, there takes shape the figure of an exceptional woman, neither wife nor girl, fearless, in whom she loves to recognize herself, flatter herself, spur herself on. For too long this essential component of living had been missing, this self-esteem: perhaps ever since the days when Cecilia Nari used to watch her as she leapt down from the bushes on the Pincio hillside towards her own window.

It was well into morning by the time she put the finishing

46

strokes to the large canvas. This time her friends had come rushing with the intention of celebrating the completion of the work which, in a few days, would be presented to their Excellencies. They did not stay still for a moment, dressed in greater finery than usual, so that their embroidered bodices, the stiff lace, the pins and the gauze quivered like the antennae of busy insects. The clear, golden light, the trembling reflection of the water on the floor seemed to dissolve all the malice, all the insinuations, prompting sincerity and openness. The white linen on which she had done the painting evoked the idea of laundry hanging out and the blood was now like cheerful, purple ribbons: then Anastasio came in. He had come so that Artemisia could check the pose for the last time and he stretched himself out quietly in his usual, weary position on the couch: he did it so discreetly that the women saw him, all of a sudden, resurrected in his place as if by magic. There was silence, and the cessation of all movement was indeed the stillness of an insect before it pounces: the merriment hung suspended and a feeling of emptiness and danger struck Artemisia in the back and made her turn round. Violante was already over at the window, next to the man: never had she dared so much before.

"Here is the place to strike," she said in a voice in which the only sign of her recent laughter was a trembling that bode ill; and she pointed with one of her marble-colored, knobby, square-nailed fingers at the man's throat. And he, from his usual supine position, suddenly sat up with an ungainly effort. At his clumsy movement Violante stepped backwards, but the others drew nearer. His rough, disheveled clothes and his swarthy skin under which the muscles appeared disproportionately huge and almost ridiculous, confirmed, with an instinctive feeling of repugnance on their part, their dangerous sense of superiority. "Men never wash, not even gentlemen," one of the Torrigianis barked, and Giovanna laughed. "Look at all that hair on him! You could comb it into curls, part it with ribbons and pearls!" "Take that big wig off him, we want to fix him properly."

47

"Who's going to be Judith?" Horribly fascinated, Artemisia, from the other end of the room, saw the flash of a thin blade in the midst of the group of women: Caterina was holding it, her fists clenched tightly as though in death, her flabby face devoid of expression and on her low forehead an unwrinkled tension. "Put your clothes on, Anastasio!" screamed the artist. The giant, who seemed to be hoping to escape by means of a foolish, servile smile, acquired the use of his limbs once more, and the gesture he made in picking up his coat and putting it on was enough to dissolve the mythical assault like snow in the sun. The dagger disappeared, the women composed themselves again, passing without transition, almost without trace, to the brazen manner of schoolgirls who have been caught red-handed but who already look like butter wouldn't melt in their mouths. And Lucrezia Torrigiani had the steady eye and smooth brow of one of her ancestors in a painting by Bronzino, while the bitter Violante did not even need to move for her widow's headdress to fall heavily into place once more on either side of her face. Some were standing, others sitting, their clothes falling in harmonious lines. Only Caterina, leaning forward on her chair, constantly wiped her sweating hands on her lace-trimmed handkerchief. The window, not properly closed, had blown open, and puffs of gentle wind stirred a slight, acrid smell of female sweat through the room.

"I've got to fly, it's getting late," said Giovanna, embarrassed and garrulous, bravely trying her best to dispel the uneasiness shared by all. Despising her for her bad grace, but glad of the excuse, the others were getting up and leaving one by one, but with deliberate slowness: it seemed as though they had never taken such prolonged pleasure in the rustling of their brocade gowns. They went out after having placed a kiss in the air somewhere in the region of Artemisia's cheek. And once again Artemisia found herself alone.

Her revenge had been consummated, her lasting shame

in Rome atoned for. Men were becoming men once more, although distant, incomprehensible shadows. Father, husband, lover: little less than names, but the first of these she loved and longed for in vain, the last had dissolved like a body in the ground. As a result, she was left with an elegiac disposition that no longer needed to be put into words, but which availed itself of the words of others in silent sympathy. The Judith had been presented, she had been paid for it and praised by everyone at Court, and now the heat bore down on the Arno, drying up its course, its waters putrid between the cloth mills. Everyone at Court had gone to the countryside, including her lady friends: and it looked as though no one would ever mention her Judith again, abandoned in the Palace in its new frame. Even her desire for success and fame seemed consummated and exhausted, nor did thoughts of a long life, of splendid new opportunities rise up to spur her on. From her soporific life in the dark, in the damp of the ground floor, Artemisia would prick up her ears to the sound of the virginal as Arcangela, the Court performer, practiced in the house next door. When it grew dark, Arcangela would come down and the two young women would lean over the river to catch a breath of coolness, and the singer would talk of her love. It was a faceless love, with neither purpose nor hope: she depicted it with mists and snow, a great river, boats with musicians, dancing on the grass. As if by chance, a name implicit in every virtue both male and human: valor, temperance, respect, kindness. "She's invented it all," thought Artemisia, but she never tired of listening to the pale girl from Mantua with the slim nose, the frequently hoarse voice, who was hoping to recover her health. "I'll try this remedy of the old Grand Duchess, my voice is certain to come back. At Easter I'll sing the Magnificat at Sant'Andrea." And Artemisia, her eyes motionless in the dark, covered in a film of tears, hoped that the remedy would work, that Arcangela would get better and sing once again over the river, amidst honest, resplendent, generous cavaliers. Up there, there is no need for daggers, no need to curse the fate of being a woman, nor command a group of savage, conniving females. There friendship reigns without sin or subterfuge and can be discussed at length, as Arcangela does between bouts of coughing, with delight.

At night, spent for the most part awake waiting for the air to get cooler and permit sleep, the darkness, both above and below, was full of whisperings, voices far and near, sometimes a soft fragment of song; an invisible hive, poor wool workers and laborers from the stifling hovels, wide awake like the two girls, on the dried-up grass of the river banks, on roof terraces, on small boats that splashed now and again as someone sleepily rowed. Humble people, unknown. And this too was a solace, a blessing, to feel united, at least as far as physical discomfort was concerned, with men and women who together, without causing offense to each other, breathed in the slight breath of coolness from the Arno. Artemisia listened and forgave. Now that all rancor was gone, she felt as though she were stretching out her hand towards the violence she had endured. She was strong now and unarmed; and men, the fateful enemy, no longer required her to exonerate herself, protect herself. They were the same as she, almost more gentle in fact, with delicate gestures of homage; like Arcangela's Luca Scotti, mild and fearless, chaste and faithful. At daybreak, once Arcangela had gone home, the sleep that Artemisia was finally able to enjoy was filled with strange, clear-headed thoughts unwinding as though from an inexhaustible, abundant skein of silk. Compassionate thoughts that passed beyond the natural boundaries of age to culminate in an old woman's lucid wisdom. Poor men, they too: tormented by arrogance and authority, compelled for thousands of years to command and to gather poisonous mushrooms, those women who feign sleep at their side while beneath silky lashes lying on velvet cheeks they harbor recriminations, hidden desires, secret plans. A feeling of widespread indulgence, as light as a bird in flight, caused her to smile in her sleep. In sleep a smile is almost as intractable as tears and must be escaped from. "But I can paint," discovers Artemisia as she wakes up, and she is saved.

With feverish haste, in the weak, watery, September sun, the peasants are finishing threshing the silted, worm-eaten grain; in haste they gather and crush the few clusters of grapes. Never has the earth appeared so shriveled and pitted, ancient, barren earth onto which the tired hand of divine indifference drops brusque, rough caresses. And the rain falls, blindly, ostensibly to wash and purify. Instead it is a diabolical instrument that, down on the ground, mixes together a paste of mud and rags, minute fragments of wood, twisted splinters of metal, slivers of glass: a clay made of the ruins over which paths are already being worn by the daily comings and goings of oblivious people. Time's game has been revealed, we can see its mechanism, a clumsy device, rusty and indestructible, its spell the only part which has been broken. Of no use are bread, a light with which to go to bed; as useless, therefore, as pen and paper, as an ancient paintbrush and the small hand which held it, freckled on the back, dry on the palm—symbols that do not rise up, seeds that the earth does not give back.

I can clearly see my body moving and taking nourishment: it is an active, stubborn master, a hard master from whom there is no escape, whose intentions I cannot decipher. It believes in nothing, the body, except in its own continuation and in a sort of silly hope for a mundane immortality. But you will die, whispers the imprisoned spirit, grown so malicious as to take delight in the shivers that run through it. Because the spirit is with the dead now, and it loathes nothing more than having to provide life, provide for life. As a message for the future, it has no respect for a testament, and the testament that Artemisia dictates to me is null. Even if I saw the lost manuscript with all its marks, its blotches, lying beside me on the grass that still resounds with the noise of the cannon, I couldn't be bothered to read a line of it. But a prisoner needs to amuse himself somehow, and I have very few playthings left, only a doll that I can dress and undress; particularly undress, until there appears the nail driven into the middle of its chest and those which hold its hair onto its forehead. If Artemisia were still a ghost and not a weighty, strange name, she would shudder at my disrespectful digressions.

When Artemisia's husband was still a boy he already dealt in nuts, holy medals made of tin, mastic for repairing broken saucepans, small wax statues to use as fetishes, and all sorts of bric-a-brac. He used to lay it all out on display on the doorstep of the house, and Artemisia, still a child and already a fellow tenant, would spit down on it from her window. He was as afraid of her as of the devil himself, and if, raising his eyes, he happened to catch sight of her, he would immediately snatch up all his treasures and hide them in the bag he always kept at his side, his nostrils quivering with emotion. He never sold anything, but he would pretend to sell, or else, trembling, he would barter with brawling boys of his own age: the bartering would result eventually in coins and was the entertainment of the swarms of street urchins. Padre Agatone, a Capuchin monk, took him under his wing and sent him to the Camilline and Oratorian fathers, dressed as a scholar in threadbare robes with dirty ruffs; he stayed at the charity schools for more than two years. They taught him to count and his father began to boast about him, whereas before, when he received reports that he had disappeared from school, or stayed away from home for days on end, he would limit himself to cursing him without getting upset. The Stiattesis were so resourceful that they contrived to follow the Gentileschis every time they moved house, finding a place sometimes in the attic, sometimes in the cellar, sometimes in huts in the vegetable garden, but always free of charge. There were four boys but Artemisia could not tell them apart, except for Antonio who was growing up, very pale: she was friends with none of them, accustomed to making fun of them and to hearing others do the same, but in her mind they figured as sort of disreputable relations, relations nonetheless, even if no one had ever explained to her how and to what degree. In San Spirito, after the scandal, they had kept their heads high and had managed to slip into a dreadful single-room lodging on the ground floor, one day friends of Tuzia's, the next enemies, all of them together custodians of the shameless hussy, as they and everyone else called Artemisia. Their raucous children were always hanging round the street door, playing and shouting, making obscene drawings on the wall with charcoal; their father pretending that he was tending the vegetables behind the house but always with the priests, as was his wont. Their mother was always coughing. Antonio had disappeared at the time.

But after Orazio had said to his daughter, "You'll have to get married," there was Antonio one morning, neatly combed and wearing a new coat, walking up and down underneath the window, as though waiting. Everything was ready in Santa Maria in Aquiro, a parish some distance away where no one knew them. "Put on your good clothes," Orazio said to his daughter who was lighting the fire; and she, who for some time had sought refuge in black clothes, dressed in black, not knowing that she was going to get married. It was so long since she had gone outside that as she stood on the doorstep she was dazzled by the reflection of light on the pavement, and through her fluttering eyelids she saw Antonio, very tall and pale, and the whole Stiattesi family all dressed up, except for Grazia who was sick in bed. They set off. Maybe the neighbors suspected something: there was a sort of whispering amidst the heavy silence, and the creaking of shutters sounded like someone furtively peeping through. They walked quickly, all spread out, but when they got to the bridge where they could no longer be seen they all came together without a word.

Antonio did not speak. Oblivious, he walked in front, with his long legs. His new coat was expensive but not made to fit, and it hung loosely on his shoulders while sticking out stiffly on his hips. His head was bare; he held his hat in his hands, a wide, felt hat with a gray plume that brushed the ground. A clump of dull, blond hair stuck up on the top of his head and the wind, blowing through it, separated it into stiff tufts. He wore spurs on his boots which jangled. From time to time he would stop to wait for the group and turn his head slightly, but without looking at them: she could see a section of his sloping cheek and his short nose. He stopped when Gervasio and Protasio, the twins, took a fancy to the gingerbread that a street vendor was selling, and when his father met a benefactor (standing with bent head, hand on chest, like in an illustration) he bent his head over his right shoulder in an attitude of resignation: he looked like a horse taking its weight off one leg in order to rest. Orazio was looking with half-closed eyes towards Palazzo Farnese, the children were getting restless, and Artemisia was pulling her shawl down over her forehead.

Did Antonio smile or not, in the sacristy, when the others had gone to look for the priest and bride and groom were left alone, face to face? The light fell slantingly from a high window, and ripples ran across his face as over a still pool: a twitching on his brow, at the corners of his mouth, at the edge of his nostrils; as a boy he was nicknamed the rabbit. Then the tiny storm was over, his features became opaque, expressionless once more, an empty mask.

Kneeling on the altar steps the bride touched a cold, damp hand from which she received a small, silver ring that Antonio slipped onto her finger with clumsy concentration, arching his long back and hollowing his chest as if it were a great effort. But, without bending over and with a free hand, he rapidly signed the parish register Antonius Stiattesi, and blotted it with sand that Artemisia could feel under the pen when it was her turn to sign. They went out by a side door without going back into the church and Orazio left them all immediately without an explanation. When they got to the Pantheon the twins went off after a street singer, at Sant' Eustachio Fabrizio greeted a man who looked like a soldier and stayed behind with him. Antonio was still walking in front, as he had on the way there, with those excessively long legs of his, and Artemisia, looking thinner than ever in her black clothes, was following some distance away from her father-in-law who was hawking and spitting. A funeral cortege with lighted torches went past. Two women were fighting on the corner near the University and further on a pedlar was exhibiting his trained birds. Without being aware of it, Artemisia slowed down, stood enraptured for a moment, and when she came to again could no longer see either her father-in-law's cloak nor her husband's green coat. She caught up with the old man in Via Banchi where he had stopped to chat with a pilgrim. She was not to see Antonio again for a number of years.

For two years, however, they lived together. From 1622 to '24? Or from '25 to '27? Thus might Artemisia ask herself when she is a forgetful old lady, raising her eyes to the ceiling, if ever she lived to be an old lady. But certainly she was able to remember far better that when her father came back to Florence he did not even unpack his trunk: he slept reluctantly in his daughter's house on the Arno that she had been so proud to show him, having cleverly obtained it from her lady patrons. The cold light of his penetrating eyes, the sharp cut of his beard and his manner of wearing it were enough to reduce the prestige of a year's pure living and the very dignity and innocence of her thoughts to frivolities and perhaps even turn them to ridicule. When he saw her Judith Orazio said, "It's good," and looked at his daughter with an intentness that to her seemed an implied reproach, so that she almost gave in to despair. She searched within herself for Artemisia Gentileschi, artist in Tuscany, but could no longer find her, she no longer had any love for herself when near this difficult, silent father. Who grew ever more silent, almost spiteful: she had not yet realized that Orazio behaved in this manner when he wanted to be free, and felt himself tied down. She understood it, but could not accept it, looking for an explanation, eternal forgiveness for her sins and worthlessness. Once again she felt equivocal, clumsy, untrustworthy; both seeking and fearing at the same time her release, which came forlorn and beneficial like the rain out of the sky and the muffled thunder over the mountains. "I am going far away, child" (he was cutting himself a slice of bread, holding the loaf against his chest like a woman), "I'm fed up with this Italian rabble. I'm going to the court of England. Whether we see each other again or not is of no importance, Gentileschi is not afraid of hell. You are a painter," and he sighed, something which he did very rarely, in a pause of the spirit that his abused body seized on to exhale its fatigue. "You are a painter, but you have a husband in Rome. Go back there, child. Even with the Stiattesis you'll be able to make a living, you always have your painting. I thought you would have come to a bad end, but instead . . . I'm leaving tomorrow, you must be patient." He drank a glass of water and sat for a while crumbling his slice of bread without touching the soup he had in front of him. There was no point in objecting, arguing or pleading; and Artemisia had never been able to cry in front of her father. All she could do was think in advance about simple things, inevitable and unbearable, all that dust at Porta a Prato where the carriages wheeled round in a suffocating white cloud and the passengers boarding and alighting looked as though they were already enveloped by the mists of distance, already unrecognizable, amidst a din of dialects from other regions and loud Tuscan shouting; and flies on the sweating horses and merchandise and luggage being rolled around, so that anyone stopping to watch, to say goodbye, did not know where to put his feet. In the end, all Artemisia's anguish was reduced to the fear that her father would not allow her to see him off, and to the pains she took to hide her unhappiness. But he was forbearing. He embraced her, lightly and fleetingly: his clothes with their smell of turpentine gave her the impression that they were empty, and already he was holding onto the handrail, already he was on board, agile and carefree as though going on a trip to the countryside. He sat down, made a light, modest bow to someone and unbuttoned his collar, and he seemed to have already forgotten her when he suddenly turned round and raised his hand in a gesture, rather than of farewell, of stopping something in the air: a sound, a word, a promise. Thus did Artemisia see him for the last time in Italy.

Carriages might travel the world over, not one of them was worth anything from the moment Orazio's had left and could not be overtaken. And to say of Artemisia, She went back to Rome, is to narrate it her way, indulging her mood of those days, sparing her. Beneath her feet the wheels turned, inside her head her brain was asleep, behind her closed lids no images could penetrate. Grief is sometimes smooth and flowing, better even than caution at protecting from ambush and danger. And if now and again her gaze wandered over the countryside, her intolerance at finding it met by another's gaze was so haughty that even a violent man would feel embarrassed. And so one morning she disembarked in Piazza del Popolo, a different woman from the one who had set out from there.

A woman: exactly that which a young girl does not want to become, no matter what has happened to her. But she has little choice, and even less in sixteen hundred and twenty-two, or twenty-five, in Rome. So Artemisia raised her head and made a mental list of her assets: an attractive face, nice hands, nice body, talent, four trunks, two hundred ducats, a husband either alive or dead—an inheritance passed on to her by that dying, heedless girl and of which she hurriedly took possession. In a flash she realized that the greatest of these assets was her husband, a necessary requirement so that the others might bear fruit. For the moment she instinctively armed herself against malice and curiosity by means of a wonderful imitation of the Tuscan ladies-in-waiting, so good at commanding respect. Now that she had come to definitely recognize her condition, suddenly strong with a desire for life and prosperity that young girls do not possess, for the first time and with a clear conscience she offered a sacrifice to guile, the goddess of the poor who do not want to die. She found a carriage immediately, obliging porters, had her luggage unloaded at once and obtained the information she needed. In less than an hour she learnt where the Stiattesis were now living, without being recognized or admitting to anyone that she bore their wretched name. The genie of furtiveness and boldness prompted her deeds and words, led her by the hand. She felt that she had concluded an obscure alliance, a sort of pact with herself, by means of a law that she had only just now discovered, a sort of second nature; and in this bustle of petty activity she found that she was enjoying herself.

The Stiattesis were living in Ripagrande, not in ordinary lodgings but, as was their wont, in crumbling, badly plastered cellars situated between the kitchens and the stables of a marquis who had set up house too hastily. Old Giambattista was still wearing the same cloak he had had on at the wedding and was holding the usual rosary in his hands when Artemisia appeared in the ever-open doorway. He had two little sniveling boys, dressed in velvet rags, their faces covered in sores, holding onto his clothes. He put on a show of indignation, raising his hands to the sky and stepping back two paces, but in the meantime her luggage was being brought in and he noticed that it was abundant: immediately he started to cry, saying "Daughter!" He began to tremble, to stumble, pointing with his forefinger to his eyes as though to say that he could not see. He shouted behind him: "Gervasio! Mariuccia!" The hovel seemed uninhabited.

And Artemisia was amazed that she knew how to deal with this man whom she had detested in her adolescence, a dirty, dangerous beast: in recent years he had been pushed to the back of her mind like a childhood bogey. Now he appeared to her exposed at first glance and the remnants of her former disgust were rekindled in the lack of pity with which she studied his rags, his gray face consumed with dishonesty. She took pleasure in speaking with the Florentine accent she never normally used, to ask, "And who are these two?" Squirming, wiping his congested eyes, he first cleared a space on a bench. "Children," he replied, "Mariuccia's children. God knows . . . " A woman charged into the room in bare feet and a brocade petticoat: her barefooted tread was heavier than anything in shoes. "Are you still here?" she shouted, curling her swollen lips: and then she stood open-mouthed and belligerent, for she had recognized the newcomer. So, this was Mariuccia, Tuzia's eldest daughter, the affected, convent school maiden who, her mother claimed, was already a saint and whom Stiattesi went to collect every Sunday, nor were there silks fine enough to cover her head. "God knows . . . ," continued Giambattista, trying to strike a really venerable attitude like the time he posed for Saint Paul the Hermit and for Saint Peter on the cross: with great deliberation Artemisia began pulling off a glove. "God knows that I'm a father in spirit to these innocent ones." And taking a proudly unresisting Artemisia by the shoulders he led her over to a corner where he hinted, with much winking, at a "fine gentleman," at "the poor girl caught in the middle," at the need for compassion and resignation to God's will. "I married her when Grazia died to get her out of trouble," sighed the old man at the end, not taking his eyes off the trunks which had now all been brought in. On their way out the porters bumped into a crippled beggar who, once inside, immediately left off his crutch and his hump. Mariuccia, from being sullen and aggressive, put on a cheerful, provocative face, patting her hair and licking her lips. "They're ready through there," she said, nodding at the door through which she had come in; and as he stood there staring at the artist, "Are you deaf?" she roared, flying into a rage, fully revealing Tuzia's peasant accent, with the heavy, guttural, raucous tones of her derisive question. At that, Artemisia looked away and, sitting down on a bench, enquired about her husband.

"A gem, that son of mine," began Giambattista, relieved at finding himself in safe waters, his eyes, a moment ago wet with tears, now already lit with a crafty gleam, his eyelids beating furiously. "A son who provides for all of us, myself, poor old man that I am, his unfortunate brothers and these poor abandoned children." He put his head round a curtain. "Gervasio my son, tell Antonio that his Artemisia is here. He has expected you every single day, he hasn't stopped pining for you. But you know how hardworking he is, and today is market day in Piazza Navona." Humming softly to himself in a bass voice that was full of catches and boyishly shrill notes, a young man came from behind the curtain, little Gervasio who had grown into an adolescent, listlessly moving his legs and reading a small book that he held right up to his eyes. He appeared not to hear his father's exhortations to hurry but he carried on walking nonetheless; and before he went out into the street he shot a glance at Artemisia, rapid and penetrating, from between his narrowed lids—he was the image of Antonio as a boy.

Signorina Gentileschi waited on the bench, uncertain and dazed inside, but to all appearances composed and calm, like a traveler waiting for a change of horses. The bench was rotten, an old church bench that had been in storage for a long time among funeral biers, candelabra and processional banners; from whence, God knows how, it had somehow fallen into the hands of the Stiattesis. The wall against which she leaned her shoulders from time to time was unplastered and there were scarcely any traces of whitewash left on the large blocks of tufa. But her mind was largely taken off her disgust at this primitive bareness by the comings and goings of a variety of strange people through that sort of cave, so that all Artemisia's attention was on observing, simply observing. Three different kinds of cripples, all carrying a haversack; a mendicant friar; two stablemen laden with bridles and harnesses; two soldiers who came in fat and went out thin. Then women, big and small, most of them old and wretched, all of them laden with bundles and packages. On one side a doorway with only half a door, and on the other that felt curtain through which Gervasio had come separated this area from that in which the family lived and where the visitors entered. They stayed for quite a while, often quarreling in voices which were either threatening or peevish, according to the circumstances, but which were all dominated by that of Mariuccia who appeared again for a moment with a notebook in her hand, her shift fallen down to reveal her right shoulder, brown and plump.

"We manage," said old man Stiattesi who had stayed behind to guard his daughter-in-law, seemingly occupied in arranging stools, in smoothing and folding a dirty tablecloth, in gathering goblets together on the table, while the two children rolled around on the floor with a cheerful mongrel puppy. One of his eyes narrowed as though winking, but he immediately contradicted its expression, muttering prayers. As he moved backwards and forwards between her trunks, he would first push back a corner that was sticking out, then remove a bit of straw from one of the joints: his fingers were trembling and it seemed that all his bustling increased proportionately as Artemisia's immobility and her calm patient manner persisted. Finally Fabrizio came in too, now a soldier, with a great show of braid on his jacket, roaring that he was hungry. The children crept off to hide; Mariuccia's voice, on the other side of the curtain, grew quieter. Even Giambattista disappeared. The soldier marched up and down, banging into the trunks, hitting his sword off them, and he began to kick the puppy. He shouted, "Is it coming or not?" and unfailingly, after every thump and shout, would look at his sister-in-law without a word of greeting. She did not move, but made herself more comfortable, leaning back with an insolent look in her eyes; she was laughing to herself inside. She was laughing at a thought that had sometimes been an occasion of remorse, all that blood of Holofernes drying on the canvas in the Palazzo Pitti. "I painted it, and it's as if I'd killed a tyrant." She was carrying a dagger in her pocket and now she caressed its shape with her thumbnail while Fabrizio hoisted up his trousers just like Cosimo the official used to. Cosimo, that other Holofernes! The impulse of her old hatred was so strong that Artemisia got to her feet and she felt she was a giant.

But she was no giant: she was a small woman and blond into the bargain, and Fabrizio's big body was so solid, standing between the bench and the table, that all she could do was look at him and hope that he was crushed by the expression in her eyes. Evening was drawing in, the sun was low, soft voices came from the riverside as though exhausted, the lullaby of prisoners. At that instant Antonio appeared.

She remembered him as thin and pale, with hunched shoulders, and thus he had remained, but with a new weightiness in his bones and with an experience of hard work that had matured him and made him acceptable just as he was. She felt she had always known the clothes he was wearing, but they fitted him well and were not ugly. He too was carrying a sack on his back and he took it off immediately, with a sort of carefree agility. He stepped round his brother, but without haste and without hesitation, as if he had bumped into a piece of furniture. He bent down to pick up a bit of string, opened a drawer. Finally he looked at Artemisia.

And Artemisia smiled at him. As though she were just born now she smiled and had no memory at all of having calculated, six hours ago, the advantages that a husband can offer to a girl on her own. She did not even remember Francesco, her devoted brother, to whom she had preferred, on her arrival, that which she considered her right, this dubious family and this man. She smiled, not feeling that she was giving in, but inexplicably free and happy. In that cavern, amidst relatives who were thieves and pimps, without a bed of her own, she felt she had been married for two years, protected for two years. The couple did not shake hands, but together, as though by agreement, attended to her luggage, to the room they would live in. For the whole evening they talked to each other in quiet voices, in harmony with one another; and with the rest of the family one would speak on behalf of the other, quite naturally. On one occasion Antonio winked at his wife, warning her of a trick of Mariuccia's, and twice before nightfall Artemisia brushed the dust from Antonio's sleeve where he had rubbed against the wall.

They installed themselves in a large room that had been used to store grain which had gone bad and the smell of it was still there. Their bed was a straw mattress on the brick floor; there was no need to climb up into it and letting oneself fall onto it from above, when tired, had a charm of its own. At its head, Artemisia's luggage, untouched and unopened, and at its foot two cords stretched from wall to wall and on them Antonio's merchandise, for he was a peddler and old-clothes dealer. Right from that first evening he arranged everything this way; he closed his eyes often between one task and the next, as though to rest, and his hands were weak, unsuited—he seemed to be dragging the heavy sacks with his nails. Artemisia stood and watched, pale with fatigue, and suddenly began to moan quietly (with whom else would she have dared?) that she could take no more and wanted to lie down. With the door closed, and closed behind Antonio who had gone out, instead of getting undressed she threw herself down and burst into unrestrained tears, almost greedily. This was another reason why she had married, in order to cry secretly, for there is no satisfaction in crying when you are on your own. Twice Antonio knocked at the door, the first time with a small table and chair, and then with a steaming cup of cocoa. The rim of the cup was very fine, so surprising in that hovel. He produced a doughnut, a bunch of golden grapes. Artemisia chewed slowly, mingling tears and hunger, while Antonio moved about the room with the long, swaying stride of a boy who has grown too tall, then sat down on the low step under the window, writing rapidly on a notepad. Artemisia did not understand how he could see to write in the dim twilight and, as there was a lamp set on the ground beside her, told him to come nearer so that they could both use its

63

light. She spoke with the falsely irate tones adopted by certain old affectionate wives, and Antonio did as he was told, crouching down beside her on a large sack before continuing to write again on his knees. He raised his head from time to time and absentmindedly watched her eat, his mind on his figures, but it seemed to Artemisia that he drew a certain satisfaction from every mouthful she swallowed, and she sat quietly under his gaze, as serious as a convalescing child showing signs that she is getting better. A great peace had come over her: the closed door and her tranquil companion gave her a feeling of comfort and warmth such as she had never experienced before, whether on her own or in company, not even with her father. She no longer remembered that she was a Gentileschi, artist and daughter of an artist. She was redeeming old debts that were owed to her, debts of family love, of family respect. She had—and the word continued to fulfill her thoughts—she had a husband.

Antonio went out early every morning. Often she did not even wake up, so light and considerate were his movements. She became aware of his absence the moment she opened her eyes more from his clothes which were missing from the cord than from the emptiness in the bed, because Antonio slept like a bird, curled up in a ball, weightless. She did not mind being left alone, not even on the first day: on the contrary, she leapt out of bed with greater freshness and energy than she would have expected, excited at the idea of being able to rummage through the things that Antonio traded in, buying and selling. It was an old desire of hers, dating back to the time they were children together, when all the kids in the Pincio district would have loved to get their hands into his sack.

Sometimes he would stay awake for three or four days at a time, for he went to distant fairs as well. By tacit agreement he left her complete freedom; and on the table ten or twenty coins. Artemisia was free to go out, stay away the whole day, see whomever she pleased. She freely helped herself to the clothes left hanging on the cord, often in preference to her own, and once she disguised herself as a pageboy, just as the ladies in the French court do, or so Violante had told her in Florence. Most of the time she would take a carriage and go to Strada Pia to see her brother who constantly asked her if she were painting and why she did not set up a house of her own, far from those Stiattesis. "A woman like you," he would say. Artemisia would shrug her shoulders without replying: it was hard to explain that for the moment she was fine the way she was, in the cellar in Ripagrande, the wife of Antonio the peddler, tolerated and amused by the rabble in the house. But she willingly listened to news of who was painting what in Rome, of new and old artists. With her chin resting in her hand and wide, dreamy eyes, she never lost sight of a vague plan for recognition and fame; of her intention of taking up her place again, of working, of traveling, for she would not remain in Rome, of that she was certain. But there was no hurry, life was long. The sparrows in the small wood in the grounds of the convent next door to Francesco's studio were settling for the night with a deafening din that traveled through the clear sky. Running barefoot over the autumn leaves on the grass, the gardener's son hurried to ring the Ave Maria: the evening bells were beginning to ring in reply. "And what about father?" asked Artemisia. He had only written twice before going to France. After that there had been no news of him. It was such a short time ago that Artemisia had believed she would die without him: instead the pain had run over her without marking her, leaving her stronger, and in particular with a better knowledge of herself and how to cope in the world. The light faded quickly at this time of year; at five o'clock it was already night, but she was not afraid to go back home alone by carriage, through the dark streets of Rome. Their conversation of the last half-hour was the most interesting. "There's a French painter who's doing large landscapes for Cassiano Dal Pozzo." "Mannozzi is painting in the Santi Quattro and brought news of your

65

Holofernes." Artemisia smiled behind her hand; her eyes remained serious. Landscapes, Holofernes. Agostino too used to paint landscapes: she can still see him, on the scaffolding in Monte Cavallo, whistling and glancing down, with his paintbrush in his hand, to see if she were looking up at him. She no longer hates him. It's as though he had never been born; remembering him now is mere curiosity devoid of emotion. "Goodnight, Francesco," she says, getting up and arranging on her shoulders the Spanish mantilla that Antonio gave her. She leaps into the carriage with a nimble sense of adventure, a lady traveling incognito. In the hired carriage that bounces over the stones and potholes she opens her eyes wide: darkness as they charge down the steep hill, then an ever-increasing number of torches and footmen, lights in roadside shrines, lamps of cautious wayfarers. But she feels safe and when she gets out at the marquis's gate (ten yards from the cellar opening) she is as merry as a masker and takes pleasure in her regal passage through the room where the Stiattesis eat, sleep and carouse, often ten or fifteen of them at a time. She does not care that Mariuccia says, "Here's that wh— Artemisia." Once the door of her room is closed, nothing can annoy her. Fine if Antonio is back, fine if he's not. Alone, she sings as she undresses, sometimes with clowning, theatrical gestures. She turns the key in the lock, nibbles on bread and walnuts, almond cake, dried chestnuts. Then when everything is quiet, when the talk on the other side of the door has ceased, she opens her trunk and takes out paper and charcoal. Just as before she draws by lamplight, but now she feels rejuvenated, carefree, getting up now and then to chew on a dry fig and peep out of the high window that looks onto the marquis's courtyard. The horses, noisily clattering their shod hooves and rearing upright before passing through the gateway, brush the grill on her window with their enormous mouths. The footmen are shouting, the torches are smoking, the red garb and florid face of a cardinal flicker like embers in the shadows at the bottom of the main stairs, while his retinue swoop down to hold up his train. And Artemisia throws herself down onto her floor-level bed to rest.

When Antonio comes home, she enjoys watching him pull out, one by one, the things he has brought back from his trip: small pieces of jewelry, filigree, miniature ivory tabernacles, rosaries of precious stones—for he does not always sell for money, and the pleasure of exchange often wins over that of profit. Antonio lets his wife handle the new objects as much as she likes and also various old-fashioned garments that make her laugh. Finally the money appears, taken out of a small, dirty bag, but at that Artemisia moves away, pretending to be busy, and he is left alone to count it, from coppers to ducats, for his wife does not want to know. For her there are always unexpected, childish gifts: fresh strawberries that have miraculously emerged intact from his sack, strings of walnuts and hazelnuts, marzipan. To please him she has to eat them at once, under his impatient gaze which he often turns suspiciously towards the door, as if afraid someone might come in. He makes the remains disappear in a flash, stones, shells, crumbs. He has always already eaten: not once did Artemisia ever eat out of the same plate or bowl as he. And then he would begin to ask, "Aren't you going to bed?" as if he found it unbearable that she were still up, sitting there, while he put his wares in order again. Only the time that he gave her a turquoise, which he did not dare slip onto her finger (the same as the turquoise that Agostino had given her, she got quite a shock), did he not seem to take any further notice of her and wrapped and unwrapped combs, mirrors, cosmetics, face powder, rapidly and with a sullen expression. But Artemisia quickly got into bed that evening too; in fact she even hid her head in the pillow pretending to fall asleep immediately, careful to leave her small finger with the ring plainly in view. After a few minutes she heard the rustle of clothes being spread out over the cord and then an unfamiliar sound like a thin, distant voice singing. Antonio was in fact singing a hymn that they had learned together in childhood, taught to all the street children by the Holy Fathers in Trinità dei Monti.

Only when he believed his wife was asleep would Antonio tiptoe over to the door, stand there for a moment listening, then turn the handle and go into the communal room. Artemisia could not resist the deception of keeping her eyes closed and pretending to be asleep, although his furtive behavior never caused her to suspect any slyness or subterfuge on his part, or that he might be scheming against her. She really was not asleep, and when the door had closed again behind him, she would open her eyes wide, as if to hear more clearly the comments and laughter which, through there, greeted his arrival. There were jeers and banter in various dialects, sometimes in different languages, and she could not understand how Antonio could expose himself to it, but she was certain that there had to be a reason for it, a carefully thought-out reason, of the sort that her husband was wordlessly explaining to her as he went along. The young woman did not like lying awake for long with the lamp that soon began to flicker, casting onto the wall strange shadows of those clothes hanging on the cord. The pleasure of a liberated solitude could easily turn into the bitterness of an enforced solitude and take her back to the unhappy times when, in Santo Spirito, she would listen to the loud babble of voices of her spiteful neighbors and, in silence, would have given anything to be able to join in. To stop herself from wanting company, especially that company, in place of her humiliating repose she used to substitute a childishly arbitrary act: she got up. She would walk round with bare feet, go up to the door, eavesdrop, looking for a crack through which to see without being seen. She found one, one rainy evening, when, to protect herself from the cold, she wrapped herself up in a traveling cloak that she had found among the old clothes. Never had she enjoyed herself so much, what with her delight in this childish game to which was added the new, spicier delight of a woman secretly spying. In the large room which was no longer

68

divided by the curtain she could see the Stiattesis' beds, big and small, which in comparison made her own seem fit for a king. Mariuccia was slowly and lazily delousing herself. She changed her bodice, combed her hair with her head hanging upside-down; then, when she stood upright again, her bright red face surrounded by her fluffed-out hair appeared dark in the dim light. The old man was writing furiously on certain scrolls, getting up every now and then to sharpen his quill, for he could never find the right knife. The children were buzzing round in everyone's way like flies in winter, dropping off for short spells of sleep, getting beaten, crying. Two tall church candlesticks lit the table where Fabrizio was playing dice, observed and admired on all sides by various cronies. The other player was dark and had a dried-up look about him; he was scratching his beard and yawning. The twins were playing a different game, but on the floor, with idlers both young and old, and this game required as much uproar and commotion as the other, at the table, suspicious immobility. A young idiot at whom the dog never stopped snarling and who wanted to join in the game too, was being kicked and slapped on the face and was screaming, while Mariuccia, her bodice finally laced up, her shoes on, a rose pinned on her breast, was going out; no one said goodbye or even raised his head. But they all did shortly afterwards, and more and more frequently, towards a sort of hatch that opened high up on the opposite wall; and Artemisia was astonished to recognize, along with the clatter of pots and dishes, the smell of roast meat and stew. There was a kitchen on the other side of the wall, nothing less than the marquis's kitchen, and the smoke from the fires, along with the steam from the cauldrons, wafted through to mingle with the exhalations of all the Stiattesis so that the room was now all foggy, like a place beside a river. "Here pussy," said a clucking, mocking voice in the distance. "Tiger, Ataturk, Tabby, Short-tail." No one in the room spoke, the children had stopped playing, the babies had woken up, the old man had risen to his feet: only Fabrizio carried on playing dice, without diverting his attention, while Antonio, who had remained sitting on a bale, to one side and as though a spectator, did not raise his eyes from the ground. And finally something heavy and shiny came flying through the hatch like a great bird and landed on the floor, and there was a sudden, silent struggle at the spot where it had fallen. The dog was howling, fists were flying in the fray, but the old man, with an obscene authority, had grabbed the spoils and was solemnly announcing, "Leg of roast boar"; everyone made way for him. Thus did supper rain upon the Stiattesis, thanks to a friendly, light-fingered scullery-boy, or so Artemisia guessed, and she would have needed an extra pair of eyes to follow the speed with which each person pulled bread and a tin mug out of his sack, demanded his portion and sat down to enjoy it. This meal, seized by means of trickery, part theft and part charity, excited them like a victory in battle; and even Fabrizio, once he had gathered up his winnings and stowed them away in a little bag of his, got up and, jangling his spurs, walked idly over to the table where the roast was being divided up, and without sitting down grabbed a portion, ate it, and wiped his fingers on Gervasio's curly hair. Then, swaying on his wide legs, swinging his shoulders, rearranging his clothes, he headed for the door that gave onto the street, followed by his hungry gang among whom was the dried-up-looking player who had been losing. They went out, they were gone, and for a while there was the sound of voices and the jangling of metal: those inside dedicated themselves with greater attention to their meal. They ate voraciously, suspicious of one another, each of them wrapped up in himself, facing the wall, perched on a rung of the ladder, or else at the table, protected by a personal object: a bowl, a glass, a knife. Those not invited to partake of the meal had pulled out their tin mugs of free soup from the monks and were working away with their spoons. Now everyone was chewing in silence while the increasing racket from the marquis's kitchen, the reflections from the great fire and the smoke were like alternating intervals of cloud and sun, the changing aspects of a sky beneath which they happened to find themselves living. The idiot was given bread dipped in the fat from the meat, just like the dog: the small children had already fallen asleep, their cheeks resting on the bones. And Antonio, who had not eaten, stood up. He had flattened himself against the wall when Fabrizio and his friends had gone out, and now he was moving about in that old, oblique, dreamy way of his, onto which had fallen and grown, like a chance seed, a peaceful awareness and wisdom. He put the children to bed, closed his father's papers away in a drawer, removed his flask from his side and, brushing against the twins as he passed, seemed to lay his hand by chance on the shoulders of the blond Gervasio, whose back was slightly crooked, and reluctantly took it away again. He went out into the street, came back in frowning as though at an unpleasant thought (Artemisia watched, learning about her husband) and said he wanted to draw the curtain because it was late: whether those who were out had come home or not. But then the quietest, the most colorless of the guests, almost an old man, seated on the floor with his back against the wall, moved his right arm and his cloak fell open. It revealed, lying flat across his knees, a stringed instrument which he plucked with his left hand, and then a deep vibrating sound like a heartrending echo of song became the new center of that late-night party. Without a word, as though remembering for himself alone, the Spaniard played quietly in an even, monotonous rhythm, an accompaniment, but the song remained locked behind his sulky, sealed lips. Then all of a sudden his hand went mad and tore at the strings with such speed that his fingers were just a blur; and from the medley of the wild chorus there emerged voices and instruments, even drums, all the flavor of a revelry. The player, gloomy, impassive, with purple lips and deathly pale cheeks, did not even appear to be listening: as for the others, some sleepily half-raised their heads, others changed position, stifling a yawn.

Antonio stood waiting, and his face bore the traces of long-endured patience. But for Artemisia, on the other side of the wall, that little bit of music was enough to remind her that there were other things, other countries, to be desired, that her father was far away, perhaps lost, that she had to make a name for herself, this strange name that she had been given and that must become famous. Her curiosity, and that small amount of mischievous animation that had kept her awake, spying, now abandoned her. She moved towards the bed, dragging the cloak behind her like a regal train. She had no further need of others, only of herself. Slowly, almost solemnly, she lay down, her movements following the humming bass notes which still reached her, muffled, "Tomorrow I'll tell Francesco that . . . " "They'll see just who Artemisia is." And so she fell asleep.

But later on, in the lightness of her first sleep, she heard Antonio open the door, close it again, come up to the bed, light a small lamp that he had: he could not sleep without a light. He undressed cautiously, sighing from time to time; his breathing quickened as he bent down to untie his shoes, and in her barely disturbed sleep Artemisia was once more overcome with the sweetness of his discreet, humble, faithful presence. She was a wife once again, and when, with her eyes still closed, she realized that before lifting the covers, he was standing for a moment looking at her, she felt a shiver run through her, a delicious fear. Deep in the night she awoke completely at least once, and the flickering light of the small lamp was the source of feelings of immediate, total happiness, warm as blood. In silence, and without moving, she contemplated this gift, this surprise, this creature that slept at her side, totally relaxed. His breathing was light, like a child's; the touchiness and shyness he had when awake were transformed into trust. Antonio enjoyed the sleep of the innocent, and an innocent man is a wonderful thing. Moved, she studied the things that made him human, her counterpart, her contemporary and her equal: his skin that was still smooth, his ruffled hair, the transparent membrane between his nostrils, his shining incisors, his hand finally at rest. At times, this noting of essential, minute details caused her to feel exhilarated and joyful, to feel that she wanted to wake him, talk to him, have him talk to her, about anything, in quiet, laughing tones, like someone blowing on a small fire that has finally caught, against all expectation. Then she would raise her arm and tuck the covers in round his neck. It did not occur to her to consider whether he was good-looking or not, or even if she liked him; hateful and pedantic seemed to her now her memories of childhood and of that faded wedding day when he had walked in front of her with his legs that were too long. Only one truth remained of that day, the page in the parish register where she is called Artemisia Stiattesi, a page that makes up for all those others that record her interrogation in Corte Savella. "How lovely it is," she thinks, enraptured, forgetful, as she drifts off into sleep once more, "how lovely it is to belong to someone, to lose one's identity, to become different, unrecognizable. How lovely is it?" The exclamation turned into a question and it was like the shadow of a dream that was just beginning, of an enchanting sadness that made the young woman knit her brow in an effort to penetrate it, to seize it whole. In the morning she had no recollection of it, not even as a dream.

This thinking and dreaming: here lay the danger. She had not had time for them when engaged in her solitary work, and in the days of her shameful confinement her thoughts had all been rigorously controlled. But now that she had paid her debt that had lasted so long, that she had overcome a certain adolescent weakness of hers which, as soon as her thoughts wandered, filled her with guilt as a sinner, it was easy to let her thoughts run free, unrestrained by any prejudice. "And what is love?" she was prompted to wonder one morning when she was feeling happy as a result of having come up with the idea of a dying Cleopatra which she would begin to paint in Francesco's studio that same day. She knew now that her duties as a wife, from which she had fled and to which she had later faced up proudly, were easy and pleasant when accepted with tenderness and love, from one weak person to another. It came naturally to her to shun the bitter secrecy of that selfish feeling which had once caused her to throw herself, as into a river, at Agostino, already impatient and distant. Agostino no longer has a face or arms, but he represented the myth of passionate love, the anguished myth to which she had attributed her motives as a girl betrayed. Does that myth still have any value? That constant internal violence, that suppressing of one's own abilities, limits and preferences? Is not love rather this unexpected enchantment, this instinctive desire to help that binds her to Antonio? She suspects herself of error, of cowardice. But now Artemisia does not close her eyes to these unpleasant facts, because Artemisia is a strong woman. So much so that she is not afraid to face certain stark truths that she invented herself, such as that it is time which makes us fall in love and out of love, time which makes us and destroys us, which we make and destroy. And she was filled with terror when she thought of how young she still was, of how many things could happen to her and seem right, and then wrong, before she died. She looked at the bed, at the odd furnishings, at her luggage all piled up, things that she not only put up with but which a feeling of superstition mingled with love warned her not to touch, connected as they were to the unspoken agreement that had rendered possible this union that kept her alive. A peddler husband who blinks all the time, who has a sunburnt neck and a white chest, who takes his box off his back with the movements of a weary laborer (the strap has etched a deep groove on his shoulder that will not go away). But a husband who takes her hand and lingeringly examines it, turning it over and over as though lovingly studying the skin, the lines, the veins, with an enraptured smile tinged with melancholy at the corners of his mouth. Secrets, impalpable mysteries which might be dispersed if too bright a light were to shine on them, and Artemisia could not bear that; which maybe even a change of clothes, a change of hairstyle might mar, or scatter, so Artemisia does not change her clothes, does not open the case in which she keeps her trinkets. Yet the day her brother offers her a lovely apartment in Ripetta with an anteroom and salon which a Frenchman is willing to let her have in return for ten large canvases a year, she does not definitely refuse. "Six at the most," she retorts, sketching in Cleopatra's clothes, with the slightly arrogant confidence which everyone except Antonio seems to expect of her. And now this idea of living in a hovel between the stables and the kitchens seems to her a childish whim.

Winter brought discomfort and hardship, and it was odd how, just when she was about to declare them barbarous and unbearable, an extravagance of Antonio's, a clever idea of his, transformed them into a fairy-tale world, magical and wonderful. An ingenious heating vent banished the cold, blowing into the room hot air in which motes of the old grain that had not been swept away danced like gold nuggets. The damp bricks disappeared one evening under a rich carpet with sumptuous colors. A fur blanket was spread over the bed which became the warmest, most luxurious Artemisia had ever slept in. Meanwhile Francesco's proposals were becoming urgent, leaving her little time to think: two weeks, one week. And it was then that the gifts in the room in Ripagrande multiplied: lengths of material, fans, small bottles of perfume, crystal jugs, silver trays, amber beads; there even arrived an armchair of gold leather and a very slim oil lamp for a writing desk. Antonio appeared very seldom, but it seemed that as the days ran out a feverish competition was taking place between what her brother was promising and what her husband was offering her. Francesco was saying, "A fully equipped house, the furniture is included in the contract, with silk door-curtains and everything you need. The Frenchman has arranged a carriage for you that will cost very little, and he will pay for the footman. You'll be able to receive ladies of rank, you'll paint portraits of the most important people here. You'll be

in his Excellency the Cardinal's service before a year is out."
And, spread out on the bed, for Christmas, Antonio left her
a dress of silver brocade, made to measure. It was his last
gift.

On St. Stephen's day, in fact, Artemisia went to visit the
new house, amid the merry bustle of horse-drawn carriages
and pedestrians, ostentatiously dressed ladies and gentlemen and busy servants, everywhere a profusion of food and
gifts, eels, vegetables, capons, apples, fresh grapes; and the
screeching of bagpipe players, the life-size cribs in the middle of the street, shouts, laughter, bright red noses. In the
extreme clarity of the winter sky the stars were already
shining and the Frenchman's footman, escorting the Gentileschis to the carriage with a lighted torch, addressed Artemisia as "your Ladyship." For the first time since his sister
had arrived in Rome, Francesco accompanied her right to
Ripagrande, got out of the carriage with her, went into the
Stiattesis who, amazed and wild, were right in the middle of
a quarrel, with Mariuccia having taken off a slipper which
she was about to throw at Protasio. "Good riddance, Bat-
tista," said Francesco, with a stern expression, for he had
always disliked this semi-relation and the time seemed right
to show it. He had taken care with his attire to accompany
Artemisia, with his sword hanging at his side, and he moved
fastidiously, like someone who does not want to soil his
good clothes. He did not sit down, he did not speak to the
others, but took leave of Artemisia with a graceful kiss on
the hand, in the Spanish style, which he had learnt goodness
knows where. For a moment it looked as though Mariuccia's slipper were going to change its target.

"I've got a surprise for you," was how Artemisia
thought she would open with Antonio when telling him
that they were moving house, that he too would be able to
enjoy lovely furniture, good food, a servant. She was well
aware of the enormity of what she was suggesting and she
tried to feel angry in order to give herself courage: "He'd
better be pleased about it, someone who doesn't even know

what a proper house is, and who, due to me, will be able to hold his head up in the world, will be obeyed and respected." But when she saw him come in with an uneasy expression, almost a presentiment, on his face that had grown haggard again in a few hours, it was forgiveness that she asked from him. And that made things worse than ever, for no one had ever asked Antonio's forgiveness, and the way his wife humbled herself like this made him feel he was in the right, a position he had never pretended to claim, so that the small mannerisms that went to make up his presence were as a result routed and his customary silence, instead of being gentle, became harsh and agitated. The burden of talking fell to Artemisia who all night long talked and wept and even lost her temper, smashing the crystal jug which Antonio picked up bit by bit. She was still talking at dawn, as the bells rang, while Antonio slept, shattered, deathly pale. He did not leave the house that morning.

Then Artemisia was caught up in a frenzy of tidying every object, every article of clothing in that crude, dusty room, as though she wanted to prove how unfounded and foolish had been her deep reluctance to change the appearance of a place where things both old and new, primitive and refined, were piled up like the accumulation of spiders' webs and dust. The first thing she did was to drag into the middle of the room the luggage she had brought from Florence, take out her Florentine dresses, the presents that she had been given by the young Grand Duchess, by her high-ranking lady friends, then she went through and sorted out her painting equipment, which included the pieces of a large collapsible easel, like the legs of a crippled insect. The cords on which Antonio's merchandise was hanging shook as she bustled past, with red cheeks and dry lips, her mouth set in its childish, stubborn pout, with jutting chin. When the lids of the crates had been nailed shut again, there was left on the floor, next to the rug, to the unmade bed, to the armchair pushed into a corner, a pile of old papers and straw, like the remains of an overnight en-

77

campment. "Now you'll come," said Artemisia, exploding in voice and manner, her head held aggressively high; and if Antonio had looked at her, he might perhaps have recognized the naughty, generous little girl who sometimes tried to wrench him from his tranquillity as a small-time dealer. But Antonio was not looking at her; he had his back to her, standing beside the tall window with his forehead resting on the iron grille which was so high up that Artemisia could only reach it with the tips of her fingers. A shout came from the courtyard, "The mules for the sedan!" followed by the noisy clatter of hooves. "The porters are here, your Highness," came the mocking voice of Mariuccia who today dared to enter their room, standing in the doorway, curious and hostile. At that moment Artemisia suddenly felt that an enormous injustice was being done to her, that someone had upset the appearance of her room, of her beloved, conjugal room. She would never have another one, of that she was sure, nor would she ever enjoy any luxury or gift as she had enjoyed those which had been given to her therein. But now it was too late to go back, to protest, to change her mind; it was too late to touch the silver lamp set on the ground, the traveling cloak she had used one evening, now sadly creased, looking like someone come back from the dead who was showing her the door. Mariuccia was looking at her, Antonio was not. "Take this, and this, and this as well," Artemisia began to order, making a supreme effort, forcing herself so that her voice did not falter. She was thinking how long it had been since Antonio had embraced her: twelve hours, twenty hours? She would have loved to put her arms round his neck, rest her cheek against his back, hold him tightly with her hands on his chest. Perhaps that was what was needed to dissipate this lasting pain. But it was like hearing heartrending music and not being able to follow it, and it was a hollow victory to pass in front of Mariuccia, her head held high, without batting an eye.

The worst was yet to come: once she had settled into the

new house, Antonio seemed to have decided to follow her, to live with her, to obey her, in short. But he was no longer her husband, her dear, strange, mysterious husband, the mercurial, gentle man who was capable when with her of acts of will and initiative that were almost imperceptible but which were as unusual as they were respectful and gentlemanly. Certain delicate, light-as-air moods which his uncoordinated limbs had been expressing more and more openly, and which consisted of states of touchy good humor and of a facade that had to be continually peeled back, had disappeared, as in the memory of a dream. Only in a dream could Artemisia believe that she had penetrated the character of the man with whom she had enjoyed living; when faced now with this present man, obtuse and uneasy, evasive and pedantic, who returned home either too early or too late, and once in the middle of the night, unsteady and knocked about; it looked to his wife as though he had been drinking.

But there was so much to be done in the new house, too much that had to be organized and overseen for them to be able to establish a free, respectable way of life; a routine of going out, coming in, working, resting, in a natural, easy rhythm; the heritage of those who have always lived in a comfortable house and felt it was their right to own it. The hours flew past, and with them the new furnishings, so that Artemisia saw the chairs, tables, crockery and full cupboards as though they were visions, or ephemeral sparks from a great fire burning far off. They appeared and were set down, only to reappear and be set down again half an hour, an hour later. Using them was a conquest, not a pleasure, so that she felt like carving a notch on their shining wood surfaces, a sign that would make them less independent and temporary. The man-servant would raise the famous door-curtains of yellow silk to announce, "Two gentlemen are coming up," or else, "Teta the washerwoman is through there," for already Artemisia was beginning to receive visitors, exhibiting the fruits of her labors, paintings brought back from Florence, now varnished and framed. But she was also beginning to be recognized and visited by importunate former neighbors and gossips who still lived in Santa Croce or Via Paolina, and who were appearing with a mixture of shyness and audacity to inquire into the well-being and situation of the little Gentileschi girl. It was unusual for the gentlemen to spend more time looking at the paintings than at the painter, and as for the gossips, they went back home saying that, never mind painting, Artemisia had found the career that suited her best. And Artemisia, retiring to what is now her room, having said goodbye to the solicitous Francesco whose savings she is spending, feels a bitter uneasiness come over her, and she climbs the steps to her fourposter bed as though descending into a well. Antonio does not share this bed with her, without an explanation he has chosen a small, dark room with a camp bed, and in the morning when he goes out he leaves not a trace behind, not so much as a pin. "You sly, suspicious, narrow-minded wretch," Artemisia says aloud, sitting alone on her big bed; but these insults do not bring release or consolation, and the chill that penetrates her curdles her tears like milk. She feels as though she were homeless, driven out from a warm shelter where Antonio's gifts, the only riches she has ever owned, have been left behind, taken from her by deception.

Crying silently, scorned, was all right at fifteen when she barely knew herself, not even her own face. Today Artemisia's suffering cannot be separated from an image that is present by itself in a mirror that never goes dark, even though the beautiful woman reflected in it—so blond, so white, such a lovely smile—is cause for suspicion and inner darkness. And too often her tears are liquid fire which light her anger, because this is not a time for suffering, but for living. Let Antonio explain himself, reproach her if that is what he wants, let him listen to her reasons, allow himself to be convinced. Already her restless limbs are getting ready to move, to take her out of bed, out of the room. But she is prevented by the darkness of the night in that borrowed, almost usurped house; by that row of useless rooms which she must pass through with the lamp in her hand and which do not recognize her; and then by Antonio's face itself, down there in his little room, with God knows what sort of expression, with God knows what staring, impenetrable eyes that would immediately disappear behind his eyelids, all of which cut short her impulse and her intentions. Impossible to believe that a month ago she dominated those eyes and was implored by them.

She lies down. Is Antonio lying down, or is he still sitting up in the cold, thinking thoughts that he does not betray, his long legs curled up under the blanket that is always too short for him? In the new street, which is noisy even at night, the carriages drive past until very late and coachmen in the service of important gentry yell raucously, claiming right of way. Laughter, wild singing that fade away, or sometimes, in the silence that beats its velvet paw on her brow, a mournful lament. From an alley, from a house, from a convent? There are so many churches round here, so many dead under and behind marble slabs. Artemisia pulls the sheet over her head, her heart racing, feeling unhappy and guilty once again. She does not care what she will say tomorrow to Chevalier Dal Pozzo, a noble patron whose support she must win, and to the Marquis Giustiniani, a sponsor who does not want any fuss. She no longer wants them to come as promised. And if she manages to calm down, to fall asleep, it is only by thinking that at least Antonio is in the house, a few yards from her, that he is her husband and that a quarrel between husband and wife is of no significance. "He'll understand, we'll be together again, he'll love me even more."

But the light of day restores her claims and her pride. Antonio must give in without being begged. Look at what he is, who I am. I must retain my pride, or else I'll lose dignity. The gentlemen arrive, they find her dressed alluringly and in the latest style: the white dress she got from Antonio is so old-fashioned. With the manner of a Queen: "Your Excellency, Marquis, you can have confidence in this woman, she will serve you as you deserve." Francesco, who is present and full of courtesy, is overjoyed: a commission from the Marquis, who has a collection of paintings of all the best artists, is the key to success. Already he can see the portrait, black and white, done in a strong, proud light, with arrogant brush strokes, the ruff around his slim neck as fresh and white as a lily. That is how kings and emperors are painted. "What do you bet that within a year one of the Courts will be asking for you?" Francesco intends saying to her as soon as they are alone, and in the meantime he enjoys the easy, daring grace with which his sister banters: poor girl, she deserves it after all she has been through, always downhearted and so hardworking. So her kind brother's thoughts run, for he is not a husband or even a father, and will not accept injustice. But then, coming from the other room—"Who's in there?"—they hear a loud thud and the sound of running footsteps clumsily disguised which it is difficult to attribute to the blundering footman, who is anything but blundering, and who, anyway, puts his head in the door and all but winks, slyly. And so Artemisia, undecided between a curtsy and a haughty glance, guesses that Antonio, who has not yet gone out this morning, has tripped over a chair, picked himself up hastily, and is running away so as not to be seen, like a wild animal: capable of jumping out of the window if anyone tried to detain him. She grows pale, her heart fluttering in indignation. "And that's my husband! That's the sort of husband I have!" The anger deep inside her no longer blazes, but burns steadily, burning the sumptuous room, the brocades, her elegant dress, the prestige of her paintings and that of the two men of rank. This is a fire that smokes and gives off a bad smell. The world to be conquered matters less than the impulse to run after Antonio, stop him, shake him, make him talk, weep, like a silly woman. She turns round impetuously and she too trips in her own skirts.

"We're not in Ripagrande now. Here you need to behave differently, with greater dignity. Greater cleanliness too," she bursts out at the first opportunity, for Antonio is sitting at the table opposite his wife, but reluctantly, all over the place as usual, playing with the meat on his plate and not eating, filling his mouth and dreaming with half-closed eyes. His hands look dirty against the white cloth. Dirty but light. This Artemisia remembers and it tears at her heart like something that has been lost; those hands, when they caress, are as light as feathers. In Ripagrande they did not look dirty, on the contrary, the grayness in the folds between his knuckles was more like an affront he had endured, a travesty. She carries on talking, accusing, so as not to feel moved, and she raises her voice and listens to herself in horror, within these walls which goad her into cruelty and spitefulness. Her young, persecuted body has no home of its own, no home for her spirit which all too often cannot find a temporal or physical setting in which to express itself, which cannot accept itself nor be accepted unless with violence and an unhappy pomposity for which it was not made. Now the words come pouring out, ricocheting off the walls; now Artemisia gets to her feet, driven towards disaster like a crazy horse. She stands erect, her hands gripping the edge of the table, leaning forward towards Antonio who does not reply. There in front of her is that face of which she has grown so fond, there is that person whom she cannot do without, whom she would never consent to losing: her husband. But the implacable voice continues, "Things can't go on like this, they can't go on," while her tongue dries up and her saliva turns bitter.

Antonio sat there, his hands lying loosely on his thighs, his head bent over one shoulder in a position of extreme

83

fatigue: Artemisia's unseeing eyes threatened, but did not pierce. But then his right eyelid trembled and it was as if he were shaking the ashes of her anger from an image. And the image thus revealed, the man she loved, was raising his arm, bent at the elbow, in front of his face, just as a child does to ward off the blows, not that he has received, but that he expects. Expects from experience.

A tumult of grief, of regret, of compassion, of love—a love that is aware of its own irretrievable loss—rose from her chest to her throat, closing it to all protest, to all amends. "No, Antonio, not like this," she wanted to say. A lock of her hair, still as blond and as fine as when she was an unhappy girl, fell down over her eyes which recognized, in that gentle gold, an appeal to the simplicity and the feminine dignity which Antonio had revived and reconsecrated in Ripagrande. But this appeal has no effect on Antonio; his recalcitrant soul has locked itself away in that crooked body which it is so sweet to have as a friend. With this new pain her earlier anger is rekindled. "You poor fool, you've let me down!" But before she can even close her mouth she is overwhelmed with dizziness; along with palpitations and a shortness of breath that she already feels instinctively guarantee her his indulgence, a happy solution. She brings her hand to her forehead in the manner of a woman fainting, feels for something to lean on, raises her fluttering eyelids: but look, there's no one there any more. Antonio has disappeared, like a will-o'-the-wisp; only his chair pushed back from the table indicates his rush for the door, his flight. The rooms are empty, there is no step on the stairs, and from the window there is no sign of him in the street. Upset, totally dumbfounded, as though she had never seen anyone get up suddenly and rush out of a house, Artemisia is on the point of screaming, of going out in her slippers to pursue the fugitive and dig him out, wherever he might be. She does not say to herself, "He'll be back." She has a premonition that she has been abandoned and lost, with her attack of dizziness, her mild fainting fit that was not ministered to by he whose duty it was. She is crying now, unrestrainedly and silently, her head down among the dishes on the table, the blond hair soaked with tears.

She is crying today too, having returned after all these months, a sudden, insistent presence that steals my words. "Oh Antonio, my husband! So gentle when asleep, you never harbored an evil thought, you used to sigh when you turned over, and if you felt my hair on the pillow you would arrange it like a bouquet of flowers. He went to get fresh water from the well for me, the night I had a fever. He used to look embarrassed whenever he blew his nose; he loved lilies-of-the-valley; he used to hold his glass with two fingers; he dragged his feet a little when he walked; I was able to recognise him by the way he coughed. Oh my husband, dead so soon!"

I recognize the tender, violent way Artemisia intervenes when she wants to force my interpretation, my memory. That obscure husband of hers, that pathetic, legitimate love of hers, she would rather have buried him than lost him. But I have to specify that Antonio was never really dead for Artemisia, even though she never saw him again and only at long intervals received news that he was alive and that someone had met him. I leave her to moan as much as she wants, her head on the laid table, back once more in that moment when she foresaw her desertion without really believing it, and gradually the tears dry on her lashes, desolate in their futility. She raised her head and carried out the simple, mechanical gestures of blowing her nose, wiping her eyes, looking round her, confused and emptied of all hope and grief. She might even have yawned from exhaustion. She touched the bread, brought a few crumbs to her mouth, her nostrils assailed by the smell of the food lying on the plate. Oh the roast that Thursday or Saturday: oh the salad grown by Taddeo, the gardener from Cicciaporci, among the brambles at Sant'Andrea! Artemisia chews, her chest still heaving: she is subject to cravings because she is pregnant. And Antonio did not even know.

Francesco had a hard time persuading her that the idea of moving to Naples was to her advantage and credit, for it is only a short journey from there to Madrid and the Spanish Court. "And you'll see," he urged her as a last resort, "you'll see if that odd husband, when he hears the news, doesn't come back to you." Artemisia shook her head in denial, intending to wallow in her despair and live—once again— like a nun. Before that, she told herself, she was going to do her worst, in deed and word, against those treacherous Stiattesis who had incited her husband. But her protests gradually grew weaker and weaker; she was slowly being filled with a great feeling of peace, she was putting on weight. Her headaches had disappeared, she no longer suffered from sudden high temperatures, and, to tell the truth, she could no longer be bothered worrying over her husband who had never come back, nor over what everyone in Rome was saying about her. Her beauty increased wondrously, but she found it exhausting doing the portrait of Signor Armidoro, a rich merchant from Genoa whom she depicted as a Turk, and a painting of Moses rescued from the river with seven women in different poses: the model for all of these was the niece of the curate of San Rocco, who had beautiful black hair. She had her brother wait on her, overbearingly calm and domineering, so that the poor fellow was not able to go back to his studio in Strada Pia, not even to sleep. The gentlemen who had taken to visiting her with the excuse of seeing what she was working on were dumbfounded and annoyed, for the woman treated them so insolently, and were it not for her beauty they would have forgotten she was such a famous artist. It was her brother who packed all the boxes and even the food for the journey; she did not move from the house. The more urgent things became, the more relaxed she grew, in the end sleeping most of the time, sending her visitors away, regardless of their rank. But three days before her departure she became once more, despite her large size, the arrogant, impatient girl who had arrived in Rome all alone, and alone intended to leave again, because she needed no one. "No one," she said firmly, with that serene face of hers, leaving poor, affectionate Francesco thunderstruck. And alone she left.

Things and people obeyed this beautiful, distant woman, so much so that never had the coach to Naples made a better journey, without even a moment's fear, not even through the woods; the horses were all strong and sensible, the postilions courteous; the weather mild. The inns, of such terrible repute, turned out to be quite acceptable, there were enough beds at every halt, and the passengers never stopped saying what a heavenly journey this was, casting frequent but respectful glances at the face of the beautiful woman, so refined in her attire, who never moved from her corner seat padded all round with cushions. Everyone was in a good mood when they arrived, and Artemisia did not have a moment's uncertainty in recognizing Padre Ilario, whom she had never seen before, a monk who was very eager to help her in any way he could. He had arranged a small apartment for her in the guest quarters of the convent of the Poor Clares, respectable, clean accommodation, with large rooms, terrace and garden: it had been vacated by a widow who had remarried. It did not cost much to smile, and Artemisia smiled, with her beautiful, blossoming, blond looks, marvelously complemented by the new stateliness of her movements that was so in keeping with the spirit of the nation. As though a noblewoman were coming among them, the nuns peeped through the grille at the arrival of their guest and the father confessor: and immediately sent her consommé, sweetmeats and marzipan. Placid and confident, Artemisia went straight to the bedroom and drew back the curtain round the bed as though she had slept there for years. "I'll need," she said to the monk, "an honest girl and a footman." With one last smile she closed the door. She was settled in, protected by walls: in the peace of her soul there rose, triumphant and sweet, an indescribably strong feeling of safety, freed from the past, satisfied with the present. In the same way was her child safe in her womb.

A life of solitude began anew, though free from restrictions, rich, smooth and easy, in this sumptuous, teeming land with its sea, its palaces, its immense hubbub, its vivid colors, its terrible smells, its extremes of cleanliness. The girl she employed was called Terenzia, not really a girl but the widow of a fisherman, an experienced woman. A porter from the market became her footman, a man who sang and told stories: he was rarely in the house, always on the doorstep polishing the copper, grinding colors or swaying on a chair as though rocking a baby. Which he did, later on, but before that Artemisia had to get through the long days in which nothing happened, apart from the evenings when, as she washed the paint off her hands, Terenzia would invite up some women who knew all about pregnancy, with the excuse of bringing a few eggs or a bunch of wild chamomile; and then there would be great discussions about what was needed to make a birth pass really smoothly. Through these humble conversations devoid of any malice, the artist was reconciled to the ordinary women of the people, the image of Tuzia no longer disgusted her and that of Cecilia and Arcangela, paragons of chastity and pure love, did not fill her with regret. Their indiscreet remarks were like caresses. "So young," one would say, "to be without a husband!" And another whispered in Terenzia's ear, "Poor girl, God knows how it happened!" In this way the state of widowhood was attributed to her without her asking for it, and she neither confirmed nor denied it, friendly and silent, won over to a sisterhood that expressed itself in symbols: refreshing brews, balsams, nourishing foods, comforts which the female species has elaborated over the centuries. As a result of these fleeting contacts with the outside world, the calm, voluntary recluse came more and more to see humanity as divided in two very disparate parts, so that her reason and her instinct convinced her that the time had come to give in and choose, to belong to only one, suppressing the burning pain of that "If only I were not a woman," that futile lament. Far better to ally herself with the sacrificed and imprisoned, participate in their veiled, momentous fate, share their feelings, their plans, their truths; secrets from which the privileged, men, were barred. Here, among the women, she listened to Nunziatina Ingroppa, a peasant women who knows what she is talking about: "When you feel those contractions low down, start walking up and down like a mule and in three hours the baby will be born." And Marchetta, mother of twins, advises her to have everything spotlessly clean in the bedroom, lots of fresh water, no shortage of freshly laundered linen, and no relics nearby, because she has seen many wealthy ladies lying in velvet die, and each time the fastidious ladies' maids were more afraid of getting soap on their hands than of the devil. The women began to grow slightly bolder, to come into the room while Artemisia was painting, and they did not bother her, paying her as little attention, after their initial curiosity, as if she had been at the loom. Only Celestina, a small, insignificant child, hovers round, always finding a way of ending up behind Artemisia and watching her work. She thought she recognized her own face in that of Saint Theresa, but said nothing, only grew bright red and covered her cheeks with her hands. There was a buzzing in her ears. Fabia, who did gold embroidery, said at that point, "I'll bring you some of my soup, after two bowls of which you'll be getting out of bed."

But most evenings, at sunset, Artemisia stays out on the terrace enjoying the coolness without being seen. She looks at the rippling, restless sea, the jousting vessels like fierce monsters, their sails billowing in the wind, bristling with masts and rigging. She is beginning to recognize the Spanish galleons, the English cutters, the French galleys, the feluccas from Genoa: she enjoys following the activities of the tiny men on the rigging among the limp sails, or watching them load the small boats that bring the merchandise ashore. Then, raising her eyes to the sky, she follows, as though in church, the play of sun and cloud, of light and shade. She watches a storm approaching from the east, swift and marvelous, the water turning dark green, then black. Terenzia makes the sign of the cross, and Artemisia thinks how these natural phenomena are studied by artists from Bologna and the north who attribute great importance to landscape, but that they could be used as background by anyone. Once the baby is born they'll see: they'll see what Artemisia Gentileschi is capable of. In the meantime she is free, under no obligation, free to indulge herself in fantasies about the color of the sea and sky as though painting were no concern of hers. She reaches out her hand for the jug of lemonade which they make so well for her here, and nibbles intently on the candied fruits made by the nuns: these cravings of hers must be taken seriously. The money Francesco gave her is worth ten times as much here as in Rome, so cheap is the cost of living in Naples. And then everyone gives credit to this beautiful Roman lady about to have a baby, no one asks her for money, not even the midwife who comes to visit her and say with the expertise of a fortune-teller, "Before the new moon is here the baby'll be born."

"I'm dying," said Artemisia, doubled up in pain as she took to her bed, at her side Terenzia and Fabia, who were not in the least worried but silent and serious: outside, under the clear evening sky, Pasqualino the footman was singing. She said "I'm dying" because she felt obliged to, but in her pain she felt strong and happy; and she was reminded of the black and white cat in the house in San Spirito who used to purr while giving birth. She took care to keep a clear head, to pay attention to what was happening to her, alone as she was in the hands of foreigners; but it was as if all unhappy thoughts were safely encased in soft, swollen clouds, summer clouds that rumbled but carried no evil, coming and going, in and out of her. It was a feeling of being a protagonist, albeit a humble one, struggling against a legendary evil that came from afar, even though born inside her. Her gestures were commanded, rough and coarse in their obedience, and they caused her waves of shame as though she had been caught in the act of sin and held up to ridicule. "I'm dying," she repeated at the last, suddenly remembering that she could indeed die, hastily taking on all the emotions of a dying person. She had lost track of time, already feeling in a state of peace, while the Sibyls grew frantic in their activities, all hands and rustling garments, while far, far off a plaintive, animal moan rebuked her. Then she felt really afraid and, aware of still being alive, raised herself up on her elbows to have a look. Before the women forced her back down again onto the pillows, she saw a small dark object, all entangled, alive only in its open-mouthed crying, sometimes on one note, sometimes shrill like a trumpet, but very effective in expressing suffering—and this she knew only too well—that has no other outlet. And suddenly it was beside her, so stiff and hard in its tight swaddling clothes, only its eyes and mouth uncovered, both closed; and big, adult tears. She clutched it to her breast with benumbed arms; it gave off a light, humble smell that seemed familiar. A childhood memory? A memory of a dream? And this too caused her shame, as though one of her bodily secrets had been revealed. In order to hide she closed her eyes tightly and said to herself, but almost without really thinking it, "What will we do now, how will we manage?" She became aware of having heard Terenzia exclaim, a century ago, "May God bless her, it's a lovely girl."

Porziella, Porziella, a sweet but clouded name, too easy on the lips, too heavy on the heart, a flower and a treacherous well for such a young mother who touches the cradle with her foot as if she were dancing, then says, "Terry, the baby's asleep, remember to give her her milk, don't let her cry because I have guests." And she descends the four steps to where the best artists in Naples were already coming to visit her, to pay her compliments, to where her model had already taken up his pose, and the apprentice boy who was in love with her, the laughingstock of the assembled gentlemen, holds out her palette already prepared, with a heavy

Spanish sigh. Down at the end of the room the groups of visitors, friends and friends of friends, form a black mass against which the sword hilts and gold necklaces sparkle; and every single time Artemisia, her eyes picking off the strongest expressions of resentment from among them— that moustache over there, that arrogant beard, that offensive, forced laughter, certain obvious allusions to the behavior of a fashionable lover, feeble or strong—halts with a sort of sudden aversion, sudden reluctance. But the time is gone when she would shun men in Via Larga or in the Palazzo: now she is Maestra Artemisia who gives lessons to young painters and is not afraid to rebuke them, if the need arises, with a tap on the cheek. She must go forward, force her way through the crowd without a backward glance, calling with all her strength on her pride, her vanity and her enormous self-confidence: then her cheeks become flushed with the small flame of excitement that suits her so well. Porziella is chubby, Pasqualino keeps her amused, Terenzia feeds her. Now that she has started walking, she sometimes latches onto the skirts of her mother who never has time for her, and looks up, frowning, as though she feared a rebuke, or desired one. She is only allowed in the salon when her mummy uses her as a model for a cherub or a Cupid, and Artemisia works intently, alone, wearing her big, dark-blue apron, her face pale, her hair unkempt; or else she sneaks in without being seen, escaping from Terenzia who has dozed off, attracted by the golden half-boots of Captain Alonso, or by the silver colors of Marquis Alcide. No one takes any notice of her as she circulates among the boots and cloaks, chasing a couple of frightened cats. Or sometimes she finds a quiet, empty corner where she stops to watch her mother who does not see her, her restless mother who bustles from one group to the next or else stands motionless, in an attitude of severity, beside an easel. And at times the light from the oil lamps casts disfiguring shadows onto her face, so that Porziella would burst into tears were she not already so peevish and secretive. Sometimes it happens that a bow made by a new arrival, or the fuss generated by an imposing cassock, reveals the child; and then Artemisia's eyes, cold and brilliant with the diligence she brings to her duty, are turned on the child just as they are, portending a reaction of such peremptory impatience and dangerous irritation that Porziella lowers her own, closes them so as not to see her mother's. And on one occasion she was seized by convulsions so that Don Alonso found her lying at his feet, nearly tripping over her. Her mother picked her up in her arms, without a word, and the child opened her eyes, calmed down: Artemisia's embrace was powerful, almost violent. In moments like these, Artemisia is aware, almost suspiciously, of an unbridled maternal vocation, a tenderness for the little girl that catches in her throat with a taste of blood. Is it permissible to love a daughter in this voracious, greedy manner, the manner of female animals and of destitute women in their hovels? Padre Ilario promised her that Porziella would be educated like a princess in the convent; but he also said that children must be made to respect their parents and behave properly particularly in Artemisia's case, a woman on her own. These obsessive longings to be alone with her daughter, for a warm, loving relationship that will carry them forward united to the grave, are not normal; or perhaps there is a place where this desire is the norm: among wild natives, or in ancient times, or a thousand years hence. Crazy thoughts, maybe even sinful, for a woman who must put propriety above all else and uphold her position, she who has opened an art school and drawing academy when there are so many worthy male artists in this city. She has no women friends and the ladies who come here would not hesitate to discredit her, declaring her to be of low and worthless character. Now and again her heart so swollen with ambition, love and contradictions sends out an imploring glance, a poor, unfortunate glance that flutters like a dove over the gathering of noblemen and painters. It asks for protection and understanding, and if anyone notices it, it is only to say, in a stage whisper, "What languishing eyes Si-

gnora Artemisia has today." And another will reply, crude-
ly, "Come on, lads, whose turn is it?" No real harm, however: Artemisia is beginning to learn about life and to shrug
her shoulders to dismiss the insolent remarks of uncouth
men. If only she did not sometimes believe that she were
heeded, respected, even beseeched by a pair of sad, mournful eyes. Artemisia has not yet learnt to protect herself from
such dangers, but no one would think so to see her engaged
in caustic repartee with Aniello, a man of great talent and
spite, and never be outdone in witty remarks, until finally
she is almost disgusted at her easy victory. "Let Agatina get
undressed," she commands in a bullying manner, "the dark
girl from Gragnano is no good for the nymphs in this Greek
painting." The models obey like sheep, accustomed to the
more polite, flattering ways of male artists: they are furious
but docile to the commands of this blond ruler, so cold, so
fragile, who fills canvases with sketches of enormous thighs
and breasts that would put Annibale to shame. "These
girls," adds the talented artist, raising her eyes scornfully,
"for every hundred that take their clothes off, there isn't one
good one among them."

And Porziella has disappeared. Maybe she is romping in
the other room with the Bolognese puppy belonging to
Don Fernando, an aristocratic pupil, or being consoled by
Pasqualino and Terenzia with songs and sweet biscuits.
There is certainly no trace of her left in Artemisia's mind,
which horrifies the soft-hearted Stanzione: this woman has
no heart, she does not know the pangs of birth, the blood
that turns to milk; she is a she-bear, a wild animal. Insinuations that are not unpleasing to Artemisia when they are re-
ported back to her, in fact they make her feel elated and help
her to appear exceptional, a woman who has renounced all
tenderness, all claim to feminine virtues, in order to dedicate
herself solely to painting. As imperturbable as a gambler,
she prepares a new palette, demonstrates how to use sepia
without letting it become dull, bites off an annoying bristle
on her brush: just look at her impasto, how haughty she is,

94

what use of color! Their voices are all in agreement, led by that of Stanzione, and Artemisia is triumphant. Oh Lord, a lover, a father, brothers, a husband: of none of these, in the end, does a woman have need. And now this daughter of hers . . .

But it is difficult to dismiss this daughter, and even just finding her behind the door, standing on her small, soft feet shod in felt—certain little red slippers—is enough to make her heart beat faster and the blood rush in her veins: this little girl of mine is growing so fast. If there is no one around, not even the servants, Artemisia gets down on her knees, brushes the soft, black hair with her forehead. She has to talk to her in the Neapolitan dialect, like Terenzia does: "Come now, Porziella, give mamma a kiss." Only rarely does the child make a halfhearted kissing noise; most of the time she turns her head away, spitefully, and looks as though she is about to cry. For a moment the soft little forehead and the solid ivory one, rather than being united, are reflected in each other. Then the woman stands up, brushes the dust off her dress at the knees, and swiftly walks away before she weakens; and from her small height Porziella can stealthily follow the bright, impassive face that is already moving away from her, like a distant meteor. Porziella and her mother learned to cross swords at a very early stage.

We are playing a chasing game, Artemisia and I. We also try to catch one another, not without laying snares, which range from the obvious and material to the most subtle. I am leaving her for my first trip since the war; from which, I tell myself, I may not return. She spills a whole bottle of ink onto my papers. And then we look at each other. She has become very suspicious about this period of her life in Naples, the turning point of her career, uncertain whether I will remember what I had written, or if I will start afresh. In the midst of so many recent deaths her second death matters less and less; there is not enough compassion left to make me conceal the sins of one who is long dead. Without a doubt it was in Naples that she accomplished deeds in the full maturity of her willpower and responsibility, the deeds which reappear, so they say, in the hour of one's death. For a moment, with a secret smile, she confides to me that this is not true, that it is a myth invented by the unfortunate living. And she shakes her head and once more lets it fall onto the tablecloth of the laid table where Antonio left her. From Naples she wrote to a Roman patron, "If it please your Excellency, let me have news of my husband, whether alive or dead." It is as though I had received a message slipped under the door: is this how you abandon one of your main characters?

I do not know if it was during the day or at night, whether at work, or walking, or making conversation, but the loss of Antonio, lost through her own fault, was a thorn that never gave her respite. At times she thought of him in a mood of righteous indignation and rancor. Often with a touch of nostalgia, but in total freedom, her own mistress. More rare, but long and intense, were the moments when her husband appeared to her in the image of a faithful, heartbroken man, with those eyes of his like a cloudy sky that said, Till death do us part. She can see Antonio as he travels along beside his donkey, or on his own, on a white road, his sack or box on his back, with his smooth, shuffling gait as though moving through the rooms at home; now and again he halts to wipe the sweat and look at the valley. Now he is taking a rest, in the uncomfortable posture so typical of him, slightly twisted, at the foot of a tree, any sort of tree, neither beautiful nor ugly, just leafy enough to provide shade and rest, the sort of tree that can be found at the edge of all main roads. He knows how to allot his time when traveling and in his gentle, passive way contemplates the distant clouds, the nearby fields, the mountain ridge; and no one knows what he is thinking as he picks up a white pebble and puts it in his pocket: goodness knows what use he has for it. Is he going to Loreto? To Senigallia? To Crema? To Varallo? Certainly not to Naples, on the contrary, he is going in the opposite direction for fear—so thinks Artemisia—of not being welcome there. He is rarely seen in Rome; long months go by with no news of him at all. And while Maestra Artemisia is painting huge canvases, he is setting up his stall laden with medals, rosaries and pictures of saints beside a roadside shrine. Saints painted by that friend of his, the slightly slow-witted lay Dominican who once knew Orazio and his daughter, that lovely young girl: now he works as the porter in a convent suspended over a valley which the sun pierces between one rampart and the other like a spit. Antonio stays with him from time to time to replenish his stock and to spend the night, lying beside the warm ashes, according to the season, or with the door open onto the steep fields full of crickets. He leaves at dawn, when there are still stars in the sky, and washes his face with a handful of dew-soaked grass, so as not disturb his host. He overtakes highway robbers hiding in thickets and their lookouts dressed as ploughmen; he brushes past carriages, still motionless, belonging to travelers who are still asleep; passes through the herds of oxen exhausted from their long journey that brings them to market. It grows lighter, he can make out cupolas and bell towers on the pink-tinged ridge. There is the cart of the traveling entertainers. The fire-eater's son has grown into a young man and is helping to repair the wheel of the comedians' cart: the women, disheveled and half-asleep, are standing around watching. How are you, Omodeo? Good morning, Romualdo! His meetings with the fake blind men and cripples are the friendliest of all. Antonio knows dozens of them, they all used to come to his father's house in Ripagrande. They go to the best known places of pilgrimage, to the most famous spas, which are frequented by sterile women and men suffering from kidney stones. He greets them, but is wary of them, for in the casket with the small compartments that he carries slung across his back are silver mirrors and buckles, gold rings, things to tempt the girls. But Antonio is reluctant to display them, for once he brought them to his wife, and now he does not look the girls in the face. . . .

97

Thus imagines Artemisia, still the object, so she believes, of the love of that runaway who, she feels, is in her debt, and to whom she dedicates various emotional daydreams, as if in conversation. "If only I had gone with him. He would have put me on a mule with a lovely comfortable saddle: being so young, I would have got used to walking at his side. In time we would have been able to buy a strong horse, a big carriage: Antonio was so clever. I would have given birth in a hut, like Our Lady. I would have been the one to paint him saints, votive offerings, and even big pictures for wealthy pilgrims. I would have been known as the traveling artist. Porziella would have grown up and sung hymns to the Virgin Mary with that beautiful voice she is showing signs of developing."

No matter how terribly hot she may sometimes find this Neapolitan land—for example, on the terrace of her new house, at siesta time—in Naples she must stay and give account of herself. It is the year sixteen hundred and thirty and there is plague about; very few people are on the roads. In the bright light of the bay the image of Antonio fades away amidst the rustling of his rosary beads, as light as acacia leaves on a slope whose summit is the sky. In those days, in well-to-do families, the father used to keep a notebook in which, for example, could be read: "On such and such a day, in the year of Our Lord, Signora Artemisia, my wife, gave birth to a female child, baptized in Sant'Angelo a Nilo with the name Porzia Antonia Orazia Cecilia Maria. . . . " So would have Antonio have written, if he had agreed to follow me, concludes Artemisia with a bitter taste in her mouth and a frown on her brow because of the sun, because of her fate. She never learned to write other than her signature and the only notebooks she possesses are for the creation of her Esthers and Cleopatras and Bathshebas—not to mention that a mother without a husband is not a head of family. Just what exactly her state is no confessor has been able to explain to her, no matter how hard she insisted; just as, moreover, no matter how much thought she gives to it, she has not managed to recognize and define herself in terms of any exemplary figure approved of by her century. Nor is this to be seen as total presumption. She is a woman who wants to mold her every gesture on a model of her own sex and time, a respected, noble model—but cannot find one. An image with which she could identify completely, under whose name she could fight: these are Artemisia's needs in her thirty-third year, an age at which she is beginning to be influenced and attracted by worldly pleasures and customs. But she is not a princess, she is not a pawn, she is not a peasant nor a tradeswoman, not a heroine, not a saint. And not even a courtesan, despite what people say about her. When she was in Florence the reputation of being noble in character was enough for her, "The shy queen of hearts, the chaste adventuress, idol of other women." In Rome she was a rash maiden, then a legitimate wife. In Naples there is no patron saint for a woman who is mistress of her art. She has to keep repeating, "My Don Pierantonio is trading far away, he sends good news and promises of gifts for Porziella. . . . " And Porziella is growing up, still slightly plump, as dark as an African; and she is at ease only with servants, dogs and working women. Artemisia's maternal love storms wildly, moans, struggles, becomes frenzied. All in silence, of course. As for the rest— her painting, her reputation, her ambitions of fame—Donna Artemisia will have to be content with improvising her own methods and rules, with sowing the seed for them that will produce, whenever it may be, the fruit which could satisfy her present thirst, but which does not yet exist. In any case, let her wear herself out, let her suffer: this is her freedom.

"Signora Anguissola, that talented artist, was already working in the Spanish court at my age; and she was offered one of the foremost noblemen for her husband. Adriana Basile, the singer who made the very air tremble, was prized by their Highnesses in Mantua as a rare jewel, and she returned to Naples a Baroness." A month after completion,

99

no one seems to remember the historical paintings she did in Pozzuoli, on such a large scale that they would terrify a giant; and as a woman she can no longer hope for any commissions in the churches of the city. That April Artemisia dressed Porziella in sky-blue brocade and brought her out with her in the carriage, giving her treats of candied fruits and ass's milk, showing off. In her drawing classes she forced herself upon the attention of visitors and friends with drawings of nude, brawny women, three times as large as life: young Cavallino, a small runt of a man, could not make up his mind to copy them. On some evenings there were only a few guests and students and in the emptiness of the room the female Maestro started talking too much. In this the season of her prime there rises a vapor which clouds the purity of her intentions and also, according to some, the mirror of her honesty, even though she guards it boldly and aggressively, at times insolently. She is harsh in her boasting, she mocks the worthlessness of the women in the house, their silly vanity: that Stanzione woman, those daughters of the Spaniard. And she goes too far, she threatens reprisals against vague enemies who insult her because she is a woman on her own, who want to give her a bad name, who want her dead. Her friends, taken by surprise and unprepared, listen pityingly but coldly, which, if it does not wound Artemisia, does at least sting her. For they are young, all younger than Artemisia; and they are men, so inevitably there is always one who winks at the man next to him as though to say, Here we go again. Talking all the time, increasingly agitated, the teacher tries nonetheless to fulfill her duty: she makes a correction here, erases something there, redraws it. But her hand trembles, her gray eyes flash, a feeling of impotent rage constricts her throat. If only she could question them one by one, these boys, evaluate their devotion, their respect, divine what they think of her. And more than once she intercepts a lazy glance that lingers like a fly on the swellings of her lace-trimmed bodice: ah no, what greater shame could she endure?

Her weapons were to paint with ever increasing boldness and ferocity, with heavy shadows, stormy light, brush strokes like the blows of a sword. These effeminate men, these pathetic painters so fond of daintiness, they'll learn. The men she paints are armed, all steel and iron; and the women are shining black, all of them rushing towards the light as though to say, Hey there, blockheads. She is well aware that these are not the sort of paintings that her father would praise at the end of the day, once work was over, as she cleaned her palette; but it was the only way to rouse the attention, or rather the amazement, of this ungrateful, un-enthusiastic public who want to be stunned, terrified, by a work of art. "Naples, stage of your marvels . . . ": among the curious who began once more to flock to her art school there were a couple of poets who composed sonnets like this in her honor, but the populace never cried out in the streets, "Long live Artemisia," as they did in greeting when the beautiful Adriana went out on the sea to sing and play on a golden lyre. No prince has yet called her to his Court; the vicereine does not want her services, despite all the presents Artemisia sends her; and the foremost ladies of rank continue to ignore her. It was during this period that Artemisia, with the excuse of a few letters that needed to be sent out, thought up the ostentatious idea of employing a personal secretary.

The Spanish cost too much; locals proved to be extremely unreliable. They demanded a whole new set of clothes, stole from the larder, then disappeared taking a couple of paintings every time; because they were so devoted, they used to say. In sixteen hundred and thirty-three a certain Diego Salato, as thin as a rake and threadbare, turned up at her school: around his neck, as well as a scapular—for he had been to the holy land—he wore a relic of the true Cross, and his family tree, which was an aristocratic one. He aroused her compassion with his great big eyes and the trembling hand he laid on his breast if Artemisa so much as went near him. Every day he presented her with jasmine and roses: he would lay them at her feet as at the statue of a saint. He fainted from hunger on the evening of his third visit, and still he said nothing. He underwent a rapid transformation from the moment she took him in, fed him, looked after him. He began to wear a long robe, indicating that he had taken holy orders, and only his large famished eyes remained motionless in his face which, like his body, was never still. Now that his slowness and seriousness have disappeared, he laughs, talks, kneels down, weeps, regains his composure, yawns and dashes off again as swift as the wind. He eats all the time but never puts on weight, is very willing and not at all embarrassed to go to the market for tender young lamb or special large eels, for he loves good food. He tells lies and then is sorry, is never lost for words, and can turn on the tears at a moment's notice. He swears, threatens to disappear so that not even the air will know where he has gone. He waves his hand in the direction of the sea, murmurs strange, incomprehensible words. Then, cold as ice, he gets ready to take dictation for the usual letter of introduction for himself. And Artemisia dictates: " . . . this gentleman, Don Diego Salato, of most noble descent, in my service . . . " The evening—the night?—will be sweet: perhaps this is the price she must pay so that a short but perfect period of serenity will ensue. "I am only as chaste as the next woman. I'm free, I'm not doing anyone any harm." Instant but short-lived justifications routed by the sound of a bell identical to the one in Corte Savella. So Lucca the tailor and Fausta the washerwoman, who testified on behalf of Agostino, both of them foulmouthed and insolent, were right after all. They were correct in their predictions: the Gentileschi girl is hot-blooded, anyone who wants can have her. "How wretched I am!" she cries out in despair, with equal sincerity, suddenly repentant, wringing her hands like Mary Magdalene whom she has painted so often. If only this fervor that spurs her on to make a spectacle of herself would last: shaven head, sackcloth, public confession, harsh hairshirts—for such a woman, such a beautiful woman.

Artemisia recovers quickly. All she has to do is raise her head and catch sight of certain aspects of the physical world, so blessedly outside herself, to feel them invade and instantly renew her, just as a beach is made clean and smooth again after the pounding of the waves. That thin crescent moon in the pale sky of early evening, already she can feel it refreshing her eyes stinging with hot tears; the line of the horizon, so simple and sparse, fills her with a forgetful innocence; that light-blue coastline over there talks to her of adventure, of freedom, of exemption from common sense. And anyway, there is no point in worrying about it, let he who is without sin cast the first stone. And since live she must, why not seize the pleasurable moments that give help and support? The wind is changing. She is receiving praise, real praise, proclaimed by people whom she may even have considered her enemies. A foreigner is due to arrive and it is well known that he has said, "The first person I visit will be that great lady artist who, I have heard, is as marvelously beautiful as she is talented." Tomorrow she is giving a formal reception; Gaspare Romer will be there too, the extremely rich Dutchman just back from Portugal, and everyone knows the affection, the special esteem he entertains for Artemisia. She will need a large number of armchairs, she can borrow them from Don Angelo Pepe who is generosity itself. Massimo Stanzione is sending some wooden chairs so that the more important artists can draw in comfort, for you never know when new ones might turn up. She is going to need musicians, she must send word to Belinda the singer. The food and drink will be provided by Padre Ilario, who has remained her friend, and his nuns. Who knows, maybe there will be a representative from court; a few noblewomen have promised to accept her invitation. Anyway, there will be no shortage of beauties. Massimo's magnificent wife has agreed to come and she can be very courteous when she wants, Signora Ribera is coming with her beautiful daughters who, although rather stupid, are on familiar terms with the nobility. And Annella de Rosa will be there too, an artist on the threshold of fame and a very attractive young woman. No one will ever be able to say that Artemisia is afraid of a new rising star: to welcome Annella and make a fuss of her will be a noble gesture on her part that will provoke everyone's admiration and make her a topic of conversation. Standing in front of the mirror with her mouth full of pins, she tries on her new dress and imagines the scene she has planned. Annella is shy, but Artemisia will go to meet her at the door and take her by the hand: what a marvelous sight! "Behold," she will say in a loud voice, and a silence will fall on the room, "behold, ladies and gentlemen, the most beautiful artist in all Naples." That will really embarrass Artemisia's supporters, who, out of politeness, won't be able to object.

But, to tell the truth, there were no objections to be heard when Artemisia, faithful to her plan, raised her voice to speak the words which, she thought, must create such a great impression. Annella's hand remained uncooperatively closed in her own, so that she felt equally torn between wanting to shake her, treat her roughly, and praise her with ever-increasing enthusiasm. One by one, she went up to her guests, even the most uninterested, and, in a conspiratorial whisper, confided to them that this lovely girl, so talented, a pearl among women, has a brutal husband who beats her out of jealousy. "Someone must save her," says Artemisia passionately, for nothing can make her draw back once she imagines that a course of action has been set in motion. Like an insolent child Annella pulls a wry expression on her beautiful, full, olive-skinned face beneath the thick black hair so badly styled—an unmistakable refusal of the compassion and friendship offered by her hostess. And the mature woman does not realize that this other, still unripe one has more friends than she and is sneering at her. She even sneers in front of Don Gaspare, the card that Artemisia did not want to play, but which, in her frenzy at excelling in generosity, she does not hold back: "I beg you, my lord Don Gaspare, to do me the honor of using the brush of this young artist who has no equal in the whole kingdom." Right at this moment, to the excited pressure of the hand which is pushing and pulling that of her protegée, Annella responds with a jerk that releases her fingers and her whole body. Annella is odd. Annella wants to leave, without any consideration whatsoever. This is the way she prepares for her present and future conquests: Massimo, the infatuated maestro, proffers her cloak, her grim husband puts it over her shoulders, everyone makes way for her, for who does not know the beautiful Anna de Rosa, the wild seductress? Don Angelo Pepe himself comes running forward, ready to offer his carriage and leave the party for her: so much for the great Artemisia.

There is no point in being mature and strong and brave if one does not learn not to give way in the most taxing situations, to which Artemisia is more exposed now than when she arrived in Naples ten years ago. Exposed, more than anything else, to suffering. Suddenly, with all the fervor of her frustrated act of kindness, she is denied that intoxicating pleasure of admiring herself in the eyes of others, a pleasure so necessary to a woman such as she, always more inclined to give and surrender than observe and compromise. It is not jealousy or envy, but the cold certainty that she does not count for anyone since she did not count for that young woman. She feels now as if she has been stripped of everything, talent, presence, beauty, fame; and even of that triumphal ability to repent and pine away, a state into which she has sometimes dreamt of withdrawing with the dignity of a betrayed queen. Repentance appears now as a luxury which is no longer for her, an ostentation of early youth which she can no longer permit herself now that she has a daughter, two servants, a house, these malicious friends and visitors; and no one to protect her, she who can protect no one. She grows peevish, starts to feel sorry for herself, loses her composure: she lavishly bestows her dazzling, open-mouthed smile on all and sundry, using it to cover up a feeling of indignation that is not really anger, but is closer to tears. "This little bit of talent that God has given me (Gaspare Romer looks as though he is listening, but is he not slightly irritated by those female hands that never stop opening and closing convulsively?), I'll tell your lordship how little it is appreciated. If I ask for two hundred scudi for a painting with eight figures, Prince Ruffo offers me one hundred because I'm a woman, and I'm not paid according to my worth." Her right hand, heavily adorned with rings, rummages inside her low-cut bodice, between her white breasts: "I'm not lying, your lordship can check for himself, here's the letter."

That maneuver of fishing around for, and finding, the letter in the gulf of Venus, as it is called; her exclamation, a short while later, in the silence of the gathering, "In my bosom lies a heart of gold"; her exaggerated curtsy to a certain Signora Capomazza, a peasant from Aversa who wants Artemisia to paint her portrait and whom Artemisia mistook for one of the Vicereine's ladies-in-waiting: the artist lucidly goes over these and other blunders in her mind once the candles have been extinguished, and, without even checking whether the door of the salon is closed—disgust and fear do not go together—picks up the lamp to go to her room. A marvelous opportunity, this lamp, held in the hand of a pale, blond woman, casting a strange shadow at every step: an opportunity to study herself in the mirror and prac- tice the style of painting as done by the Flemish artist Gerard that is now so popular. But it is late, late in every sense, and Artemisia makes her way through the cluttered, overturned chairs, the half-full glasses, the spittle on the floor, and she does not stop, her mind on her unhappy thoughts; and it is only by chance that she notices something lying in her path which rolls far away—a ball, an apple?—perhaps fallen out of the pocket of someone who had not dined, someone like Diego, a year ago. Diego has disappeared without saying anything to her, most likely gone out on some subterfuge, some dishonest affair he hopes to make money out of; for she already knows that he wants to go back to Spain with a full purse, and that it won't be his lady and mistress (as he liked to claim repeatedly) who will keep him here. How difficult it is, how costly, in this light, in this silence, to convince herself she is still a woman. The servants are asleep in the attic; she could even die tonight on her beautiful, ornate bed, her solitary artist's bed, and no one would notice. But it is not of death that Artemisia is thinking, for that is a thought that does not worry her, but rather of that clumsy behavior of hers a short while ago, of those actions and words typical of a silly woman, the worthless dross that leaked out of her from the wound inflicted by a girl with full cheeks who refused her friendship. No one can hurt her as much as another woman: this is what she ought to have explained to those men who were perhaps amused at the conflict between the two painters. "Look at these two women," she should have said, "two of the best, the strongest, two who most resemble exemplary men. See how they have been driven to being false and disloyal to one another in the world that you have created for your own use and pleasure. We are so few and so besieged that we can no longer recognize or understand or even respect each other as you men do. You set us loose, for fun, in an arsenal of poisonous weapons. And so we suffer. . . . "

No, this little speech would have been of no use either, and now, in the silence, only serves to justify and express her agonizing distress, the unhappiness that sinks into her soul like a stone into the sea; and as a result she is condemned to solitude, a sentence agreed upon by a large crowd of people to whom she wants to draw close, but who laugh in her face and slip away. The ladies in Tuscany, avid for novelty, avid for revenge when they saw the murdered Holofernes; Annella, who paints like an expert, but who jousts with her lovers at the risk of having a knife stuck into her, whose husband sends her flying like a rag doll from one end of the house to the other, and she covers up her bruises with white chalk and thinks nothing of it. And Artemisia herself, after all her pride, whom has she had to lean on, confide in, subjugate? Men, worthless men: Titta Licomodio, Tommaso Guaragna and now this Diego fellow who leaves her on her own. "I wonder who dropped that apple." Her thoughts wander as she drifts off to sleep. Porziella used to love apples when she was small, she used to leave chewed cores all over the place. But Porziella is in the convent, she belongs completely to the nuns and does not even want to come home on Sundays. "My daughter," Artemisia bursts out at dawn, waking up in a flood of hot tears incubated in her sleep, "my daughter who is now a woman and does not understand her mother. . . . "

This awakening of Artemisia's is also my own awakening. The immunities granted by war, the extraordinary freedom that everyone felt he was allowed, have ended; all the dead are resting in their final graves. Artemisia's obstinacy in making me remember her, my own obstinacy in remembering her according to my own whims, in emotional fits and starts, is becoming a game, maybe a cruel game. I was betrayed by the urgency with which I saw her, yes really saw, that she expected from me, after my grief at having lost her and the trepidation of finding her again so very much alive, that inexhaustible surge of stubborn hope of someone who continues to nurse the incurably ill. I had grown accustomed, through contradicting her and even teasing her a little, to situating her in my own time, to feeling her standing behind me, present. I was certain that she understood and needed me. I was in the habit of preparing small surprises for her, interpretations that were the opposite of what the record of her life had suggested to me; and I believed that she enjoyed it, given the fact that she had been lost. Only today, listening to the probable lament of a mother who was really alive one night in sixteen hundred and thirty-five, in Naples, a real night like the one that will be upon us in two hours' time: only today do I realize that I lacked respect in her regard and that what I longingly took to be her consent has been, for a long time now, her absence.

When was it that she left me? I go back over the events of our desperate encounter and cannot find the point. Perhaps it was from the moment at which I abandoned her childhood, the period during which, like all women of disreputable fame, she recognized the betrayed promise of a life more pure, more worthy, than the one that fell to her lot and from which I would not release her despite all the opportunities she offered me for doing so. It was a great gift: who, in fact, at the beginning of the seventeenth century, had a childhood at all? Maybe she is still on the Pincio hill outside Cecilia Nari's window, or in the act of pinning her first womanly veil over the low neckline of her bodice made of coarse material; or standing by the spinet where she posed, a quiet, secretive little girl, for Saint Cecilia, and Francesco in a nightshirt posed for the angel, so that it was easy for him to look at her with the devotion of a younger brother.

I will never again hear her protesting and objecting in that arrogant, rough, bastardized Pisan accent of hers; she will never again help me; she will never again react to the real or imagined circumstances of her life with the disgust, the shudders, that made me want to weave its rhythm and images together in a joint collaboration, active and shared, the convulsive game of two shipwrecked women who do not want to abandon the hope of being saved on a barrel. She has merged once more into the distant light of three centuries ago, a light which she shines full into my face, blinding me: the speed with which the images of her life followed each other and merged together wavers, coagulates into pictures of a lunar magic lantern, cold, flat pictures. Here is one of a blond woman, still young-looking but old in the way she holds herself and the expression in her eyes. She is sitting on a low chair against the bare wall of a large, ugly room, she bends her neck which, although firm, is heavily lined, in an attitude of defenseless prostration, almost of grief-stricken exhaustion. Someone has left her in this state, a moment ago or days ago. Maybe it was Diego who has gone back to Spain. Maybe Porziella who has returned to the convent after spending her holidays at home, bored with her mother and her painting.

I try once more to move her. I say: Porziella used to lie in her cradle as good as gold, you could not even hear her soft breathing; she learned to walk very straight right from the first; she preferred old rag dolls to beautiful wax ones; she very nearly died from the emetic given to her by the quack doctor, but she recovered in three days; she used to cry till she lost her breath but with no sign of tears; she had small curls on the back of her neck, and underneath them a little beauty spot, as black as soot. . . .

I continue to provoke her: at the age of five Porziella was already totally at home with the nuns and her face would turn deep red when they said to her, "You are the daughter of the famous lady artist." She refused to learn to draw even from Sister Assumption, who was a real saint. The abacus, on the other hand, she learnt very quickly, and also sacred history, and she knew by heart all the religious orders and their emblems, one by one. She knew how to distill elixirs better than Sister Mattea and she even did the convent's accounts the month that the cellaress was ill. She hated artists, paints, canvas: when she was at home she would hide the models' clothes and play all sorts of spiteful tricks on them which she would then boast about in the convent as if she had done something to be proud of. She admired the gentlemen, but furtively, always listening at doors, feeling the velvet of their cloaks in the hall and rubbing the hilts of their swords to see whether they were made of gold or silver. At the age of twelve she would walk around with lowered eyes, but she was able to tell you what everyone was wearing. She refused to ever sit at the table with Diego, and on one occasion she spat in his soup.

There is no reply from Artemisia; she is immeasurably distant, light years away. In the end, in my reluctance to deal with her time in Naples, even though it was responsible for her fame, I recognize an unspoken suggestion of hers. I have forced her to subscribe to the role of an imperfect, unmarried mother, of an artist of dubious quality, of a proud but weak woman, a woman who would like to be a man in order to escape from herself. And I have dealt with her as one woman to another, lacking manly respect. Three hundred years of greater experience have not taught me to release my companion from her human errors and reconstruct for her an ideal freedom, the freedom that gave her strength and elation during her hours of work, of which there were many. And now I am unable to rouse her, to make her talk, with these memories of her unhappy motherhood, the usual topic of women's conversation.

"You who have such great knowledge, such experience of research into and teaching about mothers and children, you who investigate and devise how children should be loved, how they should be brought up so that they will be healthy and loving and grateful and happy. . . . " Perhaps this is Artemisia's reply, a sudden reflex, outside my control, which through me is put into words. Words heavy with an irony that is not shrill but extremely cold and calm and yet compassionate. The sound of distant wisdom. I no longer expect any help from her friendly presence, but accept this warning and read it with the pathetic grief of someone who has to admit defeat. I now admit that it is not possible to recall to life and understand an action that happened three hundred years ago, far less an emotion, and what at the time was sadness or happiness, sudden remorse and torment, a pact between good and evil. I acknowledge my mistakes; and now that the ruins have been ruins for a year and show no sign of being in any way different from so many other, ancient ones, I limit myself to the short span of my own memory, condemning my presumptuous idea of trying to share the terrors of my own epoch with a woman who has been dead for three centuries. It is raining on the ruins over which I wept, around which sounds had a muffled, frightening quality that the first blow of a shovel dispelled for ever. Artemisia's two graves, the real and the fictitious, are now the same, breathed-in dust. We have found out once again that we are poor, and the poor must learn to persevere. For this reason, and not for any more exalted one, but in secret expiation, I will continue the story of Artemisia.

"As soon as I have finished this portrait of the Duchess, your Excellency can rest assured that I will commence work on the painting of the Baptist, the composition of which is all prepared in my head, with some marvelous landscape features. . . . " Thus dictates Signora Artemisia, and it does not matter to whom, today the twenty-sixth of July, sixteen hundred and thirty-eight. The letter is going to Rome, to one of her old friends and patrons who have not forgotten her, perhaps because she will not let them. But Rome, what is Rome like today? She hears that everything has changed, from the fountains to the palaces, from the shops to the churches, but she has never had occasion to see it again. It is particularly the artists who are in vogue there who have changed, and what with local ones and those come from afar there is now a whole throng of them. While she dictates Artemisia raises her square, stubborn chin as though the people in Rome could see her and respect her: she is still a handsome woman, in spite of her yellowing, sweat-soaked temples and the constant lines of disappointment at the corners of her mouth. She has not done the portraits of many duchesses, to tell the truth; the Viceroy's court still continues to regard her, if not with hostility, at least with indifference. But this time Artemisia is not lying, nor mistaking hope for reality. The commission exists, the lady exists, and she bears a name which is famous for the feudal domain she owns in Castile, the palaces in Naples and Palermo, a name that will impress even those in Rome: where it will be revealed and confirmed that Signora Gentileschi does not use her painting as a pretext, only in the service of men, such lies! Getting on a bit, as even her friends jokingly say, which means that she is over forty. Pride and disdain, with a touch of insolence, are still the weapons she must use if she wants to defend herself and retain her good reputation. She knows no others, even though she realizes every day that these are taking their toll on her face and her mind.

Nonetheless, there are bright days when she still manages to appear happy, and even to feel so, at least partially; days when she throws her head back to emit gurgles of genuine laughter and narrows her eyes good-humoredly so that no one can see whether the expression in them is still one of merriment or not. This Duchess is not a friend like the Florentine ladies were: his Excellency the Duke could not bear for a male artist to be near his wife, and, weary of constantly denying her a portrait, one fine day conceded, "Vamos." He sent his head footman to fetch "that Artemisia," and went out displeased and frowning, fingering the order of Calatrava that hung round his neck to ward off bad luck: let not the female artist be a sly, corrupt dueña.

Donna Virginia is sitting in her large, regal, uncomfortable armchair in a stiff, drowsy attitude that disguises her anger, for she wanted a real artist, a Spanish artist, for example that famous Ribera fellow. What is this woman daubing away at? "Vuelvase, Vossignoria, a mano izquierda," improvises Artemisia, having spent ages trying to think up a compliment to pay the Spanish woman, and finally giving up because she needs to concentrate on her work. Donna Virginia turned, as stiff as a rod, and did not reply. She was very young, barely fifteen, and her arrogant stubbornness, which deep down was really meanness of spirit, seemed to be epitomized in the way each one of the very coarse, jet-black hairs that grew on her low, spotty forehead curled upwards individually from the roots to the frizzy tips. For more than half an hour she sat in silence, but she did not sit still. She looked down at her small yellow hands which resembled the claws of a bird, nibbled on a hangnail, made it bleed, sucked the blood, constantly rummaged in her pockets, fiddled with her fan, with a box of sweets, with her ivory rosary, the beads of which were shining skulls. She even started to pray, mumbling rapidly between narrow lips and moving her eyes around so that she looked as though she had a squint. And finally she attached herself to the big bell with the purple tassel and began a litany of what she wanted and did not want, giving orders and then canceling them—still rigid and haughty, stiff-necked—to the page-boy, to the dwarf negress, to lady Manuela the dueña; all delivered in rapid Spanish but with the affectation of muf-fling the "s" sounds, and from which, from time to time, there emerged, mangled by her incorrect accent, the sound of a bastardized Italian word: "sartora," "sorbetto," "pas-seggiata."* And when all the running around, all the talk-ing, all the bowing and scraping seemed to be over and everyone had gone off to carry out her orders or else cancel them, the Duchess turned halfway round in her chair and stared at the artist who, with all her equipment neatly laid out, her canvas prepared, and the charcoal in her hand, was doing her very best to work. The look she gave her was that of a poisonous insect, greedy and unhappy, which caught Artemisia, despite all her mature experience, by surprise, so that the charcoal that was shading in the sharp cheekbone was brought to a halt. "This dress *no me gusta*," Donna Virginia said quietly, almost as if it were an effort, "can I change it tomorrow?"

She was as talkative during the second half-hour as she had been silent during the first, not with the vivacity of girls of her age nor with gestures that seemed natural, but with a sort of manic insistence, in a voice that was splendidly mo-notonous, the cry of a restless bird. A vague expression of permanent disgust continually disfigured and clouded the features of her immature, scowling, shiny face, the look in her eyes and their youthful whites, the shape of her smooth mouth. There was something brutal about this sudden fa-miliarity after such strict self-constraint, and brutal too was the choked-up abundance of the secrets that she forced

*Dressmaker, sherbet, walk.

upon, rather than confided to, Artemisia, thus revealing that she intended these as another means to lord it over and degrade her. Secrets that smacked more of bragging, of inventions fabricated to frighten her listener or herself, tragic delusions of grandeur and horror. "The Duke is madly jealous, he has spies watching every step I take, he's already had five men who were wooing me killed. The Count of Ipenarrieta was hacked to pieces simply for serenading me. In Madrid you should have seen all the noblemen who followed me to mass, a whole flock of them. I couldn't even show myself at the window. . . . " After that first appraising glance, her black pupils, nearly always hidden and almost turned back under her eyelids in her enthusiasm at her fabrications, do not once rest on the woman who, standing there, exchanges the charcoal for a paintbrush, prepares her palette, takes a step back and then goes up to the canvas. The small noblewoman does not even show any curiosity about the handling of all this equipment that is new to her, or about checking to see if the drawing resembles her, if her features that are being portrayed for the first time are attractively presented. She gives the impression of not being susceptible to the weakness of wanting to appear the way she likes, in keeping with the image she has of herself in her mind. Artemisia's attention, because it is concentrated in her eyes and her hands, has by now reached a level of such acute interior perceptiveness that she does not fail to penetrate the secret of this show of indifference; the indifference of someone who is condescendingly lending herself to receiving homage, rather than yielding to her own desires, the nature of which she would never stoop to examine. To tell the truth, the adulation wrought by her paintbrush is lost labor and futile are the sacrifices she makes to reality over that clumsy chin, that lower lip which is too full, almost drooping. Artemisia is totally wasting her time resorting to expediencies of flattery, for even if she were to put in the thick moustache that adorns her upper lip, the Spanish girl would not mind. The front of the Duchess's hair style is miserably severe, the tightly pulled-back hair revealing an expanse of discolored skin which looks slightly scabby and which the artist hides with layers of glazes. Such a pity, for she had hit on, and mixed on her palette, just the right tone for that trait of nature: any artist would be proud of it. But that's the way it goes, anyone who wants to serve the great has to put up with things like this: thus does Artemisia console herself.

On the second day Donna Virginia sent her favorite dress, covered in lace and braid, which lay lifeless on the armchair. She also sent a Spanish veil, a golden rose, a pair of gauze half-sleeves, a neck chain, a green plume. The green plume was the last to arrive and each of these objects was brought by a different messenger: Manuela, Pepito the pageboy, Tommaso the Neapolitan footman, and finally a filthy stable boy who cut a strange figure, ragged as he was, amidst all that magnificence. Donna Virginia did not come herself, but her sharp, childish voice could be heard two rooms away. Let the artist paint, for there was no shortage of things to paint, and she could have more if she wanted. The worst thing of all was that the messengers arrived but did not go away again. In fact they were joined by the steward, by the cook, by the *camarera mayor*,[*] who was even followed by the laundress; and they all talked without any consideration, especially the Spanish, to let her know that Madrid and Seville and even Burgos were the places to go if you wanted to see loads of unusual painters, but not women artists, no; they were *cosas de Italia*.[†] The Neapolitans got their own back, sniggering and winking secretly, but they were on the same side as the Spaniards when it came to besieging this woman who had the pretension to paint like a man. Artemisia, in fact, was painting furiously, her eyes half-closed, deliberately deaf, continually repeating to herself that it is difficult, but a great honor, to serve ladies of rank. The blood rose to her cheeks as it did when she was a

*Head lady's maid.
†An Italian thing.

young girl "of weak constitution." She was putting too much into it: a lock of golden hair—now pale because of a few white hairs—had fallen onto her cheek, and Captain Don Pedro, the last to come in and pry, for *Su Excelencia* was away in the country, said loudly, sucking a tooth, "Hermosa pintora,"* then turned round and went out.

But Donna Virginia reappeared on the third day and Artemisia found her sitting there as resolutely as if she had never moved. She was wearing the lace-trimmed dress and had the green plume in her hair, although slightly askew: on her face, however, was a new expression of docility, almost of dejection. No servants appeared or were sent for: her dark, prehensile hands were content to fiddle with the arms of the chair on which they rested; hands that looked cold despite the warm weather. Yet the emptiness of the large room richly decorated with wall hangings, magnificently bare of furniture, was neither peaceful nor quiet. From beyond the wide-open doors and across two immense, empty rooms there came the echo of noisy activity, of people not even trying to be discreet or even orderly: thuds, clatters, the sound of running footsteps, coarse shouts, the scraping of furniture being moved around and even laughter, even the singing of servants. They were getting ready for something: a party, a banquet, a departure? The antechambers must be full of grooms to judge from the distant, buzzing hubbub and from the frequent whiffs of soiled leather. Restricted to the brightest corner of the room, beside the excessively high window, the artist and the noblewoman look like two abandoned objects, and the dejection of the latter is so evident that Artemisia gives in to her older woman's protective instinct and loses sight of her objective, which was to finish the portrait of the Duchess in three sittings at the most. The girl seems to recover, or rather to recover her former childish severity, and the work proceeds. On the canvas there blossoms the usual pale, plump flesh that Ar-

*Beautiful artist.

temisia bestows on her female subjects, be they professional models or noblewomen; with the addition, this time, of a frowning, recalcitrant expression that it was impossible to soften and over which her brush passes again and again in futile insistence. In short, the portrait is finished and she has to speak. "Would your Excellency do me the honor of seeing if the work is to her liking?" Artemisia takes a step back, moving out of the way to make room; Donna Virginia does in fact rise to her feet, but then stands there erect, as though troubled—she is short because she has not finished growing—in front of her big chair. She yawns. She rubs her hands together. And suddenly she bursts into tears, weeping copiously, her arms hanging down by her side, not wiping the tears that run with difficulty over her brown skin. "Quiero mi madre, quiero volver a Espana!"* Those unattractive features of hers, which even her extreme youthfulness can do nothing to soften, seem to find some justification, and even a sort of beauty when convulsed in crying. "Mi madre, mi madre," she murmurs in her final sobs; and then she rubs her eyes hard, blows her nose twice in succession, in a rhythm taught her by her nursemaid, and looks round astonished, like a child, in front of the portrait that she does not even notice. "Calm yourself, Usted, your Ladyship," says Artemisia, trying to make herself understood, while a muted feeling of sadness comes over her and a confused desire to use her big, flat sketching brush to erase this unattractive portrait that bears no real likeness and that no one cares for, neither the person who painted it nor she who wanted it done and has now forgotten all about it: two unfortunate women. It is possible that a reciprocal instinct to console and be consoled could have been strong enough to cause Donna Virginia to bow her head and the artist to make a move towards holding out her arms, if they had not suddenly heard through the open door the sound of footsteps so authoritarian in their rhythm that they immediately

*"I want my mother. I want to go back to Spain."

announced that he who was approaching would tolerate no wasting of time, the master whose right it was to inquire into and censure everything. Without breathing a word or a sigh, the noblewoman slips back into her position on the chair and all that remains is an imperceptible trembling between her chin and the ruff of her dress which makes the lace quiver. An unwilling accomplice, Artemisia goes over to the canvas again and picks up her palette and her brushes. Pointless precautions, because the figure of the Duke, with his moustache, his high boots, his chain of the order of Calatrava and his cloak from Olivares, crosses the room from door to door but does not even see or take any interest in his two subjects, motionless in their corner. A minute later his voice, which seems to grow louder at every outburst of vexation, can be heard in the distance. Slowly, and with a slow sigh of relief, the artist begins to clean her palette and put her brushes away.

When she found herself out in the great courtyard once more, at the foot of the imposing staircase, her proud eyes searched and searched in vain for the carriage, or at least the sedan chair, by means of which, as was stipulated in the contract, she was to be conveyed back and forth from her own house, with honor, as befitted an artist of rank. Her glance quickly surveyed the groups of soldiers, horses, coachmen, noblemen and beggars and then immediately withdrew, recognizing only Pasqualino, the shabby, impudent servant who was enjoying himself immensely at this opportunity of mingling with the crowd. Now he comes forward with an air of confidentiality, almost winking at her: he is no longer the youth of so many years ago, he has aged badly, thin and dark, his hair already gray, wearing the tattered uniform of a street porter, an employment that his mistress allows him to engage in in his free time, to save money. He is already laden with the artist's easel, her paint box, all her equipment, not in the least surprised that today there is no carriage, coachman or sedan for her. A few glances, not too curious, not too insistent, follow the lady who is well dressed but has no escort, at her side a servant without livery; then they lose interest. In this way is she who considers herself the foremost female artist in all Italy allowed to go out into the rough-and-tumble of the streets.

It was very enjoyable traveling through the streets of Rome on her own, in a hired carriage, defying danger and risking slander. It was a real adventure to dress up as a pageboy and walk quickly, taking big, long steps. But there are neither pleasure nor risks to be enjoyed today as she makes her way through this ragged, festive crowd on Via Toledo interested only in richly turned-out equipages, in funeral corteges, in beggars' quips, in baskets of doughnuts and almond cakes. No one takes much notice of women these days, says Artemisia to herself, accustomed as she is to the eloquent inconveniences of being beautiful, and does not pursue the thought. She has a long way to go; she is not fit. At times Pasqualino walks behind her respectfully, at the prescribed four paces; at others, after having been distracted by a fascinating sight, he catches up with his mistress and talks to her with the familiarity of an equal. "It's so hot." "Did you see the face of that black fellow?" "There's a real shortage of seafood, fried fish costs a fortune." And Artemisia replies, uprooted quite naturally from the social position she always imagined she valued and which she does not even remember now. They are like two chance companions on a road crowded with people who pay them no attention: the figure of the woman, unaware of gradually looking more and more dejected, is losing its easy strength, that elastic quality which testifies how a young woman is aware of and takes pleasure in herself as she walks along, even without a mirror. And then those small, indoor feet of hers are disoriented among all the stones, holes and dust, increasingly enticed back as she goes along, to their customary immobility in the sheltered shadows of her skirts.

Soon her physical fatigue causes everything to seem distant and blurred: the colors of the crowd, of the quacks and peddlers, of the carriages darting past in the hot sunshine;

even the fiery, flaming passage of the Viceroy on horseback surrounded by his noblemen leaves her unheeding, inattentive. Not to such a degree, however, that she does not suddenly realize how unlike her usual self she has become, so that with a courageous effort she draws herself up and starts deliberately thinking that this evening or tomorrow she will laugh with her friends over this unusual excursion, confiding to Massimo and to the young Spadaro how enjoyable it really is to walk through Naples on foot: all that bustle and no one paying you any attention. But then, exactly in the middle of working out and formulating a witty, concise sentence to express this thought, her mind is brought up short, suddenly aware of a very obvious fact, a truth so evident that it hits her like a physical blow, so real as to make her want to rub the bruise. People pay no attention to a woman of forty-five if they do not know who she is: a double blow. The surprise was so great—yet goodness knows how long she had known it in her heart—that Artemisia came to a halt, slightly out of breath, and looked all around her. She saw the backs of two mendicant friars, the black plaits of a young peasant woman in a cart, and from these chance sights she tried to draw some sort of help, as though rectifying an error or a lapse of memory into which she had fallen. Her eyes went from one object to another and then turned to the high, distant sky, pale with heat, to the bare line of the coast, but she found nothing there to refute, to suppress this earthly truth, of an accuracy and mercilessness so profound that it was easy for her to trace it back to its origins, to a precise date. And she remembered that the previous year, at the beginning of May, when the Queen of Hungary had arrived, she had thought that her new tan-colored dress did not suit her.

The last hundred yards were accompanied by the following thoughts: would the Duchess immediately pay the two hundred ducats as stipulated or would she make her wait for them? Would she, or would she not, receive the fan, the box, the gold pendant which the great are accustomed to sending when they are pleased? Porziella has no dowry, she must find money. She must send a letter at once to the Marquis Del Vasto telling him that the models for his painting of Diana were costing her a fortune. She is certain not to have any visitors this evening, with this heat, and Massimo is in Portici with his wife.

These were her immediate thoughts, the first instinctive defenses of an aging, resigned woman. "You don't need to come up, Pasquale, I'll send Nunziatina down. And give my regards to Concetta." She looked at the sweating man whom she had known for so many years, who did not give her occasion for either excessive praise nor blame: she looked at him, grown pale but with new strength in her eyes and a brave smile. She was feeling weak, tired and lonely and she would have loved someone, even Pasquale, to notice and express his sympathy. "Goodnight to you," said the man, relieving himself of his load unceremoniously and, so it seemed to her, with greater abruptness in his manner than usual, as though Signora Artemisia were inevitably coming down in the world because of her increased age, suddenly become so obvious. Like the poor little woman of the people she felt herself to be, Artemisia replied, "Goodnight to you." She began to climb the stairs and, looking forward to the pleasure of a good cry, which she very much needed, thought that she would need to hold out for another couple of hours before she could allow it to herself, on her pillow, in the dark. Already she was searching for an excuse, a concrete excuse—you don't cry because you are getting old—among her collection of misfortunes: her ungrateful, unloving daughter, her distant father from whom she never hears, her husband who has disappeared. That's it: her lost husband. Goodness knows why this old wound seems to her this evening to be the most compelling, the most painful. And she does not know what awaits her upstairs.

Sitting quietly in the kitchen, in fact, in front of a lamp with a smoking wick—for he had refused to go into the salon—she found Francesco, who had just arrived from

Rome without warning. His niece, after a few cold words demanded by propriety, had left him there and withdrawn into her room as was her wont since she had been forced to leave the convent against her will. Nunziata, the sullen, gossipy servant girl who had succeeded Terenzia, had asked a few silly, prying questions and was now busying herself in the shadow of the big fireplace. From behind the lamp Francesco raised his prominent, anxious eyes to his sister as she came in. While he waited he had been reading a small devotional book, but he immediately put it down along with his glasses which were held together with black string, because he did not want to appear a bigot, just as he would never have missed the services of his religious Confraternity in Strada Giulia. At this stage in his life, he had the earthy face of a good, patient, unambitious workman: his hands, cautious and uncertain when idle, looked like they were made of dry, baked clay. "Forgive me for not giving you warning, Misia," he said as he got to his feet slightly awkwardly, as though lame. "I had to come, to see Fanzago, and I had no time to write."

All at once, at the sight of this brother of hers who has always taken upon himself all the unpleasantness, all the humiliations of their family, and now the weight of all the years that have passed, Maestra Artemisia, forgetful of her defeats, feels her youth rising up once more. They embrace calmly, with restraint, quietly happy: not for anything in the world would Artemisia lose any of her former reserve appropriate to an older, admired sister, in front of her brother. That which she seemed to be asking of Pasquale a minute ago she will never ask of Francesco who loves her and in whose eyes her life continues to be an exemplary spectacle, a wonderful performance. Now she will have no need to cry tonight, and from his friendly presence her loneliness will draw not only comfort but also strength and validity, just as when she was a young woman living on her own who took pleasure in her solitude, in defying fate. No longer sad, but relaxed and in full control, even feeling restless and joyful, she calls Porziella, urges on the servant girl, sends for new candles, moves rapidly round the dark room, breaks a glass, laughs. Her brother's face, his heavy, slightly awkward neck, typical of a sedentary worker, have restored her faith in the future, her confidence in her abilities which Francesco has never doubted. She is able to love herself once more, a strong woman who succeeds where she tries, who is exceptional in every way. She moves through the house and her deliberate, joyful movements cause the flames of the lighted candles to flicker and waver. As she gets clean sheets and a fresh, white tablecloth she tells him in a vibrant voice of her latest activities in Naples, her commissions, her hopes, the compliments she has received; and she tells him that just this very day she finished a portrait commissioned by certain Spaniards who, although of the nobility, are very stingy. Just imagine, they even saved on the footman and coach that had been agreed in the contract, for which they ought to be lampooned. Oh, how could she have let it upset her, half an hour ago? Slightly awkward and hesitant, but with the quiet trust of old times, Francesco follows her round, trying to help, as though to show, without actually saying so, that he does not like his sister to wait on him. Enchanted and happy, but certainly not surprised at her good news, he confirms and encourages with sensible, cheerful words the veracity of this picture without a shadow, of this courageous, triumphant life. And if her life is so easy and happy, why shouldn't they talk about Rome, their beloved native city where there is no doubt that an artist like Artemisia is longingly awaited and can return whenever she wants? What is the Cardinal up to? Is he pleased with these new artists? Is Poussin still in vogue? Is Bernino still in favor? What's going on in the theater? How is trade? And how are her friends?

For some unknown reason, at this point (Artemisia was laughingly trying to restore order to that youthfully rebellious lock of hair of hers with a comb) Francesco lowered his eyes onto his plate, scraped the bottom of his bowl and did not reply. Deprived of the support and warmth necessary to her cheerful mood, his sister realized that other eyes were staring at her from the other end of the table, the eyes of young Porziella, rather peeved at having had to come out of her room, but observant and critical in her ostentatious silence; and those of the servant girl standing rigidly behind her young mistress's chair, torn, in her obvious, crude way, between curiosity, suspicion and blatant irony. The artist was seized by a feeling akin to shame at having let herself get carried away, at having boasted in an unseemly manner. She felt her cheeks grow hot, and she guessed that beneath the dark hollows under her eyes her cheekbones were red and inflamed. A pitiful spectacle for the merciless eyes of a young person. And maybe even the honest Francesco dared not raise his head so as to keep intact the image he had of a silent Artemisia who, as a child, was so good at concealing her fatigue, her hopes, her pride, her despair. At these thoughts the rush of blood was halted and lost its heat but did not cool her down: her cheeks grew pale and took on a sickly yellow color tinged with purple, while her lips retained the hint of a smile which irritated the tiny lines on them. Alone, a short while before, in the twilight of the day and of her life, which she had had the wisdom to recognize, she had been on the side of right and truth: she must regain that position and maintain it. Having made her decision, she raised her hand once more to that lock of hair, but this time to straighten out and tame the exuberant, flattering curl. Not a tremor betrayed her voice as she courageously attempted to carry on the conversation and erase the memory of her over-excited, over-animated evocation of Rome, its places and people; and she tried to be impartial and modest, endeavouring to give an example of composure to everyone, especially to her daughter who once again had had occasion to pity her. Finally she grew silent and her chin dropped as though nailed to her throat, just as it used to at the time when everyone in the Santa Croce and San Spirito districts was beginning to condemn her. But only Francesco, who had raised his eyes, was able to notice this and remember: his eyes were thoughtful, yes, but he was not thinking what his sister imagined.

Porziella got to her feet, her back very straight, in fact rigid, more tightly enclosed than any other girl in her virginal, severely cut bodice. She bent forward, bowing slightly: "Goodnight, my uncle, goodnight mother." Thus was she taught by the nuns; she is very well educated and there is a cutting self-composure in the way she takes her leave that serves as a lesson to the two who remain there with their endless talk of painting and fame. Who taught Nunziatina the obsequious care with which she lights the lamp, shields it with one hand, opens the door and walks in front of Porziella to light the way? It certainly was not Artemisia, constantly swinging from being overly familiar to haughtily distant. The door closes noiselessly behind the two girls.

"I have to find a husband for Porziella," says her mother, smiling nervously, valiantly clinging to what she believes to be a display of humility, of renunciation. And Francesco finally opens his mouth, then closes it again, then opens it once more. At that moment Artemisia's heart foolishly begins to beat faster, with anxiety. "While we're on that subject," says Francesco, "I have some good news to give you. Antonio has returned. . . . "

The night that has fallen is as silent as in the countryside. There is no beggar shouting, no baby crying, no carriage rattling past. She cannot even hear the sea, the sea is calm. There is no moon in the square of the open window. The lamp smokes, in the fire now covered in ashes a still smoldering ember emits a creaking sound. Antonio has returned, returned from distant countries, some say China, others the West Indies. He has become a wealthy merchant, he has taken rooms in a palace, beautifully furnished, so they say. He lives in a grand manner and dresses in rather odd, but dignified, clothes which are sometimes magnificent. He has numerous letters of credit and important letters of introduction. And he has a woman with him, rather dark-skinned; some say she is a princess from those parts. He wants to marry her, he has powerful connections in Court circles and it appears that that hasty marriage in Santa Maria in Aquiro was defective from the point of view of form and consent. He sends this message: what has happened has happened and he knows Signora Artemisia to be a reasonable woman. He knows about her daughter and does not wish to cast doubts on that subject; in fact he admits she is his. As proof, he is offering a dowry for Porziella and a present for her mother; but Artemisia must give her consent to this new marriage, she must swear an oath, sign papers. If she needs to travel to Rome, he will naturally pay for all expenses.

"Don't you think," concludes Francesco, overcoming his usual shyness and also a sort of fluster at this unusual message that is not to his liking but which should please a woman as cold, as severe, as strong—for such has he always taken her to be—as his sister, "don't you think that everything is working out very well? Porziella will have a dowry fit for a duchess, she will be able to make a very good match. You will be able to marry again, devote your time to really important commissions with no worries about money. . . . "

The night is also cold: Artemisia can feel its icy, damp breath penetrating beneath her skin and this takes her back, dizzyingly, to bleak winter evenings when at least she could say, It's so cold. The lack of this pretext to break the silence with a cliché seems to her unbearable. Her head is bent and she does not dare raise it: her fine blond hair is smooth and tidy now, the parting that divides it is narrow and neat. She leans her hand on the table as though to push herself to her feet or as though waiting for something: maybe for Francesco to give her back the drawing she has begun or pass her his trousers for darning. This cautious immobility comes from a long acquaintance with suffering, although she has not yet realized just how much she is suffering. Instead of talking she thinks, stressing the syllables in a curious way: Antonio my husband. Antonio Stiattesi. Artemisia Stiattesi. The hasty marriage. And she does not know if it will be words that will come out if she opens her mouth, or whether by some miraculous torture all her teeth will fall into her lap, so strong is her growing awareness of a ravaging pain. All she can do is play for time and pretend to be thinking it over: a matter of a few minutes, pain like this cannot last. But instead the pain grows, it roars.

"Everything is working out well," she managed to say, in a hallucinating pause of forgetfulness, repeating her brother's words, for she was not capable of thinking up any of her own, and she even imitated his tone of voice. With a huge effort she raised her eyes and held them wide open: only in this way, she knew, could the onslaught of tears be dominated. "And it's true," she continued, empty and detached from herself, as though she had already breathed her last, but with the distinct sensation of making her way in the dark along a very narrow path, "it's true, now she will be able to make a very good match." With one last, supreme effort she abandoned the support of Francesco's words and propelled herself back to the thoughts that had been in her head a moment ago when she had rashly said, "I have to find a husband for Porziella." She strung her sentences together one at a time, feeling her way forward cautiously like someone afraid of falling, or rather of collapsing, distracting her mind by staring at any object she happened to see. "I must find a good match for her, and I have someone in mind, from a wealthy family." Confident now that her voice was able to pass through her throat that had seemed closed, she took advantage of it, speaking louder, using it as though it were an external instrument that could even be abused; and with a rush of bitter triumph abuse it she did. Suddenly she was overcome by a sort of desperate recklessness which dominated her from head to foot. She spoke at length, with a flood of clear, extremely precise words, about the Fragame family, silversmiths in Chiaja, who had retired from business and were about to purchase a title for themselves. Lots of money, an only son who is a real gem. "They have money and want more, you know how it is." But out of consideration for Porziella, who has a marquise for godmother, they will be satisfied with a thousand scudi and her trousseau. As soon as he marries, the young man will become a Knight of Saint James; Porziella will live like a lady, like the mistress of the household, for her mother-in-law is old and cannot have long to live. Her linen is ready, I only have to get the dresses: the gold will come bit by bit. They have ties with the Church, one uncle is a bishop in Eboli, and they have a cousin who is Mother Superior of the Poor Clares; she is the one who suggested the match.

Francesco cannot believe his luck, for having got over the hurdle of delivering that unpalatable message, he is now being offered the opportunity to use his judgment to work out a plan that will be advantageous to his relatives; he likes nothing better than acting as head of the family, feeling bound up with and necessary to the material life of the others. "Five hundred scudi," he repeats several times, "I've got five hundred scudi saved"; and he begins to recite the list of all the people who owe him money, of whom there are many, going back a long way, for he is very slow in collecting what he is owed. In his detailed accounts he goes over all the work he has done in the last ten years, specifying names and places which he remembers exactly, names and places which now have an incongruous, ironic, ridiculous ring to his sister's ears. Did Ripagrande with its stores of grain ever really exist? Isn't Piazza del Popolo tired of its everyday dust, traffic and people? Artemisia's fatigue is suddenly so intense that, with her elbows on the table and her hands over her eyes, she sees it reflected physically in the things and places that were witness to her difficult, transient life which is now three-quarters over. Behind her hands, she too is going over her pathetic accounts, accounts in which nothing is owing and which do not require precision, would that her memory were not so exact. Monotonous reckonings. And the sum total beats dismally: nothing, not even Antonio.

"My husband who has disappeared," the formula she had come up with this evening to fan the flames of the sadness she felt at growing old, something which had seemed to her inexcusable and almost shameful. For how long had she been unaware that he was in her thoughts? And in the depths of her heart, as on the gray sand secretly disturbed and marked by the waves, she saw the marks left by this thought which she had faithfully kept and inscribed all these years. He was her husband, he had put the ring on her finger in church, he had slept at her side. In their room in Ripagrande he used to wait on her humbly but confidently: he was her devoted servant. He used to stroke her hair, study her hand; he never wanted to put out the lamp, so that he could contemplate her. And then he had run away. She had been certain that his love, his intense adoration would last forever and run in his veins until he died. Instead: "He has a woman with him, rather dark-skinned." So nothing had been true. The faithful Antonio had never existed.

Because of her position, suggestive of deep thought and maybe even sleep, Francesco had stopped talking and showed no signs of starting again. He had always instinctively respected and feared the fragility, the weakness, the hardness, the strength which all strangely combined to create this woman he was so fond of, this unique, heartrending example of humanity. There is no need, therefore, for her to explain why she is silent, why she is shielding her eyes: ever since he was a small boy he has been accustomed to not even allowing himself to imagine her motives. The minutes pass, the quarter-hours: Francesco takes out his book, his glasses, and begins to read as though it were agreed that they had to wait patiently for something. For something: for the deep foundations to stop caving in and the dust of the ruins to settle and reveal what is still standing. Very little, to tell the truth: a few beams, a few stones upon which it will not be possible to rebuild a solid, harmonious structure. That which for Francesco is a pause not to be questioned, for Artemisia is a dizzying, speeding whirl which her mind is not able to distinguish, to contemplate; but not to despair about, for the time has not yet come for that. In the ruins even Porziella's marriage, that fragile pretext to divert her attention, that short-lived bulwark and shield against pain, has been destroyed; and her mind, so eager to endure, to persevere, to reach a decision, so quick to recover, is no more than a crushed limb beneath a pile of rubble. And yet it moves, in agony, with a monotonous, rhythmical insistence which she observes with an almost scientific curiosity. It looks like it is about to get up, move around, function. But it falls back each time, and no one hears the groans of the body to which it belongs.

She removes her hands from her eyes, finally, and looks round. She was coming back from such a great distance, where she had received such terrible blows and lightning bolts that her eyes seemed dreamy, as though waking after a deep sleep: the tears had been reabsorbed into her eyelids, heavy and bruised-looking, and there was now no sign of them. And she smiled at her brother lovingly, as though they had been working together at length or sitting up all night for some sad, irreparable reason. "I must have fallen asleep," she explained, "it really is time to go to bed." Calmly, she fetched two candles from the corner of the fireplace and with meticulous, slow care held their wicks in the flames of those already burning on the table to light them. Standing there, holding one out to Francesco, she said before she moved off: "I have a lot to do, and very little time to do it in. I didn't tell you that father has sent for me. I'll be in England before Christmas."

What terrible masters words turn out to be. By the time she wished she had never said them a year had gone by, and at her back the choppy, oily waters of the port were splashing, a pale green color between the small boats, the rigging and the sails that were being run up, so numerous that they filled the line of the horizon. She wished that she had never said them, but it was like not wanting to die when death calls you; they had dominated her and forced her, day after day, into increasingly binding decisions and actions. She had set herself time limits, she had declared them publicly. She had not gone to Rome, she had not accepted the money of that Stiattesi man, but she had placed her signature at the bottom of many long documents which she doubted, to tell the truth, would be of any use or help to Antonio's marriage plans. She had entrusted herself against her will to an efficient alter ego who had done everything for her, seeing to all the itineraries, the arrangements, the halts, the preparations, the packing. But even now, as she is about to set sail, standing on the rough stones of the breakwater that she had only seen from afar until now, what she cannot accept or explain is how Antonio, that pale, quiet boy, that faithful lover, could have repudiated his Artemisia. After a year of work, of negotiations, of endless distractions, she has not managed to erase the picture that blossomed as though from invisible ink—"He has a woman with him, rather dark-skinned"—on the evening she returned on foot from Palazzo d'Avalos, or to satisfy her enduring despair with anything other than this decree of exile. She was so harsh in passing sentence on herself that she did not realize that she was waiting for someone, or something, to prevent her in some way from carrying it out. But she realizes it now, and she only has an hour left in which to nurture this newborn hope; to devote herself, that is, to expecting a miracle. Who on earth is there to stop her going? Antonio, who has forgotten all about her and is estranged from her, will he suddenly realize that he cannot live without his difficult wife who is so swift with a pencil? Francesco, who for the first time is offended by his beloved sister because she will not let him go with her? And the more he beseeched her the more adamant she became, but that was a tearful game, a female game not to be taken seriously, and Francesco could not understand that. Some distant admirer (Artemisia is reduced to this as a last resort) who will arrive in a carriage, leap out and say: do not leave the country, Signora, I want you to stay and woe betide anyone who harms you? There is nothing more helpless, more desolate than the soul of this forty-year-old woman who outwardly displays impatience to embark, but avidly stares at every object, every person. She stares above all at Porziella Fragame, who has been married for a month now and is looking very disgruntled: anyone who follows the direction of her gaze will easily discover why Porziella is in a bad mood. The fact is that her mother's expensive dress (made of brocade that could have gone into her daughter's trousseau) is trailing in fig and melon skins lying on the ground, passing dangerously close to a pool of tar, is not lifted out of the way to avoid a filthy, stumbling porter carrying a brimming jar of oil. A small cry of vexation escapes her when a drop of oil falls onto the soft, shining hem. Were it not for her finery as a newlywed, the appearance she has to maintain in public and the presence of her new relations, Porziella would bend down to the ground, pick up that precious material in her hands and try to remove the stain: so clean and tidy is Artemisia's cold daughter, brought up by the nuns. There is no doubt that she is thinking disdainfully, "My mother doesn't care about anything," and she angrily looks forward to the satisfaction of being in command, of giving the orders in her husband's house. Porziella knows what she wants: she wanted Gennarino Fragame, with his flat, squashed face and body, his constant air of sleepiness, timid yet full of conceit; she wanted a decrepit, defenseless mother-in-law. The Neapolitans are not going to see her out and about very often because she does not like to ruin her good clothes in the streets. She brought a dowry, she brought clothes and jewelry, she wants to forget these shabby painters. "Mother, your hood!" she suddenly cries out, unable to contain her disgust at seeing that lovely garment about to fall and be spoiled because Artemisia is carrying it carelessly over one arm. The latter does not seem to have heard, but with eyes the color of deep blue sea stares spellbound at her daughter. Never before as at this moment has she seen so clearly Porziella's serious profile, the color of her skin, her prominent cheekbones so like her own, the way she carries her soft, round shoulders that rise out of the stiff bodice: a lovely portrait in the Flemish style, all that is lacking is the open window with a view of the sea. This is what going to England means: looking at a daughter's face and seeing it as a distant object, totally detached from oneself, unreachable except through the workings of memory. And, in fact, Artemisia's sorrowful observation of her daughter has already joined the realm of memory. No one will hold her back now: the Dutch ship is all ready to set sail, she knows which are the actions she must perform to carry out the decision she made as a virile woman, but already she regrets them, like so many others with which, from one decade to another—the scale on which she measures change—she has reproached herself. This time, she is certain, it is a decade that will not count for her, so she might as well get it over with quickly and leave now. She has the impression today that she is lending herself to some sort of deception and that the whole of time is contained only in the present, a present that is ground down on the millstone of the past; and in a little while she will be suspended in eternity. "But this is one of my crazy ideas," declares an internal voice which often, when she is alone, begins to visibly form words on her lips. In the meantime she is careful not to lower her head as she has had the habit of doing since she was young, so that no one will see the lines on her thin neck which she noticed in the mirror yesterday. Massimo Stanzione comes forward; he can be very gentle when he wants, but distracted even when he does not want. "England," he says, opening his arms, "is stealing our Artemisia and nothing will console us for her loss." But he is restless, he keeps turning round, shielding his eyes with his hand to look towards the city.

Eloquent gestures which express the fact that his life no longer has anything to do with her who is leaving: even the way he jokes in dialect with the boy selling lemons and whispers to one Don Giacinto from Calabria who is with him ("Let me introduce Don Giacinto, your humble servant") proclaims the elusive reality of future days from which Artemisia has been excluded and erased. For whom, moreover, is she still present? The minutes fly past and everyone finds them slow. Only Padre Eustachio of the Oratorian fathers, nervously tapping his foot and exclaiming for the third time, "What a beautiful day it is," is evidence, with his stifled yawns, that she has not yet embarked. At the last moment two youths from Apulia, tongue-tied and reluctant, arrive bearing gifts and compliments from Andrea Vaccaro, of whom they are pupils: an electuary, a silver cross, six pairs of fine gloves. Massimo draws close to see, Porziella unwraps the gifts, a few passers-by stop to watch. And this is enough for Artemisia to become herself once more, to thank everyone with a smile, as though she were happy to leave.

And now everyone, even the Fragame mother and son, begins to talk excitedly, as if drowning out an unpleasant sound; and a loud noise is in fact coming from the Dutch ship, the raucous pealing of the bell that signals departure ringing out widely over the customs area and the sea. The slight wind increased, the bellies of the vessels creaked as they rocked on their moorings, and a swarm of rowboats could be seen rushing swiftly to shore, shaving the sides of the ships, the oarsmen competing vigorously and with loud shouts to overtake each other. At that instant Nunziatina, the malicious servant who up till now has been guarding the luggage with a satisfied expression (she is staying with her young mistress who has promised to find her a husband), suddenly throws herself onto her knees, shouting, sobbing, moaning: she weeps real tears, she tears at her hair and clings to Artemisia's legs; who, through her clothes, can feel the warm wetness of that open mouth penetrate to her skin.

"My beautiful mistress, San Rocco, Sant'Ubaldo, Sant'
Agata . . . " In the village where Nunziatina was born
amidst the donkeys and pigs, this is how the dead are
mourned by women paid at an hourly rate; but Artemisia
does not know this. "Don't go, fair lady, don't leave your
servant. . . . " These are the words that Artemisia has been
waiting for for a year. Whenever the sadness became too
bitter for a woman so full of life as she, her young heart, so
stubbornly optimistic, would look forward to hearing them
and would form them on behalf of those both near and far: a
reformed, affectionate Porziella, a repentant Antonio, and
that wondrous personage, the forerunner of all those who
have said they loved her since she became a woman, and
who, as an exception, might prove not to be a traitor. But
even these words of Nunziatina's are sufficient, so that she
blushes, deeply touched, feeling sweet tears rise in her
throat and for a moment she feels consoled and almost
convinced. They have all always loved her, even this servant
whom she judged so harshly, even Porziella who is her own
flesh and blood, even Antonio who used to study her hand
closely and cannot possibly have forgotten it. As though it
were the will of some tyrant who was separating her from
her loved ones, she imagines herself as a heroine to be pitied,
the famous Artemisia setting off all alone, to the other side
of the world. Her brave smile, her air of happiness, her
boldness are all very becoming: let no one say that Artemisia
is afraid. When the time comes to embrace everyone—oh,
the sweet smell of Porziella's neck, still childish—she is
therefore in a state of elation, full of generosity at their
imagined affection, filled with an absurd hunger for self-
sacrifice which all the blood in her body would not be
enough to satisfy. The rowboat is already moving up and
down on the waves and banging against the pier, the ste-
vedores are already standing wide-legged on the benches
throwing and catching her cases, her bags, all her things
which are hidden away and which will have to wait until the
light of goodness knows what distant day to be unpacked

and used again, if ever they will be used again. Out come the hands which grasp in vain and then withdraw from the embrace all too quickly; the hands of those who are staying behind in Naples and who, this evening, tomorrow, a year hence, will greet those whom they see every day. Then the myriad inconveniences that a woman is subject to when climbing down a rope ladder for the first time in her life, unable to refuse to be assisted, handed down, unceremoniously lowered to the bottom, create a web of almost shameful dependency and a new state of dejection which makes her say "Farewell, farewell" to the sky now so far away. Nor does the trip in the rowboat from the shore out to the *Jonathan,* on the dirty, troubled waters of the port which have already taken over, erase this fear of drowning, of drowning in the future. Porziella was waving, the sun glinting on her gold bracelet; Massimo was flapping his hat, then suddenly he turned his head away; Nunziatina was beating the dust off her new mistress's skirt with the palm of her hand. Don Giacinto's wide, toothless mouth, stretched in a vague, stranger's smile, was the last thing Artemisia saw on the soil of Naples. They passed under the stern of a huge Spanish galleon laden, amongst other things, with black slaves. The rise and fall of that enormous carcass on the swell prevailed over all other thoughts.

Once aboard the *Jonathan,* as soon as she had indecently (you could see her legs as high as the thigh) climbed over the railing of the deck of black planks which the sailors were in the midst of washing down, the temptation to disembark again, to abandon the false security underfoot, to get back onto firm ground, was desperate in its iciness, resisted by her very heart which was expressing its desire to give into it, beating violently in her breast. Her trunks, her numerous bags were piled in a disordered heap around her, and already she felt she had been cast adrift in a world where there was no need for luggage, where the only thing she understood was this pathetic clinging with sweaty, tense hands to a burning hot parapet that was sticky with varnish and evil-smelling. There she stood, a small, pale woman having difficulty breathing, each inward breath accompanied by a convulsive, rearing movement of her shoulders; but no one even saw her or noticed this, she might as well have been a ghost. And even she could no longer recognize herself, panting, her mouth trembling, concentrating on enduring like a grub or a spider. Her short-lived elation, her illusions, even the image, so vivid a short time before, of Artemisia Gentileschi, artist, going off to the English Court, have all been swallowed up by the dirty waters of the port. She can no longer make out the shore through the tangle of sails, masts, curving bows; only the hills surrounding Naples bid her farewell and give her an indication of how far she is from land. The scorching heat of the wooden rail does not communicate itself to her cold fingers, with which she clenches her burning defeat. She is going off, at forty years of age, without fortune, without any real fame, without love or affection. And without even her former pride. She barely has enough of it left to prevent her changing her mind.

In this state of poverty, unalleviated by wishful thinking, Artemisia's life at sea began, a passive life, at the mercy of new, brutal needs, of external and internal fears, of the uncertainty of her rash, downright reckless decision. The ship was unfamiliar to her, the captain foreign, the language obscure, the other passengers strangers who formed a close-knit group, no protection for her anywhere. With her luggage in the hold, the objects that define her status and her reputation have disappeared: they have sunk into the eternal anonymity of an ordinary, insignificant life from which are missing, moreover, all the usual supports, so that after a year of showing how patient and reasonable she can be, there returns with increased bitterness, with greater sorrow, the pain of that husband who is erasing her, who has maybe already erased her, even from the parish register. Beyond the pain she feels there is also this test of humility for someone who has never known humility, not even when they were trying to shame her, for someone who has no experience of being humble. Accustomed to the excitement, to the liveliness of youth prolonged by her unusual way of life, Artemisia, on her own, on the foreign ship, loses all sense of proportion in diminishing her own value, exceeds in debasing herself. Unable to behave with any of her former naturalness, she dares not trail her silk skirts on the deck, nor halt, nor talk, nor decide on the sort of reserve suitable for a woman of her age, whom no one knows. She takes refuge more and more as the days pass in adopting a puerile, sullen attitude, as though she were a sick child with whom no one wants to play or live.

She refused to sit at the captain's table, but would pause to greet his second-in-command, a young blond man who could have been, so she guessed, about the same age as her daughter. Then, wary of her motives, she regretted it, imagining that everyone must mistake her for a lecherous old woman, and from then on she never went out of her cabin without the brown bonnet that tamed the youthful exuberance of her light hair. She did not worry about seasickness, waiting for it as a diversion, lying face down on her narrow bunk, where her thoughts, her confessions, her regrets, in the darkness that smelled of pepper and tar, were far more unbearable to her, though in a different way. Waiting like this for the seasickness to strike her body, she would often fall asleep with a tightness in her throat: the moan that would have escaped remained trapped there while she slept, until she woke up, and then it would burst out, not because of the discomfort in her stomach but because of the fundamental distress in her soul. "Oh Antonio, what have you done!" In her dreams it was an exquisite vase of golden hue that Antonio had smashed to pieces; when lying awake it was the secret, delicate love that he had invented, his portrait which no longer looked like him. She would wake up completely, pull herself into a sitting position on her bunk and witness, with something like amazement, the ceaseless sobs and floods of tears that left her like a wrung-out rag. And as she searched for the threads of the invisible thought processes that had taken place in her sleep, she could feel her heart beating dully in time to the rolling motion of the ship. She would press her handkerchief over her mouth in case anyone should hear her: then she would remember where she was, and throw her legs down to the floor. She would stand there in the narrow space, motionless, while her grief, that horrible infant, moved restlessly in her breast, sucking her blood and filling her mouth with the bitter saliva of tears. She would lie down again, her head spinning, the sheet under her body all wet and tangled. Finally she would grow quiet; and the weakness in her limbs, the spasms of those insatiable sobs that still pounded in her head, gave her reason to hope that she was suffering from a physical illness that her mind did not control.

The *Jonathan* sailed on, keeping close to the coast to avoid the pirates from Barbary and elsewhere who at that time of year were always to be found in those waters hunting for prey. The second-in-command informed her that they were passing by Fiumicino; there was a storm on land and big black clouds at ground level hid the shoreline. Artemisia had imagined that she would be able to see the dome of St. Peter's, and was searching for it without asking questions. But the coastline merged cruelly with the gray sky, the ship cruelly increased its speed under the billowing sails. She lifted her head then, and the incredible agility of the ship-boys among the rigging, the flight of the seagulls, the whistling wind and those enormous swollen sails flapping hard enough to tear, all gave her the idea of a catastrophe so imminent and fatal that her last hour seemed to have come. She closed her mouth tightly against the howling wind, not asking anyone for reassurance, waiting for the crash almost without fear. The sailors were running about with bare feet on the weather-beaten, soaking deck. There were a few hollow crashing sounds. A few drawn-out cries snatched away by the wind. The waves were crashing over each other, growing increasingly high and dark, drawing their stimulus from some monstrous force in the invisible black depths of the sea. If Artemisia's mind were capable of expressing anything in such an hour, it was amazement and wonder that her own end should be so portentous. And she grew inebriated at the thought, able, with a clear conscience, to satisfy her old craving for triumph.

It was not the end; in fact she later learned that it had not even been a real storm, those dark waves were no more than a choppy sea. She felt vaguely disappointed, almost annoyed. Both day and night, at regular intervals of a horribly musical precision, those harsh, inarticulate tears would return, unappeasable, commemorating her defeat. Bent over the rail, looking at the white, foaming wake on the now calm sea, there were moments when she wondered at the reason for this subterranean grief, trying to place it in front of herself like an object that needs to be carefully examined. All those years since she had last seen Antonio; all the things that had happened to make her forget him, to erase his image; for so long now all she had had was a vague memory of him. The object, identified and picked up, was so hot she could not touch it. She contrived then to recall to mind all her own faults: how she used to remain stubbornly silent at her husband's attentions; how, confident of his devotion, she would bask in it without care, almost without really enjoying it, believing herself to be free, owing him nothing in return. And how she used to reproach him for his lowly station, his wretched job, his moodiness. And how that last time, when she had been angry, she should have realized how afraid he was of her. He had left: but she had been sure of his love. . . . The untouchable, external object blocked her investigation at this point, taking over as though alive. The tears gushed forth once more, dried by the salty wind. Crying for love at forty years of age! Thus did she joust with her thoughts.

Off the coast of Elba the wind dropped. They remained motionless for several days, burning in the sun like flies in milk. Everyone slept, from the captain to the cabin boys; it seemed as though the day of damnation had come and everyone was accepting it. But not Artemisia, who had now taken to going out on deck and staying there in the great silence in the thin shade of the sails. Oh to turn back now that they were still, oh to be able to give the order. But at that very moment, with a shudder and a smack like that of a pair of huge, greedy lips, the mainsail rose and fell, then rose and fell over and over, at ever-decreasing intervals until finally it filled with wind and once more the ship was cutting through the sea. A harsh, winged force tore at Artemisia's clothes, pulling them backwards. She believed she was the only person to have witnessed the change; and her bonnet was suddenly snatched roughly from her head as if by a brutal hand. A very thin, light cloud was veiling the sun and now the sky too had turned a milky color, while the sea, on the horizon, like the abundant foliage of an uprooted tree, was trembling and growing darker. Another portent? No, it was only a hair, a shining, steely hair that the great sea beast had allowed to be plucked out. Shuddering, the ship picked up speed: it was not going to turn back.

At dusk the deck was crowded as never before, and all sorts of unusual passengers were to be seen, in particular, two young German women, very exuberant and excited, who were grabbing buckets of water out of the sailors' hands and throwing them all over each other with a great deal of laughter: scantily dressed, with bare legs, totally uninhibited, they gurgled away in their dialect like greedy pigeons. The coastline could be seen clearly and distinctly, in three colors, white, green and light blue. Someone said (and the first stars were already visible), "You can see Leghorn."

A name she knew: there had been a time when only to hear it mentioned gave her a start, made her face go red, caused her distress. That was the town in which Agostino had lived before he came to Rome ("Before I met you, my beauty"), and there had been times when she would have given anything to go there, as if she could discover the origin of her misfortunes. "Leghorn," she repeats to herself

142

today, but the syllables sound lifeless, an old fruit, its juice dried up. The coast opens up in a curve, narrows like a funnel, sailing ships at anchor give the impression of moving round the *Jonathan,* and already there are small boats approaching with naked boys selling peaches, bunches of grapes, scapulars of the Madonna of Montenero. Some passengers disembark to spend a night on land, others to visit the city, and still others hang dangerously over the side trying to catch in the air the fruit being thrown on board: particularly noticeable was the fuss made by the Portuguese priest in the black straw hat, shouting out in a loud voice for relics and keepsakes, catching them nimbly and stuffing them into his open sack. Artemisia did not want to leave the ship, suddenly feeling tired at the sight of all that dry land, dotted with small lights that were coming on one by one, near and far. She stayed out on deck all night, and at dawn, opening her eyes in the silence, in the light that was already bright but still misty, she was struck by a thought, or rather a revelation, which had been hovering over her sleep, guiding it; and it was that she never had been and never would be free of her lost husband, just as a figure can never escape from the landscape that surrounds it, relying on it, on the contrary, for air and sustenance. Her landscape was one that exuded pain and this was what she must live on henceforth. Her despair, instead of issuing from her eyes, of being momentarily assuaged by tears, sank into her chest like a stone, and she felt her heart being consumed like a candle burning in clear, still air, giving neither light nor heat.

Patience, patience: only a word, for the time being, a difficult word that already makes her set her mouth in an expression of acquired wisdom. In that big illustrated book she used to leaf through as a child were pictures of the four Virtues, each one with its name and attributes, for the use of artists who wanted to portray them. How was Patience represented? She tried to remember, with great determination, as though that clearly defined image could be a source of help and comfort for her. In the meantime the *Jonathan* was setting out once more and an obese gentleman, laden with plumes and neckchains, who had boarded at Leghorn, had taken to bowing low in front of her whenever she came out of her cabin: it gave her a bitter pleasure, she even began to think that once she was in England she would be able to marry again honorably, now that her husband had left her. Instead, however, her aversion to life was increasing rather than diminishing, a nausea that became physical and left her hanging over the rail, like so many others who had suffered seasickness before her. But the sea was calm.

Once again the planks of the deck are burning hot and the wind that arrives cool and whistling soon becomes scorching in the relentless sun, blowing through the ship from one side to the other. The soles of Artemisia's shoes burn, her hands, chin, cheekbones and eyelids become covered in salty scales, it is impossible to breathe below deck. On the coast, certain white, crystalline mountains recall, but with a cruel sharpness, the backgrounds of paintings of saints and Madonnas that used to turn up in Rome, in Orazio's studio, old paintings from Venice that her father had to value for foreign collectors. And because this is land she is compelled to look at it, to drink it in with her eyes; and Artemisia's eyes become bored, intolerant of objects imposed on them not of her own choosing, objects she would not want to paint, might not be able to paint, yet which are impossible to forget. She continued to stare at them for a whole long day of dazzling light until, amidst those slowly moving peaks and summits with their changing shapes and folds, she spotted, with the arrival of shining, white clouds, something amazing but familiar: the hiding places, the nests of angels, and then the angels themselves, huge, with immense wings, flying up and down, from valley to valley. She saw once again the soft, luminous angels that Orazio used to paint, but now grown war-like, transfigured in a silent, sky-blue brilliance. She thought she recognized them, and for an instant she was thunderstruck, pierced through by a feeling of serenity, as though she had been led by enchantment amongst these awesome hiding places to behold, to paint herself that which no one had ever painted before.

Everything made of wood, everything made of metal, even the sails, were burning ever hotter (and there were those who were badly blistered from touching them) when the ship heaved to, sucked in by the Gulf of Genoa, and the boys up in the rigging began to exchange shouts and to sing psalms amidst the flight of the first swallows from land. As the emptiness of the high sea rapidly became filled with vessels and boats of every kind, all the passengers appeared on deck once more, attired in their best finery, mingling with the barefoot sailors, and everyone was happy as though they had all attained their ultimate, longed-for goal. A serious Dutch family who had not appeared even at Leghorn came out on deck and with amazing speed made friends with their fellow travelers, even with the German girls who everyone now knew were on their way to join the Flemish army. The only people they avoided were the priests and monks; and in the excitement of arriving, the father, who was called Benjamin, had a table laid at great expense with all sorts of meats until it looked like a scene of plunder, and he invited all who were willing to eat, for it was a Friday. The mother was giving her uncovered, full breast to a baby who had been born during the voyage without, so it seemed, anyone knowing. She came up to Artemisia and talked to her in confidential tones, one Italian word to every seven incomprehensible ones. She even took her hand and put it between her shift and bodice to make her feel something that was unusual, or so Artemisia understood, for her puerperal condition; and Artemisia, very serious, was unable to understand. The woman laughed at her incomprehension, the folds in her fat face creasing in lines, her flesh extremely white, like lard.

The *Jonathan* now made its way cautiously into the labyrinth of the port, going in much further than it had at Leghorn, all sails furled, advancing solely by means of the oars; and all the passengers were ready to answer, to joke with anyone who addressed them, shouting at the top of their voices as is the custom at sea. This is what it is like when people are happy to have arrived, thought Artemisia, who would never again be happy to arrive anywhere. The workmen repairing ships, standing round huge cauldrons of smoking pitch, the men on the boats that were leaving, the boatmen on the ferries, the fishermen eating on board their vessels, all were shouting out questions, greetings, salutations. Only from the warships, two French galleys and a Spanish galleon, were there no cries, laden though they were with soldiers and galley slaves. The *Jonathan* made her way around them, passing very close, with a rather wary boldness, to the ornate griffons and the dreadful machinery of war. In silence her men paused in their tasks to look at all those soldiers, the passengers stood wide-eyed, talking to one another in hushed voices. And Artemisia watched them too, with feelings of desire, of envy, for a state so completely different from her own; of liberation, if not of freedom, whatever it might be. Instead, the moment really has come when she must assume her own name once again, assume responsibility for it and be convinced by it so that she might convince others to whom it is not known. Already the mountains around the bay are spreading out into green meadows dotted with trees that separate them from the skyline; the surface irregularities of the rocks are now visible, with their protuberances and crevices, seaweed and moss; and, finally, she is able to make out the dense mass of red-brick buildings, their walls pierced with thousands of holes for windows, and the cupolas, the bell towers, the terraces; and the swarming activity on the wharf, men and cargo, carts and carriages. The atmosphere of tired gaiety, the lively confusion of a city like Naples, so very far from Naples. Farewell to the *Jonathan,* farewell to those going on to Spain. Here she must disembark.

She was astonished at how polite everyone was, so courteous to her that she felt, as she said goodbye, that she was departing from old friends. The world had been reduced to this piece of wood on which, as Artemisia suddenly realized, her reputation had not been at all unknown. The lady artist is getting off, the lady who is going to England on her own. They all showed curiosity and concern over her luggage that was being unloaded, lest any of it be damaged. Beware, milady, of the thieves in the port. Some recommended lodgings, others advised a convent, others insisted she visit a generous relation of theirs; and the fat nobleman found a quiet moment to confide to her that he had important business in Lisbon, but intended to settle in London, where he would like to see her if she permitted. The captain gave her his arm as she disembarked, honoring her as if she were a princess, so that Artemisia felt as slender and supple as a twenty-year-old. Standing in the small boat that rocked against the side of the ship she gracefully bade them all farewell, already missing the solitary nights she had spent awake looking at the sea, the daily silence: but this is what always happens to her anyway, she only appreciates something when it is gone. There was a time when she used to say, I'll learn. She has not learnt, she never will. Amongst all the letters of introduction she has with her, she chooses the one for Gaspare Lovato, an art dealer in Canneto, a man of no great renown.

She did in fact stay in Lovato's house, which smelt richly of spices and paints and which underwent a transformation on the days he entertained guests, with all the bustle of hired servants and footmen: in the drawing room and the shop there was stacked against the walls a mountain of paintings through which he would rummage carelessly, suddenly extracting a few that he would have cleaned and framed so that they looked like jewels. And buyers of ever sort, many of them in strange Eastern garb so that she wondered why on earth they wanted Madonnas and Saints; or important noblemen, very grand and hard to please, but always polite, the likes of which Artemisia had never seen either in Rome or Naples, all came to deal in a very professional, efficient manner, like experienced merchants. The house was very tall, but it was possible to enter it even from the roof, a strange custom, and people entered all the time, quite freely, for Gaspare never turned down an opportunity to engage in lively conversation, always willing and confident of finding a specific painting, which might even have lain there for years. Sometimes he smoked a pipe, in the Flemish manner.

Giustina Lovato, who is from Padua, dresses in black in the manner of Genoese noblewomen, a privilege she flaunts. Only twenty-seven years of age, ambitious and hardworking, she has her own sedan chair, the upkeep of which she says she is able to pay for herself. She talks all the time about the women of the Spinola, Adorno and Centurione families, and not a day passes without her pointing them out to her guest with the excuse of noting their clothes, jewels or livery. She deals, buys and sells on her own behalf, going out on her own, receiving whomsoever she wants on her own, always dressed with great care, her eyes clear and sparkling, her face pale, so that everyone says she is sickly, which is not true. She wants to do everything, even humble herself, and this she does in front of Artemisia, though somewhat hastily. "Would signora Artemisia care to take a walk, have a rest, allow me to serve her a light snack?" "We female artists," she confides to her when she is pleased because she has made some money, "we female artists are not like other women"; for she too daubs away at canvases with which she fills the monasteries in Genoa. For the most part, though, she works on old, cracked paintings, restoring them to a shining, mint condition for market day when they are collected by a small-time dealer from Albissola who comes with his cart. She changes dialect with great facility from her native Venetian to Genoese, but never changes her habit of praising everything and everyone, so desperately does she want to please; and she even makes an effort at speaking Flemish, joking with Flemish merchants who feel very flattered and let her take off their hands very cheaply those paintings of theirs which are in great demand everywhere. She loves the theater, and also acts herself, at carnival time, whenever possible.

Sluggishly caught up and ensnared in all these trivial, multifarious goings-on over which she finds it impossible to prevail, Artemisia escapes by staying in her room for hours at a time, a low-ceilinged room stuffy with heat but which has three steep steps up to a French window that leads onto a terrace: at night, suspended between sea and sky, she was almost frightened by the multitude of stars that she could see. "How long are you going to be here?" She was asked the same question in turn by every single one of the Genoese artists who showed up in the Lovato household and to whom the name of Orazio was familiar as being the old maestro who had passed through Genoa, very contemptuous in manner, as proud as the devil. After asking the question they would remain silent. And Artemisia was silent too. They said she got her pride from her father; as for her ability, no one would compromise himself by praising it on the basis of simple hearsay, for Artemisia obstinately refused to unpack her cases. All these new people, these new customs and ways of life, these new names, for the most part Northern and familiar to everyone else, were too much for Artemisia, so that at first she lost her own identity, she lost her awareness of the value of her own work. She found it very difficult to conjure up in her mind the visual memory of the buildings of Naples and Rome beside these great, pale, very ornate ones; to remember the vineyards of Castelli and the sea of Posillipo beside this lovely countryside and this dark sea. It was not possible for so many, such diverse things to coexist: it seemed to her that she had exchanged the former for the latter, and that now they were gone forever, and she assiduously lamented their loss in private, as if this would keep them alive and real. Was not her talent as a great painter bound up with these things? As a result, it was days and days before she took up her paintbrush, inhibited by all the canvases, paints and tools of the

trade that surrounded her. As soon as she picked it up everyone in the house came to see; Giustina and her children who
had been trained in art at a precociously early age and who,
rightly or wrongly, stated that this painting was good, that
one bad, Gianandrea is better, this is worse than Carlone.
Artemisia did a painting of a black servant girl holding a
dove tightly to her chest; the woman very dark, the bird
very white, intending it as a demonstration of her skillful
use of contrast. And ten-year-old Orsola, who was learning
drawing and was said to be very good by all the artists,
pulled a face and said, "It looks like something done by
Sarzana," meaning that it was an old-fashioned painting in
an antiquated style. The ship for Marseilles was due to leave
soon and she looked forward to it now, it was better to push
forth into the unknown, to exile herself completely. But
before she did that she had to call on the eminent ladies of the
city.

The Centurione ladies received her between the fish
pond and the aviary. Tall ladies, with long hands, strong
jaws and snow-white skin. One of them was fishing with a
scarlet net in the green water where the fish darted about in
shoals, the other was feeding tame blackbirds with pellets
made from a mixture of worms and gum resin. They were
sisters, and they said together, with a haughtiness that did
not diminish their burning curiosity: "An artist?" "An artist!" Each of them dried her hands with a cloth made of Irish
linen after washing them in a gold basin held out by a
kneeling Moorish pageboy in purple livery. They talked
among themselves in French, then in pure Genoese: Signora
Lovato, who was feeling guilty at having introduced Artemisia, looked on in admiration, moved at being allowed
such intimacy. The more imposing of the two ladies seemed
to relinquish a little of her haughtiness, saying quietly and
dreamily, "To England!" when she heard what Artemisia's
destination was; while the shorter of the two, on whose
dark head not a single hair was out of place, said nothing, as
though to show that she had not heard. . . . Then she raised

her chin and from her light blue eyes that gave the impression of having almost been forced into position between the narrow slits of her eyelids, she flashed a look of hostility avid for a target. She said, and not without motive, "How many children, signora Artemisia?" It was Giustina who replied, "One daughter, your Ladyship," because Artemisia's attention had wandered and it was safer to forestall her. She was in fact looking at a large military portrait hanging opposite the door to the loggia.

In Genoa there were portraits of this kind in every noble household, and they were all equally fervent and highly colored, equally bright and glaring, so that Artemisia suspected that painting styles might indeed have changed while she had been in Naples playing with heavy shadows, with the contrast between light and shade, with proud heads, huge bodies. Here the churches are painted from top to bottom with a great display of strong color, very intense and lively; in this city the paintings sparkle with bright silks, shining metal and rosy flesh gleaming with health: such is the majestic style of the great painters of this nation, a style they learnt from the brush of that Flemish artist Peter Paul, who is talked of in glowing terms even in Spain. But Artemisia cannot change her style and manner, it would be too humiliating and she would never admit it in front of these noble ladies. Now the darker of the Centurione sisters is asking Signora Lovato whether the boxes from Flanders are due to arrive soon: she has been waiting for them for ages, she needs some still lifes of flowers and fruit for a private room of hers and you cannot expect anything new or fashionable from these Italians. Nodding diplomatically, the merchant's wife observed that there were a few innovations to be found even in Italy, and that she could prove it with Signora Artemisia here who had no equal among female artists when it came to painting beautiful portraits. "If your Excellency would deign to commission her . . . " The ladies were certainly not unwilling, there was a lot to be gained from a condescending acquiescence on their part and

Giustina, establishing the price, the day and the time of the first sitting, expressed her gratitude in superlative terms of a very Venetian nature. "Your most humble servant, your Ladyships." "Your Ladyships," Artemisia repeated mechanically, bowing low in a stiff curtsy. But the portrait was never done, for the lady suddenly left for Voltri and when she came back Artemisia had already gone; and no more was said about it when the cases from Flanders were unpacked in her presence in the Gaspares' house. Instead of the still lifes she chose twelve seascapes, which she later sent back as they were not to her liking.

But Pietra Spinola, sitting on her large chair beneath the canopy that protected her from the sun in her loggia that overlooked all of Genoa; Pietra Spinola, sixty years of age, stared at the artist with piercing, coal-black eyes, all the time listening intently, interrupting judiciously, and correcting the names of people and places with a marvelous pedantry. "Through France?" she pondered, asking detailed questions about the route that Artemisia had chosen to take; and she added, in a soft voice, "On your own, completely on your own?" Under her widow's headdress that had remained unchanged for twenty years her delicate face was extremely fragile, like the ash that remains when incense is burnt, expressing with rapid movements that were in harmony with her restless body, her intolerance of old age, a state she overcame by her willpower, regarding it as a trial, even a challenge; ardently, fervently. Giustina had remained at home on that occasion, for Pietra Spinola did not like her and Artemisia, on her stool, found herself talking volubly in a way that she had not done for years: when she thought she had finished, the frank expression on her listener's face (the same expression that lined her own brow) inspired her with new words. There was no need for her to defend herself or sing her own praises, but as she talked she found she was searching for, and finding, the reason for her long years of work, explaining the attraction of those manly undertakings that had always allured and tormented her, destroying her peace of mind, gaining her a questionable reputation and all the money that she had immediately spent, more on others than on herself. The sharp eyes, in whose shining gray depths numerous secret, now vanquished worries were slowly being extinguished, did not blink, so rapt was their attention, urging her, with a bitter affection, not to give in. And Artemisia did not give in, both her voice and her story unflinching, devoid of emotion, right to the last sentence. Which was, "I decided to leave in order to bring my life and my work to a close near my father." She said no more, for it was impossible to expose sentimental reasons and female weakness to such a woman as this, even though they were implicit and forgiven in advance. There remained in her throat, stuck like a needle, the phrase "my husband is no longer my husband"; and the old, irreparable grievance, "my daughter does not love me," which she had never confided to anyone and never would, except to this severe, compassionate old woman who could read between the lines. And who now was silent, lost in thought.

A servant dressed in a nun's habit came in carrying a tray with drinks and fruit. Then she brought over a long, ornate pipe lying on a purple velvet cushion; she was dismissed with a brusque, authoritarian gesture of the still white, still slim hand. With precise, impatient movements the old lady filled the bowl, pressed down the tobacco leaf, struck the flint and lit the pipe. She sucked at it with rude energy. "No woman can be happy unless she is stupid," hissed the colorless, thin lips in a muffled voice, while from the pipe which she lifted gracefully there rose to the sky fragrant, white spirals suggestive of the smoke from a mysterious sacrifice. The delicate eyelids with their small blue veins that spoke of fatigue and gave her eyes emphasis were lowered against the brilliance of the sea, every ripple of which was turned to fire by the setting sun. With the hand that was not occupied with the pipe, Pietra Spinola held out a glass of fruit syrup to Artemisia. "I met your father. He was a great man and you do him honor," she concluded, raising her voice, as though to conceal from others their secret understanding, their shared confidences; and those eyes from which the color had faded as if from the extreme clarity of her thinking or from being polished through long use, meant to give her encouragement and instead pierced her right through. But underneath that involuntary wound inflicted by someone who for too long has wielded the weapons of authority and loneliness, Artemisia perceived a heartfelt message, the farewell of a friendly, imprisoned soul, the only one worth meeting in all of Genoa. By some mysterious analogy of character, she was reminded of the innocence and purity of Cecilia. She curtsied in gratitude, but awkwardly, for her lips were drawn to that youthful, white hand; but she did not kiss it.

It was of Pietra Spinola that she was thinking, and not of her own destiny, nor of Antonio, as the Genoese felucca that was taking her to Marseilles set sail. It was a poor vessel for poor travelers who do not mind a rough voyage, and its cramped space meant that the equipment, the rough furnishings and the luggage were in everyone's way: the sailors were constantly obliged to step over it all with their bare feet. This time they sang litanies to the Madonna of Savona. It was not considered unusual even for a woman to sleep out on deck: and in fact for the women, of whom there were four in all—two maids and a pilgrim returning from visiting the shrines in Spain—makeshift beds had been made out of piles of old sails and a couple of hammocks. The women shared their first meal together, very friendly, beneath the red evening sky, and they were all as merry as though they had just been freed from bondage. The maids were saying, "At this hour Madame will be at Celle," with a sigh of relief and freedom, but from a habit of servitude they insisted that Artemisia take the wider hammock and helped her into it. The pilgrim taught them prayers that were effective against all sorts of danger and handed out extremely rare relics of Saint Casilda. The lighthouse had disappeared and the sea was black, but from the night sky came a faint glimmer of brightness evocative of distant realms of eternal resignation, of irrevocable memories. On this miserable vessel, surrounded by pathetic sleeping companions, it was pleasant to drift off to sleep with the feeling of having escaped from the hopes, the ambitions of the living, from the very faculty of suffering. Maybe even pain is a blessing to be regretted she thought when half asleep, addressing her thoughts to Pietra Spinola sitting smoking under her canopy; and it seemed to her that this whimsical, unusual idea originated not from herself but from the other woman. No other beings existed apart from the two of them, and just as Antonio had looked at Artemisia's hand, so did Artemisia feel she was examining the slim, strong hand of the old woman: so that anything that still remained of the blind, stubborn heart of Artemisia the child, of Artemisia the mature adult, melted away with an arcane sense of bewilderment, almost of love, for the eyes and the hands of Pietra Spinola who was now also far away and lost to her. "Alas, alas," she sighed on wakening, feeling herself to be not free of the past, but rather stripped of it, deprived of pain and joy, like an empty shell. The day was bright, with the silence of the deep sea, a new day just born. The other women were asleep, the maids with a tired, frowning expression, the pilgrim with a handkerchief over her face, like a corpse. The slapping noise made by the waves as the keel of the felucca cut through the sea evoked for her the image of a peaceful forest which belonged more to the realm of the imagination than to that of experience. Leaning out of her hammock and looking over the side of the ship Artemisia saw a dolphin playing in the green and white wake.

Artemisia had learned to write late in life. Her husband had taught her during the time that they lived in Ripagrande, on feast days when he did not work: she used to lie on their floor-level bed, her eyes rather lazily following the printed lines in one of the books chosen at random from those that Antonio used to bring home along with the finery, the silver

and the silks of his trade. But she was lost when it came to
italic handwriting, and from that time on had always written in capital letters when absolutely necessary. She detested
writing, it distracted one's attention from signs and drawing: the fact that she employed a secretary was common
knowledge in all Naples. And if Artemisia has sinned, it is
because of these secretaries, the last of whom was Diego.
Not a sin of lust: lucid and calm, she now admits that she
used the men as instruments of her vanity, to demonstrate
how a clever woman can have well-born but needy men of
letters at her beck and call: the other happened out of compassion, and sometimes by chance. Off the shore of Al-
benga that bright morning she also discovered that she did
not care a fig about what anyone in Naples might have said
or suspected about her. Garbled tales. Wearisome, ridiculous stories. The secretaries always ended by opening their
big mouths, like silly servant girls given the sack, and running off with more money than was their due. What has
happened has happened, she won't let it bother her any
more, not even on her deathbed: trifles to be confessed to a
priest, nothing to do with God, or even with the Virgin
Mary. Artemisia is a Roman Catholic.

But while in Marseilles she felt the lack of a secretary.
The voyage had been quick and smooth, like sailing on
milk, said the other women passengers, amazed and happy,
more accustomed to discomfort: they had enjoyed a light,
gentle wind that caressed the sails. When they arrived the
port and the town gleamed with white stones in the bright
sunshine which was, nonetheless, subdued, not dazzling,
like an invalid hoping to recover. They had been very lucky,
actually, and even the inn they stayed at was a good one,
although they did arrive in the midst of celebrations in
honor of some victorious Turkish frigates, and the merry-
making went on all night with torches and dancing in the
streets, something that was totally new to them. Having
fallen in with two merchant's wives returning home to
Lyons, Artemisia was waiting to get aboard the carriage,

sitting in the courtyard of the inn with her luggage at her feet. She passed the time watching a girl in a scarlet skirt draw water from the well using her hands and arms in a way not done in Italy. Suddenly she felt the urge not to paint her, but to write about her: "In Marseilles I saw a handsome, slim young woman with marvelously white arms who seemed to be having trouble drawing up the bucket." This picture, and this description, of such simplicity and clarity, were immediately followed by others of places and things; and she added words and phrases that she had heard, combining them all in her head to create a tale, a story she did not want to lose or forget. So that it will not be lost (she cannot tell it to anyone for no one here understands Italian) she must entrust it to someone, write it in a letter. Artemisia wants to write a letter, not one of her usual ones to Francesco, a few hasty lines, but a long, flowing letter: but she does not know how or to whom. The pulley on the well was squeaking, it seemed to her that the letter was being sung as the bright, gentle morning descended along with the sun into the cold stone of the courtyard. The girl began to sing too, putting the bucket down on the ground and drying her arms on her apron. The tune was lively and brisk but lacked gaiety, and it was totally unlike any of the songs sung in Rome or Naples. Throwing back her white-bonneted head, the girl picked the bucket up by the handle and set off; Artemisia drank in every sight and sound, and with great relish composed her unwritten letter word by word. On her tongue, engaged in its mute monologue, she relished the flavor and pleasure of travel, a totally private pleasure. "No one" she thought, "knows that I am here on this bench, in this courtyard, sitting down as though in my own home, as though I never had to move again." And from then on, for the whole journey, for as long as she could, she sought opportunities like this, occasions offered purely by chance, occasions from which there flowed letters written without a pen, substitutes for a paintbrush and companionship.

Her letter of the twelfth of September ran as follows: big

fair in Belcaire, even the rulers of this realm go to it, with peasants' stalls lining the roads, and dozens of street porters carrying big circular trays around on planks with handles, and on the trays something yellow that looks like polenta but isn't. A beautiful color, but I didn't taste any of it.

Her letter of the twentieth: we have to go slowly through these gorges of the Rhone; those going towards Italy travel by boat, a quick but dangerous journey. They flash past like lightning, and there was a cold north wind that would, as they say here, cut the face off you. Some marvelous rock formations with very strange shapes. Madame Blandina says that even the women here know how to handle a boat and make money out of it. But I haven't seen any.

The twenty-second: huge numbers of animals up on the cliffs, cows and horses. The shepherds wear leather butcher's aprons and drive the animals forward with war-like spears. In this light the white cows seem blue. There was a very small young boy, just out of the cradle by the looks of him, playing on his pipe and minding the sheep. All on his own, poor little thing.

The thirtieth: Madame Blandina has arrived home, to a rapturous reception: she has a husband and two lovely daughters. I stayed to dinner, the brunette has the same nose as my Porziella. These French really go in for kissing. Lyons is big and bright.

But on the seventh of October, a day when the sun was as sweet as wine, there was a dark sunset like in the middle of winter and Madame Artemisia did not feel like writing about how afraid she had been in that inn, the only woman in the whole place, and how the men downstairs had stared at her for ages, her and her luggage. A smelly, one-eyed stableboy showed her up to her attic room among the mice and the straw, with a door that would not even close; she had to drag a chest over against it to protect herself. She took off her shoes so as not to be heard and went out onto the gallery. Down below the men were drinking, talking now and again in brief, quiet phrases. "Belle femme," she heard and understood; and then several times, "Argent." She did not understand much French, apart from the usual phrases of the coachmen and innkeepers. She stayed awake all night, with no supper, feeling so forsaken that it did not seem possible to her that he who had loved her did not come to her assistance. "Oh Antonio," she tried saying, after all this time that she had not invoked his name, but she did not really know why, perhaps just to test herself, her loneliness and that dull, wornout pain that seemed sadly to have disappeared. Her invocation remained pathetic, futile, like a bet that is lost at the outset.

Nonetheless, it was during that night that she realized that those imagined letters of hers were in fact addressed to her husband, the only man who had been close to her who knew nothing about painting but who, with great simplicity, enjoyed various chance glimpses of things and people: snatches of conversation, ways of talking, different, unusual customs, the very things she has casually and instinctively been noting in her travels. The little he told her of his own travels through the Roman Campagna was full of tales of overturned carts, of cottages with lovely views, of beautiful trees, of rich flocks (they are worth such and such amounts). Insignificant events like a child having a bad fall and a kind passerby wiping away the mud and the tears; like a strange but delicious fish served at a meal. Traveling together, thinks Artemisia, they would have got on very well. She is so far from him now that she can no longer see the dark-skinned girl who has taken her place, and concerning Antonio she feels that she has returned to the ordinary, domestic but protected situation of the time she was his wife. Because in the long run no one has said that her marriage has been dissolved, that the new one has been celebrated. Where before there remained only ashes, a presentiment of death and a perverse ability to suffer, there now rises a stubborn hope, the desire for a tranquil, indulgent life: just as if a letter had reached the traveler to reassure her, to miraculously cure her forever.

This impression became a certainty on the nineteenth of October, during the last few leagues before Beaune where the rocks were swarming with black, white, brown and even blond goats standing still among the bushes with their beards pointing upwards as they watched the vehicle go by, just like people. The sense of well-being that was upon Artemisia was like a feeling of heat on her back and chest, and she felt the urge to talk to someone, which was unlike her, so she sat forward, keeping her head at the door, never tiring of watching the passersby, mainly peasants on their donkeys, as in the countryside around Rome; and she accepted the half of an apple that the monk who had just recently joined the carriage peeled for her with his dirty knife, she who is normally so squeamish. But all of a sudden, as the carriage turned to enter the courtyard of the inn, this feeling abandoned her like a wind that suddenly drops, leaving you wondering what is going to happen next. Her legs felt weak when it came to alighting, she was the last of all to get out and she had great difficulty gathering all her luggage together because her head was burning and aching. The inn was gloomy, already dark and cold. The fire burning in the great hearth did not give out any heat, the landlady's eyes looked at her penetratingly and the bed she finally obtained after much confused haggling was as loathsome to her as if it had been a trap. Finally on her own, she lay down, but without getting undressed, feeling herself floating, drifting, lost. Her thoughts were floating too, banging into each other until she finally managed to gather them together into a concept, a realization. She had a fever and there was the rumor of plague in France.

Maybe the evening that was darkening the windows was already her second one there: twenty-four hours, or maybe a minute ago, the maidservant had placed a light on the table, and she did not remember drinking from the half-empty glass. "I was feeling fine," she repeated insistently, as though these words might bear some promise of salvation. Was she afraid or did she take pleasure in being afraid? She

remembered that she had wished for death during the journey, for some kind of accident, and that no one would know
about it: perhaps even the fact of lying here, of being ill, was
no more than a strongly expressed desire of hers, a false
perception just like the time she had believed in the power of
the storm at sea, and it had been nothing of the sort. The
instinct to write a real letter with pen and paper (had she
asked for them) was an illusion too. Nonetheless she was
determined to begin it, in precise terms: "Dear brother,
finding myself in danger of death . . . " Did she really write
it, or was she dreaming? Someone was having trouble
breathing beside her, it was a disgrace that she was not left
on her own. Then in her dry throat she felt the last spasm of
that harsh breathing, she woke up, amazed that she had been
asleep in the middle of the day, she who never slept, even in
Naples, at the hottest time of day. But now it is not hot, she
is bathed in a cold sweat and the sun is setting once more.
The gnarled, gloomy fig tree, the tree of betrayal and remorse, which she can see outside her window, conjures up
images of death, the need to confess everything. "When I'm
better," advises a strange, optimistic cunning, prompted by
her fever which is abating. And Artemisia found herself
very weak, but restored to health once more: exhausted,
emaciated, robbed, cured without recourse to medicine or a
surgeon's lancet. And the urge to write letters had disappeared.

For twenty days she was cooped up in that mountain inn
which from one minute to the next would go from being as
silent as the grave to as rowdy as a fair. She would sit
spellbound looking at the fig tree that was now shedding its
leaves, wrapped up in coarse blankets that the innkeeper's
wife had lent her against the dampness of the place, for it
dripped water everywhere. It rained a lot, the young servant
girl was no longer afraid to come near her now that the
suspicion of plague had disappeared, and when there were
no visitors the girl would stay with her and sing certain
sad songs that had become their shared language and that

marked meal times, her progress as a convalescent and the day she was able to go down into the courtyard to get a breath of fresh air. When Delfina sang she forgot she was a servant in an inn, she forgot all about doing anything, her arms hanging loosely by her sides, and her soft mouth, gently pursed in song, would remain half open as though waiting for a reply. This was how Artemisia drew her, on a dirty bit of cardboard, while down below the coachmen and travelers were making an awful din and the innkeeper was looking for her; but neither of them was aware of it. As a result, the girl was dismissed and the Italian never even knew that she had left at dawn, in the rain, to travel on foot the twenty leagues back to her hut in the woods, there to face starvation. The young boy who was trampled on the way down the hill from Noy by the horses drawing the coach that was taking Artemisia to Dijon was Delfina's brother; he was a chimney sweep and was on his way home with a sack of oats that was too heavy for his small shoulders. When it happened Artemisia was asleep, her emaciated head leaning back against the hard headrest. She did not see the blood that mingled with the earth in such copious quantities that seemed amazing in such a small body. The postilion said, "A dead one out here, and a dead one inside," as he whipped up the horses, being in a great hurry. And Artemisia did indeed appear dead, so gaunt and white, her eyes closed.

She rested for two days in Dijon, one day in Troyes, one in Nogent, but she did not do any walking about. She had grown fond of the shabby rooms in inns, where she searched in vain for singing servants like Delfina. And then she had no money for a carriage, nor the energy to go on foot. She was becoming familiar with the sounds of the language and was finding it increasingly easier to recognize phrases and expressions that she was, however, unable to repeat, and that seemed to her always the same; especially as she got close to Paris, for everyone eagerly asked her if that was where she was going. She would reply that it was and then add, "On my way to England"; but she soon realized that this last piece of information did not please her fellow travelers and that it often gained her suspicious looks. At the beginning of November the color returned to her face and once again, but with a new intolerance, she began to hear that phrase, "Belle femme," which had first been said to her face in Marseilles by a light-fingered braggart. It was not necessary to speak French in order to understand, and for her it came as a surprise, making her rather angry; as if a rough beggar had managed to track her down again and would not leave her alone. To be still beautiful at her age, an age that showed in her face, seemed to her something to be ashamed of, a cruel joke; and it was not out of modesty that she defended herself at Provins from the clumsy advances of the country gentleman who had boarded the carriage with his dog. In icy indignation, almost out of pleasure at striking at a blow, she jabbed her elbow into his ugly face in the dark passage of the inn, and if she had had a weapon she would have used it in her fury. She felt cruel, almost bloodthirsty, once more. Had she not used the knife against Agostino? Had she not painted Holoferne's thick blood? And so once again she took her revenge for being a woman, because once again she was tired of being one.

But a woman was what she was, and when she reached Paris she decided to stay in a convent, for she felt that she should no longer rely on inns which were increasingly crowded and noisy. A cloister, a chapel, magnificent gardens, enormous rooms, but the mud outside the main door made it impossible for her to venture out on foot. As in Genoa, she had numerous letters of introduction, all procured in Rome by the diligent Francesco, addressed to the most illustrious names in the city, noblemen at court, eminent men of the Church, famous artists. But once again, as in Genoa, Artemisia grows lazy and lethargic, taking ages to get dressed in the morning, spending perhaps two hours looking out of the window at the leaves falling in the garden of the convent. To be kept waiting, to bow and curtsy, to smile, to pretend or make the effort to understand, to keep up the good name of her family, this great burden that weighs so little when she is alone, are all chores that she finds distasteful. And after all, whom does she need? She has painted more than a hundred works with which she was not displeased and which are hanging in noble houses, in good light, back in Italy. Something exists to show that Artemisia once lived, that a woman can paint like a man, maybe even better. It is late now for further ambitions, it is too soon to renounce all satisfaction. She will paint again, but not for Monseigneur de Guise nor for the Constable of France. She is on her way to England.

She is in a convent for the first time and she likes to keep it constantly in mind, to savor a state for which her father had destined her in order to keep her out of trouble, and which from time to time struck her as proof of his magnanimity, to be held in reserve for the end of her life. Despite all the bad things she has heard about them, she has always had a sinner's bitterly nostalgic respect for nuns, something that was understood by Porziella who, in order to oppose her, grew very close to the Reverend Mother, copying her ways. This latter was a fat, shiny woman with a sharp, though somewhat lisping tongue, and Artemisia was in awe of her. But here, once she had been admitted, unassisted, she was left on her own as a guest, and it was only on the fourth evening after her arrival that she saw the Mother Superior sitting behind a table covered with a red cloth that fell stiffly to the floor at the corners; and she was a dwarf. A dwarf with a deformed face, with eyes like two swollen bruises, holding in her short right hand a heavy crosier of gold and ebony. Her clothes of fine wool were horrendously close-fitting. A very tall elderly nun was hovering over her and by bending double was able to reach her ear. The dwarf was young and lively, not only answering with great rapidity but also moving very quickly, dragging herself in every direction as though on greased wheels: her lack of self-consciousness over her deformity was arrogant and lordly. Coming round to the other side of the table, she moved towards Artemisia and stared at her with no trace of warmth, an ugly expression of content and malice on her face. "Belle personne," she whispered, almost winking to herself, then she raised the crosier and headed for the door. Two white-veiled novices hurried after her, bending over to diminish their youthful height, to protect and serve that affected monster. Through the door, at the end of the room, could be seen a crowd of women, all of them widows, as their headdresses proclaimed, standing stiffly waiting.

At night, when the row in the streets had died down—for in Paris people are always quarreling—and the sounds of laughing, joking and singing had faded away with the receding footsteps of the patrols and bands of merrymakers, the silence in the convent would begin to hum with rustling noises, with knocking and whispering that would suddenly cease and then start up again from one corridor to the next. A door would bang, there would be the unmistakeable sound of someone running swiftly on bare feet. Once she clearly heard a young voice desperately imploring, "Por amor de Dios!" while the walls shook from some heavy object being laboriously dragged across the floor. During the day all is peaceful, all is order, measured by the sound of bells, the lay sisters at their never-ending work of polishing floors, woodwork and metal. Holding up her extremely full skirts so as not to dirty them, Madame de Lorré, a widow who is a boarder for life in the convent, very meddlesome in her banishment, goes past, greasy with camphor from head to toe. She is followed by the long-legged white cat with the sad, ghostly face. She stops to ask in a loud, echoing voice, like one deaf person talking to another, "Are you going to Court?" Everyone goes to Court in Paris.

But Artemisia puts off going out from day to day; she does not unpack her work, not even the small paintings intended as presents for potential patrons. "This one," Francesco had hinted, "is for Monsignor Nunzio who might give it to the Cardinal; this one for Monsieur de Bethune,

perhaps the King will see it, he should like female nudes."
Sitting once more at a window, a window with a view of
pointed roofs and in the distance Pont Neuf with its beacon,
Artemisia thoughtfully picks up her pencil and from memory does a sketch of Delfina rapt in song, with her wide
cheekbones and that wry, genial smile of hers, so sweetly
mischievous. Green, black and lead white: what other hues
for Delfina's face, the color of weary earth? At first the
widows in the parlour discussed her at length, but then their
curiosity got the better of them and they approached her.
They managed to make themselves understood, already
pronouncing her name in their own way, but they seemed
uncertain of her status. They immediately asked her her age:
that number—forty—which they seized on like an object of
prey seemed to come as a happy surprise to them and they
repeated it to one another in tones of admiration. "Widowed?" "Yes, widowed," replied Artemisia, her eyes suddenly filling with tears.

She became their plaything, they came to visit her in her
room at all hours of the day. A few paintings were unwrapped by force, and the small ones intended as gifts were
passed from hand to hand, begged for passionately, haggled
over vehemently. They arranged to take her on an outing—
You have to see Paris!—they took her to the Palais de Jus-
tice, and to examine laces and silks that none of them
bought. But they gave her gifts: delving into their drawers
they offered her an old fan, some rouge, a few medicinal
lozenges. They forced her to wait for a whole morning beneath the towers of Pont Neuf to see Cardinal Richelieu's
carriage go by. Never had she seen so many acrobats, players, lackeys, soldiers, donkeys, sheep, horses: all of them
quick and nimble, full of an arrogant, aggressive excitement, even the animals were kicking out exuberantly.
Someone stole her lovely pink silk kerchief but she said
nothing about it when she realized it was gone, although she
suspected a young servant boy with bare legs and feet, a
runny nose and frightened eyes who reminded her of Del-

fina. And while she stood looking at him, the women pulled at her skirt, her sleeve, caught hold of her hand and dragged her forward almost under the hooves of the Cardinal's horses. The carriage flashed past escorted by half a dozen red horsemen on prancing horses that struck sparks off the stones and even off the mud. Artemisia was a little frightened, feeling vulnerable in that rapacious, crowded square beneath a low, completely gray sky where no one cared that it was raining. Afterwards she recalled having seen a puppy, no, a small, white cat, very frightened, at the sparkling carriage window.

Shortly after that she was moved, without being consulted, to another room, as though she really were a nun, passing from the small cell she occupied to a big, bare room which was very cold that November: the bed was built into an alcove the size of a small room. Fifteen knights had slept there in comfort, the widows informed her, spreading their fingers like a fan, during the reign of merry King Henry. Finally they brought her to the Louvre, crowded with people who talked loudly, coughed and spat with no regard for hygiene so that the floor was like a lake; and then they all elbowed each other in the ribs to get into the gallery where the King was. Trampled, squashed, unable to defend herself from the wandering hands of the lecherous, overbearing noblemen from the countryside, Artemisia grew indignant once more, lost her patience and shouted angrily in Italian, recovering her former haughtiness. "This court is not to my liking, for I have come from a Spanish one and now am going to London." An outburst that the widows did not understand, taking these names to be terms of comparison all to the advantage of Paris. In her anger Artemisia grew very red, even without rouge, and since her companions had got the idea in their heads of seeing the King dine, it was not difficult for her to lose them in the crowd. When Artemisia is roused, she is not afraid of an army: the *petite blonde* who that evening gave Cinq-Mars, who had mingled with the crowd, a slap on the face (and he could not stop laughing about it at dinner) was Artemisia who, in the lamplight, appeared to him as a spirited young woman. And she returned on her own to the convent, did Madame Artemisia, without asking anyone the way, stomping boldly through the mud, her sumptuous skirts soaked. Indignation and disgust kept her warm even in her cold bed where she fell asleep at once.

It was lucky for her that these feelings lasted until the next day and longer, for the widows made fun of her for having got lost; for her own ends, so they said. She recovered her composure, examined her finances as best she could, decided that she had enough to hire a carriage at least for four days and finally made her rounds to present her letters, out of which she chose the least important. And so she squandered the four large paintings intended for Queen Henrietta, impulsively giving them for no good reason to people of no consequence: a protégé of Poussin's who had very recently fallen out of grace, a Milanese captain who was going back to Italy, the orphaned spinster daughter of an artist from Limoges who had been in Rome and who had filled his house with worthless antiques. With these people, who were amazed and rather amused, she then proceeded to give vent to her feelings, explaining loudly and animatedly that it was not possible to live in this country, the people were indiscreet, the roads atrocious, the bread awful, the fashions ridiculous. Despite their hot temper and touchiness, the French were slow to realize that they were being offended and to think about how they ought to retaliate. At Christmas, the captain told everyone in Milan that in Paris he had met the oddest woman in the world. But by then Artemisia had already resumed her journey.

The motion of the wheels, to which she submitted passively, began once more to take the place of activity, soothing her frenzy of words and actions which, although unconvincing, were nonetheless necessary to her now in order for her to detach herself, when she had no precise reason for doing so, from the places in which she stopped: otherwise she would never have left. From one stage of the journey to the next, sitting on worn leather seats, she indulged once again in gloomy thoughts which she monotonously wound and rewound around images of her irrevocable, discredited life that would never be free of suffering. The countryside through which they were passing was flat and bare, the people barer still in the northern cold, with gray, ashen skin and thin, bony knees, or else covered in raw, red patches. The children would come running up when the coaches halted with their wooden whistles, a peeled stick, and long-haired dogs covered in mud. They did not seem to feel the bitter wind that blew nor the heavy rain that fell. On the doorsteps of the huts with roofs of rotten thatch the mothers, fine women of tall stock, sat spinning flax while swarms of industrious little girls went round the travelers bringing them pitchers of milk, gray cakes covered in ash, and that cider of theirs. Leaning out of the door, her face once more pale and serious, Artemisia tirelessly observed these poor, haggard people with whom, so she thought, she would be able to get on much better than with the poor of Naples, were it not for the barrier of their language, increasingly impenetrable and abstruse. She was short of money and could no longer afford to give them alms, so she turned her eyes away and looked at the flat horizon: immense sky, immense earth, a few hints of pale sunshine, ponds of water everywhere and black woods on small grey hills. She drew her head in and let it fall back in that position of extreme fatigue which had dispensed her from joining in the chatter of her traveling companions after her illness in Noy. She could not believe that the end of her long journey was approaching and she began anew to dread the future when once again she would have to sustain her reputation and her name, a source of pain. They had begun to travel by water, along brimming canals, in large boats that were pulled by huge horses who were spattered all over with mud, even on their manes, blond and silver-gray.

They arrived in Calais at midday, having started out before daybreak, but the light was like that of early dawn. Another port, but the signs of activity seemed almost devoid of color, standing out against the gray air as though drawn in black ink with a few touches of yellow. Here too an intricate tangle of masts and rigging and tall bridges of ships at anchor; but the twisting, bristling convolutions of ornate prows, sails and formidable capstans seemed deadened, muffled, yet at the same time justified and consumed by the heaviness of the air and the light, by the thickness of the mist which lapped at intervals at the sea, leaving it smooth and black when it withdrew. "There's the ocean," pompously announced the Florentine who had talked the whole way, in every language, looking round, and Artemisia wished she were Turkish so as not to understand him. But the word made an impression on her. She had not stopped to consider that this sea was called an ocean, the ocean of adventurous voyages, voyages of no return. Tasting warm beer for the first time—and she spat it out into her handkerchief—at the door of a shiny, black, soot-free hut, she felt she was taking another step towards an unlimited, inhuman freedom, the release from memory. Hard to believe in the existence of Naples, of her house, of Porziella to whom she once gave birth; hard, almost impossible, to imagine that gesture of Antonio's, one so insistent and unbearable, as he touches and grasps the black girl's hand. All her memories are out of focus, from the most distant to the most recent, as though she were making her way down into a valley, a pleasurable descent, but gradually the sky grows smaller and smaller until it is reduced to the size of a plate. She hears them say that they are waiting for high tide to set sail: an expression that is new to her ears and which arouses her curiosity like a child who has no thought either for yesterday or tomorrow.

The sailors here talk very little, with short, staccato words. They move with less arrogance than the others, almost with less courage, as if they had no faith in the sea, and yet they are flying around. The ship was a small one, and she was lucky to be allowed to join it as it was sailing on behalf of certain Knights of Malta who would not accept any money and there was even a lady on board, although she kept out of sight. The order was given for everyone to remain below deck, but Artemisia chose not to understand it and remained outside, while the crew shook their heads but did not force her to obey. For company she had a black dog with yellow eyes who crouched at her feet, amazingly good and quiet, and who seemed to belong to no one, although every sailor who went by stopped to stroke him and offer him a dry biscuit. They slipped imperceptibly into the thick fog, the bells ringing continually, as though mass were about to be said. But she must not mention mass in England, for mass is never celebrated, except for the Queen who is a Catholic, this much Artemisia knows; but she did not know just how strongly she would be struck by the thought that there would not be any churches for her to go into and sit on a bench in silence, to find rest, as has always been her habit. Tales of Lutheran ferocities, of priests hanged, of Catholics burnt alive came back to her from chance references, but she found them hard to believe in this air the consistency of cotton wool, amidst these calm men with light-blue eyes. From now on any opportunity to talk is gone, as is all inclination; it is like finding oneself among birds and wanting to decipher their language. All communication with these people is carried out by means of sober, sorrowful gestures, not like among the deaf, as was the case in France, but among the dumb. Nor do they seem friendly with one another, these Englishmen. When they talk their lips hardly move and they rarely look at each other.

They had to stay on board all night long because a strong wind had sprung up, making it impossible to disembark. At sunset, which was over very quickly, she had the impression that they were in hell, forsaken prisoners. Pitch black everywhere, the lamps shining faintly like boiled eggs in the fog, and always the ringing of bells. The ship was rolling in every direction, the dog whining quietly in the dark as Artemisia tried to find her way back below deck, and she would never have succeeded had it not been for one sailor who wordlessly pushed her in the right direction. Inside, groans, sighs and the usual basins. Nothing in the way of beds, but Artemisia managed to find a space on the floor to lie down on and was confident of falling asleep: she had grown used to the crashing of the sea and took pleasure in conquering it with sleep. When she awoke amidst all those ailing, prostrate bodies, she felt fresh and full of life: the sea was smooth, gray, barely ruffled, the fog had disappeared. She saw a huge, white rock, clean and bare like an enormous bone, looming so close that she felt she could touch it with her forehead. It was the coast of England, English soil, an unbroken wall against which they would crash like blind swallows. But the ship did not crash into it and Dover came into sight, a few small houses, a deserted port.

This is a small country where distances are insignificant, where the sound of voices is like subdued humming; hills, fields, trees all look as though they could be measured in handbreadths. The sky is low here too, but bowl-shaped, its dimensions restricted in proportion with the earth, and there would never be enough room for high mountains. Huts like chicken coops, with roofs of gray thatch; carriages that were quite proper although they too were very small; and the horses appeared small too, until, as they drew nearer, every thing and every person returned to its normal size, the people, in fact, being tall, handsome and strong. But no more so than Orazio Gentileschi, who looked like one of them, as tall and erect as when he had left Italy with those gray eyes of his and that small, humorous beard which still had not turned white. He suddenly appeared before her in Canterbury as she was getting out of the carriage, and she did not know where he had sprung from, so present and so unchanged that she was not even surprised. Happy yes, incredibly happy. He placed his hand lightly on her shoulder and said, "Here you are, child." All Artemisia's troubles disappeared.

If she still daydreamed at the window, too lazy to go out, in this London palace that belonged to the Queen, it was not because she was unable to hold her own and make an impression, but because she was carefree, like a child again: whatever is going to happen will happen. Behind her back there stretched, reassuring and safe, the room where her father slept, ate and worked, filled with strange furniture in all sorts of styles so that it looked more like a storeroom than a dwelling place, although it fulfilled its role of being a home and providing shelter. Nor did it lack dignity and grandeur, for Orazio had made himself at home amidst these irregular chairs and benches goodness knows how long ago, finding the light good and conditions favorable for painting in peace; and he dominated all these objects, imprinting on them the mark of his authority which, although far from being of a rigorously domestic nature, was not in conflict with them, so that his daughter was reluctant to touch anything. Large and medium-size canvases lying everywhere testified to the labors of many years, to the level of excellence achieved by means that had a long history, a history that Artemisia was able to slowly piece together and interpret, finding in his work the reasons for his success, the triumphs of hard work, of subtle, carefully elaborated skills; so much so that it made her feel that her own methods were harsh and mechanical. It was such a pleasure to see herself, not as a woman in the presence of a man, but as a raw, inferior pupil in the presence of a master who has never lowered his standards nor relented in his industriousness and who continues at the same pace. He is more disposed now to painting small pictures, but shows them to no one; Artemisia is well aware that it is only with reluctance that he lets her see them, searching for excuses to hide them with his body or turn them face to the wall. His palette is small too, with only a few colors on it, five or six at the most; his brushes very fine, his pigments and lacquers always neatly stored away in a small cupboard, so that it is difficult for her to examine them. Orazio worked for as long as the light lasted and if his daughter turned her back on him and stayed silent, he would begin to whistle in a dull, monotonous tone; a sound that reminded her of happy childhood times and which the Gentileschi children recognized as a sign that he was in a good mood, concentrating intently and happily. With the whistling came a growing sense of peace for Artemisia, a peace that would not bear examination but was simply to be enjoyed. She did not move, aware that behind her back the old painter was using tones of green, ultramarine, soft pink and dull gold to compose landscapes and human figures, skies, silks, meadows and clear water. And it was as if she did not know how to paint, a feeling that almost made her happy, standing still in the soft light from the window as if her father had ordered her to do so, as if by not disturbing him in this way she were posing as his model. Moreover, the flat, grassy gardens, the clouds, the stones, the river all seemed to accommodate themselves to the theme of this painted order, reacting to the subdued northerly light as Orazio willed. Perhaps Artemisia would study again: was she not interested in the small boats of the milkmaids, in the river traffic with its heavily laden ferries, in the way the colorfully dressed gentlemen disported themselves? The letters that she might have written now became paintings, new signs of her renewed interest; and at times she fervently hoped so, she counted on it desperately, feeling herself young and strong again just as when, after having worked on a commission, she used to accept a holiday, looking forward to working even harder afterwards. It so happened that Lady Arabella, a great friend of Orazio's, came out onto the balcony below the window—the Queen slept every afternoon, in the Italian manner—and blew her a graceful kiss with the tips of her fingers. At that Artemisia blushed and withdrew into the room. This confidential and slightly protective gesture of approach reminded her that she was at Court, at a Court that had summoned her and now ignored her. Her mood turned once more to one of melancholy and shyness, and she took care not to show herself at the window again, despite trying not to disturb her father. And so she ended up by seeing only the sky and how quickly it grew dark, swallowed up by evening.

She learned to serve warm beer and to carve huge roasts of wild meats carried in by the pages, leftovers from the Queen's table. Orazio had grown accustomed to English ways and swallowed everything down, his mind elsewhere, confident of his iron stomach. About his daughter's life, and even about the event that had brought her, at his instigation, so far north, he seemed not to care, nor had he anything to say about her lack of activity as she sat hour after hour with a piece of silly feminine embroidery in her hands, identical to the sort he used to scold her for when they all lived together, because she was wasting time. Women's thoughts run free when they are doing needlework, but Artemisia's mind was empty as she sewed, totally taken up with certain basic designs: a narrow path, a small sparkling sword, stitches like birds' footprints in the snow. She pricked her finger often and then there would be the blood to suck as she raised her eyes, with a slight frown. During these pauses she would sometimes feel herself start suddenly, as if from an internal rebuke. "What am I doing?" she would wonder, as though she were engaged in some shameful activity. And bending her head once more, her face red perhaps, she would feel a distant stirring deep inside her, like a mechanism that is about to be released. She would have loved to stand up; but, her eyes falling on her father's curved back, she would feel calm and reassured once again.

She took pleasure in certain domestic tasks—washing hankerchiefs, polishing a box or a dish—which she gradually began to love doing for the old man, lavishing them on him needlessly; she told herself, in the manner of inveterate housewives, that he needed these things done, that it was up to her to combat the glorious dust in the studio, so that Orazio would not be living in such filthy conditions which an occasional sweep by one of the servants scarcely improved. She began to think like her countless peers, to lose respect for a man's work, which became more than anything else an object of indiscreet curiosity. And since Orazio had the habit of suddenly going out without saying where he was going, she could not resist venturing, armed with a rag and feather duster, among the stretchers, drawings, rolled-up canvases, paintings and old letters. Under the pretext of tidying and cleaning she moved and examined every object, spending ages trying to date a drawing, to find the original of a particular head, to decipher a scrawled signature; activities she performed with a thumping heart, in enjoyable trepidation, her hand always ready to conceal what she was doing and her ears to receive the string of vivid curses with which her father would once have greeted such liberties. She was, in reality, playing a game of chance and it lost all its piquancy the day that Orazio, catching her red-handed, showed no sign of having noticed, but immediately went into his corner and resumed his customary activities. Whether deliberate magnanimity or simple distraction, the effect it had was to cure her of all such female weaknesses and to reveal further depths of the stern nature of such an exceptional man; so that the slight vexation that was still aroused in her at seeing him cover his work with a hand or a shoulder slowly melted away—in its place a new understanding of the reticent ways of the loner who defends himself as best he can from the rest of the world. Living with his daughter, moreover, he was as distant from her as at the same time last year when thousands of miles separated them; not because he disliked her, but because of his increasingly rigid intransigence in wanting to avoid the waste, the pain involved in loving. He had avoided life's ambushes and resisted the workings of time. "Is Francesco well, Giulio too?" His question when they met in Canterbury had been more an aggressive command than an enquiry. He had seized on her affirmative reply, which was necessary to his peace of mind, and entrenched himself in it; and it would

suffice him—woe betide anyone who disturbed his peace—
for the rest of his life.

Not very often, but it happened nonetheless, the troupe
of artists at Court would come to knock on Orazio's half-
forgotten, half-fabled door; and the first time it happened
Artemisia feared it was an invasion of courtiers, so elegantly
were they dressed and so open in manner, a little too bois-
terous for Italian tastes. Then they all grew quiet together,
in an attitude approaching respect; and an onlooker might
have detected in this a deliberate, ironic reticence, an agreed
intention of observing, of collecting topics for conversation
afterwards. They were not at all ill at ease: they paid their
respects to Signora Artemisia who had only recently arrived
and whom the old man, in his displeasure, hastily introduced to them. The unanimous, hearty laughter began once
more; only the one called Anthony, a handsome man who
retained his dignity and never took his gloves off, did not
join in. He was Flemish like the others, but he had a palace
and stables and a lady, as noblewomen are called here, for a
wife. He spoke Italian well and talked to Artemisia in her
language, but he kept the conversation on a very distant
level and made no reference to their shared art. Orazio
spoke English with an impatient, almost angry speed, full of
errors, climbing over the words with lowered head or else
letting them fall from his lips distorted by his Tuscan palate,
repellent food. Yet the men understood him, and they began
to hand round large sheets of paper with reproductions of
the latest works of the great European artists, mostly Flemish however. Orazio took them without a word, looked at
them with his darting eyes that were always ready, like
noble insects, to run over the lines and colors: then he silently handed them back. At no stage did he show any of his
paintings; he allowed no one to turn any of them round.
Artemisia noted all this, for little notice was taken of her,
although slightly more than she thought, so she decided that
she could disappear without appearing rude, and off she
went.

Who does not know what it means to go out of a room and close the door on a group of talking, laughing people who are happy to be together? It was not just the cold of the corridors along which she moved rapidly that gave her a hollow feeling in the pit of her stomach, that made her footsteps so desolately light. She had to climb a great number of stairs to reach her room which was in a large attic where the Queen had seen fit to accommodate her along with ladies' maids, pages, old servants; people who were never quiet for a moment and whom she would meet at all hours of the day going up and down the stairs, so that she had to stand aside, the staircase being so narrow.

Her room is big and bright under the eaves of Somerset House, sparsely furnished with exquisite, unmatching pieces that might change from morning to evening due to the needs of a Court in the habit of moving furniture every day from one end of the palace to the other; for money is short and extravagance unlimited. It is not rare for Artemisia to come in and find a second bed with closed hangings, inside which some young girl or matron is fast asleep, a passing guest: a frequent occurrence in the Court of Queen Henrietta. But apart from these visitors, her room is empty, freezing and remote as though it had no connection with the crowded, bustling palace: even the cries of the white peacocks in the Queen's greenhouses barely reach her. She closes this second door behind her and has to summon all her courage not to slacken her pace as she walks over to the easel on which rests the usual unfinished painting. But the easel is next to the window, and windows are the refuge of those who are listless, unsure of themselves. From this one can be seen the same view, but from higher up, of colorless lawns, the iron-gray river, winter fog; and once again, for no reason, Artemisia stares as if spellbound. A world that is inaccessible to daily events, to the unexpected, lies in front of her, unchanging from day to day. She sits down: proud Artemisia now paints sitting down, for this small painting is proving to be recalcitrant, it is only a Susanna with her venerable old men, a small canvas, because here they do not like large ones. And then she does not have a model. The blond girl Nina, daughter of a cook from Lombardy, is kept busy all day by her father and those foreign gentlemen artists who say that she has beautiful skin tones; she has no time for Artemisia, and anyway her models have always been dark. The colors on her palette have gone dry: she tires of painting now even before they are used up. And they look dirty and dull in this climate. She feels there is a curse upon her, ever since she arrived here all her work seems to be reduced to chores: now she is scraping away with her knife at a lump of lead white which is all cracked, and to her it is just like cleaning a saucepan. In the meantime, the diffuse light on the gardens turns a darker shade of gray, taking on a sticky consistency that blurs rather than defines the outlines of things. The days are very short in this country, there is only time to paint in the mornings and even then, as soon as the painting is started, the canvas becomes smooth and oily, so that there is no pleasure in working on it. The big bell in the Tower rings, drowning out the scraping of the knife; bells so cold and so troubled in their imperiousness that Artemisia has never heard anything like it before, bells which make her exile seem so absurd that there is no point in lamenting it. Now all the bells, large and small, begin to ring from these heretical churches with their deceptive names, the happy pealing and chiming of loquacious ghosts that floats up into these foggy skies. But she will have to learn to put up with them and listen to them, if her father has been able to. With her knife suspended in her fingers, Artemisia tries hard to construct an image of herself, the image of a mature woman happily living and painting in England. Leave it till tomorrow: after all, darkness is the same everywhere, even underground.

With the arrival of the first letters from Italy at the end of winter, the world seemed to open up to her again. Not due to Porziella, who sent a string of bills to be paid and asked, summarily, for her mother's blessing, but because of Francesco who, in his usual gentle way, had overcome his resentment at being left behind and sent her his customary detailed, biased news of paintings that had fetched good prices, of flattering judgments of her work, of definite commissions for when she came back; offering once more to leave at a moment's notice to come and join her over there: "For nothing would be too much trouble for you, my respected sister," he wrote, almost in awe because of the immense distance and the address of the palace, struggling with the unwonted phrases so that none of his usual affection would be lost. At the same time the Queen fixed a date for Artemisia's introduction: in three days' time, and she was to appear on her own. There had been a time when Orazio had liked things that happened unexpectedly, he was a man who made sudden decisions and could not tolerate delays; but this he did not like and he began to mutter and grow agitated as though it were totally unexpected. Artemisia imagined she could hear him pawing the ground as he moved around among the heterogeneous clutter of furniture, banging into things angrily, pushing others out of the way, looking for this and that, neglecting his work. When, and how, he ever saw the Queen, his friend for so many years, was still a mystery to Artemisia, and any time she had asked him about it, with the indifferent air she had affected since childhood when something really mattered to her, she had come up against his old, steely inattention, a sort of invincible stubbornness in refusing to reply. "Eh?" the old man would say, without even turning round or raising his head; and he would have said the same thing a hundred times over, a sign that he was paying her no attention, if the question had been repeated to him a hundred times. But Artemisia did not repeat it. In the evenings he would be overcome by tiredness, suddenly, like a child, and would often sit at dinner with one hand—his lovely, fine hand—over his eyes, as though to protect himself from a world of sounds and events that did not concern him and his painting. Far less the chatter of a woman, but no voice got through to him anymore. And so it was rather exceptional, and, as it seemed to Artemisia, alarming, the way the Queen's message upset his usual behavior.

The disturbed dust echoed to the sounds of vigorous reprimands that dated back to sixteen hundred and ten, to sixteen hundred and fifteen; as if the years of disdainful silence, of exile, of separation and indifference weighed no more than one hour. "You bitch, will you move?" he would shout at her when his entreaties and apprehensions failed to rouse in the mature woman any signs of dismay. In twenty thundering sentences Artemisia was able to learn more about Henrietta of France, Queen of England, than she had ever thought of asking. The information he gave her was peculiar, the tidbits of a secret informer. "You must praise her hands, because she knows she is ugly, and tell her that she looks like her father." "Don't eat any of the sweets when she offers them to you, they taste like hell." "Remember, she isn't stupid, just eccentric, one word isn't enough and two are too many." "She might even give you a kiss on the face, but don't you kiss her back, I know what I'm talking about." And on one occasion, muttering to himself, "Poor woman, how many of her portraits will remain?" His words and behavior were peremptory, almost insolent, contrasting nonetheless with the impatience, with the sort of excitement with which he defined and discussed certain minute, frivolous details. He interrogated Artemisia about what she would wear, how she would do her hair. He wanted to choose something out of her wardrobe himself and his heavy tread resounded through corridors, staircases and anterooms that had certainly not seen him for years; he startled astonished pages and ladies' maids, went the wrong way and distractedly cut straight through the Persian delegation who were waiting for an audience, stood on the foot of Lord X as he came out from a privy council meeting with his hand still on his chest. When he finally reached his daughter's room he hammered on the door and entered like a thunderbolt: then he began to search delicately among her clothes, picking out petticoats and bodices one by one. He used to do exactly the same when rummaging through his chests to find garments with which to clothe a model, be it a woman or an angel, to his liking, and the linens were never fine enough, the silks never bright and soft enough. He selected a dress of blue brocade and some lace, and looked at his daughter who, in an attitude of submission with bent head, had unconsciously taken up her old pose of a fearful, slightly faithless young girl. It was this constantly suspected and abhorred faithlessness—a curse on women—that now touched the old man, in his wisdom. He laid his smooth, light hand on the cloud of bright hair that he had so seldom stroked, so often painted: it shone so tenderly. "Dark blue suits you," he murmured, engrossed in thought, and he slowly ran his fingers down her neck, down his daughter's still delicate shoulder. He stood upright again, but with a stoop, as though weighed down by thoughts too sad to bear; and then, suddenly angry and hard, he asked, "Have you chosen a painting to give her?" He looked suspiciously at the heap of paintings turned face to the wall, but not at the one that lay on the easel. He did not touch a single canvas himself, but waited for Artemisia to turn them round, one by one, with her own hands. Since she had arrived in London, he had not once asked her about her work nor to see its results. Now his examination was horribly slow, so that the pupils of his eyes, after remaining motionless and as though coagulated on a canvas, began to move, to dart about at great speed, as though reading it, piercing it right through.

Artemisia's feeling of awe, as she willingly lifted the paintings to exhibit them in the best light, and then stood beside the easel where each one was placed, had now turned into an anxious eagerness that was nonetheless completely open and full of devotion. There was nothing on any of the canvases that she would have liked to hide or conceal, nor was she ashamed of being thus exposed through her work, good or bad though it might be, the essence, the unique flavor of days when she had been happily engrossed in recreating a face or a garment, in inventing an effective light, in applying an expressive glaze. No doctor, or even confessor, would have found her more sincere or humble. One noble and secret language was spoken in an exchange of glances, a language that embraced the whole of the visible world over a long span of time, beyond the confines of human life, in an eternal fellowship of artists of which Orazio bore the mark and the wisdom. And after this necessary silence they exchanged art's free, triumphant words, establishing a rapt equality of expression that went far beyond the contingencies of age, sex and family ties. And now Artemisia is vindicated, she the eccentric middle-aged woman who set off from home all alone, for no real reason, as people might say. Now she is safe and happy in the presence of these words and gestures that are incomparably respectful, this recognition, this loyal reserve. Two minds, not a man and a woman, not a father and daughter. And the daughter, set free by this homage, released in a fervor of demonstrativeness that gives her courage, raises her head and her eyes. She explains the problems; clarifies her intentions; recognizes her mistakes without letting them worry her; enjoys her triumphs without pride, laughing about them in fact, as though they were successful jokes. She gets slightly carried away: her woman's fist is placed on her hip in a virile manner; her whole body, compressed in her stiff, full clothes, strikes attitudes that are not very feminine, but so very innocent! This damned painting! "Let me tell you that Baglione and the other Roman artists would never be capable of foreshortening like this." "No, leave landscapes alone, they're not for you." Now Artemisia's life appears as a completely harmonious continuum from the first lessons her father gave her, through the ascetic practices of her youth, right up to today when Orazio talks to her with clarity and brusqueness, just as he did to his friends in Via della Croce, the best painters in Rome. Ineffable happiness, in which the honor that was lost at such an early age is restored to a soul that had already begun to give in. It does not matter that she is a woman, often discouraged, twice betrayed. There is no longer any doubt, a new painter has been born: Artemisia Gentileschi.

At about this time news of Artemisia, news that was six months old, began to spread around the Court as though it were the very latest. An Italian woman has arrived, a famous artist, daughter of that old man Gentileschi, the Queen's protégé. She is beautiful, she is young. Well, not that young, but very good-looking and as proud as a papist devil, and she always dresses in black in the Genoese manner. No, not Genoese, Spanish. She has come from Naples, no, from Madrid, she has been sent by the Jesuits, maybe she's a spy. The ladies of the Court condescended to talk of her, pretending to sneer, each one with her own motive, and some changed the subject, talking about Lady Arabella's new monkey that has blue fur, a present from a priest who lives in Samarkand. Lady Arabella claims she is unwell, an insolent pretext to receive her intimate friends in her famous boudoir in the shape of a shell, where she lies dressed as Galatea, wearing only a transparent linen shift; just as Orazio painted her in *The Finding of Moses*. Maybe this female artist is a lover dressed as a woman? She is an assassin whom the Pope saved from the gallows. She is one of the Pope's bastards. She is of mongrel stock, a gypsy. But gypsies aren't blond. Anyway, who has even seen her?

Hundreds, thousands of them had seen her on those blessed stairs and in the low, vaulted corridors pullulating with all the men, women and children in the service of the French Queen, but they had all formulated different suppositions as to who she was, some thinking she was a pale seamstress on trial, others the widow of Smith the gardener. And Robert Dodd, an apprentice tapestry maker, took her to be a singer, goodness knows why: that evening, in the tavern, as he swilled down beer, he said that now he knew what theatrical women were like up close, they are all over the place at Court, but give themselves great airs. Now, with the craze for tidbits of news that were passed down from the salons to the anterooms, every woman was stared at and the maids jokingly said to each other, "Hey there, are you Artemisia?" "A small blond" was how Mary Bones, who made Artemisia's bed, described her; but no one believed her. But the fact was that after that no more travelers passing through were put in her room and she found the fire lit every evening. When she visited her father she was no longer permitted to stay in the background without attracting attention. The other artists made a great show of bowing to her, accompanied by their wives, Flemish women whose cheeks were of a rich, red hue beneath their large, mushroom-shaped hats gleaming with pearls. In Flanders there are no women who paint, at least not openly, and these wives, who have art under their noses all day long in the person of their husbands, grow very curious, almost covetous, about a woman who claims to equal their men. Could it be true? Is it not some trick of her father's? And they look, they investigate, most of them racked with inconfessable envy that is close to despair. Just see how Mr. Van Dyck, the Queen's favorite, treats her. He is the only one now who does not ask her the inevitable question: how does she like this city, this Court? Because even this painter of ladies has left off his gracious, haughty manner and is so friendly that Artemisia feels that they have met before in Italy, so expansive is he with her in praising that country's marvels, Rome, Naples, Palermo. What can we say about Genoa and her splendors? He knows all its streets intimately, can name all its illustrious families, remembers the perfect beauties of his time. He sighs. And then he mentions the name of the sublime Pietra Spinola, a miracle. Is she still alive? Artemisia ardently replies that she is, and her cheeks flush with love.

It was like a conspiracy to make her a success, but not without its risks of failure, an enjoyable rising out of the obscurity of anonymity, but tinged with melancholy; for in this homage and esteem which were not based on evidence of her work, she thought she recognized the terms of a dismissal that the world was offering her, unaware of the sort of person she had been, overbearing and conceited, wanting to win at any cost. And what if the Queen did not like her? She looked at her father who was impatient with all this talk, and a new, sincere cause for humility overcame her; so that that night, her thoughts full of her personal reasons for sadness, she said a painless farewell to Antonio and his dark lady, gathered Porziella to her bosom in a rush of maternal love, and above all asked Francesco's forgiveness, full of remorse at not having let him know how fond she was of him. Now she knows how it is possible to make a will, totally at peace, thinking of your loved ones who will continue, as is fair, to live: for herself, she nurtures in her heart her strong desire to paint, alone but happy in her knowledge that she can do it, as long as she still has time. What is the point, therefore, of this introduction to the Queen? She came very close to saying so out loud one evening as she served boiled mutton to her father, a dish he hated; but just then Orazio got up from the table, went over to a cabinet, rummaged around for quite a while and then came back towards the light, holding a small phial in his hand. He looked at it, held it up to the light, uncorked it, sniffed it and put it down on the table next to his daughter's plate. "This lacquer," he said, "is not available in Antwerp and there is nothing like it for the shadows in blue silk. Henrietta, you see, always dresses in blue." He winked at her and began to eat, so pleased with himself that he swallowed down the mutton without noticing.

On the Sunday before the ceremony, Artemisia had to attend high mass in the Queen's chapel, amidst a congregation composed of French, Spanish and Italians: there were very few of the latter, for Italians in London did without mass, as did Orazio. Artemisia went on foot, in lovely sunshine that was hard to believe, with the London bourgeoisie crowding round to have a look at the papists in their finery, seeming more gloomy than amused. She was given a place among the retinue of Lady Arabella who went to mass out of contrariness, her gown very low-cut and her clothes old-fashioned, with a fan in her hand. Sandwiched between two English beauties, the Italian woman felt that the pale gold of her own face must look very dark compared to these two silver flowers, their cheeks, their skin, their hair as bright as the moon, the bloom of their complexions as rigid as their expressions. They talked to one another without moving their heads, and one of them showed a flash of icy animation as she greeted two very young brothers, or cousins, among the gentlemen: like the ladies they too formed a pair, full of arrogance, dressed in gray cloaks, their coloring that of pale wheat, with full, red lips. From those snow-white brows that were never lowered at all, there flashed, at the slightest instigation, questions, answers, cruel jokes and almost frantic urgings, like unspoken hunting cries; then each one turned his pale gaze elsewhere. The only choice was to stare, as most were doing, at the royal tribune where a very fat woman, in purple and ermine, seemed to be asleep, her face lowered onto her necklaces. Two old, pathetic dwarves, one male and one female, wearing strange, tattered costumes, were evidently offering her a book and cushions: she ignored them, her top half imperceptibly swaying to and fro; her lardy fingers, resting on her stomach rapidly ran over a rosary of huge pearls. Fake pearls, fake jewels, so people said. Everything was false around the old mother of the Queen of England and the King of France, driven out by the latter, barely tolerated by the former. They say she eats vast quantities of sweetmeats and that her allowance is not sufficient to pay for even these trifling expenses. They all laugh at her here at Court. She was once the great Maria, powerful, capricious, hard to please, the richest princess in Tuscany, the most magnificent Queen in Europe. In Florence they talked about her as if she were a goddess: anyone she took a liking to was blessed, certain of being placed in Paris like a prince. Coffers full of jewels.

187

Hundreds of diamond-studded gowns, more than one for every day of the year. Now a chest full of rags, and this dusty funereal purple amidst the light-blue dartings of these neat English snakes. All she has left is her greed. She was once Queen of France, this Italian. And she is going to have to clear out very soon, King Charles can bear her no longer.

Artemisia was in the middle of a sigh when Henrietta made her entrance amidst a noisy bustle rather lacking in solemnity. She marched in as though she were in the stable yard with a whip at her side, appearing to have no neck under all the false curls. Behind her, the motley breeches of the Frenchmen, red, white and yellow; painted French ladies; then priests, monks in abundance, with and without girdles, black, white, purple and gray. The kneeling-stool had been prepared for two but the Queen took her place all on her own. In the tribune, the poor, purple parrot did not stir, looking like a stuffed bird: Artemisia could not take her eyes off her. Many years ago, one of the Torrigiani ladies had said, "Unbelievably stupid and arrogant, all she had was a nice complexion, and now all this wealth!" The mass began. Sitting down, the Queen had no legs, she was all shoulders, the shoulders of a workman under the tiny head. A large space separated her from her courtiers so that she too, like her mother, appeared abandoned and almost outcast, alone, a figure of fun.

She was not alone, however, the next day when Artemisia was introduced to her in that medium-sized, rather gloomy room, the walls of which were paneled with dark wood and hung with miniatures, those arid, old-fashioned curios so beloved of the English. Swarming around the Queen were noble ladies and damsels, with all the rustle and bustle of their duties: but one in every four was an immaculate, diligent nun, wearing an apron just like a maid. All around the edges of the room, as though keeping an eye on and besieging that nest of women, the men were pressing against each other with the stubborn urgency of hornets and three out of every seven were priests; priests without cas-

socks who were nonetheless very officious, as though celebrating mass. Artemisia was preceded by a very old major-
domo who dragged his feet, and followed by a skinny pageboy with bare, knobbly knees who carried the gift wrapped
up in a cloth; a painting of Saint Agnes with her breasts cut
off, Orazio's strange choice. Make her way through the
crowd in a royal room without losing her composure, control her excitement at such an illustrious occasion, combine
humility with dignity: these were Artemisia's aims, but she
soon had to think about protecting the hem of her black,
Flemish-style dress—a gift from her father—for never had
she encountered such bad manners. The narrow room was
seething with impetuous initiatives, decisive attacks, a
thousand turgid concerns. The painter should make haste:
no one has time to waste, but each one of them fixes her
with a gaze that is selfishly vague because, as they stare, they
do not for a minute stop thinking about themselves. Her
feet were trampled on, the lace on one of her sleeves became
caught and then tore. The major-domo turned round and
signaled to her to hurry up, but she stumbled as she bent
down to pick up a glove that ten shoes had already trampled. The stifling vapors from all those hot bodies and their
breathing was condensing, over beside the window, in the
thin air. There, in a small besieged clearing, sat the Queen.

She was flanked by four women who were so close, right
on top of her, that it was a wonder how she put up with
them as they intently sewed away at their peaceful needlework, seeming to be quite at ease, as if no one were looking
at them. Standing in front of their mother were the royal
children, pale and wan, dressed in elaborate silk, while the
Queen fussed with their shoes and their collars as though
she were not pleased with the way they were dressed. Two
little girls and the royal prince, none of them attractive. A
shabby little priest with a tattered ruff detached himself
from the crowd and came across the room at great speed:
now Henrietta was writing on a piece of paper on her knees,
like a captain in the midst of battle. "Vite, vite," she mur-

mured, but it was a murmur heard by all and sent a ripple right through the room. She raised her pale, red-rimmed eyes; and the major-domo went down on one knee, as did Artemisia, while the pageboy unwrapped the painting. The Queen rose to her feet, but it scarcely made any difference.

"So, you have come from Italy," she said in Italian, pronouncing each syllable in a sorrowful, drawling voice. She coughed. Artemisia bowed for the third time. The Queen's cough was very loose, maybe she was going to expectorate. On the floor, leaning against the forked foot of a silver wool winder, Saint Agnes, catching the light, seemed disrespectfully angry. "We would like," continued Henrietta, shaking the innumerable curls of her wig in a benevolent rhythm, "we would like you to paint our portrait." Her eyes the color of dirty water finally came to rest on the artist, but with an absent expression which Artemisia did not notice, so moved was she by those few, hazy, stumbling words of Italian; a sign of amiability, so it seemed to her, which she would have loved to linger over, to have repeated. But a Queen must be answered at once, and she began, her heart beating fast, "If your sublime, most Royal Highness . . . " She has carefully prepared this little speech of thanks, but she will never use it. A barefooted Franciscan nun, as fat as a barrel, has sprung over to the Queen's side. She leans over, whispers in her ear, raises a finger, almost a warning finger, as if to admonish her; her rosary continues to clink in the sudden silence. "Allez, allez," Henrietta interrupts her, her waxen pallor flushing with a dark purple that spreads down onto her skinny neck. The silence of the courtiers lasts another moment, but they have all heard and understood the order, and they all obey with a promptness that even the walls and the floor seem to facilitate: one door on its own could not absorb them so quickly. Weary and imperious, pushing her children in the back to make them walk on, the Queen moves away. A stool is knocked over, a box rocks, then falls, spilling out spools of thread, ribbons and flowers, objects which roll all over the floor, pursuing the courtiers;

and a golden rose lands at the feet of Artemisia, still frozen with surprise.

She finally bent down and picked it up. The room was now empty, a rather shabby room actually, nothing magnificent about it, the floor covered in rush matting dirtier than a stable. Scattered over it, as though on a lawn, were torn bits of paper, a squashed hat, a handkerchief, and even a prayer book. Two small lost dogs were sniffing around without barking, scratching, then one lifted his leg against an overturned chair. The silver wool winder had been knocked back against the wall, beneath a horrible portrait of Queen Elizabeth. No sign of the Saint Agnes; and Artemisia had to find her own way back.

The Queen sent her gifts: a small monkey from her menagerie—where she kept lions—in a beautifully worked cage (it died of cold); four silver, lidded beer tankards; ten yards—as they measure it here—of Holland linen; a clock, an ingenious device. She had not started the portrait, there had been no word of thanks for the Saint Agnes, and these gifts arrived at random and as though by mistake. Finally a footman brought her a message that was as formal as a brief, and in it was written, that in the meantime Signora Artemisia (in red letters) was to select from the royal wardrobe the dress the Queen was to wear as well as her jewelry and accessories; that she was to inform the Queen whether she preferred to depict her as a goddess, a heroine, or a saint; at what time of the day the light was best; what direction the room should face; what the size of the canvas was to be so that a frame might be ordered. The message was brought and left: the person who came to collect her reply was a strange sort of lady, slovenly, bald, bewigged, with cake crumbs on her lips; and behind her trailed a rather stupid-looking girl, the royal princess, dressed in dirty, cherry-red velvet. Their conversation was very laborious, despite the assistance of an unofficial interpreter, the Italian steward, Vincenzo Rocco. While they talked the young princess rolled up a silver sash that Artemisia had left lying on a chest of drawers and hid it in her bodice: it ended up in the Thames the following morning, out of remorse.

It was on the tenth of May that the Queen sat for the portrait. It was raining very hard on the bright green grass that Artemisia had to cross to reach the French pavilion, which was indicated to her at the last moment by the footman. She got her feet wet and her lovely Flemish dress was soaked and covered in mud by the time she reached it. In the boudoir, the walls of which were covered with pictures of saints and relics, but most of all with miniatures of King Henry, there reigned an almost military austerity, and the Queen, dressed in blue, looked like her face was made of overcooked porridge. Her left eye never stopped watering, all red around the rim, and she wiped it constantly with a lovely handkerchief. "Thank goodness for the special lacquer," thinks Artemisia, to encourage herself; but she has already been seized by that unbearable sense of foreboding which recurs with every new commission: once again she will paint the usual, bold portrait about which it is easy to boast, so difficult to feel pleased. How is it possible, anyway, to give due consideration to the setting and study her subject when you have a Queen as sitter? She will be in trouble if she does not rely upon her old cleverness, her skillful sleight of hand. She will be in trouble if she does not give a polished performance. Even the words she uses are the same as before: "Would your Majesty care to turn round." But how can she resist the vanity, risky though it may be, of touching the royal hand, arranging the fingers, one by one, around the spine of the book? Henrietta lets her do as she pleases: her mind is elsewhere, her expression identical to that of her hundred other portraits, a sort of stagnant placidity behind which it is easy for her to disguise her thoughts and which she has worn since she was a young girl. Her skin is a thick, opaque membrane and the artist tries to capture its tones on the tip of her uneasy brush: gray, lead white, a touch of vermilion? A few strokes on the forehead and chin, and then immediately onto the large dollops of blue for the dress. Will this portrait work? Maybe great artists know the answer when they begin a painting: Orazio knows. But not Artemisia: hers is an obscure, stubborn committment, she is a gambler betting on the unknown, waiting intently for luck. For as long as her talent prevails.

By the afternoon the hundred and tenth portrait of the Queen had become a mechanism that suddenly went off, trapping its inventor; a sketch that she must now stand by and have accepted. "Is your Majesty tired?" These words she had been taught to say in English. But the Queen made no movement, no reply. Embalmed within the structure of her bony shoulders, she had closed her purple eyelids. Perhaps she was asleep.

By the light of twenty-four torches hissing in the rain, that same evening the King and Queen departed, with very little luggage, a great deal of noise and confusion, and a small retinue; some said for Hampton Court, others for Norwich. It so happened that Artemisia was the last person to have seen the Queen so that quite a few people, including some important gentlemen who did not even know her, secretly questioned her. What sort of mood had the Queen been in. Had she talked about leaving? The unfinished portrait was drying in the French pavilion, the gardeners were hoeing the pansies, the does were leaping on the lawns, numerous gaily colored boats and punts were making their way down the river, for there was great merry-making at Whitehall. Serious discussions at Somerset House: another quarrel between Charles and Henrietta, the old Queen of France has been driven out and her daughter is to follow her. Enough of these papists and Jesuits and Italians. Even Orazio Gentileschi has played along with them for twenty years and now this daughter of his has come to take his place, to conspire. She's a lovely woman, however. A very lovely woman indeed.

Artemisia knew nothing of this scandalous reputation that had been rekindled belatedly at Court, and which now reached its climax. She never found out that Sir Henrich had dedicated a sonnet to her that was much appreciated by those in the know and which began, "Artemisia, who is she . . . "; nor that Jacob Mierevelt secretly painted a portrait of her. Lady Arabella, who did not follow the royal couple, visits Orazio every day but pays him very little attention, as he does her, moreover. She is interested in Artemisia, not talking to her but communicating by signs, with flashing, mysterious smiles, while her snow-white hand grows very familiar, as though it had been granted certain liberties, resting on Artemisia's shoulder, around her waist, on her breast. Artemisia's only defense is not to understand the language, and she lowers her eyes like a young maiden. Great laughter from milady. Tow-colored moustaches, ruffled, artificial-looking wigs that appear to be made out of blown glass, infernally haughty glances, thin lips in an expression of icy humor: such are Lady Arabella's followers, who often accompany her and help her to besiege the Italian lady artist. Artemisia does not try to escape, but stays silent while thinking of crazy animals and legendary fiery dragons, masters of this pale land.

She received a proposal, formal, heraldic, insolent, from a certain Pierce, a merchant much in favor, almost a nobleman, with small eyes, a fat nose and a harelip. Would the "Signora" accept a palace at Woolwich with gardens and fifty guineas a year? It was Lady Arabella herself who explained it to her, miming in a way that not even Tuzia would have permitted herself; so rigidly expressive. And it was the same Lady Arabella forty years later (for she reached a ripe old age, plastered with French cosmetics) who invented a story about a lady artist who arrived from Italy in 1640 and gave herself to all and sundry. Her nephew, a learned gentleman, swore he knew all Artemisia's lovers by name; and one of the first he wrote down was that of Francesco Romanelli, an artist who, in that year of 1640, not only was in Rome, but had the mumps.

But now her situation as a foreigner has turned to one of innocence, so that this unseasonable reputation arouses in

Artemisia no more than a suppressed irritation and a melancholy reserve. If she wanted, she could take on this world, assail and conquer it; but she does not want to. There are ambiguous compliments which are impossible to ignore, and these upset her, and once again she takes to talking to Antonio at night, sobbing. She says to him, "You, who thought I was the most beautiful, the best. You, who should have stayed at my side, loving me, until death." Once again she awakes suffocating with grief; and the moon here is not the moon, the sky is not the sky, if she goes over to the window for some fresh air. That mocking mist on the lawns. The little hills, little valleys. The desperate smallness of the infinite.

The Queen does not come back, nor the King; Orazio has withdrawn once more into his old, brusque manner. Mindful of her latest experiences, of those happy moments when she had remembered that she knew how to paint for herself alone, Artemisia locks herself in her room, opens up her boxes, tidies, dusts, prepares her work, just as she did as a young girl. And just as she did then, she chews nervously on a crust of bread left over from breakfast.

She began, at that time, a portrait without a model, done from memory: but of whom was the memory? She wondered about this as her hand gave life to a pale, warm cheek, to black hair gathered in a careless knot, falling down over the neck and ears. Remembered, not mannered: the lock that fell from the temple, unraveling down over the cheek and hiding the ear was drawn in and painted with a mastery that she recognized and took pleasure in, in a moment of pure joy. Now the shape of the small head is completed, as though the model were present, with a striking naturalness that has to be drawn from life. It is not Porziella, it is not Tuzia's daughter in Rome, her old, most frequent model. It is someone whom Artemisia has unknowingly loved, whom she has unwittingly looked at long and intensely. It was due to the peevish angle of the head bent over the left shoulder that recognition came, and with it a name: Annella de Rosa. That is her sulky mouth, her sullen eyes beneath the heavy lids; and that is why only two-thirds of her face is visible, as though she had spitefully turned it away from the artist's gaze. To bump into her like this, to stand in her way. Pinned down by the truth of a shoulder, an arm, a hand, the thumb of which is slipped through the hole in a palette, Annella cannot escape. That thumb had a short, square nail, like a man's. "Hello, Anna!" Artemisia used to say, as if she had called in by chance—but it was never by chance—going over to the shabbily dressed young woman whose clothes were neglected in her fervor of painting. Massimo Stanzione would come running over from the other end of the studio, anxious and vigilant, with raised arms, beseeching eyes: do not disturb the miraculous pupil, the beloved prodigy. Having pushed the visitor into a corner, the maestro would explain in a low voice: "She's so sensitive and odd, we must treat her with great care. An amazing talent. She uses light like Caravaggio. She has the imagination of Annibale. But the slightest little thing can make her throw down her brushes, spoil her colors, ruin the painting. Her husband is to blame, that madman. . . . " Impassive, Annella carries on working and Artemisia burns with indignation, greatly offended. She wants to see this "beaten-up" angel, she wants to give her approval, her admiration. That another woman should excel in painting is reflected glory for her; let no one prevent her from showing how generous and fair she can be when it comes to the test. "You know how much I admire her and how well I treat her; but she is too haughty." She turned and left, swearing that from now on she would ignore her. And yet, when Massimo brought Annella to her house to keep her out of the way of her husband's rages, how those young black eyes flashed with gratitude and understanding. And her mouth, still so childlike, the pink slightly tinged with purple, convulsively whispered the words that Artemisia never forgot: "There is no shortage of men painters, but only one woman, my Maestra. . . . "

So now Annella has been resurrected by chance, Annella

who would barely be thirty years old if she had not been felled by a man's dagger and left on the ground to bleed to death, as white as a Lucretia, a Cleopatra. Artemisia turns her back on the English light, this light that is so thin and exhausted that, straining her eyes against it, she seems to see the lock of black hair moving gently on the canvas.

The palace is in a state of suspension, something that rarely happens, in a hiatus of absolute peace. And remembering how on the occasion of the formal party she gave in Naples she took the beautiful De Rosa by the hand, Artemisia feels compelled to take her brush and caress that painted hand slightly more than is necessary. The heavy summer rain begins to pour down outside the open window, but she is unable to move to close it. She feels her hair standing on end even though she is so calm, so happy with her work. And the gesture that releases her from the spell is that of a superstitious woman of the people: she crosses herself. But the Hail Mary that rises to her lips is not for the repose of a soul but for the eternal image of a passionate love, for the realization of an arcane, selfless hope. And the painting lay uncovered on the easel the whole night long.

"Does it still exist?" This is not the same incorruptible instrument, the same icy voice full of impervious immortality that distinctly pronounced the syllables, "Do not cry." Not really a voice, more an internal impulse of historical compassion, devoid of worry, illusion and sorrow. Trapped in time and space like an infertile seed, I listen to a stale rustling, the dusty breathing of centuries, our own and Artemisia's combined. The breathing of sleepers whose dreams are full of imaginings that will not leave them in peace. The year nineteen hundred and thirty-nine, a royal castle in England, bleak and silent, except on Sundays when, with an almost plant-like continuity, it is invaded by swarms, clusters of humanity all obeying a series of calls that bear the name of culture and curiosity, and which are dispelled by the air outside. Already situated in the realm of memory, today they are obedient ghosts wearing out shoes and floors, reflected in the glass of the windows, then in the paintings on the walls: the wasp-like portraits of Queen Elizabeth in full regalia, the scorpion-like knights complete with spurs, a few goddesses, a few useless saints covered with the dirt of centuries, and bristling mountains and cruel, proud galleons. The Sunday eyes take on a glazed expression and move on. They did not recognize themselves, history is dead.

But higher up, hanging above the portraits of queens and warriors, a sulky young woman continues to paint as though she were alive; and underneath, in official letters, was written a name that was legible: Artemisia Gentileschi. I can assure you of this, affirm it in good faith on this page written by the light of a wartime candle. And in the air, the air at my back, the winter air of the year nineteen hundred and forty-five, there is not a breath of assent; nor do I need to swear it in letters of blood, Artemisia!

Compared to the scale of the universe, times of terrible devastation are not even a shiver, even though the universe of human memory might say otherwise. And man had trusted to paper, wood and stone, materials much more solid than the human body, so that human civilization might continue. But now books, sculptures, paintings are violently scattered and turned to ashes, while the genius who created them is reduced to a faceless entity, driven from the stone where he stood with joined feet, trembling on the edge of the precipice. So that I, alive, am almost unable to say where, at this exact moment, is the portrait of the young woman and the words: Artemisia Gentileschi.

How laboriously those English Sunday visitors spelled out her name. And just as laboriously did those others who, on numerous occasions in sixteen hundred and forty, forty-five, year after year, repeated, reread that foreign name, every time the painting was put up, taken down, exhibited, scorned, praised, rediscovered. The truth was that people liked the subject of the portrait: a young woman who paints, a woman from the south of Italy, with that untidy black hair, someone you feel you could approach freely. *The Art of Painting* was the title given to it one day by the custodians of the royal palaces. "Self-portrait by Artemisia Gentileschi," declared the inevitable descendant of Lady Arabella, a keen archivist. Perhaps he was inspired by Annella's revenge, sullen Annella who did not have time to travel, only to die young, and who slips once more out of Artemisia's hand. And with this torrid brunette's face was confirmed the reputation of Artemisia's scandalous youth, of her Mediterranean passion. "She was raped by Agostino Tassi and loved by many": thus was it repeatedly written, even in English. But Artemisia's hand is strong and Annella cannot free herself. Whether it is a self-portrait or not, a woman who paints in sixteen hundred and forty is very courageous, and this counts for Annella and for at least a hundred others, right up to the present. "It counts for you too," she concludes, by the light of a candle, in this room rendered gloomy by war, a short, sharp sound. A book has been closed, suddenly.

So the Queen does not return, the Queen has left for Holland, and no one makes any mention of the portrait slowly drying in the French pavilion; just as they make no mention now of she who painted it. When she has applied the final glaze to the work depicting Annella, or *The Art of Painting*, Artemisia puts a Saint Barbara on the easel, an unfinished painting she brought with her from Naples, but she is unable to work on it. She no longer has any desire to paint, the English summer light has become her enemy once again, and once again fills her with dismay like a ghost she cannot confront alone from her large attic window that is too far from the ground. Lower down, in Orazio's room, the light reflected from the gardens has a more earthly, less desolate quality. Artemisia goes back down to her father, but does not bring him her latest work: it is a secret, so she thinks, to be kept for later. And so once more she fills her day with humble tasks, unnecessary chores, cultivating her never-ending amazement at finding herself in this country. Exile, repatriation? Old memories of Rome, Naples, friends, flutter above her head like dry leaves about to fall from the tree. Maybe she was born here but cannot remember, lived here just as she lives now, emptied of love and sorrow, silent, beside a father who does not talk. The names conserved in her memory are ready to fall too, withered, incapable, almost, of causing her pain, and sometimes she needs the concreteness of a gesture—raise her head, stare into space—in order to capture a fleeting recollection of the suffering that nonetheless constituted living. But even loving pain is difficult, and darkness, when it finally falls, seems to absolve her from that duty. One certainty is sufficient to sustain her: her father is beside her, her father who breathes and works, who cannot die.

A man such as he cannot die, a man who extracts from life no more than abstract notions of light, color and form, a man who never errs: as long as these things exist, so shall he. For a long time now Orazio has not used up life, not been used up by it. He dozes, it is true, like the old man that he is, after dinner which he hardly touches, but only in order to obliterate the hours in which he cannot paint. Dawn finds him already up amidst his pots, bottles, brushes and paints that he prepares himself, for he refuses to have apprentices any longer. He no longer loses his temper either, has only fleeting contact with the outside world, leaves his glass half full and his food hardly touched and brushes them aside with a curt gesture when his daughter hands them to him at midday, interrupting his work. He is so engrossed in his painting that it is a wonder how none of the paint ever stains his colorless hands, now slightly veined, as though he were protected by a sheet of glass. His movements are so definite, so confident, the result of a long, unfailing experience, that they seem to emit a sort of miraculous exemption from any possibility of error which fills the air around him. Even the few painters who still come to see him notice it, despite the fact that he has ceased talking of art and of almost every other subject. They barely greet Artemisia who is engaged once again in her filial duties, treating her just as they did when she had only recently arrived. But now she does not move away as before, she does not flee. Trusting in her father, she relies entirely on the pretext of helping him; an innocent deception, for she is fully aware that it is he who is helping her.

But one evening in August, as she tiptoes towards the door to go back up to her attic, Orazio wakes up. He was in the habit of falling asleep in a large, straight-backed arm-chair against which he leant lightly, his head unsupported and erect; and his daughter was never certain whether he even got undressed and lay down later on. At the moment of reaching for the doorknob, with the lamp held firmly in her left hand, her eyes met those of her father which were wide open, as though lost in thought. Even in the half-light they shone with the brightness of enamel, every single pig-ment of the gray iris contributing to the effect; while his mouth, having lost its customary gruffness and hardness, softens, almost swells, in a new hesitancy. Under such a compelling gaze his daughter pauses, feeling that she must say something. "Father" (and the Tower bell, right at that moment, seems to be trying to drown out her voice), "fa-ther . . . " She is still in mid-step when his reply comes, not in the form of a sound, but in the flicker of an eyelid signal-ing assent. "Yes," says Orazio with that flicker, and perhaps he did not mean to: he resembles a large, gaunt, sick bird concealing its own suffering from itself by veiling its eyes. The eyelid is raised again, the iris appears even whiter, enlarged, and guides Artemisia better than the lamp as she approaches, still on tiptoe, as if she wanted to avoid the scrutiny of that old face on which she can read an embar-rassed fear and an alarmed self-examination.

And when his daughter is at his side—but before she

leans over him—the unwonted emotions that have invaded his face are joined by another, no less unusual: there is no doubt about it, it is an expression of satisfaction, of contentment; and it spreads out over his face, smoothing and lightening the deep lines, right up to the corners of his eyes which are, however, unsmiling. "Is something wrong, father?" And once again the inhuman voice of the great Tower cuts in, drowning her voice with its moving Pisan accent, that golden, unattainable town to which she is connected, despite never having seen it, by ties of blood. The old man's eyelids seem to have grown very thin, extremely fragile and vulnerable over the eyes which they crush. His throat quivers, swallows, while his ashen hand moves feverishly inside the folds of his collar, then tears it open as though it were choking him. Thus did Porziella with the ribbons of her little bonnet the first night of her life. But before his hand falls back down, to lie limply, Orazio reaches for and grasps Artemisia's, squeezing her wrist so tightly that the pain reminds her of the rope when she was tortured in Corte Savella. The daughter weeps, and she does not know whether with love or fear.

The old artist's eyes open again, and now for the first time they express a bewildered desire to share an unbearable pain, a message that is almost an accusation directed at the healthy. And after decades of exile, years and years of a virile, solitary life, the old man returns to his native dialect and moans "Aayee," a sound he must have heard as a young child on the banks of the Arno. A Tuscan mother, a sick Tuscan child are now this woman and this old man. So must Orazio have moaned as a child, so must his mother have soothed him, frightened, if she happened to find herself alone among the deserted pine forests around Pisa, at the edge of the sea, with her son in her lap. Just as the mother would have done, so does Artemisia look all around her, her eyes searching among the strange, useless objects for help. Down below in the unfamiliar kitchens of the palace, up above in the dark anterooms, scullery maids, footmen, equerries, do not exist for the two Italians; nor do Henrietta's quacks and physicians, nor their other artist friends, and there do not exist the glance, the hand, the advice of even one faithful servant. What is needed now is a familiar, reassuring hearth, a cooking pot, herbs gathered in the fields, all things that are so far away, simple things that one can turn to trustingly in times of illness, seeking the assurance that it is nothing, that a herbal infusion will do the trick. "My arm, my arm," the sick man clearly groans now, and tries to raise his free hand to indicate and relieve the source of the pain in his left elbow. With difficulty, as if in the horror of a nightmare, Artemisia fusses round him, not daring either to touch him or to leave him, and finds herself making the clumsy movements of a small child when first trying to do certain tasks, as she tries to think up a remedy. On the huge stone of the immense fireplace she manages to put together a makeshift fire, breaks an old stretcher on her knee, finds and lights the flint. "Now," she says," "now I'll light a nice fire, and the pain will soon be gone." When the dry, hostile wood finally begins to crackle in a forlorn little heap in that huge fireplace, the sight of the flames seems to fill her with a new terror, a feeling of bewilderment at a calamitous reality that is happening too fast, before it has even been announced, and which she cannot yet believe in. The most absurd wagers spring up like poisonous mushrooms: if this ember catches fire, if that blue flame does not disappear . . . The person bent over the fire is terribly intent, as though unfeeling, totally absorbed with the task at hand. In a similar manner, as a young girl doing woman's work, she used to see to the soup for her father and brothers, and night would fall before her father came home. But then there would be the sound of crickets outside the door, in the peaceful vineyards, and the bells in the monastery. And in the end a neighbor would always appear and help her to take the cooking pot down from its hook.

This is a pathetic, mean little fire, always on the point of going out, and the water which she is trying to heat in an old pot hisses and sizzles as it leaks from a crack. She finally succeeded in improvising the standby female remedy, a hot, rough brick. As she wrapped it in woollen cloths it gave off a sickly, scorched smell, the smell of Roman winters and childhood coughs, and when she looked at Orazio she saw that his eyes had grown less dilated and that his features seemed less swollen and distended. His eyes followed her movements, but without impatience: they seemed, rather, to be asking for something more difficult: a desperate closeness and intimacy. And when the red-hot brick was placed on his arm, his eyes closed again in such an unmistakeable, austere expression of surrender that Artemisia screamed. The bright irises reappeared immediately and now they were more blue than gray, color and movement wavering in a conscious, deliberate attempt to reassure her. "I feel better," the old man articulated with a careful slowness, and closed his eyes once more. But his right hand moved, again seeking his daughter's. It was trembling slightly and the veins between his knuckles appeared horribly swollen and blue. As she took his hand in hers, Artemisia was amazed at how small and light it was, fragile bones and dry skin, a hand that had worked so hard, achieved and accomplished so much. It was not so much her love for him that prompted her, more the total devotion of a pupil, and she bent down to kiss it. This had not happened ten times in their lives, and never with such a deliberate intensity of feeling. "Oh father, father," thought Artemisia, but she did not speak the words. And she raised her face so that her tears would not wet his hand. Extremely pale, with an ineffable expression of peace on his face, Orazio had fallen asleep. His body still upright, he was breathing very slowly, but without effort. His right hand, which was back on his knee, was lying open, palm upwards, the thumb and forefinger as though suspended in the middle of a delicate action, victorious in their very abandon. On the fleshy part of his thumb the calloused skin was marked by a purplish dent.

Over in one corner, beside stretchers and empty jars, there lay a beautiful, rolled-up Oriental rug; it had last been used as a backdrop behind a model. Artemisia pushed it, pulled it out, unrolled it, spread it flat. It was the same length as her body. She lay down on it, full of an inexpressible happiness, free from worry. Over her face, which was irritated by the rough wool, fell the folds of her father's coat, so close, so solid, like features of a familiar landscape. And soon the rug became forest moss, the coat rocks and the hard floor a safe cave. She felt that sleep was close. It seemed a good sign, and as she turned over to blow out the lamp that lay on the floor beside her, she bumped her head on the leg of the chair; and she nearly laughed, like a child enjoying an unusual adventure. But in the dark, sleep receded. And she lay awake for a long time, her nostrils itching and tickled by faint smells of spices and dust. Through the huge, unshuttered window came a solid, almost dirty brightness that she gradually recognized as the reflected light of the moon, the starry sky and oil lamps. A few dull, repeated thuds came from the stables, evoking images of the long-tailed horses pawing the ground as they slept and dreamt behind the thick lashes that fringed their fierce eyes. A window banged, a baby cried. Very clearly a nearby voice concluded an argument and then dissolved in a burst of laughter that was carried away and dispersed by a sudden gust of wind. Something fell from a window ledge and shattered on the stones of the courtyard. The accidental, fragile silence of overinhabited places fluttered like a veil over the sleepers, pierced at intervals by a faint, distant cry, or by an indistinct gasp, rather like the sound made by someone turning over in his sleep with a sigh. But no sigh came from Orazio Gentileschi: his daughter's ears strained to pick up the sound of his light breathing, contending with her other wide-awake senses, with the shadows, until she finally thought she had captured it in a rhythm that seemed eternal. Only then did Artemisia fall asleep.

She slept until dawn. But it was not the rough carpet or the hard floor, nor the noises of the new day that woke her, that shook her. A stillness somewhere deep inside her, a feeling of suspicion in her very soul, an awareness that she must not abandon herself nor drift in the timelessness of sleep, suddenly seized her with an icy hand; and she found herself lying on her back, eyes and ears wide open, as though she had never been asleep. She seized on external noises and flung them back again elastically with an effort of supreme attention that already trembled, palpitated. In the room, which the still air turned into a suspended, isolated world, it was as if a moth were about to beat its wings. Suddenly she remembered, leapt to her feet: there was no longer any sound, any rhythm of Orazio Gentileschi's breathing, his mouth, slack and slightly open, seemed to have swallowed it regretfully. Frightened, she leant over that mouth and in her anxiousness to find a reason to hope her forehead touched it, touched the exposed teeth. His lips were cold.

Screams, sobs, futile attempts at reviving him, grief: through the whole gamut even to the final images of mourning and funeral orations that leapt in her head in a mute, voracious dance even before anyone had said that there was a corpse. Orazio's body, in a sitting position, still belonged solely to his daughter; she could refuse his death rather than weep over it. All the forms of an extreme rebellion against a fact of nature seemed preferable to a pain that had not yet been given shape by the words of others, words so simple and commonplace, horribly new and unacceptable. So it was for the first family when faced with the mystery of death; so, for a few moments, did Artemisia consider the macabre pretense of those who cannot accept it. He is not dead, he cannot be dead; this is not a word for him. Maybe she shook her father, maybe she caressed him or hugged him, to make him think again about this weakness that was unworthy of him. Orazio did not protest, did not change his mind. Then it was time to open the door.

In the month of August in the year nineteen hundred and thirty-nine I searched, without much hope, inside and outside Somerset House, for the tomb of Orazio Gentileschi who had died three centuries earlier. A road full of potholes, boiling hot, covered in shiny, poisonous tire marks; the air laden with metallic-tasting dust. In sight of huge warehouses, I questioned the clerks in various municipal offices. The Thames, between its stone embankments, looked like a weary hospital thermometer.

And I crossed the road in order to get to the small island of pavement, surrounded by a sea of sunshine, where there stood a little church that looked as if it were made of cast iron from the spire to the railings; but did it not perhaps mark the site of Queen Henrietta's Catholic chapel? Twice I went right round the little island and I felt that I would never get off it again. If stone is recalcitrant, paper will come to the rescue: drinking camomile tea, the learned Miss Dorothy promised that she would make an exhaustive search of the archives. But I had already realized, in the glare of August, that the still air, the cruel light, the low sky with its feathery clouds were to be the only witnesses, constant and truthful, of Orazio's funeral.

And the heat. It was inevitable that the funeral preparations would take Artemisia's mind off her grief, so new and fresh, at least for a few hours. She busied herself, helping to wash, prepare and dress him; maybe she picked up her brush to do a necessary, urgent decoration, a portrait to be placed on top of the black pall. The window faced due south, the wax candles were melting. When everything was ready they had no choice but to move off, in the hot sun.

The heat of a northern climate, sudden, dense and oppressive, was the first link that bound me to Artemisia; a

207

bond of earthly discomfort as I tramped the scorching pavements thinking of she who, with slow steps, walked in the hot sun to bury her father. There were no pavements in those days; people walked in the dust of carriage ruts that in winter were full of mud. "I see," said a passerby, nodding to the person walking at his side; just as a forebear of his, Irish as well—to judge from that red hair—might have said, watching a funeral cortege that, although not very rich, was certainly Catholic, which prompted him to ask who it was for, and someone replied, "That old artist, that thin Italian fellow with the little goatee." "I see." He was holding a child by the hand, that inquisitive man: let's suppose it was a Sunday. The child was tugging at his hand, reminding him of a promise he had made, and he was a good man, affectionate and obliging. He started to talk to the child again, turning his back on the funeral, went round a corner and thought no more about it. Let the dead bury the dead.

The dust adheres to their black clothes, to their sticky skin: even the Flemist artists, so good at combining propriety and comfort, feel hot and bothered. I have to admit it, they are all there, all the Pieters, Justuses, Adams and Abrahams exiled from their native Flanders, there is the great Anthony with his flowing lace, wiping his brow with a silk handkerchief. But oh, how stiffly, how steeply do the dead man's feet in their taut black stockings point towards the sky! That mournful, grotesque proof of his intransigent attitude to walking increased Artemisia's despair, for walking is now the only thing she can do for him. Between two Flemish women in black silk, silent and sweating from the heat? Between two unknown lady's maids, suddenly filled with compassion? The road was the same as every other day, the same holes, the same stones, the same street vendors, and Artemisia's eyes that do not want to see but see just the same. The cortege was halted for a moment: a thief was being caught, a pale boy with bloody knees and on his back a knapsack containing a bunch of lavender: she could smell its scent in the hot sun. The torches, small, pale, unwavering flames, hissed, the Queen's silver and black livery smoldered on the shoulders of the pallbearers who took turns carrying the bier, even though Orazio was so light. The artist in Artemisia automatically took note of the tones, translating them into earths and glazes, the names of which rose to her lips like a prayer, a prayer for an artist who would never paint again. And who was there to paint for now, now that Orazio's eyes are made of glass, unseeing, blind to images? Andrea van Ertvelt's new boots creaked rhythmically, his breathing was labored: Artemisia has the impression that she is walking among oxen, among dumb, hardworking animals. And her thoughts turn to Roman funerals, so full of color and feeling, when the confraternity of Saint Luke would turn out in force to honor one of their members. For Orazio's funeral all the most important people would have turned up, the liveries of all the Roman families, and noblemen and princes and religious guilds. He would have slept this evening in San Lorenzo in Lucina, surrounded by his companions of old.

There is nothing that is over so quickly as a burial and those who have been present, for all their meditating and reading of psalms, do not really believe in their hearts, despite the most lugubrious evidence, that they too will fall into a similar error. For the family, on the other hand, participants in and almost party to this error, there remains an invisible inheritance to be shared, grief; to be looked after, to be tamed, to be domesticated until it crouches down, very small, in a corner of the house.

But Artemisia has no house and once the artists, the palace servants, the handful of priests and the women who came out of curiosity or because ordered to do so had left her at the door that had been her father's, there was nothing, neither person nor object, to come to her aid. Orazio's window was thrown open as it had never been before, by the hand of a stranger; and the afternoon sunlight reigned in the room, demolishing it. Someone had already moved the tables and chairs around, maybe taken some items away: the empty space left by the funeral bier was certainly enormous, and all the objects and accessories that had cluttered up a life seemed as if shrunken, pitiful and few, not even untidy. She sat down, stood up, touched the pile of canvas stretchers, ran her finger through the dust on the bottles. And then she went over to the window, as though she hoped to be able to fly.

With its cumstomary display of purple and gold the sun was setting, leaving the lawns green and throwing every single leaf and flower of the hedges into relief. The water of the Thames shone through between the trees, and from the bank opposite the palace gardens barges and boats were setting forth with people who intended to dine al fresco with their friends. Someone was playing the first notes of an Italian song over and over on the lute, always making a mistake on the same note. The Queen's lions were roaring in their enclosed cages, answered by the two eagles in the large aviary with their dismal, rending cry. And what was Artemisia but a strange creature brought from afar and chained up? Perhaps they too, the imprisoned wild beasts, see, as she does, in a stone, in a patch of grass or in the movement of two human feet down below, no more than the accidental form of their torment, of their impossible longings. Her inclination—as her eyes examined the outline of an object that might have been a sleeping dog—was to bang her head against every sharp corner just as she had banged it against her father's teeth, so hard and inert. She realized that up till then her sadness had been a pastime, almost a game: there was not a single person, animal or stone that did not confirm it, with a particular indifference or coldness, now that she had experienced death this day; as though some invisible moorings had been cast loose and she were already drifting while the others remained motionless on the shore from which she had been exiled forever. The error had been committed, Gentileschi had given in, had died. His daughter was a party to it, and was now waiting to commit the same mistake herself. Life was heavy and turbid, water no longer fit for drinking. Whether she stayed here or went back to Italy Artemisia knew that her task was to die.

As if she had been called upon to choose, as if it were in her power to agree or not, she accepted; sealing the contract on a play of light, on a boatload of happy people—three women and a beplumed gentleman—that slid gently downstream. At the same time she felt that the recent corpse, that which had once been Orazio and was now beginning to make contact with the damp earth, still warm at the surface of the grave, remained alien and indifferent to her fate: neither father nor painter nor man any longer. Only then did she feel fear: if only she could at least believe in the importance of death. In order to convince herself of it, she began from then on to imagine her own.

There were so many versions at her disposal, possessed as she was of a return journey both perilous and full of hardship. There were numerous opportunities ahead of her: the sea, hard, rocky roads, bandits' knives, poison in inns, and plague, and her weak body.

The garden and the river were gradually being immersed in a strong, violet light. At her back the room was already dark and no one came to knock at the door: the English are afraid of ghosts. How could Artemisia not look at the sky? She did not think of praying, but her despair was answered by bountiful winks from the already twinkling eye of the first evening star. "Oh you who will know my death, you who are not yet born, who do not tell me how it shall be!" moaned Artemisia in disbelief, launching herself from her own cruel, closed century towards an indefinable presentiment of some benevolent age, of some kindred spirit who alone would know how to weep for her.

It was noticed in Court that the Italian woman did not spend more than three days in mourning, and that when she came out of her room she showed no signs of grief, but behaved rather in a heedless, insolent manner, even in the presence of Her Grace the Duchess Arabella who had now returned. She avoided mixing with distinguished company and refused to sit on stately chairs, choosing instead low stools on which she sat with her elbows on her knees and her head in her hands, but without weeping. She behaved as though no one could see her, crossing her legs, placing her clenched fist on her hip or else folding her arms over her chest, deep in thought, no matter who was present. She changed the style of her hair, combing it neatly but disdaining fashion, so that her head seemed to belong to another age, although which was not clear. An odd woman, more an adventuress than a brilliant artist, and if it had not been for her father we would never have summoned her to these parts. Nothing was said to her, for she herself had already decided to leave. Her Majesty graciously allowed her to take three paintings of her father's and ten guineas for the journey. But Artemisia is busy, she is thinking about her death.

She had reached at least the thirtieth version by the time she left, as she had arrived, alone and perfectly calm as though setting off on a jaunt. As she bowed to Lady Arabella she was thinking that she would never reach Canterbury, that she would die in that flat countryside from a blow to her side, dragged along by the overturned carriage, blood mingling with the dust, a cordial that she cannot drink, horse dung beside her outstretched hand, and a daisy swaying at the edge of the road. She passed through Canterbury, and on the road to Rochester opted for a death at sea: a windy night, huge waves, the sail entangled, the mast fallen, the ship breaking up; and she could even feel, along with the sound of screams and prayers, the icy touch of the water and a sudden desire not to die. But the Channel was as smooth as a millpond, the crossing was accompanied by glorious sunshine, a real delight. Not one drop of water touched her, her appetite returned.

So that meant that she would die at the hands of brigands, in a wood, and be buried in the dark. She began to prefer night coaches, the most dangerous routes and roads. With wide-open, staring eyes she anticipated the moment when the wheel would go too close to the edge of the ravine and plunge down; she concentrated on the movement of the vehicle traveling at great speed, summoning the fatal crash with eyes tightly clenched. But no carriage ever overturned, no wheel ever broke, no lamp was ever extinguished by the wind that blew even in mountain gorges. Nights for wolves, but there were no wolves, nor men in wolves' clothing. Only extremely poor people everywhere, country beggars and starving peasants who lived on wild grasses, with swollen bellies and scrawny necks. Where would they even have room for a knife among those rags of theirs? They stood at the sides of the roads shivering with terrible fevers, with no risk of contagion, while billows of rich smoke from the chimneys of castles set in rich meadows obscured the sun. The eyes of little girls—somewhere between brown and green—sparkled happily once again with humble mischief at having obtained something to eat for nothing. That was how Delfina smiled, a year ago, and her memory, accompanied by song, sweetened the air. No, Artemisia Gentileschi was not going to die from the knives of plundering brigands.

The water in the Rhone was very low that year, there was drought everywhere. The treacherous rocks, notorious for causing accidents and fear for those who traveled on the river, were completely revealed, covered in dry moss like crumbling, dead teeth: no boat was going to crash into them that season. The vineyards came into sight once more, heavily laden: the harvest was beginning. It was still hot, people dined in the inns with doors wide open and there was always someone who remained outside on the stone benches at either side of the door in the cool air, looking at the stars. Artemisia's supper consisted of milk, as always; but on the seventh of October she could not refuse everyone's insistence that she try the hare stew and a glass of wine. She forgot about dying. Then she said she was tired and went up to bed.

In her room was a bed with a green serge mattress, just

like the one she had had in Naples. She felt she had come home and that the journey was over. Nothing had happened to her, she was alive, and for the first time, this evening, she had experienced a certain middle-aged gluttony or greed, the prelude to the sensual pleasures of old age. She was aware of this, but it did not make her sad; in fact sadness, in any form, seemed to her a state she could never recreate. Death had not heeded her, she was aware of her body as never before. She felt that she had put on weight, that her appetites had become demanding and immortal: hunger, thirst, sleep. "It's a pity," she thought, suddenly noticing it, "it's a pity about this pain in the back of my neck and my arms." She concentrated on it: a fictitious contrast to this new, obscure feeling of well-being, a small battle for her strong blood to win. It seemed to her that she had never had such copious, such strong blood in her veins. Sleep would eliminate this discomfort, she felt in command of sleep, and of waking.

Dying in bed, the only end that Artemisia had not imagined when urging, almost spurring on her own destiny. To die in bed, not as the result of a sudden accident, or tragic plague, but from a slow, vague, insidious illness that could last for years: thus do most men die. She closed the curtains round the bed, extinguished the lamp. It was a while before she fell asleep: she had a bad night.

Summer 1944 – Summer 1947

Afterword

Shirley D'Ardia Caracciolo

When *Artemisia* was published in 1947, Anna Banti (the pseudonym of Lucia Lopresti), at the age of fifty-two emerged to great critical acclaim as a fully fledged novelist. She had a very full and varied literary career behind her, with a long series of studies and research, particularly in the field of art history. The appearance of *Artemisia* immediately gained her a place among the foremost novelists of the day and the book remains, in the opinion of many, her best work. Born in Florence in 1895, she graduated from the University of Rome with a fascinating thesis on the seventeenth-century artist and writer on art Marco Boschini, and this was followed by a period of intense literary activity in Florence, where she directed the literary section of the magazine *Paragone* and, after the death of her husband, the famous art critic Roberto Longhi, also the art section. During this period she contributed articles as a film critic, discovered and reedited the *Diario di viaggio* of the Marchese Vincenzo Giustiniani, to which she wrote a preface entitled "Europa 1606," and produced her first volume of stories, *Itinerario di Paolina* (1937), as well as pursuing her academic career as a lecturer.

Her lifelong interest in art and in the seventeenth century in particular was further stimulated by her husband's love of Caravaggio, which was the starting point for her re-creation of the life of Artemisia Gentileschi (1590–1642), who was a follower of Caravaggio's style. Anna Banti was an expert examiner of old archives and while searching among them one day came across a few musty, stained pages containing the meager facts of Artemisia's life. She took these bare bones and fleshed them out into a full-length novel that occupies a unique place in twentieth-century Italian literature. It is essential to read her foreword to the reader, which contains the few basic facts of Artemisia's life, the key to the book, for the novel itself yields little in the way of the concrete information that would be found in a traditional biographical work. It is, rather, a study of one woman's struggle to live life on her own terms, to sacrifice everything in the pursuit of her career as an artist at a time when women's lives were circumscribed within the narrow confines of family life, and when a woman who lived on her own, raised a child on her own and supported herself financially through her own work was totally unheard of.

Artemisia is a very hard book to categorize, being neither historical novel nor straightforward biography, while possessing certain features of both genres. It is a dialogue between the author and Artemisia, who, in Anna Banti's words, was "one of the first women to uphold, in her speech and in her work, the right to do congenial work and the equality of spirit between the sexes." The time setting of the novel is ahistorical, bringing together the experiences of the two women, at times fusing them, blending one into the other, and the author tells us directly that she intends to share the terrors of her own age with someone who has been dead for three centuries. These two levels, the autobiographical and the historical, are apparent right from the first page, where Artemisia as a young girl appears to the author as she sits in the Boboli gardens, surrounded by refugees, in the aftermath of the battle to liberate Florence from German occupation in the summer of 1944.

The story is told in sections, reserved for the most important stages in Artemisia's life, for the essence of the book consists of the travels that she undertook in the name of art. Anna Banti did not invent these journeys, but what marvelous value she was able to draw from the few meagre facts at her disposal. From Artemisia's adolescent traumas in Rome to her stay in Florence, to her brief experience of married life back in Rome once more, then to her successful years in Naples, where she established her own school of art, and finally her long journey by sea and land to London, what holds the novel together is the tremendous coherence of the character's psychological motivation. It is, seen from this angle, the story of a life, but the emphasis throughout is on the psychological and ideological aspects, and includes reflections and discussions with Artemisia on how best to portray the key events of her life. Anna Banti constantly intrudes in her role as author, with the accompanying move from the third to first person in the narrative. Artemisia is both an object and a symbol, a real person but also a character that Anna Banti invented in her first version of the novel (which was destroyed) and therefore someone to be reinvented anew. The intense dialogue between the author and the artist is thus further complicated by the intrusion of this character from the first version. In the hands of a lesser writer this technique could have led to confusion, but Anna

Banti demonstrates tremendous literary control, skillfully juggling with the various levels of the narrative and never once upsetting its fragile balance.

The novel is, therefore, historical only on the surface, which does not mean that it is devoid of the local color and atmosphere that characterize the historical novel. Banti's portrayal of life in seventeenth-century Rome, Florence, Naples, and France is superbly memorable and evocative. Images are conveyed not through detailed descriptions but by means of dazzling flashes and glimpses of the most every-day things, which are not in themselves intrinsically topical or of great significance. It is a style that has a lot in common with film techniques.

Anna Banti was a firm believer in the literary techniques of the nineteenth century, and in particular of writers such as Manzoni, Stendhal, and Balzac, who played an essential part in her formation as a novelist. In an article written in 1949, just two years after *Artemisia,* she expressed her per-plexity at the new vogue of colloquial, rough language inspired by American writing, so in contrast to her own search for purity. This interest is evident in the linguistic style of *Artemisia,* which, to quote her own words, is "an attempt at infusing into the polluted swamp of contempo-rary literature the pure spring waters of our language as it once was." It is a style that is extremely rich and complex, very demanding but also very rewarding. This is not the sort of novel that can be skimmed through effortlessly, but one requiring great concentration and penetration on the part of the reader. Banti's is a unique voice in the literature of her time, distanced from current literary styles but not from the themes and feelings in vogue in those postwar years: the emergence of a new feminist angle on the problems of being a woman, and the themes of adolescence and the "outcast" as evinced in novels by Moravia, Vittorini, Calvino, and Morante.

After *Artemisia* Anna Banti produced a great deal of work on art and criticism, including translations from English and a profusion of novels and volumes of stories, all of which have women as their protagonists and which, despite the huge time span they cover, have one thing in common: the difficulties and uncertainties of the human lot irrespective of the temporal setting. The feminist preoccupation, whether set in the past, present or future, is always seen through a highly developed level of psychological penetration and her novels have deservedly been awarded some of the most prestigious literary prizes in Italy.

At the end of the book, Banti leaves Artemisia in an anonymous bed in a roadside inn in an atmosphere of despair, totally devoid of hope, far from everyone and everything, as she retraces the journey she made only a few months earlier to be at her father's side, seeking the affection that eluded her all her life and that she never obtained except in her work. Artemisia's return to her father at the end of his life brings the story to a symmetrical close, for it began with her learning at his side. Her end is of necessity vague, not only because nothing is known about her life after her period in England, but because the author has told the essential part of her story: she has succeeded in bringing back to life a woman whose story deserved to be made known and remembered as exemplary. We are left with the lesson of Artemisia's life, a lesson of courage as apt for us today as it was when it was written in 1947, as it was in the seventeenth century. Artemisia Gentileschi is, paradoxically, one of the most authentic and modern figures in postwar Italian literature.

Thank you: Gary I, Stan, Chris Miller, Lynn, Gail Perry, Richard Bishop, Murray Hepple, Don Bajema, Hubert Selby, Nick Cave, Bill Shields, Exene Cervenka, Ian MacKaye and Mitch Bury of Adams Mass

Joe Cole 4.10.61-12.19.91

Now
Watch
Him
Die

I am the aching negating Abyss
You can't talk to me for long without seeing it
You can't look into my eyes
Without being repelled by the desperate inferno that fuels me
A fire that burns itself, feeds on itself
Knows only its own needs
I pulled the air from the room when you came to visit
You must have thought I was pathetic
After you left I felt sick
Sick that I had filled the room with my emptiness
I didn't mean to let it out
I was going to try to fool you
I wanted you to think that I was cool
The Abyss came shining blackly through though didn't it
I don't know what I did to become this monster
Probably everything I possibly could

❧❧❧

I stood over your dead cold body
And stared down
All your mother's relatives were standing outside
You were so damn still
Were you scared like I was Joe?
What were you thinking
Did you look into your killer's eyes?
When we came into the house
I knew that piece of shit was going to waste us both
But he only got you
I've been thinking a lot about hanging myself
It's always the same white extension cord
I think of the house and the shots
The pool of your blood boiling in the dirt
It's been two weeks and you haven't called

❧❧❧

Dream 1.2.92: I'm shooting guns with Ice T. The gun I have shoots
bullets real fast.

❧❧❧

I loved a dented, broken up woman
Ravaged, wrecked and crooked legged
She was tough as hell

But she was more alive than most
She was a walking mean streak
Wrapped in a sad accident
She couldn't help but hurt me
She did the same thing to herself
But she burned so brightly
That she burned everyone that she touched
At night when I'm alone and everything is quiet
I put my hands over the scars
They keep me warm
I pull a feather from the wing of Sorrow
Just to hear it scream
And waste time until I fall asleep

◄⬤►◄⬤►◄⬤►

I am filled with horror
I can't talk to anyone up close
I'll only be able to be horrible
I'm cut off from the rest of the world
It's worse than depression
It's horror
Horror is in my blood
My silent partner
My cancer shadow

◄⬤►◄⬤►◄⬤►

Dream 1.7.92 : I'm shooting a gun.

◄⬤►◄⬤►◄⬤►

The only thing I'm afraid of is getting caught
I don't care about how much pain I might cause
The only thing I'm afraid of
Is doing hard time for shooting some piece of shit
You can do time even if you shoot a piece of shit
I'd like to make that guy shit his pants before I waste him
I'd like to make his eyes melt
I'd like to make him shake like he made me shake
And then I'd just like to shoot him in the face
Mess him up so the piece of shit that gave birth to him
Will puke when she sees him

◄⬤►◄⬤►◄⬤►

Dream 1.14.92: I am staying at someone's house and somehow I flood the place by leaving the tap on. I try to clean it up as the people that own the place yell at me.

❖❖❖

Melbourne Australia feels far away enough
It's late and I can breathe
550 people came to the show tonight
I'm back in the box
The moon is full tonight
I just came in from sitting outside
I closed my eyes and imagined Joe falling
Through the sky into me
I'll carry you brother
They won't hurt you anymore
You can't get too close to them Joe
They'll stay too long
Say too much
Drain every last drop
And then just hate your guts
You're invisible
I've got your strength
Those bullets shot you into me
I won't blow it
You'll see

❖❖❖

I'll get the wrong idea
If you're kind to me
I'll start to make things up in my head
I'll think you'll want me
I'll hurt myself trying to please you
It won't be real
It will all be in my head
I wont be able to stop lying to myself
I will cut myself to pieces again and again
I won't feel it
You can watch

❖❖❖

Living the boxed life again
Australia

Raining tonight
The room is hot, too hot
Still air and the smell of insecticide
I'm alone and far away from America
My life is now a chain of broken dream rooms
I like it that way
I can't go backwards
Death makes life easier somehow
Less choices
Less masks
Less of everything except grief
Lots of grief
Can't get far enough away

⏃⏃⏃

Joe. It's been hard since you've been gone. It's been hard on a lot of people. I'm in Australia right now and geographically it feels better than LA does but I still carry all my thoughts of you wherever I go.

I'm in a hotel room right now and I'm crying, thinking about you. I head back to LA in a few days. It's hard to go places there now because I know that just a few weeks ago you were walking on the same streets.

I have fucked up thoughts all the time, you know how you rethink things all the time like if they could have been different. I have gone through the last moments of your life so many times. I keep trying to change it so we could have tried to talk to them. But then I pull out of my thoughts and know that nothing will change the reality that you're dead. You were murdered Joe. Every time I put your name and that word together I start to sweat. I feel so dangerous these days. These people that talk to me have no idea what they are dealing with. I walk the streets now and stare through people. I feel like hurting people all the time. It's all I dream of these days. In my dreams I'm either shooting a gun or killing someone. The other night I had a dream where I killed a girl and chopped her in two pieces.

I'm doing all the same things that I usually do. Interviews and shows. The usual hustle. Only now it doesn't feel the same. I am so cut off from the world now that I don't mind working every night. I don't need nights off anymore save for rest for the throat. I just don't care about myself the way I used to. I feel like working and not stopping and going until all the parts fly off. I don't taste food. I don't think of any one person that I want to see when I feel lonely. I know that now that you're gone I'll never have anyone I can talk to. There's a lot of really great people out there but they're not you and they're not me. I find myself saying all of our jokes and one liners out loud because I have no one to say them to. I was doing it the other day in the back seat of a car on the way to a meeting and I started making myself laugh and the people I was with had no idea what I was going on about. Forget trying to explain it.

I've been out here for a couple of weeks I think. I don't know for sure, I don't look at the calendar anymore. I just find out what time and where the stage is and that's all I want to know. I don't talk to people. I just answer all their stupid fucked up questions like I'm a human answering machine. I don't care though. I think the whole year will be like this. I'll just keep going. I think if I stop I'll never get going again.

Thinking of you is hard. I have so many good memories but I know that it's all in the past. I wonder where they guy who murdered you is. I wonder what he's doing right now. I think of him all the time. People ask me if I want to kill him. You would love this Joe, I give them the rap about how the poor guy is just a victim of a fucked up system. Looks good in print. Like I really want to tell these fuck head journalists anything about you. I hope I get to deal with that piece of shit someday. I want to kill him with my hands. I would feel much better knowing he's dead. Not because it's better for society. Just because it would be good to kill the guy.

I know that it wouldn't bring you back but at this point it would be good to get some satisfaction. Fuck this.

My life will be different now. It will be different until I die. I don't care about it like I used to. I don't love it even though I tell other people that they should love theirs. It's like I'm half alive. The other half is dead and I can feel it.

◄►◄►◄►

Maybe I just need enough money
Buy a dark room and catch my breath
None of these people make sense to me
It's all just a lot of noise
Romance is out of the question
After what I've seen
I can't get rid of the horror

◄►◄►◄►

Dream 1.23.92: I kill a girl and someone I know cuts the body in two and loads the parts into two plastic garbage bags. I ask him if he got rid of the body and he says that he did but he thanked the plastic bag company on the back of his new record and thinks that maybe someone

will find out. I see police with dogs going near my apartment and I know
that they are onto me.

∞-∞-∞

I feel free like I never have before
Cut off from all of them
There are certain things
That take time
But eventually they make sense
Hell is a private place where you re-live things
It's silent and hides from the light
It lives inside and keeps my mouth shut
I watch the sunrise over the highway of another motel
A girl is asleep next to me
Club trash
She only laughs when I forget her name for the third time
My life is full of horror and shadows
I only feel safe on the road
Sleeping next to the highway
Sex with strangers who have cars
Spitting out broken pieces of bloody life
The world is smashed and scarred as far as I can see
I am merely an abortion survivor
This place makes you think predator and prey
I used to want to be the predator
Now I want to be the prey
Wary and living in fast moving shadows
Always knowing that it could end in a finger snap

∞-∞-∞

I got my cord snapped off
I float through the blank hours
I now have the mind of a shark
I have never known a freedom like this
It's not cold
It's just seeing everything with rational calm
Seeing the sun set as it rises
Seeing the end all the time
Distracted in conversation by the Abyss
Realizing that the conversation is the distraction
I am almost 31 and I feel like I've retired
It's hard to talk to these interviewers

I look right through them and forget what I was trying to say
Life is over for me and I'm just riding
A lot of things that I thought were important
Aren't

❦❦❦

Loneliness has changed its face again
Cameras in my face
Lots of noise
Isolation
Lying awake
Sweating at 3:45 a.m.
Hotel room ceilings
I've got no words
No one to tell them to
Life is hollow
It allows you to fool yourself

❦❦❦

I saw a picture of Joe's head all blown apart
I can see it now in the hotel room
I am beyond loneliness
I am an alien off a space ship
I want the rest of my life to be behind shades
I don't want friends
I want shadows
Darkness
Nowhere is far enough away
No one is anyone I can talk to
I define myself
I speak their language
It's a bad habit

❦❦❦

After shows I go right to the bus
I don't talk to anyone
I've gotten good at disappearing
I don't sign wadded up pieces of paper
Answer questions or get thanked
If I stick around it gets weird
Last night some woman got into the back room
Kissed me twice and spoke in French

I escaped to the bus
At night I lie in the darkness on a bunk
The bus slams down some highway
I press my face to the ventilator
I try to forget and sleep
I think about imaginary women and Joe
Sex and Death
From here on in it's all slow choking
The morning comes and I lie there for hours
It's dark and no one's there but me
I don't leave the bus until the afternoon
I talk to reporters and stand still for a camera
They have no idea what they're dealing with
I do though
Inside I silently scream
At this point I'm the most fucked up person I know
I don't know what to do except go crookedly onward
Nothing gets in the way of ascending plunge into the Abyss

⊲⊳-⊲⊳-⊲⊳

I'm dead to the touch
Dead to the words spoken meaninglessly on streets
Dead to the eyes I look through
I see my reflection in cement

⊲⊳-⊲⊳-⊲⊳

Wrap your skeleton around me
Weld your bones to mine
I need more than regular involvement
I need you to perform a miracle on me
Somehow still the horror inside
Please help me
I don't want to die screaming
I don't know if you can do it
Hold me in a violent grip
Outsmart me
I need something
A vacancy is growing inside me that I can't control
Fuck it
Don't even try
I'll just abuse you
It's all I know

I'm just afraid that I'll hurt you
More than I already have

❖-❖-❖

It's pathetic
The spectacle I create
It's truly obscene
All this noise
All the bother
Sometimes it's more than I can live with
I disgust myself all the time
That's why I leave silently
I don't feel glory
I feel desperation and horror
What a lie
I think it's a life

❖-❖-❖

I've been looking for a clean place to put my mind
I keep finding myself in exhaustion's ghetto
Another night I've eaten myself
I keep coming up with lean tissue
They talk to me
I always think they're talking to that other guy
Some version of me that I never met
The room is filling me again
Past one in the morning in Dublin
I can't escape the grey shadow
It follows me through these hushed frames of time
If I could only find the right way to puke
I think that everything would be alright

❖-❖-❖

Dream 2.15.92: I am walking to Joe's house. I'm right at his front steps
and I hear a sound from behind me. I turn around and see the guy who
killed him. His eyes are huge and he's staring right at me.

❖-❖-❖

I can't get away from myself enough
It all comes out sounding too close to the bone
Everything I say comes back and bites my marrow
I attack myself, even in my sleep

This planet is so lonely as far as I can tell
Maybe not but it is where I keep turning up
Could be I'm looking in the wrong places
Maybe I'm running out of steam
Maybe I'm doing it right and I'm burning out
I see through too much these days
Too cynical and paranoid
All I can think of is to keep moving and stay secretive
I feel a need to feel good for a little while every day
I don't want to be known
I don't want to be loved or understood
I want to disappear into the Abyss
I'm getting closer every day
That much I know for sure

⊲⊳-⊲⊳-⊲⊳

I'm in a small plastic box in the ground
My father bought it for me
I'll be here forever
Nothing will happen to me
Their lives will go on and I'll never know
I reach up and touch the top
The plastic is smooth
In here it's total darkness
I wonder where Rollins is
I wonder how he's feeling
I wonder if he knows where this place is
Will I be able to know if he's standing above me?
Maybe he's dead too
Why am I here?
What did I do to get murdered?
Did I make a mistake
Did I say the wrong thing?
What happened?
I hate being dead

⊲⊳-⊲⊳-⊲⊳

Dream 2.25.92: I'm fucking a young girl. I look down at my cock. It's made of glass. When I come it shoots all over the wall, the girl has disappeared.

⊲⊳-⊲⊳-⊲⊳

I have become abusive because part of me has given up
I have become full of horror because I have written my own ending
I am afraid of nothing
Dulled by everything
The shark gets shot with a bang stick
And slowly spins to the ocean floor

❦❦❦

Like a Samurai warrior
I'm walking dead
I don't care
I am ready to die
I pay homage to Death with every waking moment
Nothing they say matters
Nothing they do gets to me
You can't fuck with a dead man
We just keep going
The shitheads can run in circles
Talk shit until they fall over
Nothing penetrates my dead skin
I was lucky back there
Only part of me was murdered
The other part of me survives
I will not be stopped until I am murdered
I know I will be murdered someday

❦❦❦

Fuck you bitch
You should hear the shit fall from your mouth
You pathetic piece of stoner shit
I'd love to kick your ass
Just to see the look of shit panic on your face
Your bullshit weak ass self serving righteousness
Filling the room with hash and your bullshit bitch complaints
I'm often ashamed to be in a band with you
It's embarrassing

❦❦❦

Dreams 3.1 - 3.12

I'm trying to fire my handgun but every time I pick it up it's a plastic
one.

A series of dreams about an old girlfriend. She is with me and telling me about how she has to tell her boyfriend that she no longer wants to be with him. She lists different ways he's going to take the news.

I feel underneath a girl's shirt. She has her navel pierced. I remember that from the last time I was with her. I reach up her dress and feel that she has her vagina pierced as well. She says that she has that going for her now.

I'm talking with two girls and one is talking about sex. I don't want to let them know that I have fucked both of them. One starts laughing slightly and I remember that the last time I was with her I came on her leg or something, I hope she doesn't tell the other one.

I mouth off to a pig and he makes me plant a garden in his back yard. He says that when I finish putting the plants in the dirt I can leave town.

Something happens where a girl is trying to hurt me.

<C-C-C>

Mutilating you wouldn't be enough
Killing you wouldn't be enough either
Life and Death isn't enough to hold me
Mass murder isn't enough to help
Even a good fuck isn't enough to live for
I am alive in the world of Horror

<C-C-C>

I imagine I know every beautiful woman I see on the street
In my mind I talk to them as I pass
I make up fake conversations
In these moments of illusion we understand each other
I can say what I feel
She doesn't look at me funny
She doesn't run away
I close my eyes for a moment to try to keep it in
I open my eyes and I'm standing in the middle of the sidewalk
New York City
Everywhere is the same
All strangers to me
I don't think of desert landscapes anymore
I don't think of burning sunsets and jungle floor

14

I am no longer choked with passion
It's now just rage and contempt for life
I lost somehow
I got murdered part way
A few bad turns
Now it's all real
There's blood and Death wherever I go
No girls and stupid talk
Just tension and solitary corners
The smell of my sweat turning to ammonia
Darkness and silent horror

◁▷◁▷◁▷

So where are you tonight scar maker?
In some lit room making brain cells die?
Making some idiot lose his mind?
Have you ever seen a man tie his neck his neck in a knot?
Have you ever seen someone kill themselves with a thought?
How are your eyes tonight self hate generator?
Cutting and advertising the last chance to breathe?
When I think of you the world gets dangerously huge
My heart beats once a year
I don't know when exactly to stop inhaling
I don't know where to get off
I don't know how to not feel
I wish I could get over you
I am dangerous to myself
All of this will end soon

◁▷◁▷◁▷

Please come through the door tonight
It's so lonely and fucked up here
I'm confused and everything's strange
I wish I was just on something
You were the last woman that meant anything to me
I can't stop
I have no defense system
No attitude that sees me through
Sometimes I think that I keep getting up everyday
Because there's nothing else to do

◁▷◁▷◁▷

Looking for answers to all the questions
I walk the cities of lies
I walk the floors of rage
I pace the hallways of Death
The words mean nothing
The ruined flesh that lies behind me
The stain on my eye
It all means nothing
Because I see where it all ends up
I got here a little too early I think
Now that I'm here I might as well make myself at home
Horror takes some getting used to

❖❖❖

After life
Miles away
A life away
Up a long river
On a beach
Silent sun will watch over me
I will sleep peacefully at night
I will not hear gunshots
I will not regret
I will be free from horror
I will not have terror dreams
I will smile again and mean it
There is a place for me to breathe
It's somewhere I know it
1000 worlds beyond sickness and weakness
Unspoiled by city disease
Quietly in this room I wait
For the world to happen

❖❖❖

There are bars on the windows of my room
The apartment is surrounded by locked gates
The front door is double locked
I have the lights low and I'm away from the windows
I crawled across the room to get here to write
There could be snipers out there
Paranoia, no such thing
Can't ever be too wired around here
Can't ever be too ready

I come out at night
Behind the locks and the bars and the gates
Like living in a shark cage
Want to sleep well?
Lock yourself in good
Put your money into security
Watch out for slow moving vehicles
Death squads
You don't think they exist?
Wake up or be dead
In the end, what an insult
To be executed by someone who can't even read
At night behind the bars and the locks
I think of you
My silent thoughts are good
They don't show up on their surveillance monitors
I like this room
I always keep a little music on
Messes with their wire taps
I run outside for supplies during the day
I make sure I'm inside well before dark
They're out there
They're everywhere but here

❦❦❦

I want to meet a stranger
I want to tell her everything
I want to howl
I want her to make sense to me
I need someone
I need

❦❦❦

I was with a woman last night
Same distance as always
What's the matter with me
Why am I so fucked up
What am I looking for
Is it that I can't get over
The last time my heart was broken?
I don't know
I sure am lonely these days

❦❦❦

On the streets near my room
You might see pimps and whores
Rent boys and drug dealers
Guys who look like they would kill you quick
Wordlessly and without an emotional display
You might see danger and you might feel fear
You might see the neon and the rust of civilization
Reflected in the crime lights
Dried blood and sadness
I see sweeping eternal darkness
Enveloping doom and marrow drying sadness
All things leaning over to one side and giving up
People pushed until they act like what they fear to stay alive
To become human camouflage
My spine twitches underneath my skin
I wait for the bullet
I watch the small world wear itself down and die screaming
Alas

❦❦❦

You see I did it
I made something out of myself
I am a slave to my parents
I am slave to my horror
I mutilate myself without their help
You can see it in major cities every year
I didn't blow it
I did good can't you see
I took the punishment out on the road
I don't need them to fuck me up
I can do it to myself real well now
I have it down to a science
I don't know how I'll end up
I don't want to know anymore
I'm afraid of the nightmares I've become
I live it sickly and darkly
My saliva is black

❦❦❦

I don't know how to be anymore
When you called today and I was nasty

I didn't know how to be any other way
What a piece of work
When you said we should get together for coffee
And I told you I wanted to stab you in the face
I meant it
You said you were sorry about what happened
I was thinking
Fuck yourself you stupid bitch
I didn't say that though
You said I should call you sometime
I told you I wouldn't
I don't care about talking to people anymore
I'm not one of those people you can call and talk to
These days everything makes me sick
No more life
It's all horror walking
I wear a mask and have dreams of killing
The thought of brutal murder is the only thing that comforts me
When I walk down the street I feel safe
I'm not afraid to die
Someone without a gun would be
Fucking with the wrong guy
The wrongest guy
I mean really wrong
Oh man
You Hollywood danger boys
Move aside when I walk by
I have garbage thoughts
Of ripping your throats out
Breaking your wind pipes
I'm the ugliest person I know

<<<

It's late and I'm alone so I won't lie
If I could get through myself
And all the lies I use to protect myself
I could somehow talk to you
I could somehow listen
I could get out of my claustrophobic stranglehold
I would tell you everything
I wouldn't be so horrible

I would learn to communicate
I could maybe let someone else be strong
If I only had the guts

❁~❁~❁

I want to be in love with a woman
One who loved me
One who could show me I could trust her
One who could show me
That I didn't have to be on my guard all the time

❁~❁~❁

Been two weeks since the last show
Next tour starts in a few days
Relief
I could never deal with the room in one place for too long
Makes me feel like I'm choking
It's the only thing that makes me feel ok inside my skin
The last few nights have been depressing
I don't know what to do with myself
I'm pretty fucked up I guess

❁~❁~❁

I wish I could meet a woman that could show me something
One who could make my blood stop screaming

❁~❁~❁

Generic night
Another night in the room
It's past midnight
Waiting for sleep to take me out
All I can to do is write
I feel so wrong
Wrong planet
Wrong time
The whole thing
I am lonely and fucked up
Tomorrow another tour starts
My world will move again
I can get out of my mind for awhile
My dead friend follows me everywhere
I walk with grief and horror

I wish there was someone to talk to me
I have never felt such extinction
Loneliness, ripped away thoughts
I figure I'm allowed to write it if I don't talk
I'm ok if I keep writing and moving
I wonder if I'll ever meet someone I can be close to
Fuck it
I wouldn't know what to say
Like right now
I don't know what to say
Don't know the right thought to get me through
The streets around here
Man, they'll fuck you right up
You go out there for a little while
That's all you need
Heavy metal women
Whores and drug dealers
Police and filth
You know you're going to lose
Just by association

I love you
I have no guide to help me
Nothing to protect me from your storm
I felt like an idiot sitting in your car
Your face was so beautiful
I didn't think I could love anyone
I love you
Wouldn't be great if you would love me
Maybe you would even trust me
I need you
Because life is not enough
I hadn't seen you in over a year
It all came back
With the force of depression
I still felt the same
I have been thinking of you all day
I feel as though I have nothing
I am alone on the planet
I know this and it hurts too much
Maybe with you it could be different

I can't ask you to want me
I'll just have to see
I don't like rolling the dice again
It's hard to load the gun with a picture of your face
Spin the cylinder and pull
All my life it's been the lonely click

⋄-⋄-⋄

4.10.92
It's Joe Cole's birthday
I'm in my room on a night off in LA
Too freaked out to leave the apartment
I figure the killer knows I want to go to mail some letters
He's out there waiting in the parking garage
I have spent the last few hours crying and writing
Nothing changes
I like the stillness of the night
In a few hours they'll all be up and making noise
I don't know how I do it sometimes
I have been back in the murder mind
I see the pieces of shit on the street
I want to go up and shoot them in the stomach
Walk away and say nothing
I hate the way they look at me
I must give them the vibe that they can take me
It's predator-prey
If they only knew
I'm only afraid of guns and numbers
The rest of it doesn't get in my way
I just don't give a fuck
The part that cared
Sits in a plastic box in Burbank
I keep saying good bye
I keep getting a corpse on my porch
Every night is the same
I take it alone in silence
There really isn't any other way to handle it

⋄-⋄-⋄

One great night
I'm going to pack my belongings
And sneak out of this town

Won't tell anyone
The sun will come up and I'll be laughing
Thousands of miles away
Never to return
Not for any price
What a great plan
He never came back to California
Smart guy
He beat the game
Like you really want to die out here
Only losers finish out in California
I'll have to sneak out though
If they hear you're leaving
The killers line up to make sure you don't
Believe me
I've seen 'em
Shitheads on every corner
Looking like they own the whole game
They do out here
Kings of the shit house

❖❖❖

I am thoughtless wordless
I walk down this wet night street
I am the desert and all its sand
I cannot hold onto a thought or memory
There's no need for heartbreak
Nervous breakdown or panic
Just go on and do what you will
Don't flinch or think about Death
I can't tell you about romance
I cannot tell you how I feel
I don't feel, I'm slaughtered meat
I am the desert night and all its darkness
I'm not beyond life
Just next to it
Watching it slam down the rails
Some people need help
Some people just need
Some people know better

❖❖❖

I am alone tonight and it's a good thing too
I wouldn't want to try and talk the language tonight
I want to scream and fall into your arms
I know that will never work out
I feel like I should be vomiting right about now
Another tour starts

It's night time in Ohio
I'm in a box but it's different this time
Some of them know where we are
It's not as safe as it used to be
We don't come into town as strangers
I get recognized even at night
Somewhere they know
They could come here any time
I feel safer on the bus
Rolling across the highway at night
Curled up in a black box
Alone with my pathetic thoughts
And terrifying nightmares
I lie wake in the black box
The road under my back
I think of her
I know she never thinks of me
It is pathetic
Tonight I'll sleep with some part of me awake
Wild eyed, scared and screaming

--

He didn't do much
He just went from town to town
Did all the interviews
Shook all the hands
Said all the right things
Everybody got off but him
You don't want to know too much
If you get closer than an inch away
It's terribly ugly
I wouldn't lie to you

--

My exhaustion is nervous
I don't know why I'm running
I'll vomit myself again tonight
I'll come up with another answer
When they come up with another question
Something about all that money
All this shiny stuff
They don't know that all I smell is blood and brains
That I want to die all the time
That I had a dream about killing myself last night
How much sense it made
That an hour before the show started
I was wrapped in a blanket sweating
They don't know, they'll never know
How much of a freak I think I am
I'll never be able to explain it
I'll just scream and fuck until I die
I think that's all there is besides truth

❧❧❧

You can go see my friend's little piece of lawn
You can go for free
Doesn't mean shit to me
A nice place so the father can go
And feel better about himself
I have the horror memorial in my closet
A plastic container of the blood filled dirt
That remained after they scraped him off
809 Brooks Ave motherfucker
Right where his head fell
I had to take it before all the fly's ate it
It sits right next to his phone
In case he needs to get in touch

❧❧❧

All night blues
On the other hand fuck it
Fuck all of these late night desperation ideas
It's all self serving bullshit
Like I could really love you
Like I cold really love anything
I keep forgetting how fucked up I am

I get fooled by all the voices
I almost feel like I could fit
Then reality comes back and I know where I'm at
Stabbing you with my thoughts
Endlessly killing you
Mutilating you
The only thing that amazes me
Is how I can keep on being so fucking good all the time
I'll fuck but I won't love
I won't crawl again
I've seen life shortened by a shit head with a gun
Life's rope is too short for me
I can't be slowed by love's sick hand
There's only safety in the animal mind
Too many of these weaklings have guns now
All the time I'm looking over my shoulder
The shithead with the gun
I'm old fashioned
I miss the good old days
Punching the shit out of someone
Feeling about it
Like the other night
The piece of shit that cut in front of me in line
The only thing he had going for him
Was the fact that he might have been packing
That's the only thing that keeps me off your ass
One of these days I'm going to do the wrong thing
Not take shit from the wrong person
And get shot in a 7-11
That's how I'll go out
In a puddle of blood in a fucking convenience store
I fucking hate you all so much I can't even breathe
I'll find a way to hurt all of you

❧❧❧

4.30.92 Los Angeles California
Large buildings are on fire
The men who beat Rodney King are going to go free
Supermarkets are on fire
Pigs have shot 6, killed 1
Hospitals are overrun with injured
The news showed Westwood

A broken window
Three pigs on every corner
Outside you can smell the smoke
LA's burning
What the fuck did the pigs expect
What would they do if the shoe
Was on the other hoof
Some good may come of this
Some pigs might get killed
Every day is a good day for a pig to die

◄►◄►◄►

A super fantasy about the acquitted pigs going home
Getting ambushed and tortured to Death
Me and Cole on the controls
Watching their kids burn
Getting their eyes pulled out
Getting fed their wives intestines
They need this

◄►◄►◄►

Another night is taking me through myself
I can smell the beast's flesh cooking again tonight
Down the streets they're looting
At first it was because of the pigs
Now it's just because humans like to fuck shit up
They're all the same
Here's what:
I see this one guy go up to a liquor store and throw a trash can through the front window. A few guys standing next to me start chasing him with sticks. People next to me were yelling "Get him, he's getting away!" I didn't know who were the biggest idiots were, the looter, the guys with the sticks or the people wanting to see the blood. I decided that they were all assholes and left. Fuck this place, fuck this city. Los Angeles is for losers. I think I'll have to move soon. I don't want to live the rest of my fucking days in this decadent shithole. I don't want to die in this city. I have nothing left here anyway. I should get out of here before it gets me and kills me. But anyway, look at the shit we're in here in this fucked up place. I was leaving to go back to the room when the police came and told us to get in our homes so we would be safe. I bet the pigs love it now with the National Guard in town. I hate this place. It's getting too fucked up to live here.

I think of desert
I think of a girl
I want to know a girl
It will make me have to work
I'll have to be bigger in my heart
I doubt if I can do it
I have pulled so far back from humans
I don't know if I can come back
I have dreams of a different reality
Waking up in an apartment in some city far from here
Walking outside and not getting recognized
Knowing why people want to know me
Not getting stared at all the time
Meeting someone that will make me listen
Fuck it
In the morning I'll come to my senses
I'll know that I feel this way because I'm not on the road
When I'm on the road nothing else matters
When I sit still I get soft
There really isn't any other life for me
I wouldn't last very long with a girl in a house

❮❯❮❯❮❯

We'll get together soon you and I
As I sit here I can see it clearly
It will be pure
Animal
I'll pull your hair around my neck
We'll bite each other's flesh
We will understand each other
I'll understand that you're beautiful
Because you're alive
Maybe you'll be able to help me
I'm fucked up in the head
I'm a wounded animal
Staggering on the side of the road
Waiting for another car to hit me and leave
If you could make me cry
Make me feel something
Maybe I wouldn't want to tear my skin off
Maybe you could reach me
Please try to reach me

I think it's too late
I'm already dead pretty much
Hell with it
I'll shut up and we'll fuck
I'll leave and you'll call me weeks later
I'll be busy and have forgotten your name
I will have pulled into myself even further
You'll get a taste of how truly cold and black I am
You'll want to puke
When you think that I was inside you
From now on it's like this

<t><t><t>

Not alive
Not me
Not anymore
Say what you want
Leave any time
I don't even remember you
I'll never miss you
I'll never think about you
I'm so far past that shit
It's a joke to me, all of it
Stab your mother in the teeth
Stab mine
I don't care about anything
Except a night in the desert

<t><t><t>

At the end of all of this
I won't be wondering about shit
I won't be surprised by a fucking thing
Don't get me wrong
I'm not like you
I puke out memories
I want to hurt people
I'm negative and paranoid
I think that sex is always fucked up
A soulless cock with a mind behind it is nothing
But a tool of cruelty
I collect them and hang them like teeth
Put them in a bag and keep moving

What the fuck do you expect from a stranger
I'll tell you the truth always
You're more alone than I think you know
You're never more alone
Than when you're with me
Because with me it's different
My touch fools you
It begs for understanding and then
Prepares itself to spit on you
When you reach out to me
You humiliate yourself
I mutilate myself in front of you
You think I'm being open
I'm not
I'm being fucked and cruel
It's all I know
Animal is as animal does
Hey look
I don't ever wonder why about shit

◁▷◁▷◁▷

Deathstar CA: Do you want to die a few feet from your house? All you
have to do is move here and it all can come true for you. Do you want
to see a sea of dead eyes and toneless voices talk about bullshit? Do you
want to see millions of people waste their time when they should just
be wasting themselves? It's all right here. All the pigs and bullshit.
Every time I come back here I always kick myself. What a bad place to
be, evil place. Only a sucker would end up old in this city. Why do it
when there's so many places on the planet. 31 isn't old is it?

◁▷◁▷◁▷

Cab ride on the way to the airport
Riding down La Cienega
Looking at burned out hulls of stores
One said:
Looted, tenants upstairs
Other store fronts
With pictures of Martin Luther King
Like that's going to help
All this shit burned up on the streets
It was good to get out of all that dead cement
Fuck that dead city

It should have never stopped
The whole city should have burned to the ground
We were almost there

❮❮❮

All the parts disconnected
All the parts broken down
Another room down my throat
Slack jawed paranoia
Thinking about killing them and myself
I can't.....
It all falls into a violent display
I fall in on myself
I don't wonder why about shit
I can't find a way to get the parts together
You ever seen a pile of parts
Walking by you
Yea, it's like that
Just fucked up and thinking about Death

❮❮❮

She calls me and wonders why I don't call her
I struggle silently to remember her name
I listen to the bullshit pour from her mouth
I don't listen and tell her that I'm hanging up
She demands that I don't
She keeps talking and I'm fighting the urge
I want to tell her to get the rubber out her tits
And stab herself in the face with an ice pick
I hang up and I go back to the room
There's a gunshot outside
I see myself emptying a 9 mm in the general direction
I've been here three days
This shit doesn't work for me
Fuck it
I'll kill myself if I stay here too long
It'll make too much fucking sense
Why?
Because fuck you

❮❮❮

Mother on the answering machine

Mother through the wires
I listen to the message and I start to burn
I want to start kicking holes in the wall
A rage I can't identify courses through my body
And I just want to explode and not exist
I think about the shrink I went to
Because I was so fucked up right?
Because she was so fucked up
And now I've got this rage and nowhere to go

⊲⊱⊲⊱⊲⊱

Alive without a head
Cursed with a little too much brains
Your sight is too clear to lie your way out of the night
Alone in your room
Some fucking city somewhere
Hear the idiots outside shooting guns
Yea it's come to this
You're right in it
Trying to separate yourself
Just like me
Trying to separate yourself
Balled up like some forgotten piece of paper
I'll go to the bottom with you
I'll stand on the edge with you
You always know where you are
I'll show you around these parts

⊲⊱⊲⊱⊲⊱

Come into my room and check out some pathetic shit
Get a good seat and watch me
See me sit in here alone crying in this chair
As I go steadily deeper inside
Watching 2 a.m. turn into paranoia
Look in the closet
My friend's dried blood is in a plastic bowl
My life is pretty fucked up at this point
I re-live horror perfectly
I don't want to talk to anyone
Yet I am lonely and violent
I don't know what to do anymore

⊲⊱⊲⊱⊲⊱

At night the scars of loneliness rip open and it hurts
You look into the wound and it's deep
Put there with feeling and conviction
It's no lie
It goes beyond words
You've tried to put it down
Some piece of paper
You got so frustrated
Fuck words
Sometimes they just don't work
You have a lump in your throat
You want to break something
You wish it was different
Life I mean
You know that this is a huge part of it
You can tell that there will be many nights like this
There will be
Look at the lines in the faces
They look just like yours
In the deep wounded night I am your friend

<<->->->

I love you and you'll never know
I could tell you and it wouldn't matter
You wouldn't get it and why should you
It hurts to know you'll never know
It hurts to sit here alone and really mean it
To feel it so deeply that my bones ache thinking of you
To imagine how the conversation would go
How you would stare with your blank eyes
Say nothing until
I think you're really a great guy....
And hope you could leave it at that and just leave
And of course I would watch you walk away
Knowing deep inside that no one
Is anything but totally alone
There are some like you
Who deal with it
There are some like myself
Who don't deal with it as well
The scars are easy to see

<<->->->

Fuck it
I walked away from the wreckage
Turned my back to the waste
Staggered into the desert
You can see it in my eyes
I'm not here
Sometimes I think
That someone should love me
They really should
But then I remember how I think
Stabbing and kicking
No explanation
I can't cry anymore
I'm all dried up
All I see is the Abyss
I just keep walking through shadows
The varying shades of blindness
I end up in these rooms alone
I understand how perfect all of this is

�''⋆''⋆

Time with you was perfect
Never boring
Never wasted
You were always the same
Intense and beautiful
Amazing
I would look at you as we sat in restaurants
You awed me with your sheer presence
When I was away from you I would stare at your picture
Endlessly
Something you never got a chance to find out
Something you'll never know
One fact:
I would have done anything for you
Knowing that it all could be used against me
I know what happens when you do that even a little
I have the scars
For you I would have pulled sunlight from thin air
And lifted the curses from your life
I loved you so
It's tragic at this point

Like an ongoing funeral
You're out there somewhere
Sometimes I can feel myself dying slow
You know how those barbed and clawed nights can pass
They rip the meat off your back
Send you into a corner
And leave you with enough of your senses to realize
That you'll live to see another hammering night alone

❯❯❯

It's hard for me to talk to you
I have a problem with my face
I got shot in my left cheek last December
You can see the hole in my head
I feel strange showing myself in day light
All the powder burns on my face from the gun
It looks like someone lit me on fire
I can't make my mouth too well anymore
I have almost stopped talking altogether
I feel so crippled
All these people staring at me
They know my name everywhere I go
I wish I could show them the horror behind my eyes
Because this place doesn't care
You go looking for a hand out
I tell you man
You'll waste your life looking
You find holes in all your pockets
Nothing in your head
Except bitter memories and spent bullet casings
Be careful, so careful
Life has no meaning
The world is full of strangers
Love is a tight rope walk
The rope is made of inspiration
Intertwined with desperation
When you fall
You fall

❯❯❯

If I keep writing
Traveling all over

Pushing myself until I squeeze truth
From out of my pores
She will find me
It's worth it

⋖-⋖-⋖

I wonder if you live in a happy world. If your sleep releases you, if you have a life that makes you look forward to life. I do not begrudge you your happy life if you have one. I wish I had one too. I wouldn't want you to see mine. I wouldn't want you to deal with it for a second. I sometimes wish I could get out of existence and not have to feel. It's been a series of small abortions, inhalation of glass shards and paranoia. Insomnia and horror. I wish I had a happy life. I don't see the merit in torment. It's to the point to where I can't tell if I'm awake or dreaming of being terrified all the time. I don't mean to carry on with this bad trip. I look into their eyes and I wish I could see what they see when they smile. Last night was bad, real bad. I was overwhelmed with panic. I was in front of a lot of people and they never knew that I was freaking out in front of them wishing there was someone on the planet I could talk to. Someone to relieve the horror. Today has been strange, hanging around silently waiting for the beating. I hope you have a happy life, maybe someday I'll have one too.

⋖-⋖-⋖

6.11.92 Florence Italy: Night off tonight. We drove about 18 hours to get here. Been going since Amsterdam last night. This is a night off. Another lit box on the trail. People outside are talking loud and the traffic is whizzing by. It doesn't matter where we are tonight. I feel lost and found wherever I am these days. I don't know where I am but I know where I'm at all the time. I hang in moments. I think of other places and other times. Tonight while driving into town I thought of where I grew up and how I showed part of it to Joe and how he wrote about it in his book. I feel like dying a lot of the time now. I don't tell anyone about it because I don't want to get into a discussion about it. I don't want anyone trying to cheer me up. I don't want anyone to tell me anything. I am tired of hearing them talk. Last night there were these people waiting outside the door of the side of the building near the bus. These days people that want to meet me I automatically don't want to talk to. I know it's ridiculous but I see it as an insult. It's as if I didn't give enough of myself an hour ago on stage and they want more. I'm so tired at the end of the night that the luxury that I have is that I don't have to talk and to have to take compliments for ripping myself up every night. They came near me and I froze them out so fast that it even surprised me. Some girl wanted to give me some flowers and I stared at her so hard that she just held onto them and walked away. I figure that they shouldn't get close to people like me and I'm right.

<<<-<<-<<

Nice guys don't play good. Nice guys suck when they play. You can't be nice and be any good. The ones that make music that sticks and burns aren't nice. Charlie Parker wasn't nice. If he was nice he wouldn't be onstage with his horn on fire. These days people would rather have nice people playing music than the real thing that moves you. Music that kills the player. They'll never make me nice. Nothing will ever tame me. When these fucking journalists ask these stupid questions, I can tell that they're nice people who have no clue where the real heavy shit comes from. They wonder why the real heavy duty cats are greedy, mean assed, damaged, dangerous people that end up dying pathetically. I know why. No one has to tell me shit. Some people are born fucked up and a few of them make it onto stages. It's simple. The good ones sit in room by themselves and hate the life that they were given because they see it as what it is, an affliction. A plague. Fuck this place.

<<<-<<-<<

I am typical and I'm thinking of her tonight
I met her months ago
Spent a few days with her
Called her on the phone several times
It was good to talk to her
Pretty good
When I saw her again a few weeks later
I couldn't see why I had talked to her at all
I had nothing to say to her
Had trouble remembering her name
Couldn't wait to leave her
Haven't talked to her since
Haven't thought of her until tonight
Does this happen on Earth all the time
Or is it just me being totally fucked up?
Sometimes I wish I was stupid
Because sometimes I want to be happy
You know how hard it gets to live here
Life puts you in these rooms alone at night
Time drags you out and turns you on yourself

I wonder if I hurt her feelings at all
I doubt it
She probably already knew I was a creep
But it's deeper than that and much worse
I know that I'll never meet anyone that I can be with
I have too much distance in my eyes
Too much damage to deal with
It hurts to live beside life
Never really knowing what it's like
Yet feeling so torn and confused by it
How do you explain that to someone
Have you tried and seen the blank stare too many times?
Yea me too

<<<>

The cleaning lady wouldn't leave the room. I told her that I didn't need anything. She kept apologizing and cleaning anyway. I had slept in the bed for less than an hour and she was trying to put new sheets on it and I kept telling her that it was alright, I didn't need anything. She said that she was sorry and she would only be another minute. She left the room and I thought I was clear of her and she came back in with all her gear and started to clean the bathroom which hadn't even been used yet. I told her that it was ok and she could split and she said it was not a worry and she started to clean it anyway. She said that a younger maid recognized me when I checked in a couple of hours ago. She told me that the younger maid was replacing her and that she herself was "one of the redundancy maids" and was going to be let go next week. I looked at this older woman who wouldn't make eye contact with me at all. She diverted her eyes like I was some kind of lord. She kept running around me cleaning up, straightening the clothes that I unpacked, folding newspapers, this went on for minutes. Finally she apologized for talking and wasting my time and then without another word she pulled out of the room with her buckets and sheets.

I imagine her at the end of the day. She lies down in the maid's closet with her coat as a blanket. She steals a biscuit from the tea service and makes it her meal. A few hours later she gets up and cleans rooms all day and returns to the closet. She cleans ten miles of rooms a day. One day she cleans and there's a man at the end of the hall and he opens the door and shows her another 100 miles if hallway and tells her to clean every room and she says yes sir. She cleans the 100 miles of rooms and she gets to the end a month later to see that at the end of the hall there is an open grave with headstone with her name on it. The man returns out of nowhere and tells her to jump in. She apologizes, says thank you and jumps.

❈-❈-❈

They had just finished sex
He said that he was going "out there"
She asked him when he would be back
He said that she didn't want to know any more
That he was hollow
And that if she got any closer
He would damage her for the rest of her life
By telling her everything
He said goodbye, got up and walked away
He walked across a stretch of sand
He was met by an ocean made of fire
He turned, smiled and ducked under a wave of flame
He disappeared and the night started to scream

❈-❈-❈

Cindy Crawford
I'm in this hotel room
Smelling the bug spray and watching you on TV
I'm listening to you talk
You're one of the most intense people I've ever seen
Fascinating
You must be so great in bed
Not

❈-❈-❈

I've been thinking about your Hollywood television actor ass today. I'm looking forward to getting one of your fucked up phone calls and listening to your voice and its reading off a script sound. "Joe was my son". Where's the music. What's your motivation in this scene? Too busy with your bimbos and AA meetings to notice your son until he gets shot in the head and all of a sudden you're out of your fuckhead world back into the real world where one take is all you get and that's it. Stepping into your role as dad. Remembering the moves, making sure you look good for the cameras. Real life you piece of shit. You're so fake. Why don't you just finish the job and blow your fucking brains out and make me respect you. Why couldn't it have been you instead.

❈-❈-❈

Two strangers lie in a hotel bed
Underneath the weight of the dark
They speak their truths in hushed tones
They wrap their arms round each other
And hold tight
Because
The world is so huge

❂❂❂

Dennis Miller Show after thought
I'm not running for office
I'm not trying to make you like me
I'm not trying to sell you anything
I'm not a comic
I just wanted to take a minute to remind you of something
Life isn't short, it goes on after you're gone
Time is not running out, time just goes
It's your life time that is short and running out all the time
So what are you doing taking drugs?
Why are you putting cigarette smoke in those beautiful lungs of yours?
What are you drinking that poison for?
Weeks ago sections of this city burned to the ground
For nothing
Months ago my best friend was shot in the face and killed on my front
porch
For nothing
Life time's up for him
You're different
You're alive, you're breathing
I'd like to see you stay that way
Don't do anything for nothing
You're too important
This trip is all about you

❂❂❂

They sit across from each other and wait for the food
Several minutes ago they were having intense sex
The sweat was running off their bodies
It was mutual need nothing more
Now they sit and talk about nothing
They both know that they're looking for something
Each know that the other isn't it

Yet they go on talking and fucking
Idly
Watching out not to get too deep
Neither has the energy
They couldn't if they wanted to
Both know that the other isn't concerned too much
In the mean time they're looking
That was me tonight
I don't know what I'm looking for
In someone else's eyes
I don't know if I'd know at this point
You can get so numb over the years
You'll work, pay taxes and lie to yourself
The whole nine yards to nowhere
My eyes drifted off to the street
The lights of the cars kicked at the corners of my eyes
I forgot to pretend to listen
I was filled with emptiness
I felt old and stupid
I could do nothing but breathe
Now I sit in my room alone and I feel better
Sometimes you're faking it
Sometimes you're a coward
Sometimes you just get tired of taking the beating

<<<

At band practice today I made up a song about you. It was about the
scars in your eyes and how they alter your vision to where you think I'm
one of the ones who is going to hurt you. I could never hurt you. I think
of you all the time. I have no idea where you are but still I think of you
and the way I could sometimes see a spark in your eyes like some
diamond that didn't get crushed to powder under some man's fist. It
would never last long, it would fall from sight behind a strip of scar
tissue.

I thought I saw you the other day. It wasn't you but looking into the
girl's eyes before I had to look away in total embarrassment made me
remember you and how much I wanted to try to bring your eyes back
to life. I would live for the way your eyes would come to life every once
in a while. I miss you. Nothing much for me around here. My loneliness
doesn't use subtle hints. It comes up and stabs me. You know how the
nights are built to rip you apart. Right now Charlie Parker is soloing
through mine. Outside, Los Angeles burns and rapes. The whores are

a few blocks away getting in and out cars parked on the Blvd. This is unfinished because life is unfinished. Hot stabbing night. Past three in the morning. I am here, the pupil in the black eye.

⋘⋗⋗

Choices: Let's say you were a lonely man who once had a best friend. Months before, your best friend was murdered right next to you outside your house. Since your friend had died all of your days are full of pain. You sleep with horror and bad dreams. You can't understand why you were allowed to live and your friend was the one who had to die.

Life has lost its shine, it's not all that special anymore, you start to lose interest in things and life starts to pass you and you stop caring. Sometimes it's all you can do just to get through the day without breaking down and crying. It never seems to get better either. You realize that this will last you the rest of your life. You know deep down that you will never have another friend like that and even though you can accept that truth, you cannot find a way to deal with it. You have feelings that you are afraid to tell people about because you think that they will think you are crazy. You become withdrawn and isolated. It gets so bad that sometimes all you can do is sit in a dark room and try not to think. You feel that life is over for you and you're just waiting for it to end.

You have a dream one night. It goes like this: You are given a choice between two realities. The first choice is that nothing changes and you live the rest of your life the best you can. The second choice is that your friend will be brought back to life. The catch is that you will have to spend the rest of your life in solitary confinement in a prison. You will be shown a couple of pictures of your friend so you're sure that the deal went through. Otherwise you live alone with no contact with your friend or the outside world. The only consolation is that you know your friend is alive. He will have no memory of you or your friendship.

In a hotel room in the desert a woman asked me if I ever got lonely. I told her I was one of the loneliest people she ever met. Outside the desert wind threw sand against the glass. Middle of nowhere's nowhere. Walking the balance line between light and dark, always coming up odd. From now on life transparent and insane. I know it too well so I know too much. I am an endless choked scream. Inside I claw myself and wait for nothing.

⋘⋗⋗

Straight haired girls
With bleached brains

Walk up the Blvd
Strike poses at the corners
Trying to look like every man's fantasy
Bow legged and underfed
They look distant and hard
The street comes up to meet their rusted stare
And backs off
Hollywood

❦❦❦

I'm not going to bother with you anymore
I don't need all the extra thought
I got enough right now as it is
Not going to wait for your phone calls
Not going to think about you
And what it would be like it were different
It's not different
It's like this
I won't think of you when I'm in some shit hole
Or a rented room by a numbered highway off ramp
I will not bother to find stamps to send letters
It's living a lie
To pull myself through your studied indifference
Is to be insulted by pain
A pain that cannot teach or strengthen
Only a pain that messes with your guts
I'm throwing you out of my thoughts
You'll only hurt me anyway
I'll find better ways to hurt myself

❦❦❦

I know what I want
I want you
Too bad I'm too fucked up to do anything about it
All I could do is hurt you
I am a wounded animal blinded by headlights
This could be the universal blues song

❦❦❦

Don't think that you need me
Or that I hold any answers
Don't think of what it would be like to meet me

Believe me
I'll only let you down
You'll hate me
There's nothing I'll be able to say to make it any different
It's the oldest story
One filled with self hatred
Cannot do anything beneficial for others
When they get too close
I can't handle affection or friendship
Too fucked up and scarred
I wrote this girl a letter the other day
Two words: Don't bother
It's like talking to a dead body
Or a shark

❄❄❄

I keep telling myself:
You have to get this shit on your own
It's easy to die
People are wrong when they think they're hard to kill
Humans die easy and without much fight
If you listen to them for too long
They will sell you the fuck out
Pull back into your mind
Master yourself before someone else does
You are all you've got
You can make or break yourself any time
People measure themselves
Using the yardstick of others
Good for a while
I must maintain the One
Keep the number strong within me
It's the only number there is
People around me telling me things all the time
If I listened I wouldn't be here now
Look at them and see them
Not yourself in them
You are not them
Exhaustion level is extreme
Body pain all the time
Non stop schedule
It's my will power

Presence of mind and clarity that gets me through
If I listened to them I would fall apart
That's something they'll never understand
I fly alone in the thin air

<☞-☞-☞>

Busted LA again
I must have forgotten
Been gone from here for so long this time out
A few hours in my room and it comes back to me
The traffic outside
The chopper blades hovering near the roof
You leave this town and you can forget
It all came back to me on the plane today
Listening to the male models and call each other dude
Looking at their tinted hair pony tails
Wondering what they would do
If someone put a gun to their head
Broken lying city full of dead blood and cheap Death
I daydream of leaving
I have to get back to the east coast
Walk the streets that Coltrane, Monk and Parker walked
Listen to language that means something
Not this painted rubber killing field collection of catch phrases

<☞-☞-☞>

Alien encounters single female earthling
The idea that I had met you and that you liked me
For the simple reason that you liked me
Was incredible
One of the single most validating things
That had ever happened to me
So when you left
I really noticed

<☞-☞-☞>

Tripping on
Joe's
Dead
Body
By the time it got dead
It was no longer his

For a while it belonged to the state of California
Then it belonged to his father
Now it belongs to a graveyard
This cold slab of property
What a way to go out
Also
These people who say shit like
He's not dead
He'll always be alive in your heart
There was a reason, there's a reason for everything
This makes me want to say
See that guy over there?
Then walk over and shoot the guy in the face
And say
He's not dead
He'll always be with you
There was a reason
There's a reason for everything
And
Would you like to be next?

⊲⊱⊲⊱⊲⊱

Dream sickness
She kissed me
I said it had been a long time since I had done that
She said that had been a long time since she had wanted to
For a few moments I felt special
I existed for the first time in months
Now the hours are blank
And I feel normal again

⊲⊱⊲⊱⊲⊱

My best friend got shot in the head
Murdered
A few feet away from me
I heard his shoes shift on the pavement seconds before
I have a perspective on things
I don't have to explain

⊲⊱⊲⊱⊲⊱

I wish I could have understood you
I wish you would have needed me

It hurts to know I'll never be with you again
I think of you all the time
I have been with other women
I accidentally call them by your name
I can't help myself
These nights go by
Always different cities
But the same pain
I am becoming more familiar with myself
More strange to them
I wish I knew someone
I could talk to
I wish
I wish I didn't sound so struck, so pathetic
I should feel lucky to be alive
But I don't feel so lucky
Most of the time
I don't feel anything at all
My eyes hollow out
And the time passes unnoticed

Sitting in the box near 8 a.m. and all I can think of is playing and destroying shit. The drag is that I have to leave here in a few hours and talk to shitheads about all the little bullshit details. Press people don't get it and never will because they are press people. If they had a real life they wouldn't have to ask questions. Sometimes the guys in the band are weak and it's a drag to have to be around them. Not a warrior amongst them. That's why I spend so much time in the gym. I like being around people who are going for some pain. When I work out I don't have to listen to the bullshit and I don't have to deal with weak people. I can get off on myself and work out hard and not have apologize for the way I am. I fucking hate having to explain myself to people. I hate having to answer all these questions and be nice all the time. In the gym you go and slam the iron and everything makes sense. You pick shit up and you put it down and that's all there is to it. It's not an intellectual pursuit. It's pure animal and I can live with that.

In a small room a man sits silently and tries to forget himself and all the things that have happened in his life. He ceased being outraged at how quickly life turned on him and left him alone and broken. At first it was incredible, every day felt like crawling out of a car wreck and staggering

through the smoke past a small group of strange onlookers.

He lost touch with people immediately. At times he couldn't understand what they were saying even though they were right in front of him. It all changed on him so fast he thought that he had been transported to a different planet. Days went by like dreams. People would call and he would ask them not to call again and he meant it. He would listen as the words came out of his mouth and it was as if there was someone else living inside him saying these things. It was a relief that they stopped though. He found that talking to them only made things worse, made him more aware that he was alive. In the darkness of his room, if he sat still and concentrated only on the darkness sometimes he would forget himself.

Time went by and they stopped calling, they stopped writing. He didn't notice, all he could think about was the huge abyss inside him that was the color of the total absence of light. Soon he found himself inside this black void. He had become consumed. It was overwhelming.

◄►-◄►-◄►

The sun is setting on 9-12-92
Gold Coast Australia
On the bank of an inlet
The blue Pacific to my right
Around this time
No matter where I am
The desperation closes in
And a scream lodges itself
Like a bullet
Caught in my spine

◄►-◄►-◄►

I am a broken man
Washed ashore in humanity's
Low tide
Dislocated
I feel no kinship with humans
I do my best
To forget myself

◄►-◄►-◄►

I know nothing else
Florescent bulb overhead
A few hours until show time

The opening band's boring talk
Seeps through the walls of this room
I always end up in these places
filled with wordless isolation
Even more these days
Sounds of traffic outside
Blends with the talk
The world is out there
I have no place here
I must keep moving
So they don't find out
That I'm dead

❊-❊-❊

Nothing behind the face
I move through cities
Mixing with silence and shadow
I'm too freaked out to remember
What life is like
Without exhaustion and paranoia
Nerved and heavily charged
I go through the hours
Waiting for dreams to start

❊-❊-❊

I have new eyes
They see less than the old ones
But what they see
They see clearly
Too clearly
It's all I see
All I know
I choke on myself
My thoughts are hushed and dull
A new lease of life has been inflicted on me
I stagger
I no longer speak their language
I cannot translate what my eyes see
I am alone at all times

❊-❊-❊

Hollow night
Tonight they sprayed mace

One of them sprayed mace while we were playing
Aren't they a trip?
These fakes
Why do they bother coming
They could just stay home
Shoot themselves in the head
And spare me the drama
You can't get close to humans
Can't like them too much
Can't waste time making sense out of their emotions
All you'll do is waste yourself
Torment yourself with their image
What a cheap high
They'll either get killed
Or they'll spray mace
I don't want friends
I don't want a girlfriend
What a fucked up idea
Could you see me with a girlfriend
I remember once my father ran out of cigars at a restaurant and he
smoked one of my stepmother's cigarettes. He devoured it, the
cigarette looked so small in his mouth. He took it half way to the filter
in a couple of drags like it was nothing. That's me and a girlfriend. A girl
with her arm around a human scream pain machine. Angry when her
name is forgotten a few times, angrier when she threatens to leave and
gets no response at all. Right down to the filter in no time.
What a joke
Knowing what I know
Makes it impossible to live the life I had before
Seeing what I've seen
Makes it impossible
To let it be anything but exactly what it is
A lie
A lie that never stops being true

⋘⋘⋘

I'd rather have their money than their affection
After they spend the night spitting on me
Throwing shit and getting in the way
I look at my skin and see the scars
Cigarette and lighter burns
Chipped teeth
Stitches and concussions

If had a nickel for every piece of someone's spit
I've scraped off myself
I'd buy another planet to live on
I like knowing that I leave the hall
With some of their fucking money
I'm not one of those who thinks
That money can't buy everything
I live in the real world and I know it can
Money can buy any fucking thing you want
I don't live for the stuff
But I'd rather have a dollar
Than your phone number
Or the mouthful of beer that you spit on me
I'd rather have some dough in the bank
Than my mother's fucked up guilt ridden love
Or my father's beer soaked respect
With money
I can buy some room
And some piece of shit to shoot you in the face
If you come in uninvited
I learned early on about getting the fuck out
It's all I wanted
To have a door to shut
I feel the scars on my skin and understand
That I can't depend on you for anything
But potential harm
I'd rather have money
Than any fucking thing you got
Friendship doesn't mean shit to me

◄�►◄►◄►

I was alone in bed with a woman last night
Wondering what the hell I was doing
I wasn't there for any of it
When I came I didn't feel anything
I knew it was time to sleep
I'm just a stupid animal
Affection and attention are wasted upon me
I didn't let on though, she was nice
I am the Hollow Man
It comes in and falls to the bottom
It all falls in and disappears

I am a waste of time
Imagine having sex with a mechanical shark

⊲-⊲-⊲⊳

The power of depression is undeniable
When I'm in its grip
I don't remember ever feeling any other way
It coils around my body and holds
The room turns into a suspension cell
Outside the neon roars and people walk at high speed
In here nothing moves
All thoughts are instruments of torture right now
I fell asleep an hour ago
I woke up thinking about my friend
I cannot shake the hounds of grief and guilt
They show their teeth and jump at my throat
I hear their jaws snap as they pass
I don't open myself to others anymore
These nights are all mine
The endless replay of events
Wishing I could tell one of these humans
That I'm sorry
I'm so sorry

⊲-⊲-⊲⊳

I see pictures of myself before my friend was shot
I try to see if there's anything different about the face
Nothing
No knowledge of what was to come
Today I wanted to crawl inside one
Live in a time when I didn't know what I do now
I don't mean to be selfish
It's that I got left behind
I'm alone on the planet
And I have to figure out
What to do with the remaining time

⊲-⊲-⊲⊳

I'm dead
Don't bother
I don't care about what you thought

About what I did
Dead people see through you
I watch you on the dance floor
I listen to the shit you insist on saying to each other
I don't wonder
I don't dream
I don't know anything
I am the Death Star

◁-◁-◁▷

You have to watch out for people
I have found that they will fuck you up
If I stood too still
I wouldn't be here now
The world can fill you full of Death
Imagine a man
Living in a dangerous city
And not wanting to leave
Because he's afraid of losing his edge

◁-◁-◁▷

You were really hoping I would want to fuck you
It was painful to watch
You kept trying to keep me talking to you
There's only one thing worse than a desperate man...

◁-◁-◁▷

Her mouth is a soft explosion of roses
A burst of raw animal definition
For a few moments I was mortal

◁-◁-◁▷

Only an idiot would test his blood in the streets
There's better things to do
Than die begging for your life
There's better things to do
Than searching for a cheap ending
The night holds a knife to your throat
Stand to one side of the window
Listen to the extras in their cars
Only a fool would want to prove himself out there

◁-◁-◁▷

I am a prisoner chained to myself
I don't know what I've done
Bars will scar the windows
Of every room I will live in for the rest of my life
There's no reason I can find for all this pain
Here in solitary I can't see
I wonder if the jailer is me
In this blackout cell
I crouch paralyzed
Stricken by my own horror

⊲⊳-⊲⊳-⊲⊳

Hollowood: In the first perfect scene she finds him staring at the ground with his hands tightened into fists. She takes his face into her hands and kisses him. He takes his eyes up from the ground and looks into her's. She asks him what is the matter. Somehow he is able to tell her just what the matter is.

Life falls flat when you lean too hard upon it. They should have put up warning signs on all the bus stop signs that life is hazardous to your health. So much time spent suppressing screams that have no origin that you can find. You are continually ripped apart and slammed back together. Look at them look at you. Extras, all of them extras.

It is a small miracle. She holds him and he feels himself melting into her. He imagines their collarbones fusing together. He feels hot tears on his face. He is at once ashamed. She tells him that it's alright and he feels what she says. The screams of the beast inside him fade to nothing as the two of them stand motionlessly in the semi dark room. They are the only two people in the big lonely world that matter.

I walk by the man. He pulls out a broken boom box out of a paper bag and shows it to me like I'm supposed to want to buy it. Instead of saying no thanks, I attack him for no apparent reason. That's how he sees it at least. I hit him in the face as hard as I can and when he falls to the ground I kick him in the head several times and then run away. Attack, attack. I no longer watch out for those filthy fuckers on the street and they can see it in my eyes that I am hoping that they'll start some shit so I can swarm them without words, pure action. Pure violence. I am someone that they have to look out for. If they have a gun they'll never get a chance to use it. It will be too far up their ass.

The man to the woman in the dream: If I could find you I would love you forever. If I could find you I would do anything for you. Nothing would be beyond me. This world wounds me and I have lost words, I have lost everything except the ability to feel and deliver pain.

When it ends, it ends and the pigs come and stand around your body and talk that mindless pig bullshit. If you shot the brains out of a pig, rats wouldn't even eat them. I think that humiliation will be unavoidable at this point. I would transcend with you but my feet are nailed to the concrete and I wouldn't go anywhere without my hammer.

<e~e~e>

Trick or treat: I can only write this behind a locked door for fear of the world coming down on top of my head. I was at a Wal Mart in Joplin Missouri. I was standing in line with some shaving cream. All around me Halloween displays were up and Halloween candy was everywhere. I stood in a long line with all kinds of people. Most of them were holding bags of candy. Men coming home from work, tired eyed with slightly bent backs dressed in heavy clothing, standing in line with nothing in their hand but a bag of candy to give to little kids. I didn't think they did that anymore. I tried to imagine kids going door to door where I live. No way. Standing in line with the humans and their candy it made me feel like I came from a different planet full of bullet casings and dried blood. I am fucked up and sentimental I know. I remember how much I used to look forward to Halloween. 24 hours later I was at a hotel near the Greyhound station where drug dealers were working the parking lot. Some things are over with, really over with. Out.

<e~e~e>

I have spent so much of my life trying to get away
Throwing weight over the side of the basket
So the balloon could rise higher faster and escape
So real life could be lived before Death sets in
And slows everything down
In seemingly accidental moments of clarity
I have thought that I had seen what it was
That I was trying to get away from
But when I tried to level the foe
I found myself on the move again
I can't stop moving

<e~e~e>

I will get away from the cameras and the questions
I will find my brain again
And when I do I'll try my best to handle it

<e~e~e>

When I fuck I feel like a rapist
I equate my sexual desire with pornography

I see sex and violence as the same thing
I would never hurt anyone in a sexual situation
I look at women and feel disgusting
Like some fucked up animal
I am so far from humanity
If a woman is attracted to me
I think she's fucked up
Some one should straighten her out
I shake so many hands
The idea of touch makes me sick
I never set out to be so fucked up
But I ended up fucked up

◄►-◄►-◄►

Movieline magazine asked me if any movies had influenced my work
at all. I faxed them this: It's easy to see from even the most casual glance
over my total work span that Sylvester Stallone's staggering work in
Over the Top and Oscar, and not to mention Rhinestone, has had an
immense and embarrassingly overshadowing effect on my life and my
art. It's hard for me to admit all of this but you know, it feels good to
come right and say it. I agree with Sly when he said that if Mel Gibson
could do Shakespeare, so could he. To be or.............. line!

◄►-◄►-◄►

I fuck as an after thought
Like when I eat too much
An excess thought
A stock reflex

◄►-◄►-◄►

You always end up
Where all those bent, hit, bashed up people end up
Where ever the hell that is tonight
You'll be there
Even though you can't see me
I'll be there too
It's unbelievable how easy it is to end up there
Wherever the hell that is tonight
Do you know the times when you catch yourself falling?
Like when you freak out for a fraction of a second
You quickly recover and it's then
You realize how fucked up you are
All of a sudden it all makes sense

It's beyond words
It makes you look down at the floor for a long time
It's where you end up
At that moment you think that you need someone
Right then
Someone's eyes to somehow make it make sense
Make what make sense?
I don't know
That's the part where the holes get pounded into the walls
And life gets lived

❖❖❖

I went out tonight to feed
It's really turned into something out there
I mean you really have to watch your ass
Hard neon reflector boys manning the corners
Blocking the sidewalk silently begging confrontation
I walk around and think about how good it would be to
And how I would never be able to
In the hamburger place they sit and stare
Unknowing soldiers with corn row hair
Staring under the florescent light
Outside the streets mercilessly scream
Everything out there is screaming
A whore gets into the car and they park in front of Thrifty's
All I do is watch my ass around here
I immediately size up any males coming towards me
Look for the one good shot
Get ready to take it
Walk on by
You stupid mortal easy to kill motherfucker
Walk on by

❖❖❖

Ian sent me a clipping from a newspaper
Mr Klinger
My high school English teacher had died last week
November 13 1992
I was in Orlando and didn't feel a thing
The paper said liver cancer
Sometimes he would call me at night
From the student dorm where he lived

He would always be drunk
I never told any of the other students
I never told anyone
I used to think of how bad it would be if the headmaster knew
Mr Klinger would get kicked out of there fast
He would be disgraced
I think he was the loneliest person I ever knew
Years after I graduated
I thought of contacting him
To tell him that I still remembered the things he taught me
He was so lonely
It was pathetic
I used to sit in class and wonder if anyone else saw it
You could see the pulling sadness in his eyes
I used to imagine him riding the school bus back to the dorm
Weekends drinking himself into a stupor
Thoughts of suicide and young boys
He taught there 22 years
It was his life
Some life
He was one of the only people in the whole place who liked me
He left no relatives
Not even me

◄►◄►◄►

Inert: Now the touring is over for the year. I'm sitting in a chair in my room and it's late and I'm tired but not the kind of tired that I like. It's not the exhaustion derived from a gig. I worked out hard tonight with the Iron but without the music I don't know. I really missed not playing tonight. The next few days will be hard to deal with because I have to talk to people. It takes me days to decompress and regain the ability to act human and not blow my fuse with them. I feel alien when I come back from the road. I have nothing that I can explain to them and I can't fake my discomfort. I feel like a weakling when I'm not on tour, I will have to deal with that as well. I just feel useless when I'm not out there. If I told that to someone they wouldn't know what the hell I was talking about. There's nowhere I can go with these feelings so I sit in the room and wait for the pressure to get to a manageable level. It's times like these where I wish I could open up to a woman and be with her. I imagine scenes where I am talking to a woman and I feel good and she somehow says things that make me not feel like exploding. Someone who could remove the distance I feel. It will never happen. I try to

imagine opening myself up like that I know there's no way. Everything
I do is geared for confrontation. When you tell someone that you work
at extending your threshold of pain they look at you like you're crazy.
Of course it sounds nuts to them. But what do they know about a reality
different than theirs? Nothing, they'll never know. I'm over here and
they're over there. When I try to hang out in their world it only brings
me confusion and pain. My struggle is internal. When it comes out in
their world it comes out violently and loudly. I isolate myself further
with every breath I take. It must be what I want. It's evolution in a
lifetime. Between tours I'm not alive. I am inert and I fall prey to all the
bullshit. My life is only of use when I'm moving. Everything I do is
geared for that world. When I'm here they all turn against me. My
strength seems to attack me. To be able to keep a clear head I avoid
them and their gatherings. Avoid the parties and the endless talk that
they never get tired of. I must stay lean and hungry at all times.
Otherwise all is lost.

⋘⋙

Hack up the life and kick it from door to door
Didn't know that anyone would notice
Words fail me
Turn on me
Kick me in the mouth
I listen to the words of others
They take me hostage
I read their words
They shove me around
I wonder what life would be like
Without language
Would you still love?
Would you do anything that wasn't a pure survival move?
No smooth talkers taking the women away
From the big dick
Loud mouthed thick skull/muscle bulls
Could you think without words?
Just feel the basics?
Hunger, cold, fear, desire
I know enough to know that I know
Too much about that which matters
To people I don't know
And too little about what matters to me
They take that away from you at birth
They try to sell you their fucked up version

Why not
Their parents did it to them
And now it's their turn
I talk like he does
Same meter, tone and timber
It gets worse with age
Almost everything does

⬦-⬦-⬦

I can't get away from myself
I have tried to crawl out of here several times
I always come crawling back
Staring at the closet with Joe's stuff still in it
I have convinced myself
That the closet smells like his Death
Tonight I opened the door and the smell came out
Usually it makes me cold
Tonight it wrapped around me like a damp blanket
It felt ok
Like when I made friends
With the darkness of the basement
When my stepbrother used to lock me in
You just breathe in and know that this is it
It's your own little tragedy
A little closet full of shame
I ran all this year
Only to come back to this little room
To think about the same things that I always think about
I wonder if I'll ever do anything with my life
Except try to make it sorry it had the bad luck to fall into me

⬦-⬦-⬦

Have you ever outsmarted yourself too many times to where you can
no longer pull the wool over your eyes when you really need to? Like
when you're alone and you're thinking about someone else because it
makes you feel not so all alone and your thoughts turn to some kind of
feeling if closeness with this person. You know how it is, you're alone
in the safety of the number one. No one can read your thoughts. So no
matter how embarrassing they are, no matter if it's stuff that you could
never tell anyone for fear of them laughing in your face or being
eternally uncomfortable in the same room with you, you really let
yourself go. It's those thoughts that can really save you from one of
those severe drops into hard slamming depression. The kind that

doesn't fool around. The depression that makes you think you're some kind of diabolical genius because you could come up with something that you could inflict upon yourself that is totally and perfectly devastating. Sometimes the depression is so bad that you think that some government agency beamed it into your head because you would never level something that horrible at yourself. So have you ever gotten to the point to where you want to pull yourself out of the teeth of loneliness and you try to think of a perfect situation with one of those people out there and you are unable to do it? You keep looking at the wall and nothing happens. You just keep seeing the reality mixed with the sounds of traffic and the smell of your own skin. You see too clearly and you wish that you could soften the focus a bit so you could get a break. Yea it happens to me too. Like right now. I swear this room is the loneliest one on the planet. I don't know where you are or what you're going through but you're not here now and I'm all I've got in here and I can't go walking around my neighborhood at this time of night because the gangsters selling the drugs down the street make me freak out. So tonight I'm stuck in here looking out through the bars on my windows. Trying to think of nothing because tonight it all makes too much sense. I think right now all I can do is wait it out until I wear myself down. It's called sleep. I call it finally giving in. Sometimes it's good to get beaten.

<t><t><t>

I am glad to be alone in this room but at the same time I am not. I am relieved that there will be no one in this box with me to accidentally hear something horrible come out of my mouth. I get angry at how far I have withdrawn. I know how much of a monster I am and it keeps me to myself. I find my mouth unable to open to answer questions they ask now. I have trouble understanding what people are saying to me these days. They ask me things or tell me something and I'll just stand there and look at them and not know what to say. I find it hard to believe that they're even talking to me. I always think they're talking to some living person in my immediate proximity. I don't cry anymore or care about most things that I used to. I have become detached and withdrawn from the human experience. I wonder if they know that I'm stuffed with sawdust.

<t><t><t>

Alone in this room in Hollywood
I am afraid
I am afraid of falling apart
I am afraid of doing what I want to do

I want to be able to open myself up to a woman
Just one woman in a room
Without projecting all my pain onto that woman
Without lying
But I am afraid
I am afraid of unraveling and falling to pieces
And not being able to get up again
After a lot of years I have grown used to pain
I want to get rid of it but I know it's what makes me
When I'm cold I build fires and then don't come near them
I'm afraid of getting too warm
I harbor great conflict inside myself
I contradict myself constantly
I am addicted to pain
It is the only thing that ever told me the truth
The only thing that ever protected me
The only thing that ever forced me to move forward and survive
That's as honest as I can be right now

⬦-⬦-⬦

Makoto: I will be awake for several hours. It's as if I'm plagued. I tried to get to sleep early tonight to try to duck under the wave of depression that I knew was coming. I didn't make it. I was overcome with an overwhelming surge of depression. Power depressions, anxiety monster blues, I don't know what to call them. It got me out of bed. Here I am. Freaked out and alone.

It's early for me, only 12:50 a.m. I have been staying up until near 5 every morning writing, tying to get it out of me. Tonight I thought it was going to be different.

So now what do I do with myself? I know what I'll do. I'll be honest. The main thoughts that attack me in these bouts of depression are those of deep and terrible loneliness. During other times I can shrug off the idea of loneliness by being busy or by making tough jokes. I feel close to no one on the planet.

I have these thoughts of falling endlessly through blackness. Long trudges through deserts of night. Cold, poorly lit rooms. Arguments. The sound of my mother and father's voices. The smell of my father's car. The fear. People recognize me where I go almost every day now. I feel vulnerable all the time, it gets to me. I wonder about their lives as they stare blankly in recognition. What a strange disease life is. It gets thrust upon you and you have to deal with it as best you can. You are trained to have answers for everything and you're told you are to be able to fix yourself up when you break down. When you don't have the answers, you catch a lot of flack, or worse, you have to listen to someone else, you risk having to trust them. It would seem that everything can be explained. But it can't. Worse thing to do is walk through life thinking it owes you something. It doesn't even owe you an explanation, not even your parents can give you one. Life doesn't even owe you life, all it owes you is Death.

I know that no amount of talking will make it any better. I've tried being with women. I've tried hanging out, spilling my guts with great abandon and I felt like a damn fool. I walked away feeling like some kind of criminal. I thought that would be the answer but it never is. When I'm with them it's even worse. When they touch me I feel like I'm choking. All I want to do is be alone. When I am alone for too long I start to wonder what it would be like to be able to be with someone else that didn't make me want to run away. I start to lie to myself and invent realities in the presence of others. They try to get me to talk and I can't find the right words. I can't find words to describe the abyss inside me. Words ambush me when they come out of my mouth. I know of nothing that makes it better except working at the ridiculous pace that I do. I know enough to know that it's nothing but escape. I don't see anything real to confront. When you confront the Abyss you play yourself and lose.

So what do I do with this loneliness, this hole. I don't know. I feel like a marked man. Doomed to walk and have this gaping wound no one can see. The thing that makes me so frustrated is that I can't figure out what the fuck is wrong with me. The only thing I can think of is loneliness. But if that's what it is then what am I lonely for? What part of me is missing?

I have always kept moving. Thousands of miles and I have made friends through the years. Somehow motion keeps me breathing. I fear these still nights in the same room. I sleep better in hotels. It's a room I'm in because I'm on the move. I can deal with that much. The only way I have been able to get through life without spending all my time freaking out and hurting myself is movement and music. The fury of the music matches what I feel and I have a temporary world that I can exist in for two hours a day. Spending years on the road in search of this relief is beyond the comprehension of many. They ask me how I do it. I have no answer to that one. I amazed to survive sleep. Sleep is the state that I fear most. Insomnia and paranoia are two of my constant traveling companions. The road is the only thing I have found that keeps all the parts from flying off. It keeps the brains in my head. The idea of standing still for too long freaks me out. I wonder if I'm addicted to exhaustion.

I am afraid of losing control and killing myself or killing someone else. It's fucked up to say but I have noticed that all the stories I have read about serial killers say that they were terribly alienated from people, most all of them were loners. I was reading about the man who ripped up all those boys in Milwaukee. He was a study in depression and alienation. I feel some kind of affinity with people like that. I'm not trying to come off like I'm all shocking and shit. I'm not trying to say that I want to go kill a bunch of people tonight but I can dig the heavy choke of not being able to get along with people and having to do something to separate yourself from them all. When the man received his sentence and stood up in front of the parents and relatives of the boys that he had killed he told them all that he was terribly sorry. I believe him.

I can understand a drifter who wanders through America and kills men and women because he's lonely. He strangles a man that picked him up hitchhiking. He never even asked the driver's name. He throws the body off a cliff without feeling anything but deep and momentary relief. Crying and cursing, wishing the body was still there to kick and embrace because life is so fucked up and full of holes it makes you want to skin yourself alive. He screams through his tears and stomps the ground because he knows it will never be enough. It just makes him want to kill more. He is more lonely than he can remember. He gets in the man's car and drives off into the night. Sometime in the next 72 hours he kills again. His loneliness is an inferno.

Sometimes the only way to see any light is to get away from everyone and wait. That's all I can do sometimes, just wait it out. Keep to myself, tell no one. Tell anyone that asks me how I'm doing that I'm fine. Say as little as possible. Try not to have to explain the unexplainable. You wait for the sun to turn the sky that cold grey color and you think that it might be safe to finally close your eyes and hope that you won't dream.

In the middle of these silent nights I am alive in a small lit box somewhere on the planet. Trying to understand this deep pain that leaves me confused and scattered. Don't tell anyone.

⊲⊳-⊲⊳-⊲⊳

Saturday night in this room. The sounds of traffic have slowed down to near silence now that the clubs have closed. My neighborhood used to be dirty and full of rock and rollers with fake hair. It was a drag but not dangerous. Now the corners have Crips that have come north from south central to sell drugs. You can't go anywhere without seeing those guys. In the room, against a wall, sit boxes of mail. Talking tape letter from a manic depressive, pictures sent by models with their phone numbers and "use it xxoo!!!" written at the bottom, faxes from famous rockstars, letters from convicts doing several years and youths in correctional facilities waiting to be released in the spring. Manuscripts, magazines, cards and hundreds of letters. In this hole I sit like a sniper without the gun. Bars on my windows, locks on the door. No one knows my street address. The phone doesn't ring, nothing moves. I am unreachable, untouchable, unknown. It is somehow a relief. I have not used my voice for hours. I have sat in this room for a long time tonight just staring and thinking. The air in the room is filled with the sound of the Arkestra's Interplanetary Music and the heater. No one can help you. No one can heal your wounds. I think you get better by keeping moving and learning to take the pain. My desperation is silent and moves to me with precision. I have boxes of pictures of myself. On the floor are several crates of tapes I'm on containing recordings of music and speaking dates. Hundreds of hours of documentation of pounding blood into wood floors. In the closet is more than a decade of press articles about me from all over the world. Interviews, reviews, boxes stacked one on top of the other. Against another wall are crates of work in progress, notes, manuscripts, outlines. In piles are things left from tours that have been completed during the year. Receipts, foreign money, hotel stationery. On the door knob tour laminates hang like discarded pages of history. Then there's the dead people. In a coffee cup, leaves stained with the blood of a guy I knew who was shot to Death by a policeman last summer. In an old Rolaids container a piece of brain wrapped in tin foil from a woman who shot herself in the head with a shotgun in Nebraska 8 years ago. A plastic container of dirt with parts of my best friend's head sits in the closet next to his telephone. There's letters from dead people, a ring a girl gave to me that her dying brother wanted me to have. So the room is filled with the forgotten, the past and the dead. I sleep in it, work in it and stare at its walls until early hours of the morning. I don't know anyone and no one knows me. When I am not on the road I am here. When I am here I don't know what to do with myself except work and sleep. Sometimes I don't leave the place for days. I don't know how to deal with people. I avoid them by spending most of my time traveling and onstage. It's not the way anyone should end up.

❊—❊—❊

Sunday night in this room. I did something that I should not have. A guy I tour with was here tonight. He's from another country. I asked him if he wanted to see a documentary on LA street gangs. He said yes so I played it. I hadn't seen it since Joe and I used to watch it a long time ago. It played itself much differently tonight. When the part came where these people were walking by a body at a funeral and the face of the corpse was shown, it had the same unmoving dead look as when I saw Joe in that room nearly a year ago. Watching the show brought a lot of the horror from that time back to me. Now I'm alone in the room dealing with it. Now I'm back in that same mortal bag again. It's easy for the fuckers to take it away from you. You can have a good enough life and then some piece of shit stranger can take it all away. The guy who killed Joe is out there somewhere tonight. He's breathing out in the world somewhere tonight, right now. Like me in this room. I feel like calling somebody but I don't know anyone to call. I wouldn't call anyone even if I did know anyone I felt comfortable talking to. You can say that you have cut yourself off from people and see it as a setback but that's only if you put a lot of value in having people around that you can dump on. If you're like me and know for sure that you're really alone in the world then thoughts like these are only fleeting. They get rapidly ripped apart by the reality that rules the domain of you mind. I sit here with one small light on. In semi darkness I think about my friend. In a few days it will be a year since his Death. I remember when it was a week. I sat behind the desk of the office space I was living in and I was amazed at how unreal the entire week had been. I kept expecting to wake up from it like a dream. Now it's almost a year. 5 days away. Actually 4 days and some hours to go. I think about it every day now. I thought I had climbed a few steps out of the hole that I have spent most of the year in but now I find myself back down in it. In the last 12 months I have distanced myself from people. I will distance myself farther away from them as the years go on. I have had enough of them and their bullshit. You can call me anything you like. A walking contradiction, a bastard, a hypocrite. I am all those things and every other thing that you can think of. Now that we all know everything then there's nothing to complain about. All I know is that sometimes it's hard to leave this room knowing that there's people out there. I have no safety net because I don't lie. All that can happen to me is that I will die somehow. I've been through worse. I'm going through worse right now. The worst part about it is that I'm alive enough to be aware of everything around me. It's hard to give a fuck about a lot of things. Humanity, human values, the things they say. I walk in shadows. Nothing really gets to me anymore.

❦❦❦

If I allowed myself to care about you
I would hang myself up again
Like I have done so many times before

When I lost my self control
I would like to think that I could control myself at all times
But it just isn't true
I catch myself slipping all the time
I laugh when I caught myself tonight
Wondering if you were going to call me
Like you said you would
When the clock went past two a.m. and you hadn't called
I knew I was in one of those situations
Where I could not attach myself to it
Or let it drag me down
So I let it go
And now I see that I did the right thing
By not giving a fuck about you and your life
What was I thinking anyway?
I'm a lot of terrible things
But at least I'm not a sucker anymore

⌁⌁⌁

I learned about loss by losing: It's getting close now. In a few days it will be a year since Joe died. I am alone in a room in the middle of Los Angeles. It's past midnight. I am so ashamed. I don't know why but I am. I am embarrassed at how at this moment I have things that I want to write but I am too ashamed to. All I know is there's situations where you can lose parts of yourself and the hole the absence creates can never be filled. That's what we do instinctively. We seek to fill the holes, shove plaster into the cracks. We seek to replace what has been lost with something else. Something that resembles what is gone or replaces the way the departed thing made us feel. You know, like how someone replaces heroin with methadone. It's one of the ways we resolve the reality of loss. Well, I've been trying to replace what cannot replace and all my human tendencies are turning on me and tearing me up. Some losses you can't make up for. You just have to get on with it. I know this. I didn't before but I learned it by getting dragged through the last three hundred and sixty some nights. I know I am not capable of telling anyone what I feel and what fury and anguish courses through my veins during almost every waking moment. Sometimes I feel like I am suffocating inside my skin, like I should be ripping out of it. If I ripped out of my skin, where the hell would I go. Right. I know that I just have to keep walking the trail. I hope my fury won't turn my bones to ash, even if it does, it won't change a thing.

I remember this one time I had my arms around her and I was thinking to myself that I would never let anyone hurt her ever. I could feel her chest against mine and her arms around me, holding on. To me. At that moment her arms were holding onto no one or nothing else on the planet except me. It seemed like the most perfect moment I had ever experienced. I've never felt that way with anyone else. I still think about her and I wonder where she is. I know that no one will ever love her as much as I do. It's been years but still I miss her so much. I think about her every day. After you leave messages and write letters and hear nothing back you finally figure out the fact that she obviously doesn't want to hear from you so you come to the conclusion that you have to move on up the trail and take it as it comes. I can sit in this room and think about her all I want but it won't change a thing.

❊-❊-❊

I can't let too much show at once: I have to be careful when I walk down the streets in this neighborhood at night. I don't want the piece of shit drug dealers and scumbags to know that I only fear the fact that they might be packing a gun and that I could kill them with my bare hands and think nothing of it. When I see them look at me like I'm prey I wonder if they see it in my eyes that I know who the prey really is. That I could physically break their necks and jaw bones and there wouldn't be anything they could do about short of running for their lives. I am barely able to contain myself when they look at me on La Brea Ave. I feel an overwhelming urge to attack them savagely. Bite pieces of their faces off. I cover it well. I can't let them see too much. I hide my eyes from them on purpose. I don't want to get shot by a piece of shit. It's too easy these days. So many weak pieces of flesh out there.

❊-❊-❊

Alive inside my atomic super heavy loaded brain tonight. She lives off the guy and fucks him so she can keep the cash flow going. He knows it too but he tries to forget it. It's easy to forget when he's with her. When she calls his name in a public place or puts her hand on his arm. He thinks to himself that she really likes him. He allows himself to believe that he belongs to her. It makes him feel good about getting up in the morning. In fact the more she treats him like dirt, the more it keeps him holding on. He believes. He needs it so bad. All she talks about with her friends besides the bills she runs up when she takes his credit cards shopping is all the guys she wants to fuck.

I want to hide from all of them, they make me sick. My atomic idea is active and flashing. They will never take me down like they take down all the others. They'll never get that close. One thing my parents taught me from making me sick to my guts at the thought of being alive was to reject them before they get too close. Before they can divorce you or scream into the phone while the child watches silently and stupidly from across the room. Fuck him up and scar him for life. Fuck me up and teach me what I need to know. Break my bones and let my scar tissue mind strengthen. Show me the power of the ability to maintain distance and take the pain year after year, beating after beating. They'll take bullets to your head, they'll spend your money and watch your pain and grow numb. They'll become pigs and arrest you. They'll murder the only life that matters and leave you in a cell of your own for the rest of your life to live the horror over and over again. You can do it too, you can grow old and never live once. And you can take it too, I know you can. I have proof. Some can fuck people up and others can be fucked up and take it. Take it over and over. You get good at taking the beating.

He sits in a house because he can. He doesn't know what else to do. She's weak and it makes him feel important from time to time. He learned how to be one that carries the weak from getting injections of guilt early on. Don't try talking to me because I'll only laugh in your face and if you get too close I'll mutilate you and the only thing that will save you is a gun or a pig. I'll show you rejection. I'll show you things that you can understand. I know how to threaten and ruin life because mine is threatened and ruined every day and I've learned by punishing myself how to turn it around and put it in any direction I want. I don't feel guilt, remorse, none of it. I used to but I overcame it by getting it shoved up my ass.

<a>-<a>-<a>

The man said to the Storm: When life hands you a lemon you can squeeze it and make lemonade. The Storm said to the man: Some squeeze lemons and all they get is blood. They close their hand and the hand goes away and all they get for such troubled magic is a fist. There are some people you can't reason with because they aren't hung up in the wires like you are. The wires couldn't hold them and they fell through. They know that nothing will hold them and they never trust anything completely again. All they have to do is fall once and faith goes out the window. All they have to do is have a brief visit from pure animal panic and true horror and they come all the way back. They try to get back and part of them does get back but a large part gets stuck way back there with the fear and the horror. They see things differently. Their eyes aren't clouded like yours are and they can take one look at you and they can tell that you can't see it. That's why some people pick a rose off the bush and get a rose and others pick a rose off the bush and get a knife.

<a>-<a>-<a>

I'm in my box off Hollywood Blvd. In less than two hours it will be a year since Joe was killed. In the last couple of hours some strange things have tripped me out. I went to the store to get some food. I walked in and heard someone call my name out. I turned around and looked. It was a guy that was in a lot of Joe's video footage Modi and I had been looking at yesterday. Ron Frasca. I had never met him. I talked to him for a while. A guy with my sun tattoo painted on the back of his leather jacket walked by and watched us for second. After a few minutes I had been spotted and people were starting to come over to me. I told Ron that I would contact him later. I got my food and left.

I was almost back to the box. It was a hard walk back because no one had explained to Ron what exactly happened and I did in the store so I was thinking about it as I walked up the hill. I turned the corner and right in front of me was the Rat Sound truck parked outside a local club. The big Black Flag logo looking right at me. Joe and rode in that truck so many hours it's not even funny. I stared at the door on the driver's side and thought about how Joe had opened that door so many times and now the same door is just sitting out there on Hollywood Blvd.

Joe's father took out some big back page ad in Variety magazine. He got a few facts wrong and thanked all his AA buddies. He had some of that typical full of shit sentiment "what price life?" Whoa. I wonder why he didn't mention me. I know he doesn't like me at all. Maybe it's because I was more tuned into his son than he was. The most humorous part was his spelling of the word "homicide" as "homocide". Anyone can make that mistake right? It's fitting that Mr Cole would take out a full page to advertise his grief. Nice picture. Wonder if he'll get any work out of it.

It seems like all the progress that I made getting myself down the road from all the horror of what happened is slipping away tonight. I have been having to keep myself from breaking down a few times today.

What am supposed to feel on this night? Is it really any different than any other night? What is the difference if it's a year or a week. I guess I have a thing with years because of all the tours. I seem to take things a year at a time as far as measuring things.

⟨⟨⟨

Moving the shit: I'm taking all the boxes out of the attic. Loading through a small hole and down a small ladder and through Joe's room and through the front door, over Joe's blood and all the flies and into the truck. Joe's small room is filled with his parents and their brothers and sisters and assorted relatives. Most of them I have never met. I feel like I am in a room full of strangers talking about someone that I know. The person they are talking about and the one that I know are two distinctly different people. They are dividing his possessions, going through boxes and pulling out pictures. I show them how he had all the letters he ever got all separated into envelopes with the name of the sender on the outside. I give them out to all the people that had one. They remark at how organized he was. I think to myself how I taught Joe to organize all of his stuff so he could find things whenever he needed to. As I'm distributing the assorted envelopes of mail I notice how closely he had his things organized just the way I do. I am loading things out of the attic and I'm trying not to bump into all these people as I move box after box. I have to step over Joe's dad who is now sitting on the front steps. Sorry Mr. Cole, someone got killed here and we're moving all the stuff out as quick as we can. I have to step around him, over the blood and into the truck. I make trip after trip. The family has now parted into two factions. Joe's father only has a friend talk to the other side and to me. The mother talks to me. I am the go between for the mother and father. I am keeping busy moving all the things in the house on no sleep and no food and only the fact that a few hours ago I was walking with this guy down the same sidewalk and two guys with guns came out of the bushes and now Joe is dead and last time I ever saw him alive was when he was face down on the sidewalk with a gun at the back of his head. I remember the things I was thinking at the time. I remember looking down at him and thinking how scared he must be. I felt lucky, the guy on me only made me get on my knees.

I'm moving box after box. The neighborhood is spitting me out. It killed my best friend and now it's making me get the hell out. I look at all the people across the street watching me load box after box into the truck. Later they would fill up three detective's notebooks telling about what a bad person I was and how Joe and I bought drugs and used the local hookers. Hold on, the phone is ringing.

11:43 Don calls and we talk for about eight minutes and I tell him about the things that happened at the store and about seeing the Rat truck. He thinks they're good signs. He says he's been sitting in his place in SF thinking about what Joe and I were doing at this time a year ago. I guess that we were just finishing a ten mile bike ride on the beach. At this point Joe had about 45 minutes left on the planet and neither of us knew. There was nothing different in the wind at the beach or anything. We didn't know it was coming. Joe's Death is much more important than JFK's. I tell Don that we're in for a long night. I tell him that I'll call him later. Somehow, the fact that it's not 12:30 yet makes me feel good. Like he's still out there somehow. I know what it is though, it's the same form of denial as when I didn't sleep for a long time right after it happened thinking that if somehow I stayed up, there was a chance that he might not be dead.

These pieces of shit were kicking me out of their fucked up neighborhood. They stared at me blankly as I loaded in the boxes. I looked at them and tried to make them look away but they just stared seeming neither interested nor bored. Excuse me Mr. Cole, I have to move these boxes out of the house because someone got murdered here last night and I can't stay. Don't bother to help or anything, just keep talking like you're reading off a script. Only this time it's real.

I am the go between and as the days pass I have to be put through the ups and downs of a family that I don't want to know. That was a year ago.

Joe has a few minutes left here. I wonder if there's anything special I should be doing. Do I dare open the closet and look at the plastic container that holds dirt with his blood. Will his phone that sits next to it ring. We were in the market right now. Getting some food before we were going to watch a movie back at the house. We are probably right near the checkout now. He couldn't afford juice so I was buying some for him. He had a bag of popcorn and that was it. I remember I ate it the next day as I was unloading the truck into the storage place realizing that I had not eaten all day and was almost falling over.

For a few weeks I would go to the storage place and sit inside the room full of boxes of my old life. I felt like I was in the basement of some huge government building looking at pieces recovered from some disaster in history. I stood next to my old life as I silently inspected the boxes piled against the wall.

I remember running. I remember when I hit the back door to pull the door slightly up to get the bolt to turn. I remembered to do that. As I ran across the back yard I looked at the chain link fence thinking how the hell to get over it. Before I had finished the thought I had gone over it and was running east up the alley towards Lincoln.

I think by now Joe's history, gotta be by now, if it's not now it's within a few minutes of right now, It really doesn't matter. His ashes don't think about it. Yesterday I was watching one of his videos of interviews. I randomly pulled one out and the first thing on it was a girl telling Joe about looking at her father's ashes.

It doesn't feel like a year. It feels like I have been frozen in time until tonight. I can remember the event better than what I did yesterday.

I wonder if the guy who killed Joe is thinking of Joe right now. He's gotta be thinking about the fact that it's been a year and he got away with murder in America.

So I'm through the first year. It's my own New Year's party here in my box. It's year one in Colefornia. Nothing's different. Nothing happened. He didn't call the phone, I just looked in at it. It hasn't moved from the place I put it when I called his old number on his birthday and said hello. I don't have the strength to call him now. There's no one to call, he's dead.

Now it's 1:23 a.m. It's bit better now somehow. I think the worst part was going through the walk from the store to the house. Now that it's been almost an hour, I feel like life has come back to normal. I have a feeling that this time every year will have some kind of meaning.

So now I'll just do what I usually do at this time. Write and listen to music. I feel better. It's as if running into Ron was a life time ago.

3:09 p.m.: I fell asleep at some point hours ago and woke up at around noon. I had this bad dream that was good to be able to wake up from. It was me and this girl in a room. I knew that I loved her and I knew that she was going to fuck me up. I knew that I was in a no win situation and I knew that I was pathetic, but for some reason I kept on. I don't remember all of the conversation but I was begging her not to leave me and she was just smiling and talking on the phone and pretending that I wasn't there. After she hung up she told me that the new guy was on his way over and that they were going to be busy and that I shouldn't bother them. In the dream it felt like the world had ended or something. It was good to wake up and find out that I was still here. Can you imagine that, begging a woman not to leave you. I'll put myself in that position. Fuck that. To have to beg. By the end of all of this, I will have mastered myself. That is my goal, to master myself. It's the highest form I can aspire to.

◄►◄►◄►

Sometimes I wish there was someone I could write a letter to
I look at the piles of mail on the floor
They have someone to write to
I bet it's not a bad feeling
To be able to reach out
And believe in your heart that someone will be there
I wish I could believe that too
Isolation shoots me in the knees
Makes it impossible for anyone to believe
That all my intentions
Are good

◄►◄►◄►

The last few days have been silent
I have been choked into forced silence
I don't want to get myself too knotted
I went out there again
I had run out of food
Some guy at the intersection
Waves me over at a red light
Hey how about a signature?
Like I'm supposed to walk across Hollywood Blvd.
And serve it up
Slaves at the money machine
Blood drying on Mecca
The men that live in the cardboard boxes
Move before the club opens
The bouncers have fun kicking them down the stairs
Humanity grows dim in these parts
I don't want to test my speed
With the neon flesh reflector boys
Bullets run faster than my fear
And then there's always the pigs
The box has been good
Day after day, right here after right here
Listening to 1992 shake the bars in front of my windows
Waiting for the year to die
There's no one I miss or think about
Nothing on my mind
Without confrontation I am nothing
But this thing that breathes and waits

◁▷◁▷◁▷

It's hard to be close to one of them after the first time it blows up in your face: I don't let them get too close to me. I have learned that it only leads to heartache and self destruction. People will slow you down all the time. The more you need them the more you'll get fucked up when they do something to you. I got used to people not being dependable. I learned it from my parents. The more friends you have the more you have to miss when they're gone. I light fire to a square block of houses in Hollywood. All the people in the houses are now out in the street holding a few things that they were able to salvage from the fire. They are crying, thinking about all the things that they lost, all the things that took them all those years to get. The local bums stand there and laugh. Their shit got burned up as well, some rags, a pair of shoes, a blanket.

They never had cars and pianos to lose. Nothing devastates them. I don't want to love someone. It puts me in a sucker's position. There I am waiting to get ripped apart. It happened to me a couple of times and to this day I regret ever having made the contact in the first place. I must have been bored or crazy. I keep my distance. I get more done and I don't get played like a fool.

◁◁◁▷

At this point it would just sound like a confession
Some man talking with his eyes glued to the ground
Not knowing what to do with his hands
Barely able to get the words out of his mouth
Never feeling right where he should be anywhere
Only stopping to prove myself for no reason
I'm no fucking musician
I stand next to music and watch it while I scream
When they talk to me
They don't talk to me
From now on it's going to get deeper and more painful
I'm going for the bone
I have no protection left
I am stripped to the truth
Rage, fury and Death
The rest doesn't figure in anymore
I have freed myself from my illusions
Straightened myself out from all the bullshit
I was desperately clinging to
I am not interested in impressing anyone
What a waste of time
I am heading to the Abyss once more
And this time I'm not going to miss

◁◁◁▷

The cartoon version is probably better anyway:
I can see someone looking at me
Saying to his friend:
Let's cut him

◁◁◁▷

Cast iron body suit
Think about a fish
Swimming around near the surface of the water

Swimming weakly and slowly
Pulled slightly off center
Because the leech attached its side
Is filled with blood
Think about your life
Your compromised vision

❀❀❀

Go for the Visa card, the car, the works:
Set him up slow
You might have to put out a little but it's worth it
Talk to him and make him feel good
Make him think that you look up to him
Validate his stupidity
Ask his advice on almost everything
Feign astonishment when he tells his stupid stories
Let him flex worldly knowledge he got
Through all that abuse and violence based experience
Widen your eyes in amazement
Play him like a deck of cards
You got him where you want him right?
Because he's stupid, right?
Because he wants the same thing they all want right?
Who cares about loneliness and pain
You got your place in the sun
He's breathing easy
You hate him so much now you can barely stand it
Ok, quickly now
Take him down

❀❀❀

Listen to the lines as they fall out of her mouth
How many times have you heard this
You wish she could be a little more creative
You need what you need
Life is short
So you say the things you should
Pretend to eat the bait on the hook
Swell up with false bravado
Put on a good show
Run a good con on the con artist
Take it to the limit

I mean really take it to the limit
Get what you need
Malice makes it even better
Then start laughing as you turn your real face to her
Throw a few crumpled bills at her face
And tell her not to call you again
Fuck these people
Some of them
Beg to be ruined

◄►◄►◄►

Night time in the box
Same thing always happens
I'm right about to fall asleep
I start thinking about Joe
Standing paralyzed in the living room
Hands in the air
A bag of food on the floor
Thinking desperately what to do
If we go to the back room we're dead
What can I give them
All of this in the space of a few seconds
Listening to the gunshots behind me
My eyes snap open
I'm awake and alone in the world
It's dark and it's 1992
I close my eyes and I'm in the room with Joe's body
He doesn't move
I've never seen anything in the world so still
I look at the hole in the left side of his face
Mortician's clay packed into the hole
Dotted with ink to resemble beard stubble
Straightening his hair with my hands
Touching his cold face
Half afraid he's going to jump up
I open my eyes again and I can't sleep
Afraid that if I do
I'll wake up and it will be longer since he died
That he'll be even more dead
I lie on my side
I wonder how much pain and horror can be contained
In one human mind

I turn on the light
All I can think about is going somewhere
I feel like a target
I feel aged and no one can tell me anything
I feel hard, jaded and partially dead
Then my eyes start to ache and get moist
There's nothing I can do to change what happened
Sometime later near dawn I fall asleep
I get up and go out there
Go through the motions
Trying to look like someone
Who's alive
Inside I'm screaming all the time
Everyday dealing with the many shades of horror
There's nothing anyone can say to me
Nothing anyone can do
I am that which survives
You know that quote about that which does not kill you
You don't want to be made stronger like this
It's all I can do to control myself
Ripping someone apart
Myself or someone else
At this point it doesn't matter
It's all life and Death to me

⟨×⟩⟨×⟩⟨×⟩

1993 go
I will continue to pull the muscle from the bone
I will find out more
I will grow stronger
There's nothing else to do
No other place to go
I am in Detroit
Getting ready to go out and see the Beastie Boys play
1993 is a few hours away
I can't wait to put this year and its faux, hollow glory behind me
All the facts, stats, numbers
Want to dump it
Too heavy to carry
4 trips to Europe
2 to Australia
Japan

Singapore
182 shows
400 + interviews
I shook 1992 by the neck
The road shot into me
Now there's only 1993
Don't attach
Hit hard
Disappear into the treeline
Keep moving
It gets harder to get up in the morning
Lines on my face
It should start getting interesting right about now

CITIES

1.17.92 Sydney Australia: Five in the morning LA time when I walk onstage. Eyes hurt and I want to puke. There's a dead friend in my thoughts. He'll be waiting for me in my room if I ever get through this gig. They yell and I can smell the beer coming up through the rug. Earlier today it was interviews and heat. Small hotel room and loneliness. It's what I know. It's all there is.

1.18.92 Sydney Australia: The room smells me. The room knows me. It doesn't wonder why I don't go outside. The room knows that I don't want to talk, don't want to know. I talk to interviewers. I feel dead. I know I am and I'm amazed they can't tell. I figured that when my hand turned black and fell off the one guy was going to say something. The lady interviewer shifted in her seat when I shot myself in the head. These rooms always smell like insecticide. I share the room with hundreds of dead insects. And one dead man.

1.19.92 Melbourne Australia: I stood up there and told them what I knew to be true. If I think about it too much I want to scream and run away. I throw myself out like the trash in cities all over the world. The cities don't care. They don't even notice if you live there, leave there or die there. They really don't care, they really don't. Don't let the world break your heart too many times.

1.20.92 Melbourne Australia: Sometimes I feel like that guy at the end of the movie Runaway Train. You know the part where he's standing on top of the train and the train is going into the side of the mountain and you know he's going to get crushed. That's how I feel up there. Standing there with lights on me and my guts flying into the Abyss. The Abyss laughing at me the whole time. Laughing at me, laughing with me, laughing every step of the way. Look at the idiot up there ripping himself to pieces. He comes so easily. What a good dog. He's satisfied with so little. After the gut dump was over I came back to the box here and inhaled the bug spray and thought about you Joe. I thought about you and kept right on dying. Invisibly bleeding and re-living it. Sat outside for a while and looked into the sky and thought about you Joe and I felt huge and empty, I felt enormous and desolate. I am living inside my skin. I am next to life but no longer in it. I walk beside it staring in silent stretched horror and shock.

1.21.92 Adelaide Australia: I skipped this town with the band last time we were here because of the bullshit that went down. We were playing James Brown and Parliament and people in the crowd were telling us not to play "that nigger music". Really great. I wonder what the show will be like tonight. I'm in the bug spray smelling hotel room looking at footage of a man digging up his parents in Hungary. They were executed. This room is cold and it's raining outside. The last few days have been hard. I wonder if the rest of my life will be like this. The last month has been unreal. Like walking through a dream. Later: I'm back in the box. The show was really cool actually. More people showed up than when the band played here. They were a good bunch as well. I told them why the band didn't come to Adelaide the last time we toured Australia. I told them story about when I met Dion and he told me about touring the south with Sam Cooke. So now I'm back in the box and will be going to Sydney in the morning. I'm glad no one is here right now. I have a feeling that I will be spending a lot more time alone now.

1.24.92 Brisbane Australia: Been back and forth from Melbourne and Sydney. In the hotel room. The opening guy is sharing a room with me but he's gone out to drink with his friends so I moved out into the front room so I don't have to listen or smell. I am the one who's a fool. I got no life. I should get one sometime. Sick of answering drunk's questions. The road and the cities will conspire to kill you. They'll get you and they'll always win. I could barely contain myself around them tonight. Question after question. I wish I could have vomited as hard as I felt like so they could get an idea of how I feel. I kept tripping over his body onstage tonight. They watched and talked and called out. I'm a million miles away from them, they'll never know, No matter how I try to make it different, they'll never know. Maybe I'm wrong, maybe it all waits for me in the next city. I have nowhere else to go.

1.26.92 Sydney Australia: Last talking show in Australia. Soon I leave and the entire year starts kind of. I don't know. Everything feels new in a strange way. Joe has been all I think about. I talk at these people, I do interviews. I stare at the ceiling in my box at night and it's all the same. Inside I'm screaming. No one will hear me or see the difference. Perhaps something strange or unsettling in the eyes will give me away other than that it's all in my head. I see them from ten miles back in my skull.

2.1.92 Trenton NJ: Tonight was good and one of the only times I've ever felt a bit nervous about going on a stage. There was more people there tonight then when the band plays. About 700. I told them everything I knew. I really like the Trenton crowd. I have been doing talking shows on that stage since 1987. After the show Death overcame me again. People were around me all talking to me at once I did my best to hear them all and talk to all of them. It's hard after spilling your guts out for over two hours. After that, useless sex in a roadside motel somewhere on Highway 1. These nights hammer me. I wonder why I don't wake up with blood on my pillow. I figure my brain will break some day. I guess I am hanging in here because I am into self torture. I will not allow myself to burn out. The ones who burn out are the lucky ones. Then there are the others who hang in for the long haul and get really chewed up. I know something about this.

2.2.92 New York NY: It was hard. Sitting at the bar waiting to do the thing knowing pretty much what was going to come out of my mouth because right now there's nothing else on my mind and there's no way I can stop it and there's no way I'm going to be able to deal with it very well. Also knowing that when I'm done I will return to a room next to the road and wait for the next thing to happen. I sit at the end of the bar and watch the place fill up. A while later I'm up there talking away. It's pretty amazing what you can take and still keep going. I see now how much of life is auto pilot. You can get by with a lot of your controls down. The last few days have been walking through the cold getting to the right place by smell, by taste, by memory derived through repetition. After the show I was trying to get out of there and deal with people who were being really nice to me. It seemed that the nicer they were the worse I felt. I am often taken aback at how kind people can be, I don't see this kind of thing in myself so when I see it in others I am startled.

I said thank you a lot and tried to be cool but inside I was confused and dying.

2.11.92 Rotterdam Holland: I just want to hurt them as much as I can tonight. I look at the press and the way people hang around and I want to freak them out and destroy them with sweat and pain. I workout in the dressing room. I can feel the pain in my arms. 60 minutes until we play. I love opening sets. Something about them makes me play like a motherfucker. We open for the Chili Peppers for the next few weeks. I have trained for this and I want to bum out their fans. I want to be a clean annihilating force. First show of the year and I couldn't be happier to be anywhere else at any time. Did a few days of press and all that did was piss me off and make me wish for this night and all the nights to come. It's not even about music to me. It's about rage and feeling it. Fuck them.

2.12.92 Hamburg Germany: First of two nights in this place. The Peppers soundcheck with a Stooges song and it makes me mad. I'll just have to wipe myself all over their nice little fans and bum them out. Finished the set. It hurt and the lights were hot. They just watch, it will destroy you if you try to make it mean anything to anyone but yourself.

2.13.92 Hamburg Germany: Second night in this place. Played better than last night. Got taken out to dinner by people from the record company. Ate with a bunch of drunk Germans that were really cool and that was it. The only thing on my mind is playing well. I love opening. I can't wait to hit the Peppers fans again, they're so nice. Fuck this shit. Let's be honest. The Peppers are cool people and they kick the hard jams, but all I want to do is blow their asses off stage every night and that's the only reason I'm on the this fucking tour. Wish I could see more of Hamburg but there's no time of course. Doesn't matter. All I'm good for is playing doing interviews and sleeping in my black box.

2.14.92 Gronningen Holland: A show on our own without the Peppers. I don't know how many time we've played this place now. Always the same people who work here show up. Pretty cool place they have here. Trying to play hard and have a life. I think of my friend. He was in this place in 1987. Everything has changed for me. The way I do everything is different. I don't know if I'm better or worse or what. I wonder if people notice anything different about me. Place was hot tonight, I don't know if they liked the gig or not. I never know in this place. I like playing on our own better than playing a short set opening for the Peppers fans. Some times all I want to do is kill.

2.15.92 Deinze Belgium: Woke up in the bus in some parking lot. Staggered in and watched the crew build the stage for the night's show. Did interviews all day long. I am an enemy of my brain because I know at this point it hates me for putting it through all the questions. Made sure I played hard as fuck tonight. I tried to pack a full show in the six songs that we played. All I want to do is pound the audience, damage them, show them something that's not nice, fuck them up with a feeling. Later the Peppers went on and it was so loud that even behind the stage it was painful, I can't see how they can take it onstage. Soon I will go into my black box bunk. I will do my best not to think of anything so I can get some sleep. Try as I might I know that I will soon be thinking of murder and loss. We go to Paris next.

2.16.92 Paris France: Woke up in my box. Parked on the side of the road near the faceless huge venue we played in tonight. Interviews all day. I played hard as I could tonight. Opening for the Peppers is a constant inspiration. I see their backdrop and all the people with their Peppers shirts on and I feel like Tyson coming out of the corner after the bell in the first round. Just wreck the fuckers. Destroy them with music and a sheer love of animal pain. After the show no one knows us. We pass through the halls invisibly, nothing exists except the Peppers. We are the faceless opening band. I sit in the back room and sweat onto the floor. Hit and keep hitting. I'm not expecting anything to happen. I'm not looking for success. I get what I need every night. Animal pain. The rest I don't need. Imagine me in a stage costume.

2.17.92 Amsterdam Holland: I woke up in the morning in the black box. I got out and found that we were parked at a rest stop. I went and got some coffee. When I came out I found that the bus had taken off without me. Luckily I had some money. I took a cab to Breda and caught a train to Amsterdam from there. I had enough to spare to get a hamburger on the way to the club which I happened to know the location of. When I got there the bus was there and the others were sitting on there, no problem. I was right in time for soundcheck. The gig went well though. I don't like playing that place usually. The stage is hard to hear on and the staff is pretty lazy. Most of the Dutch people at clubs are pretty fucking lazy. The people at this place make me want to randomly smack them. It's hard for me to help myself at this place. They piss me off and I react poorly. I usually regret it later but I can't help myself.

2.18.92 Nijemagen Holland: I think if you give people too much sunshine and clean air, remove a large percentage of the violence and crime from the streets then the people get bored from not having to watch their ass. That's my opinion anyway. Like Greg Ginn once said between bowls of pot: *In the absence of intimidation, creativity will flourish.* You can see how it flourishes here in Holland. How the crowds just stand there in their silly pants and dumbass hair cuts and tell you what songs they want to hear. Little do they know that the singer would like to randomly smack them when they tell him what to do. They never get to find this fact out. That's why shitty music comes out of this country, there's no tension on the streets, there's no angst, nothing. The fact that the Urban Dance squad comes from Holland is a miracle. Yea we played and they watched like they always do. I liked it better many years ago when Black Flag played this same hall in '83, there were fights and people throwing shit, it kept us on our toes. Shoot pigs in the face.

2.19.92 Munster Germany: Another show in Germany. I wonder what they think of us here. I can't always understand Germans. I like this country because the people leave you alone when you're on the street. Pretty dead crowd tonight. I play right through them, right over them. I play for myself. They have no idea how heavy this trip is, they just smoke and look on. I used to get mad at this but as long as they don't get in my way then I don't care what they do. I have been seeing things differently these days. You do everything for yourself, even when you're doing something for someone else, you're doing it for yourself. So now I just play from the bone marrow out and not bother with the rest. I think that will make me play better. Now when people yell at me I don't have to let that matter. I know now that the music does not care about attitude, the music is pure and the more attitude you throw at it, the more it will become clouded. You have to approach the music with a strong thought, with a clear mind. Music will tolerate no shit. It will always throw itself back in your face and show you out for the fool you are. If you serve it then you will be rewarded by the lesson of strength that it endlessly provides.

2.20.92 Kassel Germany: Same as last night. I get up and play. They watch and talk and drink and smoke. I wonder sometimes if I have ever lived in real life at all. I go through all these towns and I don't notice the years pass by unless I am told how many times I have played in a certain place. I could get lost in the countries of Europe. Never come back to America's killing machine again. I've seen what it can do. I've seen it and I can still see it. It sells you out and leaves you on the sidewalk so a bunch of pigs can stand over your body and talk a bunch of pig bullshit. I am covered with blood and they can't see it. I am full of screams from a horror show and they'll never know. Best thing to do is to keep on playing and pulling in the pain. Maybe someday I'll just explode up there and then they'll see something.

2.21.92 Hannover Germany: A guy got up onstage tonight with a sun tattoo on his back that was bigger than the one I have. It had all kinds of fucked up colors in it. Green, put on all crooked. Sometimes this shit trips me out to the point where I can't get myself out the door. A lot of people at the gig and they were onstage all night. I wonder how much sweat comes out of me a year. When they talk shit about me in magazines that's what I think about, I think about all the sweat coming out of my skin and landing on the floor. They'll never know anything. Moving across borders totally unknown. I feel like I am on tour with Joe's dead body. I keep expecting to see the corpse on my bunk in the bus. I drag it with me from town to town. It's been hard doing all the press and getting asked about him all the time. I think the whole year will be like this. I don't know how I will get through it.

2.22.92 Saarbrucken Germany: Woke up on a deserted road in the middle of nowhere but now I find out it's Saarbrucken. I walked to a gas station and got some food. Peanuts and orange juice. I came back and found that some of the other bus dwellers had gone into a local bar and were getting some coffee. The place was already full of old guys drinking and arguing. So hours later we played and they watched and that's it. I managed to play hard enough so that I thought my bones were burning afterwards. I took a shower in the backstage place and it was cold. Now I'm on the bus listening to people knock on the windows calling my name. I am playing a tape of Miles Davis. Waiting to leave down this dark road. I have some shitty food that I got in the dressing room. It's good enough. My body feels like it has been beaten by strangers. It's me though, always me. The emptiness after playing is huge. The vacancy inside is enormous. I try to describe it so I can somehow deal with it better than I do now but perhaps it's just what happens with this trip. I have stopped questioning a lot of things. You can do almost any damn thing you want. You can play your ass off and you can get shot in the head. People think that everyone else gives a fuck about them. I know different.

2.23.92 Zurich Switzerland: Cold out tonight. I was outside the bus working out with dumbbells for as long as I could without getting frozen. Interviews most of the day down the road at the BMG office.

They wheel in one after the other and we have a fake talk. They stand still tonight like I have never seen them stand still before. Tonight is the thirteenth show straight. I feel good. I walked off stage and minutes later I didn't remember playing the show at all. All the faces fell away as I watched the sweat run off my legs and felt the pain and chill bite into my ribs. What a strange way to live out a life time. If the music doesn't mean everything to you then you lose because you're just doing it for them, handing your guts out to strangers without getting to take a bite before you pass the steaming entrails on to those who walk over them and never know.

2.25.92 Munich Germany: I work out all the way up until the doors open. I feel like a coiled spring. Sometimes I find it hard to control myself. It's a good thing that there's the music to pound into. I have headlined in this place a couple of times before, it's strange to open for the Peppers here. A gig is a gig. I'll take it. I don't care who it's with, same thing happens every time anyway. As we played I wanted to bite them in half, to squeeze their collective necks. To savage them into impotency.

2.26.92 Munich Germany: Night two felt better than last night. I watch the Pepper guitar player stumble around in a pot and wine stupor, I could do a lot better things with the money. Flea and Sim do Monk's Bemsha Swing at soundcheck. Other than that it's a lot of playing. I only know myself through playing shows and traveling. I couldn't tell if I was being distant to someone, or rude or even hostile. I only know a good night and a bad night. I know that I remember the bad night longer than the good night. Touring is more important than love. If I didn't know people than I wouldn't have to feel anything when they get murdered a few feet away from me. As it is now I play and get back in the bus. On this tour I am learning because I know that the Peppers audience doesn't give a fuck about us. I get off only on the music. That's all there is for me. The crowd is just a distraction, an expanse of flesh that throws cups and ice. They were lucky tonight. There was a barrier to keep me away from them as I know that I could casually release short controlled bursts of body damaging violence to strangers without raising my blood pressure one bit.

2.27.92 Frankfurt Germany: The Marines up front made it hard to play tonight. They look at you and tell you to "kick ass" and that "None of these assholes know shit man!" Too bad they don't get it. There's always a few of those guys at our shows in Germany, they figure that since they're fellow Americans that we're going to be all buddy buddy with them. I don't know if they have any idea how sad they are. They were the security for the show for some strange reason so there was no way to get away from them. It was a good gig anyway. I went to catering afterwards and ate and went to the bus. This is the biggest place we've ever played in Frankfurt. I've been here so many times at this point. I was sorry that we didn't get to stay over night in our usual dingy hotel by the train station where you can find any drug or trade you want.

2.28.92 Innsbruck Austria: I did a talking show here in this place before. In the bus today Chris played a tape that Joe made him of himself talking. It was strange hearing Joe's voice. It was hard to take. He was being funny as hell and that made it worse. I sat there kind of laughing and kind of bleeding out the side. I listen to dead people on records all the time. It's not hard to take when I listen to Coltrane or someone like that but it's different with Joe. Eventually he took the tape off. I sat in the backstage area and stretched and waited to play and wondered if the crowd was going to be the same bored looking bunch that always seems to go to our shows in Austria. We played hard and they watched and that was about it. Went back on the bus and waited to leave. The mountains were beautiful today. I cannot imagine living in a place like this, having a view like that everyday. I wonder what that does to your mind if you were born and raised in clean air and streets that were not violent. I wonder what they think of people like me who come in from a different world.

2.29.92 Vienna Austria: We played in this club in 1987. It's small and it's pretty much just a disco. Better than an night off. The Peppers have a night off so we're playing this club that we played in about five years ago on our first tour here. The show is over and it was alright. Sometimes it seems like the Austrians are not even at the show. They just stand there and talk. Like last night. I don't know what gets them off. The place will be packed and I don't know if they like us or what. Doesn't really matter. We just play right through'em every night. Getting used to opening for other bands, it's good training for what I don't know but I'm sure it's good training for something. It's a good test.

3.1.92 Milan Italy: I'm glad this is a Peppers show and not one of ours. I don't have to worry about the bullshit of "Fuck we're in Italy nothing works and the crew are the laziest pieces of shit known to rock and roll." I can just go out and play and not think about the fact that every other time I've ever played here it's always been such a load of bullshit just to get onstage. I had to do a press conference. I counted the tape recorders, there was 15 of them in all. Some others were just writing shit down on paper. Whatever. What the hell are they going to use it for anyway, I would be surprised if they can get the printing presses to work. I watch the Pepper crew agonize with the local crew people who are dropping delicate equipment and thank my good luck that I'm only in the opening band. A security guard tries to stop me on the way into the back of the hall. I laugh in his face and walk past him. It reminds me of the scene in Saturday Night Live when the crew comes on the set of Star Trek and takes down all the props and Chevy Chase tries to put the Vulcan Death grip on a guy and the guy just laughs at him and says back off joker. How can you take them seriously when they barely have any shit together. They make this huge arena right next to a church. The nuns won't allow much noise so you have to run the sound at way below normal level. How typically Italian. I heard that and laughed. Perfect. Hours later we play and it's a great time. I sit on the bus wait to go and eventually have to leave and wait in the parking lot because there's so much pot smoke that I fear getting contact weakness by being around people who are so weak they have to smoke it in the first place. At least it's a nice night to look up at the stars.

3.2.92 Lyon France: This was a show that the Peppers were supposed to do but for some reason they didn't do it. We did it anyway. They moved us into a smaller hall and we played in front of about 200 people. It was a good time. For some reason there was a television crew there filming us. Of course Andrew had to fuck up things by not bothering to play and pose out in front of the cameras so much that I had to ask them to stop so we could get through the songs. No matter what, Andrew will always sell you out. I feel like beating the shit out of him all the time. He waits all day to act like a dick onstage. I wish he could get it out of the way in the morning in his bunk or at lunch but no! He has to wait until we're trying to play. He always talks about how he's always into playing. He's so full of shit. I came right here to the bus after we played because I didn't want to talk to anyone. I was hanging out in the dressing room but there were these drunk assholes who somehow get themselves in and were getting themselves groomed for an ass kicking by someone who won't tolerate the hazy out of focus world of the alcoholic. There were people out by the bus and I did my best to be nice because they don't know the black box that sits on my head and the Death and horror in my brain. Soon I will get into my little black box and dream the same dreams and feel the same tears go down my face.

3.4.92 Birmingham England: We have to be good tonight. We're in Sabbath's home town. Walking the same streets as Geezer Butler, Ozzy Osbourne, Tony Iommi and Bill Ward. The mightiest band there ever was. Later: We played hard as hell. I don't know what the Peppers are going to do. The place is so hot that the walls in the dressing room two flights up are sweating. The stage temp has got to be insane. As soon as I went on I knew we were in for a hot one. People were cool and seemed to like us. I was afraid that people on this tour would be giving us shit because they were only into the Peppers but they seem to be into us enough to tolerate us. You can tell the girls are bored and wish we were out of the way but what the fuck. I could feel the day off kicking my ass. It's a good lesson in how fast the body forgets all the training that you put into it. If I don't stretch for a couple of days, all the flexibility I had goes away. It's like I never stretched once in my life. A few songs in the pain starts. It comes as a stranger every night. It's like I have never felt it before but then a few songs later it feels like I have been that way all my life and then I really start kicking it. It's like my little secret. I don't know anyone who plays with pain. I never heard anyone in a band talk about it. It keeps me at a distance with people. They don't understand why I am in a bad mood before shows. They don't know that I am trying to get my mind ready to take on a high level of pain. I snuck out of the hall through the hello Cleveland route and got to the street without having to sign any autographs. I feel good when I can play hard and walk out and not have to talk to anyone or get thanked or shake anyone's hand. I am trying to feel better about everything and have a life. I'm really trying. I am feeling a little better as we go down the line with these shows.

3.5.92 Liverpool England: The Peppers production guy tapes up a sheet every day in the dressing room telling stage times, after show travel plans, etc. Today's said that the "punters are mental" here in Liverpool. The hall is freezing. I am told that even in summer the place is cold. It's got to be at least two thousand years old. Looking forward to playing. Later. The crowd was really cool. Easily one of the best crowds I've been in front of since I've been coming to the UK. Being in the opening spot is a good way to start a long tour. It's good to get out in front of an audience that is not there to see you. Tonight was one of those shows that you do and then walk away from. Sometimes the opening slot leaves me a bit unsatisfied. You never get to really expend yourself. I finish and sit in the dressing room wishing there was another gig across town. The shower room was in the front office for some reason. This shit doesn't matter. I see how tunneled out I can be. I wonder what I would be like in the real world.

3.6.92 Dublin Ireland: I spent the day doing interviews and had to go to Windmill studios to do something, I think it was MTV. It's the studio that U2 bought and their idiot fans have made the place some kind of mecca. Every square inch of wall space on the entire street is taken up with messages from fans to the band. "We traveled all the way from Sydney Australia because seeing you 11 times there wasn't enough, we love you always." Shit like that. It was pretty intense. I hope the camera got all the footage of me spitting all over the walls and kicking them. I hate that band. What a drag that they own Windmill. It's where Thin Lizzy recorded some of their albums. Much later I'm at the gig. I didn't know what to expect. They ended up being one of the greatest crowds I've ever been in front of. I laid into Bono and crew almost immediately to see if that would get a rise out of them and they were laughing immediately. The rest of the gig was good. I told them about Joe. It was a good show. Another night of leaving entrails on the floor. Nearly got into a thing with some piece of shit outside the place. He told me that he was the guy that threw a beer mug onstage when I did this show in San Francisco once. It missed me and broke on the floor and exploded and sent glass all over these girls who were sitting on the stage next to me. I told him to walk away before he got hurt. He told me that he wasn't aiming for me, he was trying to get me excited so I would do a good show. He also said that the glass didn't break. He wouldn't stop talking to me and I kept trying to get away from him because I don't want to get arrested for fucking up one of the pieces of shit. He eventually went away. I was relieved. I am now back in the cold small box. I am waiting for sleep to come.

3.7.92 Dublin Ireland: I did an instore experience today. The people were really cool but the whole thing was unnerving. I eventually had to slip through the people and leave. After an hour in a tiny store with people all around you it gets to be a bit much. The show was real good tonight. People really like the Peppers here, it was pretty insane when they came on. I like those guys ok. They're easy to tour with, all the people in their crew are great and the guys in the band are cool as well. The high point of the night was meeting up with a man named Smiley. Smiley was one of the Thin Lizzy road crew. Apparently he worked with Phil and Co. for quite some time. He told me some cool stories. He said that Phil was a great guy, really big hearted but in a lot of pain. It's kind of what I got from listening to Thin Lizzy records. I listen to Thin Lizzy almost every day. I never get tired of them. Phil had it right. That song Running Back from the Jailbreak album is a perfect song, that's a great album to have out on the road. Smiley said that I could come by his place the next time I'm in town and see some stuff he has from his years on the road with the band. Now I'm in the tiny hotel room that will house three of us tonight. Me and Chris are here and we are giving the floor to a friend of ours that has come from England to see us. I am trying get out of the hall as soon as I can after I play. I find that the more I'm alone, the better I feel. I am trying to deal with the dull haze that I find myself in almost every day. It's like I have a lead cloud over me all the time.

3.8.92 Belfast Ireland: Most intense border crossing I can remember. I was sitting up in the front seat with Tim the driver. He told me to be cool and always show my hands. We were met at the gate by a terrified teenager holding a rifle aimed at our faces. We told him that we were in a rock band and that we were playing with the Peppers. He immediately put the rifle down and said you're in a band? Right then all these teenagers in fatigues came out of several hiding places all over the roadside. We had been in front of half a dozen guns the entire time. They came on the bus and we gave them some shirts. They told us that they would love nothing more than to be at the show tonight but they had to be here. There was a sign up that apologized for the wait at the gate but said it was because of the terrorists. It's no joke there. We get to the gig and it so happens it's right near the place where some bombs went off as couple of weeks before. Finally we get to play. The crowd was tense and wild at the same time. Got hit with some spit, I didn't think they did that shit anymore. We were so far from the crowd and the stage was so high, I don't know what they saw of us. The bouncers had this system of grabbing kids. One would get the kid in a head lock and the other one would put two fingers into the kid's mouth and pull his cheek back and the two of them would take the kid out real hard, then they would come back and laugh about it. All of this was going on the whole time right below me. It was hard to take. I sat in the dressing room until it was time to go. I didn't want to be in the bus if it got fire bombed or some shit. They have security out there guarding the tour busses because they were afraid that someone might put a bomb underneath one of them. It will be good to get out of here.

3.9.92 Glasgow Scotland: The band has a night off and I have a talking show. The first thing I did was tell them the reason why I haven't been back to Scotland for 8 years. I walked out in front of a bunch of people that were there to see a spoken word show and one of the first lines that came out of my mouth was "I think you all are fucked." I think they liked me after that. A night off from the band in Scotland and I find a way to make trouble for myself by not being able to say no to a gig. I must like what I'm doing. The only thing that was troubling was the young man that came up crying and hugged me and wouldn't let go for what seemed like an eternity. He has no idea how much it freaked me out to have someone touch me like that. I am a haunted house. I am a freak show. I am all the police line ups. I am good at being a witness. I am good at being a victim. It's in my DNA. I was always good at watching them do everything and me doing nothing. I was always good at letting the world do what it wanted to me. I learned to take it from my mother and father and the people they fucked. I am trouble, big trouble. I can't control myself like I used to. This is a strange time. I have been cut loose to swing in the darkness of the Abyss. I do interviews all day long talking shit to people I don't know. It's like a fast fuck. Always business, never personal. I don't know anyone and I know too much because no one can tell me anything.

3.10.92 Glasgow Scotland: I was figuring that were going to get pelted, spat on and all the rest. It was a great gig instead. The place is a famous venue called the Barrowlands. Real good sounding hall. The load in is a drag because there's several long flights of stairs and no elevator. The loaders are famous for getting gear up and down the stairs in no time flat. Since most of them are psychotic biker motherfuckers, you stay out of their way. I watched the Peppers play tonight. I have never seen anything like that. The place was packed to capacity of course, and everyone there was jumping up and down at the same time like the whole thing had been choreographed. I thought the floor was going to break. Now I'm in the dressing room which is cold and smells and the shower only gives out cold water. I'm not lonely because I'm not human. I am this thing that plays shows and gets it going on every night. No matter what happens to me, the music and the road don't care. The road is always waiting for me to throw up my hands and walk off. It's always trying to tell me that I never really had it, never really meant it. You have to keep rising to the occasion, that's what it's all about, you have to be ready to go without to get to it. That's why I don't hang around for the talk and adulation fests. I know better. The road watches and laughs thinking that it's going to take me out. You stick around and congratulated and patted on the back, then you lose your edge. That's what these bands don't understand. In order to give it up you have to be pure. The impurities are what wear these rockstars down. Most of these people with guitars are so lightweight. So fake. They don't rise to the occasion. The road chews them up and spits them out. They complain about the road being hard. It is hard so you have to be hard. It's so simple, either you go for it all the way or you pose out.

3.12.92 London England: Did two shows today. I did a talking show at a club for press and record people. I talked about Joe, what else is there. I don't know if I bummed them out too much. I felt strange talking to these people in the middle of the afternoon and then going on to do interviews and another gig. The crowd tonight at the band show was limp. I didn't understand what the deal with them was, I would look up and they were just standing there. We had to take breaks between songs because drum mics kept falling off and that kind of thing always fucks us up. Nick Cave was at the show tonight. It's strange, he always seems to come to shows that I don't like as much as the one before when he wasn't there. It was cool to see him there anyway. It's cold out and of course it's raining. We have two more shows here in the UK and then we're out. Nothing much on my mind tonight. I am burned out from the interviews and the fact that I did two shows today. I guess I'm doing good because if at the end of the day I'm so tired that I can't think then I must have given all I could. I am unable to protect myself. I don't have any shields up anymore. I just take as best I can. I don't know what else to do except play.

3.13.92 Brixton England: Just got back from the first of the two shows at the Brixton venue. I think we played well. I got a workout in before we went on and that was a good help to me. I like it when I can hit the weights before I go on. I feel better about myself. I feel like a slob when I don't workout. While I was hitting the weights, Andrew sat on his ass and smoked hash. Typical. If Joe saw that he would have laughed so hard he would have fallen over. That's Andrew, he smokes dope and cigarettes, drinks, kicks back and complains. He plays bass sometimes. I want to get a different player in the band. I'm tired of this lazy piece of shit. He wants to have a meeting with me and Gail tomorrow. I hope he wants to quit. I know he'll be complaining about something, he always does, nothing's good enough for him. I really don't care at this point, after what I've been through, bullshit is nothing to me. It's not like he's getting his head blown off on my front porch or anything. I did press for hours today. I did radio, television, an instore at Tower. The press was hard to do, I was at it all day right into sound check. Right after that I worked out and went to play. Now I'm back. I think nothing of it. I don't care. I'm still standing, I can still work.

3.14.92 Brixton England: Last night with the Peppers. All the Beastie

Boys showed up. Now that was something. One of the only bands that matter. The Pepper guitar player walked into our dressing room and mumbled something about it being a beautiful experience playing with us. I guess he was stoned. Seems like a nice enough guy. I never said a word to him the whole tour except for hello in passing. Andrew is all bent out of shape about all kinds of stuff and asked to meet with me and Gail and when I said ok let's talk he has nothing to say. It's always the same bullshit with him, he never confronts. Fuck it, I played hard as hell and gave it up. This has been a good tour I think. It was hard to look at all the Beasties in the room hanging out and not think of Joe and how much he would be getting off on all of this. I have to go to New York and do press for the next few days. Night after night and I'm still here. You have to keep coming back and hitting year after year. You need to be unbelievable. That's the part that a slob like Andrew will never be able to get to. You have to have a great deal of straight up pride in what you do and realize that it matters more than sleep, more than anything. I have Samurai in my blood. The hall here in Brixton is cold and the rooms smell. Some guy that we remotely know from London came in here and started to fuck the place up and I had to throw him out. Drunks are so pathetic. I can't take them. If I know someone and they get drunk and get in my face I no longer respect them. Somehow I can tolerate when someone in the band gets drunk because they never do it onstage but I can never respect someone that drinks and gets drunk as much as I cold someone that is straight. If you really want to destroy then you are straight all the time and you get it done. Otherwise you're just talking shit.

4.1.92 Fullerton CA: We played outside today at Cal State Fullerton. It was good. A few songs in it started to rain. We kept on playing. It really started coming down. But we kept playing. I fully expected to get shocked and killed. There was a girl up front grabbing me and she had on all this lipstick so I wiped it all over her face and wiped it onto mine and went for the scene with Frank Booth in Blue Velvet where he's kissing Jeffrey. I was telling her that I was going to send her straight to hell fucker. We finished the gig and like rockstars left the equipment behind for the road crew and went to the Dennis Miller show where there was more gear waiting for us and we soundchecked and then played Tearing on the program. I hung out with Dennis on the talk show scene for a few minutes and it was better this time then the last time. I feel ok, nothing really on my mind. We go to San Diego in the morning for two shows. Strange day. One set outside with people watching from all sides, no walls, the music just flying into the trees and into the air and then a television show, all in one day. Now I'm in my box waiting for the road to begin.

4.2.92 San Diego CA: First night here in San Diego. The opening band was crap. It had the old singer from TSOL, I think his name is Jack. He's the same bullshit as he always was but now he's overweight. Whatever. These punk legends are hilarious to me. Punk rock! Anyway they sucked and were quickly blown offstage. I remember I was here a few months ago doing spoken word with Don. As far as the gig, the only stand out thing besides playing our asses off was some large punker guy insisting that he jump off stage and squash people and then tell them that it was better in eighty something. Thanks Punk! Don once told me that the nights in San Diego are the best in the world. It's great outside tonight. I wish I wasn't so tired. It was hot onstage tonight, the heat beats the hell out me every year. I always wonder why my tattoos don't melt off my body. After shows I am filled with emptiness. I have no idea how the will to play comes back every day. Strange how at the end of the day all I can think about is getting to the stage and playing. I figured I would get tired of this trip after a few years and now I know nothing else, for me there is nothing else.

4.3.92 San Diego CA: Played hard tonight. The sun is coming up and I am writing. A girl I met is sleeping in my bed. It was a good night of playing. A band from the old LA scene opened tonight. Actually, it was two bands that have taken members from both and made a band. One band was The Controllers and the other band was The Skulls. They have a band called Skull Control. I think they were a little surprised that I knew their old records. I have all of them from both bands. I thought they were cool. If I see their name in the paper I will go check them out. I don't know if the crowd could get to them but it was great to see them go for it. I did 9 interviews. Sometimes I amaze myself at how I can do that shit and still play, I don't know how long I can keep that up. With the schedule that's up for this year I'll get a chance to find out.

4.4.92 Los Angeles CA: Instead of a night off we are playing at the Palladium as part of the Magic Johnson AIDS Benefit. Should be cool. I'm taking my bike down to the gig, I live close enough. That will be a first for me. Later: Had a good time with the whole thing. Hung out with the singer in Fishbone and did some pictures. Did some interview stuff with MTV and radio. Porno for Pyros played tonight, I think it was their first gig. I'm not too sure but that was what I heard. I thought they were cool. It was hard to watch them from out front because people kept coming up and talking to me. I had to tell some people to leave me the fuck alone. I really wanted to see Perry do his thing. I think they will be better when they get some more shows under their belt. When Perry hit stage the crowd went off. People really get off on that guy. It was like there was some kind of magnet at the front of the stage. We played after that and it was ok. I have a problem with short sets where I tend to come out of the gate too fast and blow my pace a little. I tried to cool it before I went on but I was so fired up I was punching the wall and hitting myself in the head but I pulled of the set ok. After that I hung out for a while and then split. I can't stay around the LA scene thing for too long without feeling like I am getting drained. It's bad for you to stick around and listen to that band bullshit and even start talking about it. The more you talk to others, the more you become like them. You don't want to get on topics of "common ground", the best thing to do is to do your number and get the fuck out into the night and disappear. The only thing I should be thinking about after a show is the next one.

4.5.92 San Francisco CA: MTV is filming a couple of our shows. Luckily for us they are cool people so I see there being no problems. It's hard to be in the hotel that we're in because it looks out across the street to the apartment building of a girl I used to go out with up here. She doesn't live there anymore. I can see the window that I used to look out of though and it's a drag. The gig is hours away. Later: We played a good one I thought. The place is the same place where I do the talking shows up here. I gave it all I had and it was a great time. Last time I was here Joe was videoing me right to my right side. Before the show we were talking to these girls doing one of our typical good guy bad guy routines. They didn't recognize either of us and we were asking them how they got here and what they were expecting and we told them that we knew that Rollins guy and that he was pretty fucked up and that he had killed a bunch of people and no one knew about it and that they should keep it a secret as well. Andrew's brother played percussion with us tonight and Morgan played violin too. We went for a Sabbath sounding jam that felt good. Now I'm back here in the room. Soon I will go into another room and have sex with this girl who's name keeps escaping me until the last moment. It will be meaningless in typical Californian style. I will become more hollow. My eyes will fill with the local night. Syringes, hookers, garbage on the streets. The old words from the place across the street. Ghosts and gunshots, horror and dried blood.

4.6.92 San Francisco CA: We played with Morgan and Andrew's brother again. Another great night in SF. After the show was over I was walking Morgan back to her car and this guy came out of nowhere, he had a poncho on and I couldn't see his hands. He came up and said hello and I was getting ready to see the gun come out and ready to be held up again. His left hand came out of the poncho first and I figured that the other was going to come out with the gun. The other hand came out and there was nothing in it. I had an overwhelming urge to attack him and take him out before he could do anything to me. Do it to him before he could do it to me. Eliminate him without asking any questions. He turned out to be some street guy looking for change and he was very cool. He had no idea how close I came to attacking him. Like a shark, like a pitbull. Like the most terrified man on the face of the earth. It's all I know. I know panic and hotel hideouts. Sometimes I really think that I could rip the flesh off my bones. I get a few seconds out of every few minutes. I watch the time go by in strangled increments. I meet people that call my name and it all sounds like screams and terror to me. Compliments sound like threats, like the great send off going away party to the Abyss. The music makes me more berserk, you shouldn't talk to me tonight because there's not much I care about and a whole lot I don't give a fuck about.

4.7.92 Los Angeles CA: In LA the blood dries at night because the streets never cool down. The sound of helicopters fills the ears and send knee jerk shots of panic, paranoia and animal savagery through the veins of the shuffled extras too numbed by glamour overload to notice that there's not a single intersection in the entire city where you can stand and not be an animal waiting to see your own intestines slide down your leg from a stray bullet. In this city they kill for the fuck of it, fuck for the hell of it and live for no reason. If I could have a nickel for every siren I've heard go screaming into the distance to some scene, I'd still be here, still be looking out the window of my room, still laughing at the fact that I can't get my window open very far because the security bars get in the way. Every window in the apartment has iron bars across them to keep me safe. I don't feel safe. I don't feel safe anywhere. I don't feel safe and I'll attack you because I'm scared and full of fear like the next guy, like the next dead guy, like the next guy who knows he's nothing, nothing but a piece of meat waiting for something to come around and charge him double and scar him for life. I played tonight and challenged my muscles and pain threshold and I won again. I think about a sword and its brutal simplicity. I temper myself in the furnace of these hot boxes all over the world. I come out stronger and stronger. I will outlive the fear, the spent bullet casings and the ravaging heartbreak of this city, any city, every city.

4.8.92 Los Angeles CA: Got back here a little while ago. Another good night at the Whisky. I had a good time playing. We had Chad and Flea from the Peppers and Steve Perkins from Jane's Addiction out there as well. Two bass players and three drummers at once, it was really cool. It totally worked. Last night was cool as well Perry came out and did vocals with me on Obscene. It was great to share a stage with him. I did an instore today. It was a drag. The people were really great as they usually are but there were so many of them. I was there for nearly two hours. I don't think I'll let them put me in that position again after the ones I promised I'd do are over with. I don't like putting people in the position in line to talk to me. I can't take it. I wanted to bolt out of there a few times today. It's hard because the people are so cool and they like you and I want to give them everything. I don't know why I'm like that. I hate myself when I think that I left anyone out. I could never hurt their feelings. The pigs called me today and asked if I wanted to see more line up shots. I told them that I would do what I could. So far they have no leads that they would tell me about. Just talking to them put me back in that pig frame of mind. I have a day off tomorrow. I'll get in a good workout. Looking forward to that. Looking forward to getting left alone as well. I will do the best I can to get my mind to myself. It's hard with the pigs bearing down on me all the time. I feel like hiding out and protecting my thoughts from all these people that seem to be so interested in all the pathetic little details of my shallow, blasted life.

4.11.92 Phoenix AZ: Played at this outdoor radio get down with all these bands that would never play together if it wasn't for this. Imagine us with Social Distortion and the Sugar Cubes. We didn't get to use any of our own equipment and it was a drag for the rest of the guys. It didn't help that no one really knew what was going on. Our dressing room became the designated area for all these coked out DJ types who think we're really impressed and don't realize that we don't give a fuck about anything but playing the gig. So we get to play and we gave it up as best we could. Hilarious, I wouldn't want to have been Social Distortion going on after us because they got their asses blown off stage so hard their socks landed in LA. Now I'm in the hotel box. Some girl slid pictures of herself under my door and she'll be over in a few minutes. Sometimes you get a break.

4.12.92 Dallas TX: At the instore I stood next to a table with a pen in my hand watching the line not end. I looked ahead of me. There were people with posters in their hands and they were looking at me and I was signing this stuff the best I could and I was trying to be cool but it was hard because the line never stopped. There's no real time you can say to one of the men that are working there if they can cut the line off at some point. It's a great way to spend an afternoon if you want to learn to hate your own guts worse than you do at present. Nearly two hours of it and I felt like asking to get my hands chopped off. The PA blew up during the last song so there was nothing we could do about it and the coolest part was that the audience understood. Sometimes it's hard to tell an audience that the PA that's in the club is not so hot and it blew up and it's not the band's fault and there is nothing we would rather be doing than playing. Sometimes they flat out don't believe you, like you tried to blow it up or something. Hot place tonight, sold out and people all over the place nonstop. Just another night on tour. Was stressed out after the instore thing and started running a fever after soundcheck. Managed to fall asleep in the bunk for a little while. I woke up in sweat. Outside people were lined up to get in. When you get out of the bus they stare at you like you're coming out of a spaceship. No matter how low key you try to get out of the bus it looks like some bullshit grand entrance and I'm sure that people start hating your guts before they even get a chance to find out what a fucked up, dented, tragic wreck you really are. I wish there could be something amazing that could happen every night on tour. Something to make me remember the name of the town we're in. So many nights are the same. I pull in, get taken away to do interviews with people who don't know me from spit and do the soundcheck and then you hang out and then you get ready and then you play. The playing is the total reason for living but then there's the emptiness that keeps me up until near dawn. The only thing that makes it better is the chance to rise to the occasion again and again. To challenge the pain threshold nightly. It's a heavy way to get off. I'm confused and tired, is it showing? All I know is that I feel empty all the time. In the last two weeks I've been with some great women and it never seems to make me feel any better. I always feel the same distance. I never felt that with the girl that dumped me. I bet I was just fooling myself though. But the other night I was in a hotel room with a girl and for a little while I felt somewhat close to her. It wasn't for long though. It would be cool to meet someone that I could identify with. Fuck it. I'm a loner all the way. I don't understand why I keep trying to deny it and get out of it. I always end up alone. I always end up insulting them and pissing them off. I'm better off alone.

4.14.92 Cincinnati OH: I think tonight was the first show where we broke 1000 paid in America as a headliner. I don't know if that's important but it put some shit into perspective one way or the other.

I thought we played good tonight. It was a trip leaving the place. I walked out into the cold only thinking about getting on the bus and getting some sleep and there were all these people out there waiting to get their stuff signed and all. There was a lot of them too. I did the best I could. I'm standing there shivering with my wet shorts and the rest of my shit on the ground between my feet and I'm telling them that I'm really cold and I have to get on the bus and they just stand there unmoving. I don't know if they hear me or not. They just stand there with their stuff in their hands and they're not going anywhere. I did the best I could and then I finally got on the bus and I felt like throwing up. I am not the rockstar type. I don't want to bum any of these people out. How can you <u>not</u> like them? They like you, they came to your gig. It's hard for me to not like young people and it's hard not to like someone who likes you, even a little, even if they're strangers. That's my problem. I can't help but like these people, even though I don't know them. I think that's the part that's the hardest. I don't like myself as much as they like me. They have no idea how fucked up I am these days. How hung up I am with Joe and everything else. Some nights when I'm standing there like a cardboard cutout, I have to wonder who they're talking to.

4.15.92 Chicago IL: I am in one of those ruts where I can't think of anything to think of. I played all the way tonight and left my mind on the stage. I don't know how I do it night after night. I figure that at some point my head will explode or I'll have a heart attack. I think people in this town are cool. I always have a great time playing here. Tonight was no exception. I feel like I have been hit on the head with something. I think a lot of bullshit during the day like if I could meet a woman that could help me take my mind off of Joe. Not that I want to forget him at all, it's just that it's wearing me out. I'm never very far from losing it. It's become very hard to find inspiration. I used to think I was pretty unstoppable. Now I see that I was wrong. People are stoppable as hell. It doesn't take much. I'm a walking laugh riot I know. I feel different than I used to. I somehow feel like I live right next door to life. I think I have enough Death in me to disqualify me from the status of the living. I just don't feel like I have anything in common with anyone alive. The world has shrunk around my neck. Become a small and lonely place not suited for disturbed loners anymore. I'm going to keep playing and see where the hell it ends up. I've got nowhere else to go.

4.16.92 Chicago IL: The guy walked up to the whore and stared at her. He walked around her and put his face within an inch of her's. I thought he was going to inhale her. He pulled back and said "I don't wanna fuck you." She told him to come back but he had already gone across the street and was headed for another girl in high leather boots. Before that we played at Medusa. I like Chicago. Me and Joe were talking about moving here few days before he got killed. We figured that we should be out of LA by the spring before the place really got to us. Some timing.

4.17.92 Detroit MI: Over 1200 people at the instore. 800 got in. My intestines were on the table. Can I hug you? I held their flesh, held their babies. Outside the bus they wait for me to sign something. 30 minutes until we play. I don't remember getting up. After the show my belongings are scattered mixed with flowers, phone numbers and pictures. I'm afraid of vomiting in my sleep. The restaurant makes me feel like my eyes are resting on desert crust. Some guy asks me how many times I have found myself in a diner in the middle of nowhere after two in the morning. Over a decade. I think of one girl in particular. Please be with me for a little while. You don't have to do anything, just let me be next to you. A second later I'm 100 miles past loneliness sitting in a moonlit desert, alone and breathing. I snap back at the sound of my name being called. Some guy wants an autograph.

4.18.92 Toronto: They'll drink themselves to Death like their fathers did. They'll end up like their hammered old men fathers before they know what life is all about. They'll do their time in jail and lose their fear of it before they even get a taste for the hard stuff and when they finally do it's all over. They'll never get out, they'll just end up. I end up with one of the rare ones in a single bed late in the night. She tells me about Death and how long it takes to get over it. She kisses me and I know she's right. She is one of the rare ones. I am too dead to fully notice. I fall into her breasts and nearly pass out from the sheer weight of the bliss. Death on the road, safe in hotels. Spitting out pieces of glass and million year old cigarette smoke. I fall through everything. You get a taste of the Abyss and nothing gets in your way after that.

4.19.92 Toronto: To do something that will reduce me to a bag of flesh that wants nothing more than cold water. Might be the act of a fool. That was me tonight. On the last song of the encore I wanted nothing more in the world than a large container of cold water. I know what I am. I am animal. They'll never take it away from me. I'll keep it in my teeth and shake it to pieces before they get it from me. Fuck it, they'll have to kill me.

4.20.92 Washington DC: Parked the bus in front of the bank I walked past for years on my way to school and work. The hotel is in my old neighborhood. My home town. Walked down my old strip of Wisconsin Ave. Most of the places I grew up around are now gone. I feel old and homeless. I am homeless. I don't know any of these buildings. I didn't know the old ones either. It's all a damage report. I don't want to be a casualty. How many hours sleeping on the bus from Toronto. Will I ever love a woman again. The spring air reminds me of growing up and spending time outside on these streets. I cannot smell the blood on my hands. I can feel my mother on these streets I can sense her heat. I bet I could cough pure car exhaust if I wanted.

4.21.92 Washington DC: The line at the instore never ends. Girls there since the place opened so they could be the first in line and they didn't make it. I sign stuff and shake their hands and look into their cameras. It's all I am these days. I know nothing else. The heat at the show cannot be translated. At some point I stop being hot and become heat and then I can play. It's getting to that point that hurts so much. I made up a song during a jam. I wished you loved me, why don't you love me. It worked itself out right there. It's raining outside and I am thinking about how I made my escape tonight in a friend's car. At some point I have to just walk away from all the voices and questions and hope they understand. Out here is endless. They don't know me and I don't know them and that's all the space I need. Tonight my mother hovered in the dressing room. I left and sat shivering on the stairs. I don't want to know anyone, the very idea that I know anyone at all is a lie that I will not take.

4.24.92 New York: First night in NYC down. I had a great time playing. Vernon Reid came down to soundcheck to play with us. He brought a riff with him and we played it later on that night. The place was packed and there wasn't a great deal of air up there but we played well anyway. The encore with Vernon was great. It's so cool to play with him. He's a real good guy. Earlier in the day I did an instore at Tower. I stupidly said yes to doing these and I have several more ahead of me. It's a drag to stand there like a stuffed human xerox machine signing stuff. The people there were great and real nice to me and all but it's hard to stand there and smile and say thank you. I feel like a dick for being something that you can stand in line and see, something that you have to stand in line to see. After I do the ones I have agreed to I will never do them again. I like the people that come to them but I don't want to meet them like this. It's degrading to them and myself. It makes me feel gross. Other than that it's good to be playing well every night. It's good to be alone in this room and not have to see anyone. It's scary to deal with the thoughts that go through my head all the time now. It's somehow better to be alone even when everything in me wants to be with someone.

4.25.92 New York: The boy in the room next door has been screaming for the last hour. I've slept a few hours and some press people will be here soon. It's Saturday and I'll be doing press until soundcheck. I don't have a life. I've totaled 8 hours sleep in the last two days. I can feel my eyes ache. I want to kill someone. I hate the way this shit makes me feel. My throat is coming off. The boy is screaming at his mother. A lot of people live in this hotel full time. It's all bug spray and bad heating. Too much breathing in this place will kill you. Hours later I am finished playing. The place was hot and packed tonight. Had a good time playing. I remember melting onstage and looking out at all the maniacs. Vernon Reid jammed with us tonight on the encore again and that was great. Iggy Pop and Alan Vega showed up a well. At one point they were standing together talking and I wish I had a picture of that, two of the greatest singers ever. I am exhausted and braindead from the interviews and playing. I have to get up in a few hours to shoot a video for the song Tearing. It's going to be live in front of an audience. It's going to be raw playing all day on no sleep. Just thinking about it makes me want to puke.

4.26.92 New York: Shot video all day on 90 minutes of sleep. Want to throw up. Sitting on a monitor between "takes" talking to the "audience" that was "invited" to the gig. Played the one song over and over live and synched until I could no longer remember the words. We were onstage for about ten hours today. The room waited for me until I got back. I cannot translate the language of exhaustion. I feel alone but I'm not lonely. The walls understand me better. I don't know anything. The more they want to know the less I know. Words make me forget all I know.

4.27.92 Atlanta GA: I fall asleep on the chair in the hotel room before I do anything else. The phone rings and it's time to go to some radio station and talk shit. I don't have a life. I listen to the bullshit come out of the DJ's mouth. She asks questions that amount to nothing. I notice that her hands are shaking. Everything in me wants to sleep and vomit. The pigs are trying to shut down the place we're playing. Too bad because the people who run it seem like good folks. I don't remember how the last shows have been. I am beyond loneliness. All I want is sleep.

4.28.92 Atlanta GA: My legs won't get loose. I do the best I can at the instore, they give me things and I promise to the best I can to read, listen and use it all. If they only knew the language that I use in my brain. The language that screams with clearly formed words yet will not come out of my mouth. I stand there like some guy waiting to get smacked. I wonder if I'll ever get shot at one of these things. I hear these girls say ohmigod it's him. I realize that they're talking about me and I want to hand them my lungs and make a getaway out the back of the store. Tonight I'll play harder than I did last night. I remember the other times we played in this town. They just stood there and watched. This time they know all the words and they move and they even sent one of their women onstage to touch the wounded animal.

5.4.92 Menomonie WI: The sky is huge and filled with dark clouds. The hotel is in the middle of nowhere. I like it. They find me still. Call me in the room and ask to come over. I dodge them as best I can. I feel watched. I sit in the diner across the road and listen to the low rumbling of the truckers over in the smoking section. Better than the fire filled streets I left behind in LA. The only break is that I get to keep moving. Have to move like I have to breathe. To those that don't feel this, no amount of explanation will make them understand. I love the big sky country. The night air is fresh. Tonight's theater was packed. I told them the truth. I pulled out my guts and we watched them steam in the lights. I throw out my entrails and pull them back in at the end of the night. I go back to the room and wait to move to the next city. This is fine with me. Nowhere I'd rather be than on the way to the next city. How many of their fathers blew their brains out. How many sons came back to this town from some steaming jungle with an American flag over their remains. How many rapes, how many heartbreaks. What happens in a town this size when someone is murdered. I am in a lit box with a parking lot outside the window. Across the road are fast food places and small time desperation.

5.5.92 Chicago IL: You can hear the L thunder by every so often. I stood and sweated in front of them. The lights peered into me. Afterwards they looked at me and spoke to me and shook my hand and I did the best I could. This city passes quickly. Not enough time to see any of it or remember any of the moves. It's just another room, like so many boxed nights on this trail. It's near one in the morning. Wish I had the energy to do something like think. Times like these make me think that someday I'll get it together to where at the end of the night I can have a brain to use instead of this hollow shell I keep going to bed with.

The L train runs echoes through me. My head is full of nothing, crammed full of their nothing, all their words and sounds. Laughter and clapping and words, so many words, words piled on top of each other. Stranger's words escaping from their mouths, seeking refuge in my brain. What they don't know is that I hear it all the time and they got here too late. The sidewalks take the taste out of my mouth.

5.6.92 Cleveland OH: Flat and the dirt clings. Been here so many times. Stayed in one girl's house while her boyfriend who hated me shot junk in the other room. Another city gets stuck in my throat. Another flesh wave stands in front of my face. Heat, I sweat through my clothes. I shake their hands. The city waits outside the doors of the venue. Another night on the trail. Another city in the life. I don't want to know them like they want to know me. It never works out. I sleep off heartbreak like you wouldn't believe. I can't translate.

5.7.92 Denver CO: Empty streets except for hippies and homeless. Nazi stronghold here. Trees and streams, skiing and nazis. Old hippy people named Dale and Dinah. AA, NA, health food. Nothing moves, it's hard to breathe. When I'm here I can't wait to leave. I fear places that don't move. The creepy conservatism, racism. They're hiding and even the young can't escape the bullshit of these earth shoe wearing motherfuckers.

5.8.92 Salt Lake City UT: Spaced out on too much wide open and sunlight. They simmer in their own self righteousness. I see the sky so huge and the mountains so high and yet I feel stifled and freaked out. They look at me strange when I get coffee in the local diner. They really don't know what they're fucking with this time. The mountains scream. I've never felt at home anywhere. A city looks best to me when I'm leaving it. Dry heat and a show tonight. Two boys in heavy metal shirts tell me it's great to have me here. After them a group of boys comes over to the traffic light and tell me the same thing. It's good at least to be able to be something that someone looks forward to. I wonder about living a whole life in a place like this. Not my life, someone else's.

5.28.92 Los Angeles CA: I imagine watching myself from the back of the hall. I see a man with a bucket of his guts throwing pieces out to an audience. The bucket seems bottomless. The entrails never seem to stop coming. I feel sorry for the guy because I know that when the seemingly bottomless bucket is empty and he walks off stage to the basement and listens to the feet of the audience above as they walk out of the theater he will look down and see that there's blood all over his shoes. He'll look under his shirt and find that he has no more guts left. Confusedly he'll shake the hands of people who are for some strange reason in the room with him. He'll feel nothing for these people because he has no feeling in him whatsoever, he has no feeling of himself, for himself. He speaks thoughtlessly, the words fall out of him as he tries desperately to make these people who are saying things to his hollow frame feel at ease thinking that it will somehow make himself feel something. Soon they are gone and he stands in the room alone. He is as alone as he was several minutes before when he was in front of so many. He leaves the theater and walks unrecognized past people that are waiting to meet him. They imagine he is so much bigger than the average height and build human that quickly walks by them, a broken machine on two legs. He returns to a small room and waits for sleep. The phone rings. It's someone he doesn't know who got his number. The stranger tells him that he was at the show. He asks the stranger, this person out there somewhere on the end of a curled black cord. "Was I good?" The stranger says yes. He hangs up and unplugs the phone. He feels like the only person in the world, so remote, so horribly singular. He knows that all the pain and bloodletting in the world won't get it out. He'll wake up a few hours later and he'll be full of venom and guts and poison and he'll have to find another place to get it out before the pressure becomes too much.

5.31.92 Berlin Germany: Sitting outside a coffee place looking at what's left of Check Point Charlie. Some sections of the wall are still standing. Looks stupid now, like you wonder what took them so long to tear the damn thing down in the first place and you know why, but still. Small painted versions of the wall stand in gift shops. The sun sets and she and I talk about getting out of America alive. She lives here now and has no reason to go back. I think of America and it becomes a horror filled murdering plane. Blood, glass and needles. Lies and sorrow. Larger than Death, so much larger. Seems too big to go back to, like it's the last thing you would want to do. The sun disappears and the night hovers above us. It's one of those great nights that happens around here all the time. I hear about her roommate who was from the East. Her brother engineered wire taps on her to turn her in for the state. You have to wonder about the ones who know how to use a title to their best advantage. Like he'll never sell you out, he's your brother. Sure he will, your brother's human. So's your mother. What about a place where you could go and pay a small amount of money and sit in a room with someone and trust them completely and then after the time was up you would leave feeling like there really is someone out there that you can depend on. You would feel good about it because you had paid for it. I don't trust anyone and I don't ask anything from anyone I don't pay. Do you? What a mess we're in this time.

6.3.92 Dusseldorf Germany: My skull exploded onstage last night. I wonder if anyone in the crowd saw it. I saw bright lights and smoke. I felt my heart scream and die. It was so hot and the weight of the music was heavy. It occurred to me that there could be music that was so heavy that it destroys the people that play it. An honor to be destroyed by music. Build the body up to withstand the music that you took part in creating. Music doesn't care. Music will rip your guts out and laugh in your face. The heat made me a visionary. I heard the dead of Vietnam scream and I answered them with my own. No one would believe me if I told them. I looked up into the lights and felt so alone.

6.4.92 Stuttgart Germany: I don't know, all I've seen is the parking lot of the venue. I don't remember when we got here. I don't know the name of the city that we're playing tomorrow night. I didn't even know we were playing here until I asked someone this morning when we were pulling in. I have no context. All there is in the world is this hall and the show that we'll play in a few hours. I know nothing else. I have been thinking too much. All last night during the show I was screaming I want to die. I did. In the last few weeks things have become too much. I have been having a hard time handling. I don't know what to do. I am dealing shit that's too strong for me. Cities will pull the brains right out of your head. I don't want to know so much all the time. I hate my loneliness and sorrow. It cuts deep into me. It defines me. They can't see it. I do these interviews and scream underneath my skin as I give them some kind of answer. I need something badly and I hate to think about it. Some things that don't give a fuck about you: Cities, money, numbers, roads, time, life, Death. I can inhale shared breath and exhale a naked vision of the Nile, pyramids and stars. I can wrap my arms around a stranger but the horror will never leave. I don' know whether it's patience or tenacity that keeps it near. I don't understand what my next move is. All the lessons I learned in the past fall flat and watch themselves bleed to Death.

6.5.92 Bielefeld Germany: Saw a little bit of the city when we were coming in. Don't remember leaving the last town we were in. I fell asleep in the same parking lot I woke up in that morning. Another grind with a twist at the end. Walk into the place, wait for the coffee to come out. Drink it out of habit not for any other reason. Walk around the venue and try to pass time. I feel stupid and dull. I am looking forward to playing. I don't remember what it feels like even though we played last night. It's coma to coma. We go to Eindhoven after this. I am dislocated from myself. I don't know what the lady was asking me today during the interview interrogation session. I looked at her and wondered what she thought of this guy she didn't know anything about who looked through her and talked about horror and Death. I'm a silent crisis center.

6.6.92 Eindhoven Holland: I finished the show. Gave it all I had. I don't know these people and the stupid shit that comes out of their mouths just makes me meaner. Some guy comes up to me tells me that a woman that works at his favorite bar told him that the band I'm in sucks and women are just into me because of my body. Like I really have to hear this shit. I looked at some woman that was standing there and said that I was heartbroken because I thought that women liked me for my mind. Then I said that I should start stabbing common bitches in the face. She bummed out because I was staring at her when I said it. What the fuck do these people expect from me. Do they think that I'm some nice guy who they can talk shit to? Fuck these people. I don't care what some woman wants me for. Mind, body, who gives a fuck what someone wants. Remind me to not give a fucking woman the time of day for a few years. I think that more people should start getting stabbed in the face with screwdrivers. Fuck all of you, I hope you all get raped and murdered, fucked in the ass and slaughtered. I left out the back door and didn't have to say shit to anyone. I looked at the signs for the highway as I walked. I have played almost every city that was listed. People fuck with me too much. I am good for a few things. I am good at being that thing that you can throw peanuts at. Other than that, you don't want to know me.

6.7.92 Rotterdam Holland: Waiting to play I get bored. A few hours to wait until we hit. The wait makes me crazy. Finally we get to go and it's a relief. Been walking around the outside the club for what seems to be forever. Nothing to look at. Blank faced people. Another show, it could be anywhere. They don't come to the show for the same reasons that I do. I don't connect with them because I know the truth. I know how fucked up I am. I feel the cage. I wanted to wound them. Afterwards I walked around and looked for food. I sat in some cheap lit place and stared at a table full of people until they looked at the floor. I don't know whether dragging my life through these cities is the cure or the problem. It's the process of examination. It destroys me and I know the truth so I don't care.

6.8.92 Brussels Belgium: I will not lower myself to lust anymore. I don't want to love anyone. I don't even want to fuck anyone anymore. I don't want to kill them, I don't want to know them either. I don't think there is a more honorable way to go. All the talk is just time wasting. I was thinking about it on the way to this city. The jazzmen knew. That's why their music killed them. They went deep inside and explored and the truth that they pulled out killed them. Ate them alive, destroyed them piece by piece. I was thinking about the weight of this and then the non-weight of trying to talk to a woman and how the sound of the horn is more beautiful than a woman could ever be and maybe that's why those guys played the damn thing in the first place. Where they got to was a better place. It was so good that it killed them.

6.9.92 Paris France: I'm looking through the skylight of the bus as traffic on both sides roars by. The moon is almost full. So What by Miles is playing on the stereo. I think of all the greats that saw Paris at night. I think of Monk and Coltrane, Art Blakey, Parker, Miller. I wonder what made Miller stay here for so many years. I don't know the people. The ones that came to the show tonight make me wonder why they bothered showing up. It's hard to know where others get off. After the show the backstage was filled with people that I didn't know so I came out here to be with the night. There was an old man sitting in the park near the venue today. He watched a young couple walk by and he called them over. They came and he gave them a piece of plastic jewelry. At first they didn't want to take it but the man insisted and they finally did. He smiled and waved at them until they crossed the street and then he looked down at his feet and shook his head. I wonder if he saw himself in the young man's eyes. Maybe he had taken a walk with a young girl on the very same path decades ago.

6.10.92 Amsterdam Holland: I'm sitting in the basement of the Paradiso. I look over to the corner and can remember seeing D. Boon standing there from when I played here in February 1983. I walked along the streets here this morning. I looked at the girls and they looked good but I don't lower myself to common lust anymore. We were here at this club a few months ago. I wonder if anyone will show up. We woke up in the parking lot of the club again like we have been doing for the last several days. I walked into the city and tried to think straight but was in such a bad mood from the dreams that I had that all I could do was trip. I have found a good way to deal with the loneliness that always follows me on the roads through these cities year after year. I knew I would come to some kind of answer and in the past I had thought I already had but it was not true. I always thought the answer was in some kind of hardlined tough guy bullshit but I have found that not to be true for me. I now see it as a relief of sorts. When I let it go a little, it lets me go a little and so I get to breathe a little easier. I don't have to thicken my outer shell as much as I have to understand myself better. Some people are not going to fit into the world as others do. There's nothing wrong with this as long as you can deal with it if this happens to be your reality. I know it's mine. It took my friend dying to see what really being alone in the world is all about. You don't know loneliness unless you're around a lot of people. You can pass them in a hallway or stand with them on the bus and you'll feel it. People are the root of loneliness. When I am by myself for long periods of time I feel better about people than when I spend long periods of time amongst them. I know what I want to do with myself until I die and it took me a while to find it out and it doesn't involve me dealing closely with many people. I have to re-learn all the things I've taught myself and I have to re-evaluate all the things I've seen. It will take me a long time to learn how to not slow myself down. Other's expectations will kill you and waste your time every time. You have to learn to fly alone if you want to get a lot of things done.

6.12.92 Florence Italy: Shit doesn't work and you know you must be in Italy. Didn't see much of the city, didn't want to. Something about this country pisses me off. Maybe because no one ever seems to have their shit together. They get mad if you get mad at that fact. For me I don't care. I'm good at lying awake in that bunk compartment re-living Death trips over and over. Making up bullshit conversations with women that don't exist. Thinking of ways to try to fool myself into wanting to live. I like it in there in that hole, that dark box. I don't have to see anyone and I can breathe easy. I have become an enemy of language. When people talk to me I hate them for using the language that brings me pain. I don't want to talk. I want to get away from anyone that wants to know me. When someone tries to talk to me I only feel the emptiness of the language, the desperation of words. The hunger of the need to communicate. I know my truth in that I know I'll never be able to say anything back to them that isn't coming from the dark room that is my mind. All I know is horror and ugliness. I'd rather keep most of it to myself. It's like diving on hand grenades. I went out earlier and tried talking to the guy selling the horrible bootleg shirts outside the show. It was a great conversation. I told him he was a fucking thief. He smiled and shrugged. I told him to get the fuck out and he said he couldn't, he already bought the shirts. I told him he was fucking with our trip. He told me that he was sorry but this was his job. I told him I was going to beat the shit out of him. He begged me not to. I took a big pile of shirts and threw them to people in the street. He ran around trying to get them back and I grabbed him and wouldn't let him take them away from people. I told him to look and see how happy we were making people by giving them free shirts. There was really nothing I could do to persuade this guy to leave and I really didn't hate him, he seemed like too nice a guy to get mad at. In the end I don't really give a fuck but the shirts are so bad, I feel sorry for anyone who bought one of them.

6.13.92 Fribourg Switzerland: They are drunk against the Alps. They stand complacently against the clear blue sky. I feel nothing. I sit in the room and look out the window and wait to play. Dead time. The opening band is playing and I'm waiting through dead time to get to play. I'm hoping the music will somehow cure me of the pain that keeps my eyes to the floor and makes so fucked up. I feel far away from everything. Nothing reaches me. I try all the normal things to get myself out of the haze but nothing works. I am an experiment. I no longer feel like I'm part of life. I am walking along beside it. I wonder if they can tell that I'm half dead. Finally we play. They watch and talk and it all seems to bore them and then you realize that they can't identify with any of it because they don't come from a polluted crime ridden land where paranoia is the landscape. It's not America that I'm speaking about. It's my mind. They have no clue. I am a different species and that makes it alright because for the evening they can hang out with an alien.

6.15.92 Sheffield England: Fucked up buildings. Every other block looks like it just got shelled. The people on the street look depressed and mutated. If I lived here I would get the fuck out or start killing people. All the restaurants smell like grease. The air stinks. The bands suck. The place is like a leech. It drains me every second I stand here. The shows at night are the only release. Waiting for them to happen is the drag. Nothing works, it's always fucked up every year. Like a sucker I keep returning to test myself against this bullshit machine. I can't help but hate all the shit around me. If I don't hate it then it gets too close to me and I go down. Fuck this slump backed shit. Fuck this leeching bullshit polite backstabbing population. I'll ignore it and play right through the fuckers. You can't let them grind you down. They won't care of you die in right front of them. If you're looking for someone to care about you then get the fuck out of music. When you let that idea go then it lets you go and you can really let it rip. I see no other way to go.

6.16.92 Newcastle England: The Beastie Boys soundcheck inside. I am in a cold trailer out back. I wish there was something on my mind. I hate the times when the brain is cold and dead. I avoided walking around the city. I don't need my mind polluted. There's nothing that I want to see in this city at all except the stage. I don't want to meet any of its inhabitants and I don't want to talk to anyone if I don't have to. I just remain inert until playing time. It's the only time that matters these days. I am going to learn to live with less and less as the years go on. I want nothing to hang onto me. I want no one to hang onto me. I think that's the thing that keeps people fucked up all the time. I want to empty myself of all filler.

6.17.92 Glasgow Scotland: I went from the bus to the venue. I have not seen any of Scotland. I don't want to know anything about it, I just want to play and leave. The poison thought is that I will be playing several more shows this year. If I look at the schedule it will kill me. So many nights of getting ripped apart by the music. The music never misses ever. It will always try to kill you. The music is pure and it exposes all that isn't in you. The music takes me out every night and beats the shit out of me. Trying to help me out. I know what there is for me now. I can't fight the music. I was fighting it without realizing it. Music is one thing that never cares about your bullshit. It will beat the shit out of you with your own arms if you lie to it. Doesn't matter what city it is. If you look too much at the scenery, it will ruin your day. Too many moving scenes over the years make the mind insane. I can't talk, I can no longer speak in a language that I can use to talk to people with. I fake it and use their language instead. It makes me lonely for other planets, other deserts. Sometimes I'd rather just howl.

6.18.92 Birmingham England: Couldn't sleep last night because I was too busy planning how I'll kill myself very soon. Spent the morning in the dark box not knowing that we were parked in the hotel lot. I Thought of a girl while still in half sleep. I think I was begging her to stay with me. All my money disappeared from my pants pockets tonight backstage. Lost, stolen, I don't know. I am choking inside myself. I don't exist. I breathe. I went and signed bullshit in a record store today.

Everywhere I went I was asked to sign shit. I had to talk to employees in record stores while I looked at records, they wouldn't stop talking and I wanted them to die because all I wanted to do was look at the fucking records. They have no idea who they're talking to. They don't know that I'm not listening, that I'm screaming inside at them to leave me the fuck alone. They can't smell the animal that's standing next to them. I don't want to know these people that take my money and fill the world with talk. I'm sitting in the hallway of the hotel. The man in the room across from my feet is vomiting violently. I can hear him as he lets go over and over. No more autographs, no more contact. They take money from me, they should stay away. The shithead couple that got backstage and wasted my time. The man has no idea how close he came to getting maimed. Fuck this country and all the begging pathetic little thieves that occupy it. I am filled with horror and don't want to know anyone.

6.19.92 Manchester England: Don't hold onto time. Just let it go. Don't even look back unless you want to scare the shit out of yourself. I don't look back over the calendar these days. I don't want to remember night after night. I was there and that's good enough for now. Time will kill you. Standing next to the bus in a gas station on some highway on the way out of Manchester feels good. No one knows where I am and those who do don't care. I hope my brain doesn't leak out of my head. Manchester was a stage to play on and a small fucked up room to wait in. That's all I know. I woke up in the parking lot and didn't ask. I don't want to know anything about England. I could count how many times I've been to this country but I won't. I don't want to let time own me more than it does already. We drive tonight and wake up in London. After that we go back to America. It's all the same to me. I play and it doesn't matter where anymore. If you want it to matter then wake me up, get me out of this suffocation mind. It has all run together and no one touches me. I lie in that bunk and make up stories about suicide and mixing with the earthlings that talk to me. It's possible to be dead and still be filled with horror, this is what I have found.

6.20.92 London England: I don't know how long we were out here in Europe. Doesn't matter. We leave London tomorrow. Just back from the only food place open around here. Men staggering drunk. Three ugly limey shit bags try to talk up a whore in front of the kebab place. A man who can barely stand up urinates in a doorway. The show was a lot of steam and sweat. I don't know if it was any good. I gave it all I had. Did interviews today. Don't remember what I said. It doesn't matter really. I get up in a few hours to go to the airport to fly to New York where I will have my only day off. I have nothing on my mind. Back sore, elbow smashed, face a mess. Stressed out and a long string of lit boxes are just up the road. Bury me.

6.21.92 New York City: It seems like I have a lot of friends in this city. Every block or so someone comes running up to talk to me. It's scary. I walked the streets for hours looking at the people. I wish I could share the city with someone. I see people walking together and I wonder what they're talking about, what they're thinking. I wish I knew someone here, someone to make the city seem smaller and more understandable. It doesn't matter does it. Tomorrow I'll be in an office a few blocks from this insecticide smelling room talking to strangers on the phone about bullshit so it really doesn't matter about this fucking city and the size of it and finding someone to share it with.

6.24.92 Los Angeles CA: This place is so dead except for the murderers. Whores on the corners, pigs everywhere. Burned out buildings. Piles of rubble. Men working in the hulls of huge structures with smoke marks all over. Friend in the hospital, the city is killing another one. My room smells of Death. I can smell him in the closet. I can smell the blood. I can smell the brains. I leave soon. This city starves me for real life. It's a heartbreaker and all the inhabitants will die horrible Deaths. I will not be one of them. I am a road man and get out whenever I can. You stand around here long enough and you'll get murder one done to you. Believe me, they're all scum.

6.26.92 Houston TX: I wouldn't want to die here, live here or anything else. Texas has always been one of those places that I'm glad to leave. I remember all the fights I've been in here, the heat and the bullshit. The redneck motherfuckers and the pigs telling us to take our van and get the hell out of town. Desert sprawl. I don't see how they do it year after year. Where the hell can you go. I wonder what someone from here would think of a place like Chicago. Instore. They want you to sign this thing and then stand still for the picture. I do it and I feel like I want to crawl away. If they only knew me they would never come as close as they do.

6.27.92 Dallas TX: A lot of people look and talk. The heat is something you can see and touch, the heat is so much a part of things here that it has its own phone number and tax bracket. I find a way to look through them and sign pieces of paper. I mutter and try to disappear. The more they like me the more I want to break things. I hung out with a girl afterwards and it was no good, I was still locked up inside myself. It was good to leave. I wonder if there's a way to get though life without hating it all the time.

6.28.92 Austin TX: I'm talking to Selby on the phone long distance. He's in the hospital. I listen to his voice, it sounds far away and tired and beat. It's hard to take. He plays it off like it's nothing and asks if there's an opening in the band for a trumpet player. I think of the one partially collapsed lung he's breathing out of and it hurts. I want to give him one of mine. I can tell how hard it is for him to talk. Every word seems like an effort. I am getting upset having to stand in this abandoned strip mall and listen to this fading voice. I start crying while talking to him. A guy is standing next to me trying to get my attention so I can sign some picture. He and his friend both have cameras and they're taking pictures of me on the phone. I want to beat the shit out of these guys. I tell Selby that I have to go to soundcheck and that I'll call him tomorrow. I get off the phone and they're on me. I want to tell them that I was just on the phone with someone close to me and how could they stand around me like that and can't they get lives of their own. Instead I just sign the fucking pieces of paper and stand for photographs. Later on the show proves to be one of the hottest onstage temps that I have ever dealt with. The Butthole Surfers come out and play with us, it's amazing. After the show I have to hide from the people because they want to talk and I want to kill. Gibby wants to have a boxing match with me for charity. He needs three years to train and he says he knows he'll take me out because he has an eighty inch reach on me. I listen and laugh and wish Joe could be here listening and laughing too. We get on the bus and leave.

6.29.92 Oklahoma City OK: Tonight was definitely a rock experience. A girl got onstage and we were making out like it was some movie. The whole gig was like a movie. A 90 minute MTV video. People all over the stage, flying through the air. It was hard to get any playing done because it was just all I could do to keep out of the way of the people running into me. So many nights now turn into the mere execution of the set list because of the amount of people getting in the way of the band. They really have no idea how much it fucks us up. It's the worst thing to take a night out of your life, a night you'll never get back and have to throw it away because people won't let you go all the way. I don't think they have any idea what it's like to walk off stage and feel totally ripped off. They wouldn't ever think that the band might feel ripped off for not getting to play hard. I'm not going to stand up there like some asshole telling them what and what not to do, I didn't get into this shit to be a cop. There were people all over the place in the parking lot when we pulled in for soundcheck and it went from there. After the show some young teenage girl was hitting on me enough times to where I had to walk away and stand on the other side of the bus. I think she may have struck a deal for the exchange of fluids with another member of the band, of course this could all be a bunch of smoke, I mean I don't know for sure and at the end of the day who gives a fuck. I don't see what it is about bands that make people who have lives of their own stand around in a parking lot and stare nervously at you for half an hour and then go home.

6.30.92 Columbia MO: Everyone makes me crazy and mad. They more they talk, the more I get twisted inside. I sit by myself and they keep coming up with words. I wish I wasn't so fucked up so I could talk to them but I'm fucked up and I can't talk to them. I play an hour later and I don't know how it is for them. I know that they can't be getting the same thing that we get. If they did, they wouldn't get on stage and fuck us up. After the show I'm sitting in a place eating and a woman sits down and tells me that she likes what I do but the only thing she didn't like was what I said about pigs. She's a pig herself and she says that she's an individual. I tell the pig cunt that when she puts a uniform on that she loses all individuality. I told her that I party down when I hear that a pig has gotten wasted. I hope she goes out and gets shot in the knees by some low rent motherfucker who laughs in her face. She really thought that she was a human being. I don't know how they brainwash these shitheads into being so self righteous about being a bag of shit that should be taken out and shot in the face. Fuck these people. You never know when they are pigs in disguise. Fuck you, you stupid pig bitch, I hope you get Magic Johnson disease and die in some ward. I wonder how long I have left with this shit.

7.1.92 St. Louis MO: I had sex with a girl in the club shower. It was good. Then we played. I think we played well. It's hard to tell when they don't let you play as hard as you can. They get onstage and they fuck your shit up. We finished the show and I sat and waited for them to leave. It was hard as usual to deal with them after the show. I can't talk and they just make me mad. After they left me and the girl went back into the bathroom and had sex again. It was good again. She said that she was sorry that my friend had passed away. I told her that he didn't pass away, he was murdered. Whatever, the flies ate the blood anyway.

I went to the backdoor to get to the bus and saw all these people waiting by the door of the bus. I pulled back in and snuck around to the front of the club and the bus picked me up and we got out of there. I don't know what they get out of the music. I think about it more and more seeing how many of them get onstage and stomp on people's heads. Now I'm vacant and waiting for sleep to take me out. The sex get off was mutual. I had to wipe my come off the floor so no one else would slip when they came in. Another page of life has been ripped out of the book.

7.2.92 Lawrence KS: A girl got raped at the show tonight. She was taken into one of the toilets and raped and had cigarettes put out on her flesh. She does not know whether she will press charges or not. In bullshit land I woke up in the bus and was told to go to a room in a hotel and do interviews on the phone. I talked and slept in the minutes between calls. I am in the bus and numb from playing hard as I could. I stink and I don't know how many shows I have done so far on this trip. I worked out in some community gym today with the hayseeds. Ghosts. There were ghosts at the restaurant this morning. I looked out the window to the parking lot where in 1986 the Rat Sound truck was parked waiting for the band to eat a late meal. Joe and I sat in cab and played Mississippi Fred McDowell and waited for them. I looked at the place where the truck had been and thought back to a few weeks to when I saw the Rat truck in the back of a hall I was doing a talking show at. I looked into the cab and looked at the big fucked up seat and remembered all the times in 1986 that Joe and I sat in there and drove down the road. So many thousands of miles we drove together in that truck. So now I don't want to know about their lives. It hurts too much sometimes. I have invented a new kind of loneliness for myself. It is an animal that lives inside me. I must stay away from people because they only make it mad.

7.3.92 Omaha NE: When people like us that much I always think it's the prelude for them hating our guts that much as well. Hard to get through the set tonight. People onstage all the time. They wait outside the door of the bus, the dressing room, the side of the stage, they're all over the place. They came early to hang out in the parking lot. I was as nice as I could be. I like these people, I can't help but like them, there's nothing not to like about them. She asks if she can hug me and I tell her that I freak out if people touch me. It's true. I don't like it when they want to touch me like that. I waited in the room for them to go home and go to sleep. I waited for a long time. When I left, they were out there. One had a tape recorder on and read aloud everything I wrote on their ticket stubs and other assorted things. I hate autographs. I hate compliments. They'll never know how fucked up I am. That the only reason I do what I do is because I'm damaged. Still I like them. I get exhausted after playing. They have no idea what the entire day has been like, what the horror dreams of the night before were about. They don't know shit about me, it's a lonely gig.

7.5.92 Denver CO: Thin air for us tonight. Hot lights and sweat. I sat in an alley after working out. A few of them came and stared and asked meaningless questions. After that they left as silently as they came. We drive tonight. I am not thinking, I am not knowing, I don't remember how to feel. I thought of nothing all day. I don't remember anything except some panic stricken man on the phone wondering why I didn't know about some interview. My life is bullshit sometimes. We go tonight to Salt Lake City. That's all I know.

7.6.92 Salt Lake City UT: Something about this place I don't like. It's the Mormons. Fucked up conservatives. The promoter's boyfriend is one of these pieces of shit. I know that they're both fakes, brainwashed, uncreative and hypocritical. We played our asses off and I don't know what they thought of it and I don't care. I have the intellect of a shark and that's good. I don't want to take all of their bullshit onstage or anywhere else. I have to keep away from their words. I have to leave them all over there so I can get on with the real thing. They talk too much about nothing. I sit outside and I listen to them talk about getting fucked up and how much they are drinking tonight. I can't talk to someone like that. There's nothing we have in common. I don't have any energy to do anything. I get up in a few hours to go talk bullshit to interviewers.

7.8.92 Seattle WA: Joe's book came out today. I pulled a copy out of the box here in Seattle. It's great and horrible at the same time. I almost don't want to see it. It's a great book but I would like to be able to give him a copy and show him that he made it happen. It hurts to know that he'll never see it. I sat in the box and read the foreword that I had written for the book on his birthday on April 4. It hurts so much. I looked at the back cover at the two of us looking like we knew everything. Life is so different. I looked at the book and all I could think of was not wanting to live anymore. I can't explain to anyone how hard it's been to live. I feel like I'm going to explode sometimes. I know that everyone feels like that all the time but it's hard to do all this stuff and think of Joe. Tonight it's hard to read his book and laugh at the great stories and realize that he died thinking that he was a failure. I was hoping that this book was going to be the first of many things that we were going to do together to get Joe going. I know he would have been so thrilled to see the book. He would have wanted to send it to people and he would have gotten great mail and he would see that he could do many things he didn't think possible. I promised him that I would publish his book and I did it. The show was ok. I talked to the singer from Pearl Jam after the show and he's a really good guy. Saw one of the Soundgarden guys as well, they are good folks, they like to play and they're not into the bullshit. Now I'm in this box with my brain. I miss my friend and it's hard for me to be strong. I guess I'll have to lift more weights and play harder and wear myself out and fall over. End.

7.9.92 Portland OR: They never stopped getting on the stage and jumping off. I don't know if the show was good or not. The audience seemed to like it. It was hard to get into it knowing that no one cared about the music, they just cared about getting on stage and jumping off. I guess the music doesn't matter to them like it does to us. It's hard to talk to them after the show because I can't take them seriously at all. We come from such different worlds. She said that I had influenced her whole life and that she had read all of my books and that she knew everything that I thought. She was drunk and kept shaking my hand every few minutes and telling me the same things over and over again. She would get mad at me when I would have nothing to say the third time around the same thing. Finally she told me to fuck off and staggered away. After that I now know that I don't want to know any of these people. I play my guts out and tell the truth and then get told to fuck off. I need that like I need more bills. I'll do my thing and avoid them. I won't be able to go out before shows like I want to. I won't be able to warm up on the sidewalk like I usually do anymore. Things have changed. Next stop is California.

7.11.92 Sacramento CA: The pigs shut the PA off a few songs from the end of the set. Too bad the place was near the pig station. I was getting shocked for the last few songs. The pigs turned the lights on and freaked people out. It's a drag to be back in the police state of California. I will move from this state if it's the last thing I do. I will not live in this motherfucker. I was careful to stay away from people this time remembering the girl in Portland. They frisked people at the door. I can feel the laid back paranoia with every set of eyes that flash in front of me. I like them but I don't know who's packing. And then there's the pigs, they're all over the place and they know that everyone hates them and they love it and can't wait for one of these punk ass motherfuckers to step out of line so they can give it to them like their fathers did in their nightmares. I made an exit to the side door after the set and nearly got some people hurt because I started a crush of people trying to get to me. I made it outside and some vacant girls tried to fill me with hopeless night almost dead words. Party conversation. I knew I was back in California. The land of the paranoid and almost dead.

7.12.92 San Francisco CA: Over a thousand people in the place tonight. Gave them all we had. San Francisco doesn't count on the California is fucked up scale, for some reason this city escapes that. I'm in a hotel room that looks out at the apartment that used to house a girl I was too stuck on. Today I looked at the window and remembered all the great times I had with her there. I am sorry that these things can run too deep. I fall too far and hit the bottom too hard. I thought about her all day today. Nothing I want to admit to. Makes me feel too exposed, like anyone could come by and cut me if they wanted to. All there is to do is lift and play and tell the truth. We go to Santa Clara tomorrow. Who the hell knows what that will be like. I bet the audience looks like the cast of River's Edge. Doing shows in California isn't like being on tour, it's just getting out without getting any on you.

7.13.92 Santa Clara CA: After the show she comes up to tell me how her brother saved her life and died doing so. She was getting raped by a man when her brother stepped in to protect her. His throat was slashed and he died. She wanted to give me his ring that he was going to give me the first chance he got. I sat with the ring and looked at it and listened to this girl talk. It was hard to take. He was only 15 years old. She feels guilty and the pigs have been asking her all the stupid questions that only pigs can. They're so good at that. I left the hall totally empty. The heat was incredible. I was kicked in the shoulder at one point. I can't understand what they see in what we do. Thinking of them leaves me in a darkness of my own.

7.14.92 Santa Cruz CA: It's the place you want to plow under and then move into. Some of the staffers cannot hide their cocaine habits and contradict themselves. An hour at the venue makes me wonder how we're going to pull off the show having to work with people like this. The sun is shining and the palm trees are green and it would be better if it were a slum so these hippies would have to die of all known diseases. The audience. When they weren't fighting, they were making stupid comments and wasting our time. The most shallow people I have ever been in front of. A waste of a night. We played and I don't remember any of it. After the show they wanted to talk to me and I wouldn't do it because I felt like they should go die instead of wasting my time further with their vacant no brain no soul white trash bullshit. Be back soon? Never.

7.15.92 Los Angeles CA: Night off in LA. Got here this morning. I don't think it was a good idea for me to come here for this one day. I feel weak being off the road. It takes so much compression to get through the sets that when I'm not near it feeling the pressure so much that I stop feeling it, I fall apart. That's how I am tonight. Sitting here in my room wondering if I'll be able to do it tomorrow night. Knowing that I have to. I was with a woman tonight. I don't think it was a good idea as good as it felt to be with her. It fucked my head up to where all I can feel is the exhaustion that makes my bones ache from the marrow out. All I can feel is the need for my body and mind to get away from this for a little while. I also know it's greatness calling, seeing if I have what it takes. Greatness is seeing if it can weed me out. My room is the siren song calling out to me to stop what I'm doing. Trying to separate the eagles from the birds. To do this you have fly in the thin air. One cannot surround oneself with friends and feel that fake support. It only breeds a false sense of security. The only thing that will get you through this shit is to pull inward and harden and move forward. The less friends and words you exchange, the better. I have at least 50 to 60 more shows to do this year. If I don't do it just right, I'll wind up in the hospital with a nervous breakdown. This is my hardest year yet. A lot of things are going against me. It's greatness calling.

7.16.92 Phoenix AZ: In the middle of the first song a guy jumps off stage and smacks his head on the floor and we sit it out and wait for the ambulance. We eventually come out and finish playing. People are being thrown out left and right. I spend some time with a girl at the hotel. Didn't sleep until near six in the morning. Had to get up at eight to leave. I talked to her. I don't know if she knows that I told her things that I never tell anyone, you can do that with strangers. She probably thinks I'm some maniac. I will never see her again so it's just another human experience. All these words they mean nothing, they mean everything. It would have been the time where the brains blow out of the side of the head. She would be sleeping and be awakened by a gunshot in the bathroom. There I'd be, all over the walls. No note just a freak out. She would get treatment. Possible one word notes to leave when you kill yourself: Broken, Mother, Finished, Sorry, No.

7.17.92 Santa Barbara CA: The P.A. shorts out and the audience is kept waiting for nearly an hour as the sound team desperately tries to fix the system. People are packed in and pissed off. Finally we play. They never stop getting onstage even after they are asked. They don't care. They don't take the music seriously so I don't think about them at all. I find a place near the drum riser so I can do my thing and get off and not have to think about them. Before the set I hid from them. When they call me dude I want to hide. Nothing's more depressing than the trash that falls out of the mouths of guys who call you dude. I wait a long time to leave after the show so I can leave without having to sign autographs. They are in the parking lot waiting. I try to be cool but something comes over me and all I can do is run through them to a waiting car. They must think I am a total asshole. I think about this as the miles go by the window. I don't want to be like that but at the end of the night there's nothing left to give them and they'll never understand.

7.18.92 Tijuana Mexico: Knocked to the floor in the second song. Smacked in the head. I remember trying to get up. Everything moved slow and I heard people in the audience telling me to get up. The rest of the night was a balancing act of trying to sing and not puke. I kept it all in. Later on in the set some guy got onstage and tried to tackle me but only knocked me into the drums. My head was ringing all the way through the set. After the set I just sat and waited for them to leave. I had been called dude all day and it made it worse. California is a disease. Due to getting smacked in the head I don't know if anything else happened.

7.21.92 Los Angeles CA: Hot onstage. I actually felt pressure tonight. Something about the size of the place and all, I was wondering if we were going to get swallowed up in there. Body Count was in the house. Played hard but I don't know how it went. Dave Navarro came out for the encore jam. What a great guy, good to see him again. Looking forward to getting back on the road. Something about playing in California doesn't seem real to me. So many people, they come out of the cracks, they spill over the edges, they are everywhere. I like them more than they will ever know. I don't know if I'll be able to tell them the way I want to.

7.23.92 Anaheim CA: Live shoot for television. I don't remember much of it. Felt like band practice with people standing all the way at the back of the room. Had a good time though. I hid from the autograph guys as best I could but they found me anyway. We leave in a few days for a long time. It was strange being in LA this time around. The place alienates me. Looking forward to getting out to Florida and wherever else we're going this year. Nothing here but loneliness and sorrow, dried blood and shallow breath.

7.27.92 St. Petersburg FL: Outdoor gig. Lights went off a few times. I don't know if they even heard us. They felt so far away, more concerned with beating the shit out of each other than anything else it seemed. I shouldn't be near people after I play. The farther we go the worse it gets for me. Sitting slumped over in a chair smelling the sweat turn to ammonia, catching breath for the first time in two hours. Listening to the ringing roar thundering in both ears, louder in the right. Feeling an immense emptiness. All of a sudden there is a poke in the ribs. A pen is being shoved into my side. Could I sign this piece of paper? I should be put in a cage and rolled out because all I want to do is kill this piece of shit. I can barely get out the words. I sign the paper. The guy looks at it and says "That's all you're going to write?" This is the point where a punch to the throat is the only thing that I can think of doing to help this guy out. Like I said I should be put in a fucking cage and hauled out because I can't deal with these people.

7.28.92 Miami FL: The best line all night was the guy who told me that I would be soon out of a job because I told the stage divers to cool it. Some skinhead asshole telling me that I'm going to be out of a job because I want to play music instead of getting out of the way of punkers all night. He should get his own television show. I like Miami. It seems like you could killed here real easy. Haven't been here to play with the band for years. After the show there were record company people with their pictures to sign, some terrified radio guy apologizing for all kinds of shit he isn't responsible for. I was so angry that I could barely make words come out. I said hello a little above a whisper and they took the hint and left. Some people will not give up and will stay there and wait until hell freezes over to meet someone. They came in and got their books signed. I tried to be as nice as I could be. I couldn't wait to leave. I talked to a girl outside the hall for awhile. I don't know her name. Now I'm inside the bus waiting to go to another city and I don't even know which one it is.

7.29.92 Gainesville FL: It's hard. It's hard to get the music out when they're stepping all over you. It's hard to make it matter to anyone if you can't make it matter to yourself. No matter where you go they will grab you, shove the mic into your teeth and smack you in the head. Sometimes I hate them, I hate their fucking guts and I can't believe I'm stupid enough to put myself in a situation where I can get picked at like a piece of meat in a field of crows. There's no way I will ever be able to explain myself to them. I now avoid them and their questions and compliments and small talk. It's hard to like them when one of them uses you to climb onstage and knee you in the balls. It's hard to see individuality when one of them swings at your head. The more they compliment the more sick it makes me. I saw them coming after the show. I was in the dark in the back looking at the stars, thinking about how good it was that I decided to let go of the idea that I will ever be close to someone. I was feeling good in my thoughts. I figured after playing over two hours of music that people should leave me alone. I saw them coming and I ran and hid. One guy came after me to tell me every time he saw me and he was in the process of telling me all the times I was on some television show and I asked him to stop talking. I told him that compliments make me want to tear my face off. Near two in the morning and they're still out there knocking on the window. They have no idea how fucked up I am, no idea at all.

7.30.92 Pensacola FL: Hottest show I can remember. It was like breathing your own flesh. All I could do was try to stand. I hid from them tonight knowing that I was in no shape to even shake anyone's hand. I woke up in the parking lot of a hotel with interviews starting soon after I walked into the room. I worked out too hard. Losing weight. Nothing but that. Didn't talk to anyone. Came here and played and now I'm leaving. I don't know if the people at the show have idea what we're about but they seemed to like us ok. I am pounded flat and totally useless.

7.31.92 New Orleans LA: They never got off the stage except when we played a real slow one. I don't know if it was respect, reverence or boredom. I don't remember anything about today except waking up and walking into the phone. Interview with some stupid bitch who wanted to know if I hated some rockstar. I think I will have to start doing less interviews. They are getting to me. A guy asked me about Joe today and I told him that I didn't want to talk about him. I think that's good. It does no good to talk about him anymore. I don't want to wear out the memory by talking about him too much. I was thinking about seeing him dead while I was in my black box bunk last night. Thinking about it now it seems too incredible to be real. Just seeing him there like that. Tonight I sang about him. About living in the form of ash in a small plastic box. I think we go to Tennessee tomorrow. I don't think matters anymore where I go. I just go. I am unattached and falling forward. Nothing stops me anymore. Not to say that I'm unstoppable, it's just that I have thrown out a lot of my thoughts. What a thought that is.

8.1.92 Nashville TN: We played and they stepped all over us. What does it matter to play when all that happens is your ass gets knocked around all night. It was a waste of time. I only got to play two songs all night. The rest was just going through the motions of playing, looking out for the guys who have to get onstage every three seconds. Trying to get the words right and trying to find a place where they aren't. That's all that happened all day. Got in a workout that was more meaningful. Next is Minneapolis where there will be some air to breathe and maybe we'll even get to play some. What they don't know, what they'll never know is that they push me away with every word, autograph, with every handshake I fall further away from them all.

8.3.92 Minneapolis MN: 1800 people in the big room. More than Black Flag ever had in there. I watched the equipment come in and all I could think about was loading the gear into the small room a few years ago. Taking shit from the 135 in attendance as they got shitfaced. Tonight we played hard and it felt good to be set free from bullshit thought. Throw out thoughts that you don't need, what a great idea, what a time waste eliminating lifesaver. Went to a thing to meet people from BMG. Not my kind of thing. Standing around saying thank you. Thank you, I'm glad you like the way I'm fucked up. I'm not good for much but what I'm good for, I'm really good for and that's all that matters. The rest is just bullshit.

8.4.92 Racine WI: Watched some people get the shit beaten out of them as we played. People jumping on other people's heads and then getting hit in the head and then people seeing it and hitting them in the head. Same guys getting on top of everyone and rolling over their heads. I wonder what goes on in the minds of these people. What would you talk about with someone like that. I wonder if they have shit for brains.

8.5.92 Grand Rapids MI: We played hard as hell and no one got in our way. It was a good day and a good night so nothing must have happened. In a hotel tonight. I have thrown out so many thoughts in the last few weeks that all I think about is playing and Death.

8.6.92 Pontiac MI: Played outside to over 2000 people. They were all over the place. He has been waiting for three hours by the gate to talk to me. His father left him when he was five and now he lives down the street and won't return his phone calls. As he tells me this stuff, other people are listening to the conversation. I feel sorry for him and respect his guts. I don't know what to say to him though. Hours later we finally get to play. The only reason I'm in this city at all is to play, the rest means nothing to me. I don't think it's necessary to talk to anyone, shake anyone's hand. Not every fucking person is suited for the ritual bullshit of civilization. Some people just want to play and get on with it and not talk about it. Sharks don't talk about ripping someone's guts out for lunch, they just rip. After the show they wait endlessly outside the tent. I walk outside and tell that I'm not signing shit and it's late. I leave and go to the bus. I hate myself when I have to be like this. At this point it's just survival. I can't give them anymore. There's nothing. What they don't know is that I couldn't talk to someone to save my life. I can't talk to people I know. I don't return phone calls unless it's business. I don't like compliments. I don't think I'm above anyone, that's what makes it so hard to listen to them. There's so much bullshit out there.

8.7.92 Cleveland OH: Sometimes I think that I don't have long have long for this shit. When the music becomes a secondary issue to the bullshit I think it's time to move. Watching the youths beat the shit out of each other. Having to endure the ego mood trips of the bass player, whatever. Tonight was a lost night. Having to watch out for them, it seems incredible to me that I have to look out for them. So it was a night that I will soon forget. We played so what. I tried to be nice to all the people that were waiting at the bus. All I could do was look at the ground and sign their pieces of paper with silent submission. I hate it when they beat my spirit down like that. They won tonight.

8.8.92 Columbus OH: Played as well as I could. The monitors were not so hot. I worked out and went to soundcheck. We sold out the place that Black Flag never could. Nothing happened tonight besides a great storm. I am exhausted and blank. I don't remember what I ate today, what I said, what I did besides the show and the workout. I am boring and hulled out. I miss no one, I think of no one.

8.9.92 Pittsburgh PA: It's a shame to have to put up with the bass player's infantile shit night to night. It would be great to haul off and bust the bitch in the face but I can't do that because we have to do the dates. Otherwise it was a good show. It's all I remember of the day. Got here too late to workout so I was on edge before I went on. My head is exploding from a headache. I feel like I got kicked in the head. I played as hard as I could, trying to get the bad blood out of me. Trying to get my mother out of my system, trying to kick my father's bad blood out of my veins. On good nights I get a drop or two out. The rest of the time I hemorrhage and get thanked for it either way.

8.10.92 Buffalo NY: Played as well as I could. A lot of people onstage tonight. Somehow they were cool about getting onstage over and over. I don't know why they didn't piss me off like they usually do. After the show some girl tried to pick up on me, not a good start asking me if I was in the opening band. I didn't talk to her much because I didn't want to know a damn thing about her. Some woman told me a few times that her infant loves me. She was amazed that I had not much to say about it. I am amazed at how my face freezes when someone wants to talk to me. The worst is when someone wants to kiss or hug me. I feel like a human stone. Got in a good workout and that makes the day easier to handle. Otherwise nothing happens these days. Tomorrow there is a day off in Canada. I am feeling pretty good about being alive tonight but I don't know why.

8.12.92 Toronto Canada: Woke up in a woman's bed after a day off. Back into harness once again, felt strange to be out of the zone for 24 entire hours. Did a small press conference and then went to the venue, to a gym and then back to the venue. Phone interviews with Australia after soundcheck. Short sleep and then got ready to play. 2100 tickets sold out show. By the time we went on the walls were sweating. There were no moments when the stage was clear of people. Tonight I tried a different tack. I stood in the middle of them and got kicked around for two hours. Sitting in the bus with no liquid left in my body. Sometimes the days turn into non-events. A day like today leading into a night like tonight where you get up and stagger around until soundcheck and then wander onto the stage, do your trip and wander off again. I stayed inside the venue until they all left. When I emerged from the hall no one was on the streets, it was as if the whole thing never happen at all.

8.13.92 Ottawa Canada: Tonight was like trying to run through water. Every song fought me. I looked into the blank faces of the audience and remembered the last time we played in this town to about one tenth as many people, it was the same. It's like the town that time forgot. After the show I avoided people as well as I could knowing that I wouldn't be able to deal with their questions very well. One guy came up and told me that the fact that one of our CD's is only one track for over 70 minutes is a "spit in the face" to the fans. I told him that spit in his face is a lot different than his CD and would he like to find out about that. He went away. After the show my entire body started to ache from the bottom of my feet up. Now I'm waiting for sleep. Beep.

8.14.92 Montreal Canada: Better show than last night. Did interviews most of the day and then went to the gym for a bad workout. Walked the whore filled streets near the venue looking at the ugly women for sale. One looked at me like she thought I wanted to fuck her. I looked at her and tried to imagine sex with her ugly junkie ass. Later on we play. It was good and we gave it everything. After the show I walked around some more and watched the freaks. I know that it's all about Death and that's all it's about. Nothing occurs to me at this point. Playing empties me out all the way. Fatigue has set in and I am now a product of all its traits. I'm looking forward to getting back to America. Canada has too many of those long dead punks that still breathe. There's a day off coming soon, night after next. I don't look forward to the days off like I used to. I would just as soon play. Sometimes this is a boring trip I know. The last few days have been dull and have embalmed me.

8.15.92 Providence RI: Back in club land again. Nothing works, no food, same old shit. Played this place a year ago or so and the only thing different is that the place has gotten dirtier and more fucked up. Got to the place and went to the gym and then to soundcheck. Mitch Bury showed up so we had a star guest for the evening. Nothing happened that I'm aware of. We played and that was it. I think people liked it. I went into this thing about tough guys and how they aren't tougher than a 9mm bullet in the face. I think I bummed out the skinheads a little but the truth is like that. After the show the same drunk psycho who kept trying to talk to me all through the set kept trying to talk to me and eventually went away which was great because I couldn't figure out for the life of me what was on his mind. After three in the morning we're sitting on the bus and there's still a group of people standing out in the rain. They waved at me to come out and sign their fucking baseball caps. I wouldn't wait in the rain for ten seconds for some fucking guy in a band to sign my anything.

8.17.92 Richmond VA: Parts of this city look like a movie set for some old drama. Run down buildings, poor folks, people standing on corners doing nothing, waiting for who the hell knows what to happen. We played, they yelled and got onstage all night like we weren't even there. For the life of me I don't know what they get out of all this. I wish I could hear the music that they hear when we play. Tonight they are pretty lightweight on the soul level and it's hard to take them seriously at all when all they want to do is knock you over while you're trying to play. Finish playing and go back to the bus an await blast off to the next city. Don't want to talk to anyone, don't want to know. It's raining outside tonight. I was born and raised 90 miles north of here, the weather reminds me of a long time ago. I am looking forward to leaving. I'm always looking forward to leaving. I don't think of my room anymore. I used to think of being alone in my room with my records and typewriter but I don't remember what it feels like to be there so it might as well not even exist. That's good for me. The less I have the better. The less I know the less gets in my way when I need to hit it. I don't miss anyone or anything and that makes me a good touring machine and right now that's all I want to be.

8.18.92 Philadelphia PA: Got to this city. Woken up by the road manager. Interviews started a few minutes later. Later I left to go to soundcheck. King Sunny Ade was standing out in front of the hotel. I spoke to him briefly. Made my day. Went to the hall and did soundcheck. Was told that I had to go back to the hotel to do more interviews. I'm in here now waiting for the fuckers to call. I don't know why I am so full of rage. All I can think of doing is ripping that hall apart. Interviews have nothing to do with what the music and the Death trip are about. Sitting in this fucking room watching a bunch of soft boys on MTV waiting for the world to start. Hours pass and finally we get to play. It was good when they weren't onstage. They were pretty good about it. After the show they were waiting outside. It reminds me how alienated I am from them. Signing autographs is so fucked up, how could you ever be friends with someone who wanted your autograph? Nice enough people but why they need to get something signed is beyond me. I can see meeting someone but that's it. Whatever. Now I'm back in the box. Vacancy is filling my life. The playing was good but that was all besides meeting King Sunny that happened today. Interviews don't count. My mother showed up tonight out of nowhere and it threw me a little but I still pulled off the show.

8.19.92 Baltimore MD: Played tonight with the Beastie Boys. L7 opened, they are as boring as ever, at least they're consistent. I don't think we played all that well. We didn't get a soundcheck and it wasn't a great set up with the monitors. I gave it all I had but I don't know. After the set I went outside and talked to people that were leaving because they didn't want to see the Beastie Boys play. I told them that they were missing a good band but they didn't want to see them. Ian showed up to the gig. As always it's good to see him. I wish we could have played better. We drive to New York tonight. I am sitting in the bus and there are people outside knocking on the windows. It never ends. You spend a good portion of the day and night dealing with all these people and they don't know about all the shit that you have been dealing with before they came up to you and they don't know what's going on in your head. Bullets, brains, headshots, horror. They don't know and you can't get mad at them for not knowing but you somehow wish they could read your mind. If I could open up my head and let it all fall on the ground it would make people throw up. There's nowhere to go on this bus where people can't see in and know you're in here except for the bunk you sleep on and the bathroom. I honestly don't see why anyone would want to meet me. I wouldn't want to know me.

8.20.92 New York NY: Did interviews all day right up until soundcheck. First thing was talking to Gilbert Gottfried the comedian for some television show that I have forgotten. After that was talking to a bunch of young people about drugs and stuff for PBS, that was great to be around positive people like that. Then an interview with the television show that shot the show tonight. After that there was an interview with Harper's Bizarre. Then soundcheck and then time to get ready to play. The day went away. Playing was great until the bass player decided something was wrong and pulled an attitude and walked off stage one song before the set was over. It would be so cool to punch him out but then there would be no bass player for the rest of the tour. We are held captive by this child. I was hoping to be able to meet a girl but I never got out of the dressing room, I can't go out there without having to talk to all kinds of people. I hung out with Alan Vega and that was cool. Now the show is over and I just got back to the box that smells like bug spray. My body is full of pain and I am five pounds lighter than I was last week. I can feel my body feeding on itself. I felt bad on the cab ride back here. Tomorrow is more press and a gig.

8.21.92 Asbury Park NJ: Did a photo shoot for Harper's and then went to the gig. Got there late and made soundcheck. Asbury Park NJ is a hard place. The club is a depressing dive, don't know how the evening will go. The boardwalk is empty with only the occasional jogger to break up the lack of humans. I got stomped on, kicked and whacked around by people getting onstage. Managed to play anyway. I don't remember waking up this morning. I have started to think of women again. No one in particular. It doesn't matter anymore. I am thrown into the fabric of the road and I am not anyone that anyone will ever know. When I think of other people I know that I'm from another world. I'm too tired to think of anything to write. We played and we were good and I'm alone as always and sometimes it's hard to take. My body is in pain, I am still sitting crooked from the kick in the ribs I got from one of the people who claims to like us so much, yea right.

8.22.92 Trenton NJ: I got kicked in the mouth and spat blood on the stage for a few songs. Otherwise it was a good show. I watched some guy walk on people's heads until I told him to stop. He did. Did some thinking today, most of the shit that occupies my mind space is dragging me down. Nothing is on my mind at all now. We play the same place tomorrow night and then I'm off to the UK. I'm looking forward to walking the streets of London by myself and getting some time to think. It will be good to get out of America for awhile. Now in the box waiting for sleep to set in. Had some meaningless sex a few hours ago. Learned a good lesson there. It's not worth it. The need for female companionship that I was feeling last night is gone. I know now that it's all in my head. It's like I've been saying in that song Almost Real. People need to make life seem large at times just to survive it at all. We use lies and dramas to keep distracted from the fact that life itself is without moral or meaning. The very act of sex itself makes me see that. I don't know maybe it was just a bad night.

8.23.92 Trenton NJ: I am looking forward to getting onstage tonight. I am because I am curious to see if I will be able to do it. I feel so shitty right now I don't know how I'll be. I am exhausted. I don't know whether it's the fact that it's the last show or that I'm beat. I'll feel better when I get to the hall and smell that fucked up club smell. Later: I got to the place and that was all I needed. We were going to be filmed for a show to be televised in Spain and Portugal. The opening band was so bad that it got me in a great mood to play. I was sweating before I was on. Played hard and that's all there was to it. Spat blood most of the night from getting hit in the mouth last night. After the set I walked around the side of the club so I wouldn't have to go through the crowd. Sat in the backstage room and sweated into the carpet. Two sold out nights in Trenton. Body was wracked after show. A few days off now. Hoping to get some rest in the next few days.

8.26.92 London UK: Tonight was a talking show. 600 People sold out. All day long was interviews. I managed to get away from them for awhile and went to a local gym and got a good workout in. Before I knew it I was at the venue nearly falling asleep with little time before I went on. I did well. Went for about two hours, didn't notice. I emptied myself out and left the venue depressed and blurred. I don't know if I can do these shows anymore for a while, they get to me. I walked around the streets for a while after trying to get something of myself back. People passed in cars and told me it was a bloody good show. The air is nice out tonight and I would be out there walking still if I wasn't so depressed and tired. Tonight's show ripped a hole in me. Another night on the trail.

8.28.92 London UK: Interviews all day. Taxi cabs, people stopping me in stores for photographs. Shitty club PA and monitor system. Stinking back room with fucked up food, oh yeah I forgot we're in England. Played with jet lag pounding my legs. Did the best I could while people rolled past me. Don't know what they thought of us. After show were leg cramps and people's cigarette smoke, no room to move around and a bunch of people that I don't know in my face. Depression set in as I walked around the streets before soundcheck. Thinking about Joe too much these days. It gets to me, I miss him so much sometimes, it's unbearable. I never think about him while I'm playing so that's a temporary escape. I don't know what to write, I don't know what I feel right now. So many things have fallen out of my brain. The cities win always. I am blank and beyond loneliness, I am full of horror and it keeps me on my own planet.

8.29.92 Reading UK: Reading Festival 1992. We drove past hundreds of people who were doing their best to look fucked up and filthy. It looked like they had rubbed shit into their hair. We got to the compound and waited for our passes. The press bullshit never stops, Started as soon as I got my pass. Talked to the shithead from Kerrang and he has no idea how close he came to getting smacked like a bitch right in the teeth. He's asking me all this shit about now that I'm a big rockstar he reckons all of our new stuff will suck. If I was going to interview someone, the last thing I would do is try to get on the guy's nerves. I got suckered into a tent with a bunch of people who wanted autographs. I stood behind a table like a propped up asshole and signed pictures like a human xerox machine. All I could think of was getting on with the gig. Finally I got to get ready and hit stage. Played as hard as I could. Sure was a lot of people, about 30-40 thousand. As far out as I could see there were people waving. After the set I had to do some photos and then I got the fuck out of there. I was amazed at how hard it was to do the autograph thing, it was unbearable. The people were cool and all but I can't stand making people stand in line to meet me and get their little thing signed, it makes me feel like such an asshole. I'm out of here.

9.11.92 Brisbane Australia: Brisbane is always a taste of the waste. On jet lag I was sleeping up until an hour before the show. I woke up in a dark room with the show yet to do. When we got there, it seemed unreal. Like this whole evening had been going on while I was asleep. I looked out at the other band and watched the stage divers push them around, it looked like the band didn't give a fuck about it either way. The people at the show were either beating the shit out of each other or beating up the bouncers or throwing up or drinking. Tonight was no exception. Not as many fights as last time. There was about 1500 in there tonight, I think they all got on stage at least once. I played a little. I spent most of the time at the back of the stage keeping out of their way. What utter bullshit, having to stay out of their way. I don't care about them because they don't care about the music. So we played and I stayed in the kitchen until nearly three a.m. so I wouldn't have to meet and speak with drunks, they always make me mad with their slurred speech and bullshit talk. Finally we leave the kitchen area and I look on the floor of the hall. It's covered in beer cans. The green Victoria Bitter can was all over the place. Over 2000 sold tonight. One girl told me that she stocked 2400 cans herself earlier in the day. I'm glad to be by myself right now. I hope I don't dream tonight, the moon is full and it's shining down upon the water. I wish someone knew me.

9.12.92 Burleigh Heads Australia: Tonight was pretty much like last night but without the belligerence factor. Instead it was the annoying youth must get on stage all the time thing. We played well and I got off, but when I know the music isn't being taken seriously then I start getting annoyed with how lightweight people can be. Someone will think nothing of getting in your way all night and then expect you to be nice to them when they ask you a million questions. I stood outside hours before the show and watched the sun set against the Pacific Ocean and waited for the show to start. For several hours I was in the club, watched videos until too many people would notice me then I would have to move locations. That's how it is these days. I have to keep moving every few minutes otherwise I have to answer all these questions and I'm tired of answering, answering, answering. It's the truth. It's not "part of the job" either. So I had to just sit in the small room backstage and wait. Can't go anywhere around the venue. They get into back slapping here. People come up from behind you and slap you on the back and start in with the questions, startles the shit out of me. I wiped my shorts on some guys that chose to sit on the stage. I don't think they liked my sweat being scrubbed into their heads, they got off stage. If only they knew how heavy this trip is, but they'll never know because they're too busy with the bullshit. Life will pass them by like it passed their fathers and mothers by.

9.13.92 Sydney Australia: About 3000 people in a hall where you could see your breath. We were the last of four bands. I played hard as hell. I watched bouncers cheap shot young people that were giving them no resistance whatsoever. Drunk people backstage afterwards. Some guy back there with his compliment machine coming out of his mouth. I always wonder how they get back there. I think you should never ask for autographs backstage. If you somehow get back there, you should leave the bands alone, at least leave me alone. They have no idea where you're coming from, they never will. I left as soon as I could. Now I'm back in the box. Every part of my body is sore. It feels like someone has been kicking my legs all night. Sometimes this happens, my body gets sore from head to toe. Tomorrow is a day off. I went and found food after the show. The man behind the counter at the all night place had a blue dot tattooed on the tip of his nose. As I ate I wondered what the blue dot was all about. I thought that maybe in his younger days he had it on there so people would say Hey you've got a blue dot on your nose and he could punch them out for laughs, you never know, Australians are pretty hard bastards. I sat on the edge of the bed for a while trying to understand what my problem is. Sometimes I feel so lonely after shows that I get desperate but at the same time I am so relieved to be alone. I am afraid that I would freak someone out if they got too close. I wonder if you could shoot enough people to make the horror stop. If you could find a space that was large enough to where you could get all the bullshit out of your mind. All the sounds of traffic and screams and television static. What if you could live on the moon.

9.15.92 Canberra Australia: Today we drove from Sydney, we saw kangaroos and desert. The air is so clear here. I thought about Joe and what he might think of this scene as it flew by the window. Another night of them getting onstage all the time and me getting out of their way instead of playing as hard as I could. We played well anyway. After a show like this one I will not talk to them, I will not sign anything. I take it personally that they will not let me play hard. They don't respect the music so I can't respect them, end of thought on that. Too bad though because last time we played here I remember it being a lot better in that respect. Maybe I take this too seriously, I don't think so. Life is so short, why fuck around. Charlie Parker, Coltrane, Miles, Monk, Hendrix, they didn't fuck around, I must aspire to that weight at all times. Tomorrow is a day off. I go to Melbourne to do press. I see things differently now. Press doesn't matter, the punters and what they think doesn't matter, the only thing that matters is the music. The rest is just ego and entertainment. I think you can do a lot more if you sidestep the ego trips and the entertainment bullshit factor. The music is enough, if it's not then you're in the wrong business.

9.17.92 Melbourne Australia: It was another night of them getting onstage and the set not getting very intense. I have bruises on my hand from hitting a guy in his face. I watched some guys beat another guy, about four on one. I don't understand the need for them to antagonize the band. I thought that they would have come for the music. I told them a few things. I told them that I wished it was one of them that got killed and not my friend and I told them that I'm not impressed by how lame they are. I'm not. Fuck these people and their lightweight bullshit. I'm tired of dealing with them. The music doesn't mean anything to them so they get onstage and waste my time, I can't be expected to take them seriously at all. Too bad that the music isn't enough for them and they have to bring their bullshit with them to my world. We should put a fence up and let them deal with themselves. I'm not part of them and they're not part of me. I don't want to know about their drunk pathetic lives. I don't know them and I don't want to touch them and I don't care about them. Perhaps it's time for me to stop being around people. I guess I'm frustrated at how weak people are. I think that people should have more soul. I can't see how they settle for so little. I don't like feeling like this. I don't like being mad at these people. I don't want to carry around this negativity. I don't know how to deal with people anymore. I can't understand them at all. I come from a different planet. No relation whatsoever. Alien blues is what I play.

9.18.92 Melbourne Australia: Same shit as last night but the place was different and they couldn't get onstage as easily so it was a good show. Someone still tried to fuck it up. A few songs into the set I started coughing and I thought that I had something in my throat. I looked into the front row and a lot of the people were coughing as well as the bouncers. Something about the air seemed strange. All at once it hit me that someone had sprayed mace in the air. I told the fuckers that they had their chance and they blew it, they should have killed me last year. Fuck you, you didn't stop me. I coughed and kept on playing. My eyes were burning and it was hard to keep my breath but I kept playing. Later on in the set it was sprayed again but a little stronger but I concentrated on the music and I kept playing. After the set was over I left through the back and was barely recognized. I didn't want to stick around. I can't talk to any of them. Any one of them could have been the one that had the mace. Having to deal with any of them would have been a weakening experience. The only thing that would have made sense would have been to smack the shit out of the first one who said shit. You always lose when you touch them, when you punch them, when you push them out of your way when you're trying to play, you always lose. Their weakness beats your strength every time. Best thing to do is leave and get back on the trail and move out. They aren't individuals to me. When a few get onstage all night and turn the whole thing into a lightweight pose out and spray mace then all of them are those people. I can't separate. It's them and me. Fuck you all, you should have killed me last year you human pieces of shit. I would like to get Sonic Youth, Nirvana, get all those bands on one gig and open for them and run their shit up the flag pole. I guess I'm like Mike Tyson, I guess nothing blows me off a fucking stage, I guess I'm pretty unstoppable when it comes to this shit. Fuck you. I'll be at that gig tomorrow bitch.

9.19.92 Melbourne Australia: No mace today. We played an early show. I was amazed at how well behaved the audience was. Sometimes I think they know the exact time to get onstage and fuck me up. It's always at the one point where the vocal stands alone and I have to be careful, like in Blues Jam where there's that part where it's just me and I want to get it good, right then was when the guy got onstage and stomped on my foot. Perfect. Flowers in the dressing room with a card that had a girl's name and address and the words "Try me" on it. I left them in there. Someone left flowers in the lobby and called me twice to ask me what I thought about that fact. I told her to leave me alone. I don't think that she got it at first but I straightened her right out. I talked to the man in the lobby and he told me that all evening he's been kicking people out of the lobby who were looking for me. When I walked in there was some guy in there waiting for me and I got rid of him by the elevator. I don't know what it is with these people. I must not like myself very much because I can't see why anyone would go to the trouble to bother with flowers and all the other bullshit. That's all it is to me. I don't want to know anyone. I just want to play the music and then crawl away. I don't think that anyone in a band has to be a nice guy. If I was a nice guy then I wouldn't be playing the way I do. Fuck it, it's not worth going into. I would like to go out tonight for a walk but I don't want to because I don't know who might be outside waiting for me. I don't want to hurt any of them, I don't want to do the time. Some people are better left alone. I sat in here tonight and tried to figure out why it makes me so mad when people give me things like flowers. It makes me lose my temper. Shows of gratitude angers me and I don't know why. Something fucked up about me, pick a number and stand in line. People like me don't have friends, believe it.

9.20.92 Hobart Australia: As we were starting the set, Sim looked over at me and said that he was reminded of Budapest. He was right. Strange vibe in this place, you can tell that they don't get much music here, not stuff like us at least. They were drunk but ok. We played pretty good. I had a good time playing, it would have been better without the barrier in the way but still it was ok. I barely remember getting here in the early afternoon. We leave in a few hours on an early flight to Adelaide, one hell of a depressing place to play. I hear that bands avoid the place big time these days. I remember the first time we played there. The first thing I thought as we were into the first few minutes was that we were going to have to endure two nights at the same venue. The bouncers had lead pipes and were fucked, but then again so were the people at the show. The air is cold and clear tonight. On the way in to the box I was reminded of a night on the road with Black Flag. It was 1983 and we had no place to go. We were driving to a town in Germany called Osnabruk where the owner of the place we played a few days before told us that we were welcome to stay there any time we wanted. We went there to see if she was going to make good on her offer. I remember sitting in the back of the cold van with a stash of yogurt and bread and cheese that I was keeping and trying not to eat too quickly because I couldn't be sure when we were going to eat again. We were playing a tape of the Velvet Underground and it was depressing in that van with the cold air and the headlights and all the miles to go and not knowing if we had any place to go and knowing that we didn't have much money and just sitting there knowing it, feeling like a piece of old shit. These people can't tell me anything at this point that can make me feel bad about myself. I was good tonight, I kept my hands to myself and when I did deal with them I was cool. One for me.

9.21.92 Adelaide Australia: For some reason they like us here. Last time we were here we played two nights and no one showed up and this time we sold this big place out completely. Go figure. It was uphill for me. I just stayed out of their way all night. People seemed to get off on what we were doing, or trying to do. A band called The Mark of Cain went on before us, they were great. I was distracted by having to look out for people all night. On the good nights I get to go into my own world and play from in there and play my guts out. Other nights aren't as good and all it amounts to is getting through the set as best you can and not get hit in the head. I am alone in the box and am glad. The questions wear me out. I had to wait for a while to get out of the hall tonight. It was question and autograph time until I went and hid in the backroom. After a while I hate the sound of my voice. I hate having to explain myself to people all the time. I'm wearing out piece by piece. I keep writing so perhaps I will have some kind of map to use to re-trace the steps if I ever get time to go back and pick up the pieces that are scattered on the side of the highway. Blank.

9.22.92 Perth Australia: All night long they were onstage and who gives a fuck about the music besides us. At some point I apparently pissed off the bouncers by taking a kid away from them and not letting them beat the shit out of him. I told the kid to jump off stage because the bouncers wanted to beat him up and he took the tip and did but then the bouncers went into the crowd and beat the shit out of him anyway. The opening band's singer was saying shit like "The music is black and that's the way it's going to stay", or "Our clothes are black and that's the way they're going to stay." Something like that and then they would plunge right into another Metallica sounding song. Of all the bands in the world why would you want to be like them? It was a bad scene all night. I didn't get off at all. All I did was try to get through the set and get the fuck out of there. After the show, the bouncer that was pointing at me during the set came back and got in the promoter's face. Fuck all of these people. It's not worth it, it's not worth trying to play music with all these lightweight people who can't handle it. Tonight it really hit me. I was sitting backstage thinking about how much bullshit we go through just to play. So much bullshit just to play music. I asked them to let us play but they are more into the bullshit pose than the music, some nights it's hard to take. Right now I don't want to know anyone, don't want to play music in front of anyone. After the show people were trying to talk to me but I just walked away or told them to leave me alone. Fuck them all, the bouncers, the bullshit artists, all of them. All I want to do is play. Tonight I think I should just get a job and get the fuck out of sight. I think I'm in the wrong place at the wrong time because I don't feel anything for these people.

9.25.92 Sydney Australia: The day started out in a television studio. I didn't want to do this shit but we were doing it anyway. It was Andrew who really wanted to do this. I knew it was going to be the same bullshit as it usually is. If every piece of equipment isn't exactly what he wants then he throws a shit fit. He was told that the equipment for the tv show was going to be the best gear they could get and he said that was ok. I knew that it wasn't going to be ok. I hate listening to the complaints. Of course there was the prima donna bullshit, no surprises there. Tearing three times and Low Self Opinion three times and then on to the hall for soundcheck, then back to the television studio to do it again as a dress rehearsal and then through it again "for real". After that back to the hall, a little before midnight. Stretch for a few minutes and then go out and kick it. Spit, ice cubes, beer, the endless chain of bodies onstage. A guy who would fill up beer cans with water and bring them to the front and cover our equipment with it. Can't play too hard because that would involve too much concentration and that means taking my eyes off of them for a few seconds and like the ocean, you can't turn your back on a crowd like this one. I spent the night looking out for the flying beer can or the ice or the punker. At one point I told the people up front that I wished they were all black. I knew that would piss them off and I was right. Funny as fuck to see them get mad like that. Even with all this lightweight element at the show we still rocked out. I don't stick around after the last song is over. I get the fuck off stage, I can't be sure what they will be planning. Maybe that one shithead is waiting to throw his glass right on the last note and there I'd be standing there with a fake ass grin on my face like a sitting duck waiting to get what I deserved for giving them an inch. So I play and split, make the hit and leave. I learned that this bunch isn't about music so I do the trip and get the fuck out. Might be a long time before I come back here again.

9.26.92 Manly Australia: Tiny stage tonight. Played ok and had a good time. Set clocked in at over two hours. One of those nights where everywhere you go someone is waiting to gawk at you for unlimited minutes. Young folks never get tired of seeing some old man warming up his body to go play. I always tell these young guys not to bother watching me, but rather they should go out and check out the women, they never take my advice. I like these people but I can't take the talk, I always come off sounding like a grouch. I avoid them because I know that I don't work well with people. I hate some of the things that come out of my mouth. I am good at being a tool and that's it. On-off, the intellect of a shark. I'm not good at hanging out. So as far as gigs go it was a good one. The crowd wasn't as belligerent as they were last night. Good for us. Put in a hard workout today so I feel tired from that. The next show is in Singapore. There's only one way to walk this line. It's all in your head. You can have all the good sleep you want, to do this all the way, you have to have the one idea. One strong thought is all you need.

9.29.92 Singapore: Nothing worked well tonight. The bass amp blew out a few songs in and the bass player made a big scene out of it, as if it wasn't bad enough already. He was told that this gig was going to be a wastey one and he still wanted to do it. So the gig gets wastey and he can't handle, typical. There was no real PA and it was a drag all the way through. Didn't see much of the city since I did interviews all the way up until soundcheck, which lasted 4 hours because we couldn't locate a bass amp. It's as if everyone in the country needs an autograph, they come from everywhere, they all have cameras as well. The BMG rep who was driving me around to all the radio stations was a nervous guy that had a tape of Suicide going for him and that was about all. It was a long day. People were waiting for me everywhere it seemed. My heart is heavy and I don't give a fuck about anything but the playing. It's the only thing keeping my head on straight right now. The interviews are getting to me. Tonight after the show we went and got some food and we saw a car crash. Mo said that it was going to be a hassle. I said "It wasn't us." Me and Joe used to say that to each other all the time. "There are going to be a lot of dead people around after we get done and none of them will be us, so it's cool." Now it is. Now it's us, now it's me and I want to die all the time. It's all I thought about today while I talked to these journalist fakes and watched the nervous BMG guy walk around the room. Now it's me. I wish I could throw this night out. We leave for Japan in two hours and fifteen minutes and I don't even care. I'll play Tokyo, Pittsburgh or Hell, it's all the same to me.

10.2.92 Nagoya Japan: Finally a gig where no one got onstage and we could play. The rented gear was the stuff that we asked for and the gig went without a hitch. Between songs it was so quiet. I couldn't even hear a single conversation. We finished playing Blues Jam and they just stood there. I don't think it was apathy, it seemed more like respect or something. During the lowdown parts of the songs they were dead silent out there. It really let us get deep into the music. I had a great time playing. People were pretty cool to us as well. The hang up is the way people follow you around and want to meet you but when you say hello to them they shrink back like you were going to hit them or they are too afraid to approach you. It makes me feel uncomfortable. I like

Japan. These people try to play you off like they like you and they're your friends but I know better. They are cool professionals and I like that but I can see how it would be easy to take it the wrong way and think that they're sincere about they way they act. Like they way they are all running over each other to get you shit. Fuck that. I know better. You're not my fucking friend, so just do your trip, whatever it is, promoting, interviews, whatever. I like it because I see the real you and you don't even know it. It makes me see the girl I went out a long time ago differently. I see where I got fucked up. I would like to play here more and shove it right down their throats every time. I think it's funny when people front themselves and they think that they're getting away with it. I don't trust anyone in this business except myself.

10.3.92 Osaka Japan: Tonight was another good playing experience. It feels great to rock hard and not have to think about getting whacked around. Some kids kept flying over the barrier and as they flipped over their boot tips would slam against the stage and if my feet were there they have been broken by now. Japanese fans are the most intense I have ever encountered anywhere. I did an instore appearance at Tower today and it was a heavy experience. People out of breath when they would come to the front. All of their hands were cold and wet when I shook them. They were everywhere even at the train station when I was on an early train I took ahead of the guys to go to Osaka from Nagoya. After the show we went to the van and they were there and there was one guy crying and telling me he loved me. Tonight they were in the hotel lobby as well. I took the stairs, twelve flights just so I wouldn't have to wait for the elevator and get told that someone is sorry again. They always say they're sorry when they want your autograph and picture. They were in the lobby of the hotel when I got there this morning. It would be too crazy if you were in a big band and came here. Imagine someone like David Bowie or Prince, insane. After the set we went and ate food in a restaurant where you take your shoes off and sit at a low table and the ladies come out with the robes on and all, it was great. If I had a real room to live in that's what it would look like. I got a good workout in today. When I got to the gym they wouldn't let me in because I had tattoos and they had some problem with my shoes. They had a discussion about it and they gave me a sweatshirt and some shoes that they had around. Some gym. These guys would shit themselves if they went to a gym in America. In the gym here there were no weights that were heavy. I was doing shrugs with a couple of hundred pounds to warm up and I looked behind me and all the people had stopped and were staring at me. One guy came over with a calculator and showed me exactly how many pounds I was lifting. No one made a sound except me. They looked at me like I was some kind of monster. Honestly it felt good. The gym is the only place where I feel totally at home. People in a room sweating, lifting up shit and making animal sounds. I don't have to apologize for the way I am, I don't have to be nice to fragile people. It's the only place where I feel natural. I like working out better than sex, it's only second to music. Right before we went on this strange thing happened. I had bought a Jane's Addiction bootleg CD in the store underneath the club and I had the DJ put it on. I was standing in the hall and the CD came on. At first it was just the sound of a huge Jane's audience waiting to see the band. The bass line for Up the Beach came on and the crowd went nuts. Every time I ever saw them that's the tune they opened up with. For a split second I thought I was at Lollapalooza. It was an intense flashback. It only lasted a fraction of a second but it was intense. I'll have to tell those guys about it if I ever see any of them again.

10.04.92 Tokyo Japan: Another great night of not getting bugged while playing. The only pain in the ass were the Americans up front showing off the fact that they thought they knew us. Last night there was some English guy talking shit and I said "Shut up round eye" and the place broke out laughing. Dave Navarro just happened to be in Tokyo and he came and jammed out with us. We did Crazy Lover, Move Right In and On the Road. I hid from the autographers pretty well. Playing the same place tomorrow night, looking forward to it. It's the only thing on my mind. Let the fucking bull out of its cage and get the fuck out of the way.

10.05.92 Tokyo Japan: Tonight was a good time. The only hang up was the American element of the audience that feels the need to show off the fact that they're major assholes. I kicked them back pretty hard. I'm too good at verbal abuse. I learned from the best. Dave Navarro played with us again tonight. We did Killin' Floor, it was cool. After the show there were girls waiting in the rain to get their paper signed. I did press all day and went to soundcheck. Now I'm back in the box. The rest of them leave tomorrow. I stay to do press for another two days. So what else is new. Burned out and blank. Didn't go out to eat with the rest of them because I just wanted to be alone. I am finding out things about myself more and more. I am sometimes dismayed at how hardened I have become but I guess it's part of the process. I don't care. If you stick around too long you get your ass shot off that's all I know. I'm glad we're getting out of here. I like playing here but the apologizing nature of the Japanese fans I don't like and I don't believe. I am reminded of the line from Blue Velvet where Frank Booth says: Don't say please fuckhead!

10.09.92 Honolulu HI: Back in America. Playing here feels like playing in Santa Cruz or San Diego. The PA was onstage and it made the entire stage shake. Couldn't hear any one instrument, just heard a huge dull roar. Still got off on the playing though. People in the crowd were cool but I could tell that they didn't know what to make of us. After the show I stood on the second floor and watched people dance. Some girl that had passed a note backstage came up and started talking at me. I kept telling her not to talk to me because I was dead. Finally I ignored her and she still stood there. It's at the point now where I cringe when they want to shake my hand. I find myself wiping my hands off on my leg. Their hands are always moist. I play and the rest is bullshit. I like to play and then I like to shut the fuck up. Standing around shaking hands and saying thank you has nothing to so with the music. I wish I could vaporize into a bloody mist after I play.

10.10.92 Honolulu HI: I go to the toilet and they come in and start the talking, we're in a toilet and I have to answer questions. I am a fucking idiot for being in a place where this can happen to me. They yell we play, what the fuck. I had a great time tonight. They throw ice and yell the stupidest shit I have ever heard but they stayed off stage and that was great. The guys always want to touch me. After the show they find their way backstage and put their arm around me. A woman keeps patting me on the back and she tells me that from what she heard me say tonight she thinks I would be an interesting person to talk to. I just stare at her until she leaves. What did I say tonight? I asked if there was a difference in the smell of rape and normal sex. That I didn't want to unite with anyone because humans smell like blood and brains. I am the Death Star and everything that comes out of my mouth is from darkness.

10.25.92 Tucson AZ: I don't know if they know. The sun sets and I sit outside waiting for the soundcheck to start. Small groups of youths come up to me and stand around like I am some museum piece or some wall hanging. One will speak and I will stare and use one word answers. One by one they will go away wordlessly. I don't know if they know. Pain is the only thing that will tell you the truth about yourself and the rest of them. The pain shot through my body like electricity tonight. After the show I sat in a puddle of my sweat on the floor of the arena. People looked over the barrier and yelled shit I couldn't understand. I felt like a boxer, I don't care what they yell, I'm just an animal. Just meat, experienced meat. They don't know that underneath my skin the pain is screaming the truth to me. So loud that it shuts out anything that they are yelling, they don't know that. Pain is my friend because it has never lied to me. It never leaves me for long. When pain is with me everything becomes clear and life has meaning. I know something about myself, I see deeper. Pain makes me stronger. Fire fills my body. After I get dressed I walk out and talk to people from some radio station. They are alien to me. Pain is the great isolator, the almighty truth teller. Fuck spirituality, it's all in the flesh and how much you can take. You want to transcend? Burn.

10.26.92 Albuquerque NM: The reverb in the hall was over five seconds in decay time. One of those places where you play the song and you hear it off the back wall for a few minutes afterwards. We played a few blocks away from where the Bush rally was. I went over there and listened to a man talk over the PA system about how we have to get back to christ. He said things were looking bad when they hand out condoms in schools. A smattering of applause. Secret Service men all over the place. A bad scene. After I left Bush came onstage and kicked some spoken word. Tonight's show was good. Played hard despite feeling the shortness of breath that comes with the elevation out here. Some drunk guy shook my hand four times until I finally told him to cut the shit. I wince at the thought of shaking hands these days. It's like having to kiss strangers. I don't like having to touch strangers, it's fucked up. What if you were running for office, you would be doing that shit all day every day, working hard to get people to like you. I can't see how you could live with yourself doing that shit. Now I'm sitting in the bus in back of the enormous reverb chamber waiting to get on the road to Dayton, Ohio. The bouncers were fucked up tonight, strong-arming kids out, they have no idea what their job is, none. I am tired and sore, looking forward to getting some sleep. The last time I ever saw D. Boon was in this town. In fact I walked right by the spot today. It's so good to be out on the road again. I was home for two weeks and it was apparent to me that I can't handle that life. I was getting more bent out of shape as the days passed. Couldn't get good sleep, couldn't think straight. There's nothing like warming up getting ready to play. Nothing like being out there kicking it live night after night. You either do this all the way and take the pain and learn to be it all the way or you step off. I cannot see any other life other than this one.

10.29.92 Dayton OH: Another night at the Hara. Played here with Jane's Addiction a while back. Tonight was nowhere near as crowded as when we played with Jane's. I gave it all I had. The opening band is this rap group from South Central LA called Da Lench Mob. Ice Cube came out and sang with them tonight. Even he couldn't save them.

They suck flat out. They are on the hate whitey trip. Apparently a few of them were talking about kicking our white asses. They carry guns and are no doubt some bad motherfuckers who can kill you like it's no big thing just like they say in their songs. With all the guns in the world they still suck. They have to go up against the hardest band there ever was and they lose every time. It was great to walk by them tonight when we finished. Fuck that rap shit. They can't cut it where it matters, live. All they do is that wave your hands in the air shit. Losers. I will keep playing and I will keep destroying all these weak fucks. After the show I try to sit in the bus but I can't because there's all these people outside banging on the window. I go out there and sign things and say thank you. Nice people but I can feel my skin crawling and I have to fight the urge to bolt. I can't believe how much that shit upsets me. I don't want to be that person that gets thanked all the time. I will forget who I am if I can't get away from the rockstar bullshit. I have to work hard to keep away from them. They don't know what I know.

10.30.92 Kalamazoo MI: The best part of tonight's show was the part where we're playing and I see that Ice Cube is watching and between songs I say in a cracked falsetto "Put your hands in the air and wave them like you just don't care!" And then started laughing in my own voice. He got up and left. The playing was good. I had a good time. We got a short set but still it was cool. The opening band has some piece of shit song where they name off people that are on the "on my shotgun" or some shit. Apparently they have used my name in their list a few times. Not even the use of my name can help them. They still suck and they still get their shit shown up every night by us. I'd love to see them have to do a real set. That shit is so boring. A bunch of guys posing out, singing to a tape. How intense. Tonight the crowd threw shoes, shirts and hats. I spat on them and threw them off to the side making sure they never get them back again. Tonight there was one of those "meet and greet" radio things after the show. People call in to the station and win a ticket I guess. They come back to meet the band after the show. This kind of thing rubs me the wrong way. The people are always really cool but I feel like an ass hanging out making up fake conversation. No one told us about the one tonight. I was on the bus and someone came and got me. I went back into the hall and into the dressing room and there were a bunch of people standing around. I immediately felt uncomfortable and my mouth shut tight and I couldn't get my eyes off the floor. I stood around for about a minute and then a few of them came up to me and stuck their hand out and I shook it and I said thank you a few times and then I kind of drifted out the door. I told the road manager that I don't want to do that anymore. I think the playing is enough. I don't want to be someone's expectation. You can see that they're nervous and you want to make them feel ok and you don't want to bum them out, at least I don't. I don't know how to handle these situations. It's a drag to see that these people know how tired you are and they don't want to be a bother but at the same time they are thrilled to be where they are and I want it to be a good memory for them but I don't know if one of the requirements of being in a band is to be a public relations man. I do the best I can.

10.31.92 Indianapolis IN: Happy Halloween. The crowd looked the same as always. Kicked it as hard as I could. Now I am the hole. After the show I sat shivering in a corner and shook my head no when they came to interrogate me. They take and take. They can't get me all the way. You finish playing your guts out and you're sitting there steaming and they will come up immediately and start in with the questions. I get sick of my mouth. I get sick of answering endless questions, some nights it's all I do. Scratch, pry, dig, scrape. Sign this. Wring his bones until there's no juice left. No. You won't get me. The radio guy comes out of nowhere and tells me he has some people he wants me to meet. I tell him that after shows all I want to do is kill people. He goes away. They have no idea. You work with people for years and they have no idea what's going on with you. You just go on talking hoping that somewhere someone gets it halfway the way you meant it. Wince when they don't, run and cover when they do. Some Nation of Islam guys were here tonight, they were an intense crew to say the least. Immaculately dressed with bow ties and full length leather coats.

11.1.92 Chicago IL: We get to the venue and there's kids outside waiting for something. There's no tickets and they stand there in the pissing rain all day. Hours later soundcheck starts. Tonight they're up close and they throw Oh Henry candy bars and tell us that we suck. We play hard and I can't tell what they're saying. The bass player pulls one of his infant attitude trips for the encore and no one kills him. That's it. It's a good thing that I do this for myself because if I was an entertainer I would be looking for their approval. How fucked up is that. They would hand me my head. Steve Albini was at the show tonight hanging out with the opening band I guess. I never met the guy before but once read an article he wrote that put me down. I was considering breaking his face up for him but when I moved in on him I saw that he was just a skinny punk. It wouldn't have been a good kill so I let it slide. He'll never know how close he came to getting his face fucked up in front of his friends. After the show is over I leave the venue to get some food before we leave for Toronto. People are outside waiting in bad weather. I sign whatever they got and do my best to be nice to these people knowing they have no idea how much I want to puke my lungs out of my body when I get asked to sign an autograph. I go to the restaurant up the street and people put pieces of paper in my face as I'm eating. I get on the bus and we leave.

11.2.92 Toronto Canada: We get to the venue after a drive that ends up taking about 15 hours. People are waiting for the bus in shitting rain and wind. I go to the dressing room and shave. People are looking in the window. Hours later the doors are about to open and someone throws a rock through the window and covers me with glass. I notice that "the Da Lench Mob" as we now call them has incorporated a "We love y'all" rap into the show. No doubt high management has told them that they need to cross over and kiss some white ass to make the record and t-shirt sales go better. The audience eats it right up. Finally we get to play. I give it all I have. By the end of the set my bone marrow was screaming. Pain makes it go better. I get out of the shower and I'm still out of breath. My legs are burning. As long as I can maintain the present pain threshold, none of these fuckers will ever get to me.

11.3.92 Montreal Canada: There's something about us that the Beastie crowd doesn't like. Tonight they spit and flip me off. Good thing there's a barrier. It would be pretty satisfying to meet up with one of those spitters after the gig and show them something. Again we play hard and right through them all. Tonight was the end result of four interviews. Sometimes I think if I have to talk about myself with one more stranger I'll explode into nothing. After the show I'm eating and I get called outside the bus to meet this guy who is partly retarded. I talk to him but his friend is freaking out and yelling so the retarded guy apologizes to me. I shake his hand which is covered with something that smells like rotting milk. I try to wash it off but it doesn't work. The smell makes it so I can't finish my meal so I throw it out. You get too close to people and they will cover you with themselves, with their lives. I don't want to touch. I want to play hard and play through but I don't want to touch anyone and I don't want to know what they want to tell me. I don't even know what I think anymore. I feel tired after saying thank you. I want to puke and sleep.

11.4.92 Durham NH: The DLM couldn't go on at their correct time because they were afraid of the check that the university was going to pay them. We have to wait for them to get their shit together, finally we are allowed to play. I guess they don't know that universities never pay a band in cash. These guys are amateurs and won't even be around next year so who cares. There is a similarity night to night on this tour. People up front who are waiting for the Beasties are not tolerant of our brand of music. They have proven to be very abusive. Tonight they were in full effect telling us to get off stage and that I'm not as good as I used to be but looking at the age of the crowd I don't think they ever saw me the way I used to be, however and whenever the hell that was. They tell me that I'm a junkie and all kinds of other shit. I asked them how many of their fathers are in the Klan. I called them all white boys and that bummed them out big time. It's easy to get a rise out of people like that. It's a good thing that we don't play for the people and that we play for ourselves. Grab your dick whiteboy here comes the next verse. That was a good one. I played my ass off anyway. It was good to get out of there, you get the feeling that you would have to show one of these dung producers some real hostility. These food wasters are lucky that there are laws and barriers keeping me away from their necks. They have no idea how close they are to getting hurt by someone who wouldn't give a fuck if they died. I remember the Canadian guy who was giving me all kinds of shit one night in Rome. He walked out of the venue and got his drunk ass run over and killed by a guy in a car coming around the bend. Sounds like the Death of an asshole to me. So I played another show and I'm still alive.

11.5.92 Boston MA: Andrew pulled out all the stops on this one. He lies down to play, he solos through all the songs, he jumps through rings of fire, anything but play with the rest of us. He always talks about never selling out and he's the biggest sellout there ever was. He's so full of shit, no matter what he'll ever say I'll always know that he's weak. I am proud of myself for not attacking him. I know the importance of completing the shows that we have in front of us. I would like to swarm him so hard he would have to get his crippled wife to feed him. It's a disgrace to watch this punk make our stage a disgrace. There is a friend of the band's that's up here from NJ. He came to the show tonight and told me he was disgusted with the bass player's bullshit. I felt bad for him, worse for myself however, having to put up with him until the end of the tour where he will be unceremoniously dropped. I played hard as I could though and had a good time. At this point I am pretty hard to stop.

11.6.92 New York NY: Good time playing tonight. Got fucked up on the time because we played one song too long. Met some people. Met Ron

Delsnor the promoter, he was really cool. Lenny Kravitz had some pretty woman with him, I talked to him for a second. Other than that, it was just a night. I didn't watch the Beasties because I kind of got trapped down in the basement with these people. I should have left the place as soon as I finished playing. It's a bad idea to stick around. You have to talk to people and get thanked or whatever. A few girls asked me out tonight. I did my best to be polite and say no without making a big deal out of it. Walked back to the hotel through all the people coming out of the show. Slaps on the back and clapping follow me down the street. I like the people here. They are cool and they don't hang on you, they have a sense of themselves it seems. Another night on tour.

11.7.92 New York NY: Here for the second night of the NYC shows. I would like to live here. It's great in New York. I walked by Carnegie Hall last night wondering if Charlie Parker had stood where I was standing. I tried to imagine standing in line to see Miles play there. Down the street a man was lying in the street, hit by a taxi cab. Police were there, several onlookers watched the man cry out in pain. They all came to New York. Miles, Parker, Coltrane, Roach, Monk, Mingus, Gillespie, Ayler, Coleman, Shorter, Prez, Blakey all of them. The longer I make the list the more I show my ignorance by the number of greats I would be leaving out. I went past the Village Vanguard club once, I remembered the photo of Coltrane standing out in front of the place that's on one of his records I have. I tried to find the exact spot on the sidewalk where he stood in time. I walked outside today until it was too cold to go on. The sun is setting and the sirens are screaming by. It's dangerous to live here. Don't fool yourself, it's dangerous to live anywhere in America now. They all want to kill each other it seems, hell me too. I want to see some of them dead for sure. Later: Did the show tonight and it rocked hard. I played as hard as I could. Vernon Reid came out and jammed with us at the end of the night and that was great. Iggy was at the show and we hung out and talked for a good while. He's so cool. It means a lot to me to be able to hang out with him. He's going to come to our show in New Orleans and play with us if he has time, he'll be down there recording. Iggy said that he wants to do a lot of shows when his new record comes out, he says he's feeling good. He was looking great. Other than that it was a good night. Some pretty women backstage, I guess they were there for the Beasties, all I know is that none of them looked at me twice.

11.8.92 New Brunswick NJ: Many were politically correct and a little unsure. I never seen so many youths in baggy clothes. Hide the body's form and remove the idea of sex. Remove the threat of sex, something that might kill you. Campus anxiety. Young people losing the language of their bodies, sexuality muffled, stifled under layers of clothes. Nice people at the place tonight. Same security crew as the guys in NYC. Now that is a great crew. They know the difference between being a bouncer and being security. These guys do not get into hurting people, they are total pros and they like the people that come to the gigs. I talked with several of them, too bad we can't take them with us, it would be great to not have to worry about aspect of the shows. Played as hard as I could, kept slipping on the carpet but what the fuck. Other than that there was nothing to remark upon. We came to their gym and we played and I left several minutes later. One of those gigs that are good but don't leave any marks. As I drove back to the city I thought about this girl that I actually loved. The pain of some of that shit never goes away. It sucks to be mortal and to have a heart that can break.

11.10.92 Raleigh NC: Played hard as possible. Ran out of time before we got to finish. Showered and got out of there. I don't know what else happened, been playing hard to the point to where it blasts out the rest of the thoughts that I have. After the show was over I sat on the bus and waited to leave. People looked inside for a long time. I felt like I was living on display. It was good to leave. I am falling apart in some ways.

11.11.92 Atlanta GA: Another night of good playing. Crowd was great. Not much to remark on. I didn't get outside much after we got to the gig. I got in a good workout in the gym they had there. After the show I watched people leave the hall, I feel so far from them. I don't know the language, I don't know the moves, I don't know anything about this version of the world.

11.13.92 Orlando FL: Outside gig tonight. First night with Cypress Hill. Good band and cool people as far as I can tell. I played as hard as I could and watched the Beastie Boys play as well, they were great as usual. They don't play bad ever, if they have I've never seen it. The backstage area is just a bunch of fences so as you stand around, people from all sides call out to you and then you realize you're just on display like some fucked up zoo trip. I guess it doesn't matter, in the end you're just ashes to scatter. Another show down. I like playing as much as ever but it's the other stuff that I don't handle well.

11.14.92 Miami FL: I sat out back of the exit door tonight and watched groupies wait for the Beasties. People disgust me sometimes. They tried to play that weak shit with me and I told them to get fucked.

Played hard tonight and I think we really bummed out a large portion of the crowd. I like the idea of us and the Beasties playing together but I don't know if it makes much sense for the person in the audience. I can tell that we are too heavy for people coming to see the Beasties. I kind of feel sorry for them to have to sit through our set when they want to get into the party mood. After the show I was sitting on the side watching people do their thing and a few of them started coming up to me. They were Beasties people, people waiting around for the poor guys to come out and go to their bus. They were talking to me and all I wanted to do was hurt them. People were asking for my autograph and I was telling them no, that the autograph thing was stupid. I see things clearly. It's not about signing shit and being all charming to women that you want to fuck. It's the sword, following the sword and adhering to the line of the blade. That's all there is for me. When I talk to people I disgust myself. When they anger me I disgust myself further. Finally I got so sick of watching the women and their antics that I had to walk away. I sat for minutes thinking that all I wanted to do was give away all my possessions and throw away all my meager savings and get a job as a dishwasher. Perhaps be in a place where people wouldn't make me hate so much. As it is now all I want to do is play and get away from them before they make me do stupid things. I feel dangerous and devoid of sex appeal. I feel like the definition of the word ugly.

11.15.92 Tampa FL: In the parking lot of a hotel waiting to go down to the venue. Tampa is beat down. The streets are tired. No one knows it yet but America is worn out. I see it when I come to Florida. The coasts are going to go down first and the rest will slowly fall apart as the years go by. The midwest will end up being as bad as Los Angeles in a short while. I don't think I've been through Tampa since I was here with Black Flag. It's a Beasties show so I don't think there will be any bad experiences with the skinhead boys. Not many shows left on the tour. The year is winding down. I don't remember a lot of it. I wonder what next year will be like. I wonder if I can keep this up or if I will fall over. It doesn't matter because I know that in the end I will keep on going insanely until Death. Later: Did the show and had a good time. Cypress Hill were great. I gave it all I had and felt good afterwards. I watched the Beasties for a while. I was on the side of the stage when some girl was looking for a good place to see started stepping on my legs. I kicked her legs off of me and told her to get the fuck away from me. After that I couldn't have a good time watching the show so I had to bail. Now I'm on the bus listening to Clifford Brown play with Max Roach and Sonny Rollins. I'm alone and all is well.

11.16.92 Jacksonville FL: Gave it all I had tonight. Got in a good workout before so my spirits were high. The rest of the day I forget. I woke up in the parking lot of the hotel that also is the parking lot of the venue. Tonight is the first night the place was open. They were still building the front today. So we played and I don't know what they thought about it. Another night on the road. It's all starting to run together. I know you can go until the muscle falls off the bone and no one would notice. The road is open ended and will allow you to do every stupid thing to yourself that you want. I'm burning out slowly but I still want to keep playing, it's just now getting interesting. I'm beyond loneliness and my thinking is short term but clear like a real animal. There was a beautiful moment tonight when my body was screaming in pain and I kept riding it. I did not back off. Through loss and the Iron I have learned to make friends with the pain. It is my only friend at this point. I came up with an idea while we were in the middle of a jam about how good it would be to be able to have my own skull in my hand and still be alive. I would have someone to talk to. I am like all of them in that I am a desperate animal trying to escape fear.

11.18.92 New Orleans LA: Iggy Pop played with us tonight. It was cool as hell. When we were in New York he said that he was interested. He came to soundcheck and we kicked a blues jam that felt good. After that he asked me if I wanted to come sing some on a song he was working on. I went with him to Daniel Lanois studio and he and I sang on this song called Wild America. It was great to be standing next to him singing along. We did it without headphones, using the monitors over the desk. It was one of those situations where you are trying to concentrate on the work but you really can't believe what you're doing and who you're doing it with. We were just going for it and it was a great time. I hope that they keep my vocal in when it comes time for the final mix. I went back to the hall and got ready to play. I gave it all I had like I always do. The bass player was playing so loud that in some of the songs I thought my ears were going to explode. Can't wait to get that guy away from me. During the last song the generator blew out and we had to wait for them to get their shit together. It was wild to be waiting to play and see Iggy on the side of the stage with his shirt off jumping up and down waiting to get out there. When we finally got the power on we hit it and it was great. Iggy was all over the place. I'm glad Ricky Powell got it on tape. Crowd was pretty boring but that's ok, I don't have to live with them. It's a bit of a drag being in the band with this bass player but his days are numbered so it's no big deal.

11.19.92 Dallas TX: It rained all day and I watched the men load the gear into a fucked up old wrestling arena. I sat in the bleachers and thought about how many times people had sat there and yelled for one redneck to rip the head off another redneck. Water was coming in through the roof. There was a hole in the floor right in front of the stage. A girl I know came early to talk to me and I was lame and had little to say. I felt like a jerk sitting there not being able to say anything. I don't get along with people as well as I used to, it's like I have turned into another person. Right after Cypress Hill finished the barricade was broken almost immediately. Great to see it handed piece by piece across the front of the stage. After a long time and a lot of people onstage talking to the crowd telling them to get back we finally got to play. Our set was cut to 45 minutes. We pulled off a few songs and did the best we could to get the crowd to be cool. It was like one of our regular shows, people all over the place. Other than that it was a good night. The Beasties were great as usual, it's great to see them every night. I didn't have to talk to too many people after the show and that made things pretty easy to deal with. I find it hard to say thank you over and over. It makes me want to rip my lungs out.

11.20.92 Houston TX: Tonight was Mike D's birthday. The Beasties were great tonight. They brought out a cake and smashed Ricky Powell in the face with it. Mike D sang Georgie Girl. Cypress Hill were great tonight as well. I wish they could play longer but they only get 20 minutes. I wonder what it's like to play for that little amount of time. Eric, the percussionist with the Beasties played Obscene with us and both he and Mark the Beastie keyboard player played Next Time. It was a good set and I had a good time playing. After the show I sat and shook the hands of people that I didn't know and I noticed that without thinking about it I always wipe my hand on my leg. I get tired of people touching me. They were outside near the bus tonight screaming my name. You would think that they would have something else to do than to stand outside and wait for fellow humans to walk ten feet out to their bus. Now I'm in the box. We play in San Antonio tomorrow night without the Beasties or Cypress. There is only one thing to do and that's to keep hitting it hard and not let the normal bullshit hang you up. You have to keep away from the women to keep clear minded. I'm only interested in being relentless. The rest is just bullshit.

11.21.92 San Antonio TX: Tonight was a headlining show as the Beasties Boys are off tonight. The place stinks and it's cold like a lot of places in Texas. Hours pass and I go from the bus to the backstage hopping from one boring environment to the other. There are only about 400 people tonight. Not such a big draw in old San Antonio. Finally we get to play and after straightening out a few stage divers we had a good time playing. Played a long set too. It was a good time and the crowd was very cool. After the show they were waiting around the bus in cold weather so I talked to a few of them and tried to talk them out of the autograph thing that makes me so sick. I stood there in this alley and told them the truth as best I could. I told them that I like them but the autograph thing makes me feel like an asshole more than usual. They just stood there and laughed nervously and held out the pieces of paper anyway. Some girls took us to a Mexican place and we ate a lot of food. It is now past six in the morning and I can't sleep. I will be in my own bed tonight. In a few hours I fly to LA and have all of Sunday to myself. I'm looking forward to being in my room alone with my stereo. I will try to get in a workout in as well. My body is sore and I am tired but unable to sleep. I missed the presence of the Beasties and Cypress tonight as the opening band was crap. Not much to tell. I feel good inside myself. I feel fucked up around others though. I can't handle women very well anymore. When they want to hug me it makes me freak out. I think they're control freaks. It's hard to talk to them because they are always talking shit to me. It's never real, always some bullshit trip. I don't do well with people and it makes me mad because I don't want them to think badly of me. But I am tired of answering the questions all the time. I know how fucked up I am. I am fucked up with other people's trips. I like the work and that's all. The rest is too exhausting and sickening.

11.23.92 San Diego CA: We played outside. People were cool. We played well and it was a good night. One of those ones where you play and nothing happens besides you going out and playing. That's it.

11.24.92 Los Angeles CA: We start playing and Chris' guitar lead starts to cut out and we have to stop through a song. We start again on another song and already the set is losing a little steam. Another song goes by and at least I'm going for it as hard as I can and someone throws a shoe at me and hits me in the face. It rings my bells good. We keep playing and a guy up front spits at me and it goes right into my mouth. I take the mic and swing it at him and hit him in the face and call him every name I can think of. Fuck these people. Take them out and shoot them. We finish the set and after the show the bass player starts talking shit about what I did. He always does it the same way. He walks away while he's talking and gets to the punch line when he's out the door. He never confronts. I can't respect him because he's a bitch. He lies down onstage, he solos through entire sets. He does all this sellout shit and then he tells me how fucked up I am. He's so weak. It's pathetic. Tomorrow is his last show with me. No longer will he disgrace my stage with his weakness. Let him do it to someone else. Hell of a gig though. I am unstoppable. Fuck you.

11.25.92 San Francisco CA: They threw large plastic containers of pepper, garlic, you name it. There were about four spices thrown up there all in all. Missed my head a few times close. I caught one. I spent the gig watching the crowd, inhaling pepper and waiting for the next projectile. I got hit in the head with a coin. Good shot. Tried to play with all I had but couldn't because of a few pieces of shit in the audience. Play all year and it comes down to your last show and they shit on you all the way. It would be nice to have a way to shit right back on them. It would have been so great to have found the guy, imagine the hospital bill. So like Iggy said: "You're paying five dollars and I'm making ten thousand so screw ya." I hopped a ride with the crew bus and wound up at the airport in LA and I took a cab to my room. We saw Ray Charles at the airport, it was cool. He was being led by this guy. They were walking real fast. Sure was a good year for playing. It was great playing with the Beastie Boys and Cypress Hill. I wish we were playing tonight. I don't know what I'll do with myself.

HOLLOW MAN: 55 NIGHTS

#1: I keep telling myself that if I keep to myself a little longer everything will be alright. I don't know what this feeling of alrightness entails. I don't know why it occurs to me that I must be alone as much as possible to feel better.

It seems to me that the best thing is to keep things to myself. I have tried to explain myself to others and it always ends up being an upsetting waste of time.

My loneliness has never burned with more intensity than now. I wish there was someone that I could identify with. I don't look because I know how I am. I want something and as soon as I get it I don't want it anymore . If some woman told me she wanted me I would immediately go as far away from her as possible. But alone in this room alone on the planet, the way I always find myself, I wish for a warmth that speaks to me. I don't know where it would come from.

Sometimes I think that I have been cut out of a mold to perform some duty or task. I'm not talking about some kind of weird destiny bullshit. It just seems like all the things that have been happening to me are part of some story. All the bad things that have happened recently are like the plot to a large drama.

I am not one to take things as they come. I don't have the time. I have learned that one can be put in situations where one must hang on and keep from going overboard into the raging torrent of life's events.

The loneliness that I feel fills me completely. I feel it in everything I do. I don't mind loneliness anymore. I have made friends with it and I can handle. Loneliness adds beauty to life. It puts a special burn on sunsets and makes night air smell better. It is the only thing I've ever really known besides pain.

#2: I called your number tonight even though I know it's disconnected. I just wanted to hear the sound of the tones the buttons made. I thought if I called maybe you would pick up the phone even though you're dead. Maybe I could hear you being shot over and over. Maybe you would answer and tell me that you don't understand what all the fuss is about. You would tell me what it's like to be, dead.

The guy from the LA Weekly left a message on the machine telling me that they want to pay me for the obit that I wrote about you. Isn't that something. I can call in and they'll send me a check. I'll call them in the morning and tell them that I don't want any money from them.

As a reflex I called your number again. 392 2063 just to hear the sound the tones made. Now my eyes are stinging. I'm glad no one's here right now.

#3: The other day I was doing a video in Los Angeles. A few hours into what would be a 14 hour work day the pigs came by to show me pictures of potential suspects in Joe's murder. I spread the pictures on the floor and looked at 8x10's of fucked up guys who were too stoned to focus. After looking at their faces for a while and knowing that I'll never be able identify the guy I gave up. One of the pigs said that by time that all of this was over they would know as much about me as I did. Some of the shit that comes out their mouths is hilarious. I can't wait for them to find out everything about me. I would like to help fill them in on how much I think pigs should be taken out of circulation.

After we looked at the pictures one of the pigs took out another notebook and showed me pictures of the scene of the crime. He turned the page and came to a few pictures of Joe lying on the front walk with a sheet over his body. The white sheet covered almost all of him except the back of his head which was torn up. He looked so pathetic and small lying there. So lonely. His body fell in this fucked up position that made it look like he had been thrown to one side like some piece of insignificant garbage. He looked like an afterthought. I wanted to crawl into the picture and get him out of there.

Soon after the pigs thanked me for my cooperation and left. I sat in silence and thought about the picture. Seeing Joe like that made me want to die. Soon I was in front of a camera screaming along with some song. Every time I looked into the lens all I could see was that white sheet and Joe underneath it.

That was weeks ago and now I'm in Europe. I spend most of the nights trying to get to sleep in the bunk of a moving bus. I close my eyes and try to get to sleep. All I can think about is Joe and I start to cry into the pillow. I don't tell anyone about it. I keep seeing the sheet. Tonight I was in a book shop in the train station here in Munich. I saw the sheet on two books that were in front of me.

Tonight is a night off, the first one in two weeks. I wish we were playing so I wouldn't have time to think.

I am totally cut off from the rest of the world. I think of what it would be like to try to communicate with someone and I can't see it. I don't even want to anymore. I just want to keep moving. I feel good when I'm moving.

Tonight I was thinking, wondering if I will regret staying to myself all the time like I do. I wondered if I would look back and think that I blew it and should have ventured out into the world more. I look at women and some part of me wants to be with them and then see how at shows they don't come near me and never talk to me. I see that animals, dogs for instance will instinctively stay away from certain people. It's as they sense something about them. I think women do that with me.

Honestly I don't care. I am how I am and I should learn to live with it. Some part of me feels that I'm missing out on something. I realize that I'm a fucked up workaholic. I also realize that to do things you have to sacrifice other things. I can live with that.

What's hard to live with is my friend's Death. I have been putting miles on the road ever since it happened but it doesn't do any good. I hate to admit how much it still hurts like it did right when it happened. At this point I can't tell how it will change how I live. I feel deadened and at the same time resolved to move forward towards my own Death.

#4: I'm fucked up and changed since my friend died. Part of me died too. I see now that it's bigger part than I can fill. I don't give a fuck about anything anymore. I know that's bullshit on my part, it's weak, all the things that I say I hate so much I am becoming. I am becoming a total hypocrite. It's hard to function with a broken heart, a shattered spirit. I feel so frustrated all the time. I just go with the program. I am the Hollow Man. I am the hollowgram. Fuck it. I have no hope, I have no one, nothing. I just walk with the wind. I am becoming smaller and smaller as times goes on. I don't remember how it feels to feel good. I look back at the writing that I was doing before Joe died and it's a lot different. I have less to say now. I think I should just stop. I can't write about anything except feeling hollow because that's all I am now. I am turning into a ghost. Soon I won't exist. I'm fading away.

#5: I feel guilty for the very fact that I'm alive. Today it really got to me. I no longer feel I have a purpose in life at all. I walked the streets today trying to get away from myself. It didn't work. I feel bad that I breathe. I keep thinking about my best friend in the plastic box. I no longer feel like a solemn warrior like I used to. I just feel depression, rage and bitterness. I feel let down that something like that could happen to someone like Joe. It gets harder to take as the days go by. For a while it was ok but in the last week it's been getting to me. I don't know if it's the exhaustion getting to me or what. All I know is that my life is dark and plain. I know that others have gone through much, much worse than this. I don't know if I feel or if I'm numb and in shock. I feel out of energy. I have been doing all the regular things I do but this time it's with a broken heart. I can't make things matter. It all seems so fucking stupid. Everything. Makes me think that all I do is take up space because I'm not in love with life's lie anymore. I used to feel like I should be doing things all the time and now I just do things to get away from myself and to get my mind off killing myself.

#6: At this point no one can tell me shit and have me listen. I'm tired of the words. I'm tired of the isolation sickness. I only get it when I'm around them too much. When I'm alone I feel alright because I can forget that I'm alive for a while. For now this is the only way that I have found relief. I do interviews, go on television and look into camera lenses. I heard once that Indians hated getting their pictures taken because they thought it took away a layer of their souls. I thought that for a few moments once. Seemed romantic. Now I know different. Nothing can take you out besides Death. They can roll all the tape they want and it doesn't fucking matter. You can fuck all you want and it doesn't matter. None of it matters. You'll do what you'll do. You can fall for years and never hit the bottom. You can kill until you get caught. It's wide open. So much of what held me together I see now as total bullshit. A romantic dream. In search of some kind of approval. I don't care about it now and I'm more powerful than ever. I'm free and I'm over the edge looking back at them all. I'll never come back. They'll never, I'll never, nothing will ever bring me back.

#7: Back in LA for the first night in weeks. Rain has been hitting the streets for hours. I walk to a food place. The rain soaked sidewalks seem to take people's voices and fill the with a violent jagged current. I hear the words come hissing off the side walk and turn into threats hanging in the air like knives suspended. I sit in the food place not wanting to be near a window. I really do think of drive by shootings these days.

This is the place for paranoia. I think about the guy I nearly took out in New York the other night. He was hitting me up for change after I got out of a cab. He came around behind me and I thought he was going to jack me and I was going to try to kill him. I thought he was going to go for me. He would had no idea what he was messing with. Not a clue. At this point I don't either. I think about the man I nearly hit at the record company office a few days ago. He was talking shit and I started staring at him, through him. He got a worried look on his face, I don't think he really had any idea what he was fucking with. This city rips the heart out of humanity. It reduces people to desperate fear merchants. I want a gun so I'll never get messed with. I am scared of walking into a hold up in every store I go to. I don't want a gun because I don't want to end up one of those people that have guns and get their heads shot off. I want a gun because I feel the need for one every time there's a knock on the front door like the one that happened three minutes ago that I didn't open. My immediate impulse was to open the door and attack. Instead I sat stock still until the footsteps went away. I will try to sleep tonight. I wrote a girl tonight but didn't send the letter because I was embarrassed at the things I said. I was embarrassed and I pitied myself. I wish she would walk through the door right now and put her arms around me and never let go.

#8: Letter to a woman that scars the flesh and soul when she comes to mind. It's Friday night, a little after 9 p.m. March 20. I got here to LA this morning at 2 am. I went into this new apartment. The book company has moved into the living room. It's really good. My room was nothing but boxes and ghosts. A plastic container of blood and brain soaked dirt from Joe's head and a roach the size of a mouse was my company. I worked through the night unpacking all the stuff and building shelves. 14 hours later I finished. There were two milk crates of mail on the floor waiting for me. I found a letter from you. I was surprised.

I got back from tour last Sunday. The record company had me land in NYC and do 4 days of interviews. It was pretty fucked coming off a tour where I was on the road for 5 weeks with three days off. I wasn't in the mood to do stuff. It was hard to deal with all these people every day when I was trying to come down from tour. It's something that I've never been able to explain.

I am sorry for the last letter that I wrote you from Munich. If you got it or not it was pretty fucked up I guess. It's been difficult for me the last few weeks. I have a lot of things that are trying to rip me apart and I confide in no one so I spend a lot of time on my own. Whatever.

I am confused as to why you are writing me. You never really come out and say anything. You always seem to come off as vague. Perhaps I just don't understand. I would like nothing more than to understand you. I wondered if you were writing me letters to hurt me. If you're doing that please don't hurt me. When I think of you too much it hurts. It's embarrassing to say how much. It's pathetic at this point. I don't think you would want to hurt me.

Seems to me that you have been put through a lot of pain at other's expense a lot in your life. I imagine it was all men. You were probably a lot nicer at some point but some one whacked it out of you or scared it out of you, or humiliated it out of you. I don't know if you're mean or not but I think you're tough. I meet women when they come up and want to talk to me and they don't have it. They have nothing, so boring, so shallow. They make the world such a lonely place.

I don't know if it's a good idea for me to write you anymore . It's hard to think about you and not lose sleep. I have a bad enough time sleeping these days as it is. I have terrible nightmares now. I do all nighters now like I am doing right now because the dreams are so fucked. Going into the second night of not sleeping. I did a good workout tonight and I still don't feel tired. I have a headache that won't quit though.

These letters always go too long. Have you ever seen the Kurosawa film "Ikiru"? I imagine you have. If you haven't then you should. I have seen it three times now. I don't think I'll be writing you anymore , it hurts me too much. At this point I can't take it. Hope all's well with you.

#9: When I looked back I saw that the mountains that I had spent so much time climbing had turned to piles of sand. The first gust of wind reduced them to desert. So much for glory and the past. Nothing to do but move on. The pack grows heavy at times and I wish there was some place to put it down and catch my breath. I look around as far as I can see there's no place to rest not even for a second. I shoulder the pack and keep walking the trail of scars. My journey is to the wound, the great wound.

As I walk the desert spreads and grows before me. I see a man ahead of me shoot himself in the mouth and drop. He turns to sand and blows away before I can get to him. When I look for solid ground I start to sink. Only when I move can I survive. To be still is to know suffocation. I had to get away from your eyes. They were killing me. All I have to do is think of you and I start to choke.

I am the Hollow Man. I leave the hollow stare that stays with you long after I'm gone. I'm always gone. I am the echo on you phone. Your broken that heart that leaks your blood is my sound track. I am the annihilating silence that fills you with horror.

I can't look back. I can't take the pain. The trail's pull is so strong that to look back is to be emptied all the way. My heart was broken so many times that I went from shallow to hollow.

The urban landscape is my horror backdrop. The nights are filled with my loneliness. I long for a voice, a touch. I know that it will never come. I want to die all the time. I know that I will die pitiful and insane. Hollow.

#10: Just take me out and work me to Death. I can't love anyone. I'm good for taking pain and dispensing rage. The nights pass and they remind me of books I have read about the ones that got fucked up in a war. I can't call anyone. I try to and then at the last minute I just put the phone down. I'm afraid of bumming them out. They might catch some of the horror that has taken me over. I feel like I have been dropped off on some other planet. I don't speak their language anymore. I feel better in the room staring at the walls, trying to make words work. I am the Hollow Man. I will be empty at the end of the trail. Nothing witty to say. I got bucket of dirt that's soaked in my dead friend's blood. I keep it in the closet. Tonight the whole room smells like the dirt. It's hard not to go insane. I think I slip a little every day. I must be. As time goes by I feel less and less. I sink and become more hollow. Soon the sun will shine right through me. Pure.

#11: Tonight during one of the songs I talked about Joe. It was a whisper, the whole place was silent. It was like I wasn't even there. I just listened to myself tell the story. After the show I sat and let the sweat dry. I usually feel lonely after shows but not these days. I feel totally inside myself. I don't want to know anyone, I don't want to talk to anyone. I feel fine on my own. Some girl wanted to talk to me. I just stared at my feet as she went on and on. I have no idea what she said. She was talking to the wrong guy. I'm always the wrong guy. I got out of the venue and there were people standing in the rain waiting for me so I could sign their tickets. I looked at them and could barely speak. I just signed the stuff as quickly as I could, tried to get my name right, said thank you and left. I don't know what to do in those situations. I like them but I don't want to know them. I don't want to know anyone these days. I don't even want to know myself. Sleep is my escape. It gives me a break from the ceaseless self awareness that I choke on. I used to think of a woman and that if I could be with her that things would be better but now I know that that's just a dead engine in the desert. Just a burnt corpse that never gets discovered. It's nothing. I could never be there for anyone. I couldn't do anything with this girl that would change the way I am. I am the Hollow Man. I can barely be there for myself. I have to pick myself up off the floor all the time now. Sort through the pieces and figure out who I am underneath all the ash and sweat. I am disgusting. I want to end. I want to be one with the shadows. I want to end the scream that tears at my guts. I will travel on a moving bed tomorrow night. I will feel safe knowing that no one can touch me. It's the only break I can see.

#12: Just for a little while be with me. Just sit next to me, I need you. Not anyone. I wish it was that easy, there's a lot of them around. It's you I want to be with. I don't think it will ever happen. I was with another girl today. I've been with a few girls in the last week. It's not the same. They're nice, real nice but they're not you. I know I could walk up to you with an arm cut off and blood pumping out with each heartbeat and you wouldn't notice. I know how you are, you're not bad you've had it hard. You need someone to help you, if you would let me get close to you I could heal all your wounds.

#13: While I stagger away to puke. I put a wall behind me and a wall in front of me. The wall behind me has bricks three deep and no light comes in. The wall in front of me has peep holes so I can see out. I don't want to talk about back there. I don't look behind myself unless I can be alone and scream. My horror isolates me and leaves me stranded in the middle of my brain. No matter what I do or say I'm always alone in this room puking and screaming. Sometimes I feel nothing at all, nothing. I can't talk. She could touch me and I wouldn't feel anything. I can fuck but I can't feel. I can puke but I can't feel. I've been falling for a while now.

#14: At some point you'll ask yourself why she left you. You will not play all the typical games in your mind where you make her something that lives below you, cold and inhuman. You will sit in your room and stare at the floor as you turn over every time you talked to her. You'll try to remember what it was that might have made her leave you forever. You can't find a single thing. In your mind you are wounded and in pain. You cannot find an answer. You will find a lump in your throat because you feel so stupid and vulnerable and alone. You'll remember everything that you said and meant as being pitifully stupid and embarrassing. You hope that she'll never tell anyone the things that you told her. You become suddenly angry at yourself for ever having told her all the things you did. You accuse yourself of being weak and lame, unable to face the world alone. You feel overwhelmed at your own inability to handle anything. Life sucks since she's been gone. You can tell how good you felt with her by how bad you feel right now. The radio will play a sad song as if the DJ knew you were in there and is trying to get you to cry. You feel the lump in your throat swell and you cry. Hard and short, the tears fall from your eyes onto the ends of your shoes. Your nose becomes clogged and you wipe your face with your arm. You will not tell any of your friends about this part of your life. They have probably been through the same thing as you although you never talk about the naked lonely moments that you do on your own. Totally on your own. Like no one's ever been there before, not like you have. Everyone has a desert that they go to watch the moon paint the sand. When she leaves you will feel the miracle of humanity. The horrible intellect that you possess will turn you into a self torturing machine. You will feel the hollow bones in your body. You will know me and the depths from which I come to you always.

#15: I look into the mirror and think of what my face would look like if someone had shot me in the left cheek with a gun. I think of what a fragile thing the skull is. I think of my face shattered and mutilated. I'm lucky to have a face and that thought makes me want to erase my face.

What an awesome trip to get murdered. Stepping over the line. Stepping into nothing. To be dead, to be murdered and die.

The faces and the streets are blank. The words are meaningless. The world is extinct and dead. I have found the meaning and it's meaningless. I don't have emotion to rekindle. I'm in a walking coma. Partly dead. From now on, it's just documentation. I am beyond heartbreak. I am extinct but still breathing. I stab myself with my senses yet I feel no pain. My body keeps breathing even though my thoughts are dead. It's funny how I am able to live this lie. How I can go out there and talk to them and then come back here to this room and break down all on my own. I am alive enough to feel the pain in my face when I look off to nowhere and start to cry. My eyes burn at first and then it's easy after that. I can't talk because I'm cold and made out of wood. Part of my face has been shot off and I can't talk like I want to. I can't let the words go. They stay inside and kill me a little more every day.

#16: To the Hollow Brother. I see you in the mirror as I contemplate another night on the killing plane. So many years here. Neon sprawl, littered with humans. Broken and twisted. I saw a woman come out of the bushes near a highway overpass today. She was pulling up her pants. She was as ugly as the concrete she was walking on. She was as beautiful. She sat down on a bucket and held up a sign that said : Please feed me and Joe. I guessed that Joe was the small dog at her feet. The car ahead of me must have said something because she screamed Fuck you, you son of a bitch at it as it made a left. Now it's night and no one's here except me and the hollow pattern of my breathing. I can't hold onto the flesh lies. I don't call them, I don't need them. They fell away from my eyes. I could no longer live in their world. I live in the hollow desert. The howling sonic expanse. Rage is my sustenance. I cannot use their language to speak. I lie whenever I speak because it's their words, they will never be their words. The words were here before me and all

I can do is use them and get used by them. I'd rather be here in the horror worlds of my screaming desert night.

#17: I passed a woman tonight as I was riding my bike the wrong way down Hollywood Blvd. Our eyes met for a split second. As I sped down the street I looked behind me. She had turned to look at me. I thought of what would have happened if I got off the bike and walked up to her. Hello my name is Henry, I don't like the name but it's the one that they gave me. I hope I'm not scaring you. I swear I won't hurt you. You have such a kind face that I felt ok about coming up and talking to you. Would you like to come to my place, I swear I won't hurt you. We could talk or what ever you wanted. I could make you some food if you were hungry. I just came from the store. I'm so lonely in this city, so lonely on this planet. I don't want to die but I can't stand it sometimes. I wonder if someone could meet someone else and have their life turned around. Do you think that kind of thing ever happens or is it just something that we tell ourselves to keep hanging on. We tell ourselves certain things to keep the carrot dangling in front of our faces I know. It's a fail-safe that keeps us in pain. I don't know if I'm living real life or a movie. I don't know where I fit. Are you like me? Do you feel need like it's trying to kill you when you're alone in your room? Do you think it's possible to meet someone on the street in a city past midnight and make some kind of connection that could last? I missed this car that was pulling out from the curb by that much. I think it's better for me to keep my eyes on the road.

#18: She got up about an hour after I did. Everything I did pissed her off. Why don't you listen to me when I'm talking to you, where are you? You're so fucked up! For a moment she made me care. Care enough to contemplate wordlessly killing and dumping her after dark in the parking garage. All I did was tell her to shut up and get out. She said is that it? That's all you're going to say to me after we spent the night together? You're fucked you know that? I didn't say anything. I was miles beyond caring at all. I didn't even notice when she left the room. I heard the hard slam of the door as she exited. I am hard pressed to remember a thing of what she said the night before. I would just nod my head and stare off into my jungle. I don't remember the sex, I don't remember anything except the things that I want to forget, those things I remember with alarming clarity that makes me forget everything else.

#19: I want to write you and tell you everything, that's how desperate I am. I don't even know you. You're just a face that talked to me, a voice that had a comforting tone to it that made me want to stay with you so

I could hear you say more things. It wouldn't have mattered what you said. It's like talking to a dog. They listen to the tone. I think that loneliness is disgusting and it victimizes anyone it comes near. I feel lonely and I project it on you. What an insult. If I told you I wanted to spend the night with you, you might think that I felt something for you but that's not the truth. The truth is that I'm looking for way to get through the time left on the planet. I don't know you, I don't hear your words, I only hear the tone. I talk to myself while you talk to me. I don't even need you here, just leave your tone and your body in this dark box with me and I'll clutch it and listen to the tone and lie myself into a coma.

#20: Then on the other hand you have to remember the reason that you do anything for. Even the smallest thing, you must know the reason. There's always a reason. That's the only way to deal with this meat mutilation existence. Like it should matter who thinks what. I never lived for them. I never lived until I lived for myself. The rest of the time was just that, time. Doing time in the darkness. Not waiting for anything, anyone, nothing. I could pour my blood and guts out all over the place for them, for you.....would it matter? Yea sure it would, I would get sold out in no time. It's lonely here but it's alright if you know how to deal with the time.

#21: When you think you have no more guts to be gutted, you find out that you have a few more chunks that they can rip out of you. If you think you're all the way empty, you're wrong, you'll run into one of those people that will be able to press you flatter, to squeeze out a little more juice. The pigs were in my room the other day asking the same questions again. I kept telling them the same things over and over again. I don't deal drugs, Joe didn't deal drugs. I looked over on the carpet, there was Joe's body lying there with his brains all over the floor twitching every time the pigs asked more questions. Finally the pigs told me that they wanted me to take a polygraph test. I told the pigs that I couldn't wait. I'll take any test they have. I hope they ask me if I hate pigs so I can scream yes yes yes until I pass out. Every time I think that I'm building myself back up and putting things into myself that no one will be able to take away from me so I do not have to be Hollow Man. They come in and squeeze it out of me and drag me back into the world of pig horror.

#22: You asked me what I wanted so here it is. For a little while, sidestep the scars and the past and love me. Put your arms around me. I need you so much. It's hard to breathe. I feel so alone. All these people pass me and I don't know any of them. They talk to me but I don't understand anything they say. I hear but do not listen. I smile and shake their hands. They empty me, they pull my guts out. My mind is hollow, I cannot lie. I have been broken down. My shadow has been stolen. I can be your friend. I know they have hurt you. I know you expect things to go wrong. I know you expect pain first, so much that you create situations where it will be brought upon you so you can get it over with. You have been taught by example to take the beating. I could never hurt you.

#23: She was able to turn herself into plastic whenever she wanted to. I would put my arms around her and all of a sudden she would get hard and slightly cold. A few seconds later she would turn back into flesh and everything would be alright. She liked being plastic better then being flesh. I would wake up in the night and she would be sleeping plastic. If she sensed me looking at her she would turn to flesh in the speed of an eye blink. We would never talk about it. I was afraid she would leave me. I thought that if I loved her she would remain in flesh. If I ever brought up subjects that were too intense, she would look away and her skin would take on a slight sheen as her pores disappeared. Sometimes she would go between plastic and flesh with every breath as if she couldn't decide which she preferred. Nothing I did was enough. Too many beatings and abuse had scarred her forever. From my dark box I wonder where she is now. I wonder if there was anything I could have done differently to have made her stay with me. I know that love has no great power in the world. The wrath of abuse and pain are far more decisive influences on the flesh. We will go to great lengths to deny and hide. She is living scar tissue.

#24: I'm losing tonight. I'm in this room in Seattle and I'm looking at Joe Cole's book and it hurts. I have a lump in my throat and I want to die because I miss him so much. I look at the picture and I read the words and it hurts. Sometimes I wonder how I'll make it without killing myself because it's all I think of doing a lot of the time I'm alone at night. I am finding it hard to give a fuck about anything at all. I miss him. I don't know what to do with myself. I can't find a way not to lose over and over. Sometimes I feel like I'm suffocating inside, like I want to scream but I can't because there's so much scar tissue in the way of my throat. I'm lonely and fucked up. I'm losing this round. Sometimes I feel like I can deal with it and then there comes a night like this and it's hard to take, so hard. I think that the things that happen to people on this planet are enough to make you want to die fast. I will not talk to anyone about anything, I will write like hell and tell the truth. There is nothing else. They ask me how I can do what I do and I can't explain to them that I have no choice. I'm a wounded animal caught in the headlights.

#25: I leave another heartbreak hotel and make my way down the road. I went to the town thinking that some thing good was going to happen, something out of the ordinary. Didn't work out like that. The streets and the room all told me that I'm in a slow desperate moving psychosis. All I can do is move. I looked into her eyes and knew she didn't get where I was coming from. I am from the still moments that go unnoticed. The emptiness and the silent sadness. I couldn't say a word to her. I have no language that works with these people. I told her that I come from a different planet and I knew I was right. Hushed voices wait for me at bus stops. They see me and I hear my name behind me. The planet and all its cities wait for me. I know I won't be here long and that's fine. The silence and the alienation are refined. The blades are sharp and I never run out of blood.

#26: The airport makes me think that I can breathe again. Always good to see an airport especially on the way out. Going out. Escaped from another city before it killed me, wore me down and ground me out. I leave today to go to more dead cities on the planet. I like the idea of leaving cities. The freedom is in the movement. Between cities they can't touch you, they have to leave you alone when you're above the clouds. It's good to get off the earth for a while.

#27: I can hear the dirty traffic through the window. The sun burns my feet as I sit on the end of the bed and think about the idea of sleep. I can hear voices and movement out there. I want to walk around but the lack of sleep is getting to me. All I'll do today is sleep to get ready to do press. I will see nothing of Madrid except from the back of a car. I already know this. Cool and the Gang posters up everywhere. The room waits for me to fall and then closes in with paranoia dreams of a killer chasing me. Hours later I'm semi coherent and they come and take me away to answer all kinds of questions. I wonder if the sun shined out there today. I wonder if I could have had a good time if I could have been there to know anything different than all these rooms look the same after a while and that you can get used to being all alone all the time.

#28: I thought I recognized a street as we sped along. I realized that the street I was thinking of is in Zurich. They all look the same after a while, you can go fast enough, long enough to where it's all the same. The guy next to me looked out the window at a large building and said that it was too large, a fascist building. I was going to say something about the building not being bigger than Guns and Roses, their logo loudly adorning the back of his jacket. I looked at the buildings flying by, lit up for the tourists. Last time I was here playing a boy was hit by a car and killed outside of the show. Outside my window they scream at each other and beep their horns. I do interviews most of the day and then fly to another city. I am homeless, hopeless without care or love.

#29: Hollow recollection that drills me alone in this box. I'm standing in front of 25 plus press people answering questions. I wonder what the fuck I'm doing. I look out the window and see all the people that have heard that I'm in Rome at this record store doing a press conference. They watch from outside and try to catch my eye by holding up records that I'm on. I finish the press thing and there's record company people running around asking me if I'm alright. Yea sure it was just some questions what the fuck. They open the door and the others come in and then I'm signing things. Some piece of shit tells me that I only played the shit holes all these years so I could play with the Chili Peppers in front of several thousand people. He said I used the shitty punker dives as a stepping stone. I tell him to forget the rest of the speech and let's go outside so I can smack him like a bitch. He bails. Smart piece of shit. More record company types rush over to see if I'm alright. It's just a piece of human garbage, what's the problem? I go to the airport. I am picked up by two young pigs with machine guns and am told to unpack. They are mad that I'm not scared. I want to punch the pigshit out of them. Finally they let me get out of their city. I leave the city, another one waits for me always.

#30: Hollow memo. I was riding in the back of a car going through the Alps. I had pulled out of Munich an hour before. The moon was staring in the window. I faked falling asleep so the record company lady wouldn't ask any more questions. All of a sudden a thought hit me. Something that I've always known but never thought about in a different way. I thought about Joe's mother Sally. She has been working so hard to keep it together. I never really knew her before Joe was killed. For no reason at all of a sudden realized that she lost her only son. Her son was murdered and she'll deal with that for the rest of her life. She'll go through it every day. She must feel some kind of horrible failure for bringing up I started to cry. It was so fucked. I felt so totally alone in the world. I hate this place so much.

#31: 2:46 a.m. Paranoia, depression and exhaustion have a hold on me. I was staring into the black of the room sweating and thinking that I would like to get some time off so I could go out and blow my brains out. I am hungry and there are places open to eat but I'm too paranoid to go out there and get food. I'm not doing too well I guess. I should have not come here for my day off. I sit in my room and I freak myself out. I wish to be happy but all I can do is make myself more angry and full of rage. I have no one to blame but myself. I am not looking for anyone to blame but I desperately need some kind of relief. I don't know how to get it and I don't know what to do with myself now. You can get so tired that you cannot sleep and all you do is get more fucked up. Believe me it's true. You can withdraw inside yourself further and further to the point to where you won't even be able to listen to a voice on a record. I get quieter every day. I don't know what to do. I don't want to kill myself but sometimes it's the only thing that I can think of. I have interviews starting in the morning and then I go to Arizona to play. I fear for myself. I don't know how I'll get through the next few months.

#32: In a hotel room far away from the real world I sit and think to myself while she is in the bathroom. There is only them. There is never anyone that is as close as a life away. I think about the stranger in the toilet. I think about what she's thinking, what she thinks of me. If she feels freaked out by the things that I have told her in the last hour. I wonder if she's scared of me and wants to find a way to get out of the room. I wonder of she's in there freaking out thinking that I'm going to hurt her. There's just them. No matter what you say, you'll always be on the outside. Always a stranger. All of a sudden life becomes a disease that rips you apart and leaves you on a strange planet. You go along with it because you know nothing else. If you think about it too much it makes you depressed because you see all the things that you have to do to keep your mind busy. You try to talk to someone and almost always you regret it afterwards. I think that I will hate myself in the morning. The comes out of the bathroom. Everything I say and do from this point on is desperate and pathetic.

#33: I am a stupid fuck up with no life. One more night here in my room and then I leave to go out there again for a long time. I'm glad that I'm leaving. I like my room, with all the music and the door that I can close.

Mostly the music though. I like listening to Charlie Parker and Coltrane at three in the morning and getting left alone. But. I don't belong here. I have been here a few days and already I'm getting fucked up in the head. My problem is that I have no idea how to get along with people. All I can do is play and move. I try to get along with them and it fails. I'm no good at being in one place. I get lonely on the road like anyone else but there's something about the movement that keeps me in one piece. Here I fall apart and I talk a bunch of stupid shit and I get weak and the loneliness gets to be too much. I was in rare form tonight. I tried to talk to a girl and all I did was insult her terribly. If I had the courage I would talk to her and tell her that I am sorry, that I acted in a dishonorable manner. Maybe tomorrow night I will. Of course I won't because by tomorrow night I will have found some way to justify what I did and I'll just say fuck it, so what. The only good thing that I do is cause myself pain by playing my guts out and pushing weights up and down. These people will never know how fucked up I am because I don't have the strength to kill myself or the intelligence to render it with words. I'm caught in the middle. Too stupid to do anything and too smart to know that I'm nothing but a no one.

#34: I dreamt last night that I came into a room and saw a girl that I used to go out with lying on a couch with my father. She was laughing in my face and treating me like a child. She was acting like my stepmother. I can't remember what my father looked like but I remember him staring at me and laughing. I won't see him again unless it's in a dream. I don't know what to do with myself except to make myself as hollow as possible whenever I can. The less I am the better.

#35: I'm getting good and empty. I have never been so empty in all my half life. I lie in my black box and I don't think about anything except killer's eyes. I have become comfortable with his eyes. I look into them and I wonder where he is and what he's doing. What he had for breakfast and if he thinks about what he did, if he has dreams like I do. I used to think of women I knew and now I don't. I came upon the great idea that unhinged me from life as I knew it before. The days are passing me and I can't tell one from another. They give me things and as soon as they leave I throw them out. I can't hold onto them and be free. You even touch them and you become part of them for a while. It's hard to get them off you. You have to be careful because they will kill you with words and actions. The only way to be free to live the half life is to be hollow. Otherwise it's just a gut stomp that kills you always.

#36: Night off in a New York box. Spent hours walking the streets. Students talking about "gender sanity". An old woman pushing her cart, me walking from street to street not knowing where the hell I'm going. No one recognizing me, thinking of things:
I don't want my brain to explode and all the murder to come out
I don't see any other way other than to put their brains all over the street
I don't want to hurt anyone
I know I'm the kind that hurts people
Stupid animals know not what they do to others
The two guys staring at me in the diner make me want to reach over and grab one of them by the throat, the feeling immediately leaves me. I don't want to hurt anyone, I don't want to touch anyone and I don't want anyone to touch me. I see a sign with a picture of a father and son weather forecasting team on a local news station. The father has his arms around the son. I think of my father touching me and it seems unreal that it ever happened. I makes me think of my mother and the rage that she makes me feel. Hours pass and I'm back in the bug spray smelling box. I am determined to write truths from my guts that will make me sick and violent when I read them back to myself. Stab that shit talking bitch in the stomach so many times that she'll never have children. Never being touched by one of them again. I inhale the bug spray and feel the claustrophobia of the room set in. Have not slept in a day and a half and I feel fine. I'm free, that's the thing I've got in my favor tonight and all nights from now on.

#37: I told her: Most of the people that I know I pay a salary to. I would never ask you a favor unless I was paying you. Like if I was hungry I would ask you to get me some food and I would pay you for the food and your time. I pay the guys in the band because I know how fast they would be gone if I didn't. My parents taught me from an early age to depend on no one but myself. I never felt they supported me in any way besides the food and housing. I pay people to do things and I usually only know others from business that I do with them. I told her that the phone doesn't ring at my place on the weekend. She started to cry. Right there during an interview on camera. I don't understand the problem. Seems to me I have rooted out the truth pretty well. Some life.

#38: I am doing the best I can to strip away the excess and get to the point. Existence is the muscle pulling away from the bone. Pure animal pain. The rest is just television to me. Death is the only thing that I answer to. Death calls out to me at all times. I am always aware of its presence. I have made friends with my nightmares, they are just dreams now, part of me. I fully understand what Kurtz said about making friends with horror and moral terror. They were my enemies and they plagued me and now they are my friends and they are my allies. They do not judge me like people do. I am of horror and terror.

#39: On the nights when we're staying in a hotel and not on the bus moving across some black highway I will have short moments of panic right before I fall asleep because I don't know where I am. Right before the eyes close I'll choke from not knowing where I am in the darkness. It happened the other night in London. I looked into the darkness of the room and started to spin for a few frantic seconds I didn't know if I was alive or what. Geographic location was secondary to just being alive. Wouldn't be great at a moment like that to be able to have someone with you to tell you that it's alright, some kind of human buoy, a reference point. Someone who wouldn't laugh at your cold-skinned horror life. Someone to tell you where you were. Someone to take away the panic need to blow my brains out right then and there feeling.

#40: I just came back from a woman's house. It was a good time with her. She is beautiful and kind, intelligent and has a great sense of humor. I am glad to be back in the room. I have found that I prefer to be alone. I have taken this thought further and found that I like to be with the dead. I like to be alone with music and memories of things and people that are no more. I am playing Thin Lizzy in the headphones. I have to use head phones because the human shit bag upstairs freaks out when I play anything past a certain hour. Phil's dead, Monk, Miles, Trane, Parker, Lightnin', Joe Cole, all the greats, all dead and here with me. I feel closer to them than I do with anyone living. I wonder if there's anyone else like this out there. It was good to be with the woman but I feel separate from her, the closest I can get is next to her. I feel like a dead person next to her. She really has no idea what my reality is. I don't know what her's is either. We are equal in our strangeness to each other. The dead will take you just the way you are and there doesn't have to be any lies or game playing. I think more about dead people than I ever do about the ones that are living. It's good to be in this box alone with Phil. In the morning I do a television show to talk about Joe's Death so they can show it and try to stir some kind of local conscious-ness to inspire someone to come forward and give information. It will be ok, I'll know what to do. At this point I know a lot more about the dead than I know about the living. I am beyond life. It was horrible at first. It felt like a curse of some kind but steadily it became a welcome fact. I feel good somehow through all these empty nights.

#41 For the last two nights the old Black Flag truck has been parked outside the apartment building I live in. This truck belongs to the sound company that supplied Black Flag with its sound system for three years from 1984 through to 1896. This is the truck that Joe and drove in almost every day for 7 months in 1986. Last night it sat outside the building like some huge black horrible reminder. I imagine that the sound company is working at some local club off the Blvd. It seemed like a bad trick. Maybe it drove itself over there and was waiting for me to come out. I wanted to walk over to the window and look into the cab at the place where we sat and spent so much time running down the miles. The Black Flag logo was still on the back. I sat on the steps and looked at it for a long time. I don't know what I waiting for. Maybe I was hoping to see Joe in there waving me over so we could get on the road and get out of here. It sits outside the building watching me. I know how stupid this all sounds. Sometimes I feel so ruined. I can't sit still for too long or it gets to me. I have been throwing out memories as best I can. Sometimes I'm not hollow enough. I'm working on it.

#42: Hosted KROQ's Love Line show tonight. It's the number one show in the city of Los Angeles. You call in and talk about your hang-up no matter what it is. High lights include: A 14 year old girl caught giving her boyfriend head and has no been kicked out of the house and can she have some tickets to the band's show tomorrow night. A 15 year old girl that gave 8 guys head and wonders about the legion of sores around her mouth. A white guy who is scared of getting the shit kicked out of him by her black girlfriend's brother. The manic depressive boy who is scared of what he might do to his girlfriend. Endless faxes come in from people all over who are listening to the show. Afterwards people call in to talk to me while I'm waiting to get out of the station. At the ground floor we are informed that there are people outside that have been waiting all evening. I duck them and we see them as we go speeding out of the parking lot. I get back home and go out to the store to get food. I go by the diner where the blond was a few months ago. She's not there tonight. I go west on Sunset and look at the whore come out of the car wiping her mouth. I go into the supermarket and someone in each aisle knows me. One guy says he's just moved here from Buffalo and he trips out on seeing famous people. I give him a confidential look and tell him that WE ALL shop here. He says "that's cool" and leaves. I get back on the bike and weave through the whores and the drug dealers and go back to the apartment.

#43: I sit in this room in a silent clear eyed state of horror. In my mind my mother walks towards me with buckets of aborted children. She screams at me that she hates me for surviving her. I see cameras and my friend's blood being eaten by flies. Police fucking with me. I sit in the room and wait for the night to go by. I sometimes wish for someone who could help me but I have tried that and I know that you ride out horror on your own every time and you never talk about it because no one gets it unless they've been there and if they've been there you don't want to know them and they don't want to know you. You can smell it on each other and you both know the same dull ringing ache and the insanity that you've been through and continue to go through. I constantly amaze myself that I'm still alive. I know that the most dangerous thing to my health is me. I know that I are capable of great harm to others. The ones that I like and the ones that I don't. I only hurt the ones close to me as well as the ones at arm's length. I see people stepping over bodies to get on the bus. I'm in bed with a woman and I roll over onto Joe's dead body. I turn into a silent human scream. If you understand then I feel sorry for you because you're fucked up. If you don't, then I suggest you stay away from me because every move I make is a warning signal, a prelude to violence.

#44: Sometimes life is a recurring nightmare. Sometimes every thought that comes through my head is horrible. Like right now. I'm in Sydney Australia. I have the curtains shut and I have been in bed for a few hours just lying under the covers trying not to think because the only things that come to mind are Joe Cole getting murdered and this woman that I wanted to be with that didn't want to be with me. Death and rejection. I don't care how it sounds or how it looks. Earlier today I went out there and did the work that I needed to do and now I'm back in the box and feel no need to ever leave again until the morning. I feel safe with myself, even if I feel like killing myself all the time. Behind the hollow eyes there is a hollow, thoughtless desperate scream. I've been dead for months and none of these people can tell. A few of earth's women have fucked a dead man, it wouldn't have been the first time.

#45: After the night they spent together he thought about the woman constantly not knowing what she thought of him or if she even thought of him at all. She called him and told him that the night meant so much to her, that she had been waiting years to be close to him and even though they had met on several occasions she had never seen fit to tell him of her feelings. She had kept them to herself for years and finally told him. Now she calls and tells him of all the times she had watched him when he didn't even know she was there. She tells him that she wants to know where he's at with her because she doesn't want to lead herself on. She is open and totally honest. She tells him that if he just wants to be friends with her, to please speak now and she'll tone her feelings down and not hope for anything. He likes her, he really likes her. He knows himself well, so many empty miles have hollowed him out and he knows that he'll never be able to be there for anyone else, he can't even show up on time to be there for himself. He has no needs and no longer has understanding of how deal with anyone else's. He stammers and tries to find a non committal answer that will give her hope and keep her around but will allow him to get out quick if he feels he needs to, like he knows he'll need to a few weeks later. He knows well the suffocation that he always feels when he gets too close to one of them. When he gets too far away from himself. Too many years driven like a nail into himself. He never gets too far out of his head. He breaks the silence and listens the words come out of his mouth: No, I don't think I could ever be more than a friend to you and not a very good one at that, I'm not very..........I'm just not good with......I'm sorry. He tells her that he'll see her next time he comes through. He hangs up with relief and slight pride from having told the truth and sparing someone his beneath the skin behind the eyes desperation that spares no one. Ever.

#46: In a box in Melbourne Australia. It's too late for a lot of things. Too late for me to care about the things that don't matter because I have seen them with my hollow eyes for what they are. I smell my own fear and coiled animal panic when I think of my father and my mother's boyfriends. I can't give a fuck about what happens to them. All I can do is be ready if any of them come forward to try to destroy me. I cannot love and cannot be loved. Love is for humans. I know what I am. I am a sociopathic predatory animal. Either you're looking to make the kill or you're looking to get killed. I thought I loved some people before but I now see that I did not. It was just one of those things that happens when there's nothing else to do. Just something to take up the time until Death comes. With my hollow eyes I see you, with my hollow eyes I see myself, falling away. Human pain is 99% bullshit. I have freed myself from human pain. All I know is animal pain. If they hit you, you have to take it because it's illegal to kill them when they fuck with you. You have to take it and swallow more animal fear and grow more scars. Life is hollow. Leaves in a box. The shrink's office was in her house. I used to sit in the shrink's waiting room and watch her children come though the hallway on their way home from school. They would look at me and laugh. I wanted to kill them and the fucked up shrink bitch that was picking my brain. I would go home from that and listen to the bitch mother tell me how much money she was paying to have the shrink bitch tell me what my problem was. I would see my father on the weekends and he would tease me about what a sissy I was to be getting talked to by a shrink. We are now partners in mutual disgrace. The only thing we have in common is self disgust.

#47: Hollow walk on late night streets. Charlie Parker in New York. Bloody explosions of liquid fire scorch the sides of my skull. Dead men in cars drive by looking for the meat sale. A group of men come out of a bar smelling like aftershave and scuffling feet quick violence. They expand and contract near their car. The two men look at me in the diner. They talk to each other and look back and laugh. Blocks later, groups of men pass by and the smell of beer comes off their clothes. I fool myself and think that I'm invisible until a few people call my name out and then I see that it's the wrong planet for me. Charlie Parker nodding off on the bandstand, sweating backstage. His music full of beauty, fury and Death. Why can't they see it in everything. Why doesn't it drive them to small rooms all over the world. Why am I so alone on the planet. Blocks go by. I see Death everywhere in every-thing. I see them walk by on the street and I think of savagely attacking them with blunt instruments. Tough guy in a coma, put there by a guy who cared less than anyone he ever met in his half life. I think of women that don't exist. I kill strangers in my mind and walk late at night in bad neighborhoods because I am a bad neighbor. The pigs filled up three notebooks on me from all the things that the people in my old neighborhood said I did, said I was. Now I'm hollow for all to see. Thoughts explode and disintegrate in my head as I listen to my footsteps hit the street. I feel like stalking them. I don't look for friends anywhere. I don't look for kindness because I know more about humans than they do. I've had my head blown off by words for years. The only thing that could make me notice is guns. That's what it's come to. The words are meaningless when they fall out of their mouths. They love you, they hate you, it's all the same in the real world. Don't cling, don't attach to them. You'll rip yourself to pieces. Let their words fall to the ground, let them break at their feet so they can see where they are. Let them break their own backs, if they don't, the only back that will get broken is yours. I'm waiting for the world to fall over and quit. I'm waiting for the sun to run itself into the ground. There's that scene in Deer Hunter where the Green Beret is sitting at the bar and the guys are trying to get him to talk and all he says is "Fuck it" and keeps looking away. That's all there is to do, keep looking away, right through the bottom, right into the eyes of the Abyss. Call nowhere home. Unhappy misanthrope kills them to ease the pain. Finally he kills himself.

#48: Singapore. Tonight as we were walking out of a restaurant we saw a small car wreck. Someone said what a drag. I said that it wasn't us. I felt like something had kicked me in the side. I remembered how me and Joe used to say that to each other all the time. We would read something in the paper about something bad happening to someone and we would say that it wasn't us so we really didn't care. We thought everything was funny. That's all over now. I've never felt so alone in my life. I am Pain's errand boy.

#49: I'm surrounded by car exhaust and neon. Night time in Tokyo and people are all over the place, walking and laughing and breathing. None of them know that Joe is in a small box in the ground and the silence and stillness in the box would be enough to give them nightmares for the rest of their lives. I am pretty pathetic at this point, I know this.

#50: In a box near the airport in New Orleans. Walked along the highway looking for a gas station to get something to eat. People were inside but all the doors were locked. People are afraid of getting shot in the head. Afraid of men coming into the quikmart, looking past them and all of a sudden telling them to lie down on the floor or they'll get their fucking heads shot off. Afraid of a man that wants to kill for the fucked up sake of killing. The smart ones know that others will do that. Paranoia is everywhere, it's been hammered into a reality. In fact it's no longer paranoia that we feel. It's the honest knowledge that things can happen to anyone any time. Paranoia used to be something that would crawl up the back of your spine and bite, now it's just the weary reality that violence never sleeps. I walked along the highway. I was alone and hollow: I don't want anyone to know me. I don't want to know any one of them. I want to speak in hushed tones and avoid the light of day. I feel hunted sometimes. They know me, I don't know them. They have the advantage always. I used to think that if I knew one person that I would be alright. If I had one person to talk to that all things would be well with the world. I know now that you don't need anyone to get by. All you have to do is know how to duck and avoid places where they can see you. If I'm alone I start to forget. I forget myself. I forget my mother and father and I forget all the things that the humans have said and done to me over the years. I forget all the things I have done to them. I usually regret dealing with people. I lose my control and do things that I hate myself for later. It's obvious to me that I don't know how to be around them. When they come to talk to me I keep my distance and treat them like a curator at a museum talks about the paintings on the walls. More so around women. I feel that if I don't keep my distance that they will think I want to rape them and they'll call the pigs on me and I'll go to prison. When they talk to me I either cross my arms or put them in my pockets and I try to be as unthreatening as I possibly can. Sometimes they ask if they can kiss me or hug me and I politely say no because I don't want any of those fucking women touching me and then telling the pigs that I tried to do something with them. Sometimes they give me notes and ask me to go out with them so they can talk to me. They want to take me somewhere so they can have their own personal interrogation session. I always say no because I don't want to talk to them and I hate answering questions. I like walking alone on the highway at night.

#51: Rebirthed after Death. My father hacked out my lungs and stripped me of courage. He gave me only fear and a few words to live by, words like: Yes sir. My mother and her boyfriends ripped my arms and legs off making it hard to move. I learned to crawl very well. I gave the guts my parents gave me at birth to strangers from the stage at an early age. I had to grow my own guts to replace them. One time I took out the intestines that they gave me and nailed the end to the edge of a stage and let the audience pull them out and take sections home as souvenirs. I dumped all the brains out of my skull and grew new brains. I lifted weights and pounded words into the air and onto paper and learned about pain, the first thing that was truly my own. I forged myself out of a vacuum. I crawl along the highway on hacked off stumps year after year. Some wonder how and why. I never do.

#52: So I go out and smash myself all the time. I put myself in places where I'm up there and they're down there. I put myself under their scrutiny every chance I get. I get spat on, dented up and hollowed out. I hit myself in the face while I play to make myself play harder. I sing and wreck my throat. I see through people when they talk to me. I have the nerve to wonder why I'm so lonely and isolated from people. It's funny sometimes I'll feel like some kind of victim, like poor little me. It's no wonder anymore, I do this shit to myself and that's what happens. Right now I'm sitting here in my little box thinking about the piece of shit that spat one me tonight and how I cracked him in the face with the mic like it wasn't anything big. It wasn't. I don't wonder why I couldn't talk to this girl I know after the show. How I just looked at her and said some bullshit hoping that it would relieve her of any stress I might have put her under by being so weird. It was easy to see that I had confused her by being fucked up. I excused myself and left. I am banged up and smashed up. I don't make sense and I shouldn't get too close to people because there's just no way it works anymore. I talked to one guy I have known for a few years and he wanted to hug me and I felt myself want to run. I could tell that had alienated him as well. I can't help it. I didn't want to talk to him but I did anyway because I could see that I was freaking him out a little. He asked me how someone could get in touch with me on an intimate basis, he said he wanted to phone me because we lived in the same town and he shouldn't have to write me. He was right but all I could do was stare at him. I wasn't going to give him my phone number, hell he might use it some time. I was too fucked up to talk to this guy and even be a human being so I walked away. I go out and smash myself around all the time. I pride myself on being able to take a lot of pain on a regular basis. How the fuck can I expect myself to be able to be cool to someone else when all I do is self involve myself. I get lonely and have the nerve to wonder why. What a joke. I should get off the bullshit and get on with it. If I wanted to do something different with myself I would. If I'm going to go this route I should go, go and take it and deal with it and not complain that I'm not getting the comfort of the world that I left behind. How typically weak of me. I must get stronger. I must listen to my scar tissue and follow the silent instructions and cut the bullshit.

#53: All the hollow nights filling me. I have been back here for a few days and tonight it hits me how useless I am off the road. I wake up in the morning and work at things but I can't remember any of it. I look through the mail and all the voices from the letters crowd me and I have to put it down. I have all the time I want to do whatever I want. I keep myself busy as best I can. I try not to think. The night comes and around 8 p.m. I start to feel nervous even though I have worked out hard a few hours before. There's no gig, no chance to push against myself. I fall in on myself. I look around my room and don't recognize any of the belongings. The only thing in here that doesn't belong is me. Someone calls me and it's all I can do to get them off the line and turn the phone off. I'm too fucked up. I sit still for a few minutes and then look for something else to do. Somehow experience has failed me. I am a bullet lodged in a wall. Time spent moving constantly makes sitting still all but impossible. I have painted myself into the corner of a portrait of myself. Discipline and repetition waited and got me into this room before they turned on me. Experience has made me into a confrontation addict.

#54: I didn't want to get off stage tonight. I'm in the box inside Hollywood. I felt like my guts were flying out of my body. I've been cooped up in the box for a few weeks and tonight I was part of a benefit and I got to do some talking for 15 minutes. It wasn't enough. Now I'm back here and I want to break shit. I don't know when I'll be getting tired now. It was hard to be back in my element for a little while and then to get ripped out of it and thrown back into the box where nothing moves, nothing happens. I still smell like tobacco smoke. I want to be on tour. I need to have more self control. I am afraid that I am addicted to touring. When I'm home I can't deal with things. People are either to hard or too soft. Too soft in that they can't deal with it or too hard in that you can walk outside and be in the wrong place and have some 18 year old example of the species shoot you in the face. It makes me hostile and confused. I have thrown out the idea of what is fair. I'm in this box right now and I want to be out there. I need relief. The year is almost over. They didn't kill me. To paraphrase Ice T: they should have killed me last year. I feel inadequate and I don't know why. It seems like I can't get hit hard enough. I feel out of place in this day and age. I have pulled back. I got sick of getting pinned to the floor by midgets and being in a position where I was forced to care about things that didn't matter. It's a weakening experience. I've go to get back on the road, I can't stay here too much longer fooling myself every day. It's a trip realizing that there's no other way for you to go.

#55: 1992 staggers down the hallway clutching its side where it has been stabbed. The lights are growing dim. The drug dealers and the whores in my neighborhood know each other. It's the only community I've seen on the streets near my house. Ugly, fat women in hot pants standing on the corner laughing and talking with quick faced young men always looking side to side. They talk and laugh and inhale car exhaust and watch the lights change and then a car pulls up and one of the whores gets in and waves goodbye as the car pulls away. Shucks, so heartwarming. The other day I watched two pigs with their guns out in the parking lot of the video store, they were looking into one of the stores. One pig had a shotgun and the other had his handgun out. All the drug dealers just stood in the parking lot and watched. I don't want to live around here anymore. 1993 is almost here and I find myself in Hollywood and out of Venice for a year. I never liked Hollywood but here I am anyway. I moved into the present box because it was there. I had nowhere else to go, all of my stuff was in storage and this place became available. The nights here pass slowly. Sirens and chopper blades. Don't know how long I've been here this time, a few weeks, a month, I don't know.

1992 feels old and haggard. 1992 feels betrayed and tricked, no one told the year that it had only a year to live. I stay up nights until the sun is almost coming up. I like to get up early and work during the day but night after night I have found myself unable to sleep even after a hard workout and a day of office work. I stay up and look at the wall. I barely know this room. I have been out on the road almost all of this year. I feel like a fish out of water. A bullet lodged in wood, inert and unmoving. I imagine exchanging words with a woman that understood me. I wish I had something to say that I wanted her to understand. I feel bad that I am so empty that I can stay in this room only to leave and lift weights until exhaustion makes my limbs shake. Then it's to the kitchen for the same food every night. After that it's back to the room and wait for sleep. I search my mind for something that doesn't make me recoil in shame, rage and horror. I come up empty. Touch me. Lie on this mattress with me and do something that makes me feel something else other than that I've made a big mistake letting you come here. I'm stupid and I don't know what move to make. Teach me how to think again. Please. Please. Please....leave.

1992 hears people in all the apartments celebrating 1993's approach. 1992 lurches to the side and collapses gasping with the roar of cheering and clapping ringing in its ears. I throw out magazines without bothering to read them. The animals out there. The animals driving by in their cars. The animals mistaking me for prey. I don't know which one has the gun in his pants. I don't go out there much anymore. I go out there every few days for food and then right back to the room. Out there they come up and ask questions. They touch you in the supermarket Touched by a stranger on the streets of Death. I'm sorry. Please understand me. I don't mean to harm, I don't mean to do damage. I am an animal in pain, stricken with fear and I will fuck you up. If you love me I'll let you down. I'll turn on you and make you hate me. I'll do it because I'll think it's what I have to do to survive you. I don't trust love. I feel hands around my throat. Mother's boyfriends. Father, stepbrother. You can have it, save it, shove it, taste it until it makes you choke. I sit endlessly. I wait to leave again and again. I live the same horror trip over and over. I have to move so I can unplug myself from thought and disappear into action and pain. The rage builds again obscuring any thought of balance and self control. I want to feel muscle pull from the bone. I want to make my body scream. I want to learn the lessons in pain that expand me. Last longer, move faster with more clarity. I will go until my body quits. Panicked and charged with blind fury the bull sees the gate come up and he stomps and bellows in an arena full of strangers. It was always simple combat, one against all. One never relenting, knowing no other way to go but until collapse. 1992 dies.

LIVE DATES 1992

BAND DATES

February
11 Rotterdam Holland
12 Hamburg Germany
13 Hamburg Germany
14 Gronningen Holland
15 Deinze Belgium
16 Paris France
17 Amsterdam Holland
18 Nijemagen Holland
19 Munster Germany
20 Kassel Germany
21 Hannover Germany
22 Saarbrucken Germany
23 Zurich Switzerland
25 Munich Germany
26 Munich Germany
27 Frankfurt Germany
28 Innsbruck Austria
29 Vienna Austria

March
01 Milan Italy
02 Lyon France
04 Birmingham England
05 Liverpool England
07 Dublin Ireland
08 Belfast Ireland

10 Glasgow Scotland
12 London England
13 London England
14 London England

April
01 Fullerton CA (also Dennis Miller show taping)
02 San Diego CA
03 San Diego CA
04 Los Angeles CA
05 San Francisco CA
06 San Francisco CA
07 Los Angeles CA
08 Los Angeles CA
11 Phoenix AZ
12 Dallas TX
14 Cincinnati OH
15 Chicago IL
16 Chicago IL
17 Detroit MI
18 Toronto Canada
19 Toronto Canada
21 Washington DC
22 Washington DC
23 Boston MA
24 New York NY
25 New York NY
27 Atlanta GA
28 Atlanta GA

June
02 Berlin Germany
03 Dusseldorf Germany
04 Stuttgart Germany
05 Bielefeld Germany
06 Eindhoven Holland
07 Rotterdam Holland (plus day show at Dynamo Festival, Eindhoven)
08 Brussels Belgium
09 Paris France
10 Amsterdam Holland
11 Florence Italy
13 Fribourg Switzerland

15 Sheffield England
16 Newcastle England
17 Glasgow Scotland
18 Birmingham England
19 Manchester England
20 London England
26 Houston TX
27 Dallas TX
28 Austin TX
29 Oklahoma City OK
30 Columbia MO

July
01 St. Louis MO
02 Lawrence KS
03 Omaha NE
05 Denver CO
06 Salt Lake City UT
08 Seattle WA
09 Portland OR
11 Sacramento CA
12 San Francisco CA
13 Santa Clara CA
14 Santa Cruz CA
16 Phoenix AZ
17 Santa Barbara CA
18 Tijuana Mexico
21 Los Angeles CA
23 Anaheim CA (cable television shoot)
27 St. Petersburg FL
28 Miami FL
29 Gainesville FL
30 Pensacola FL
31 New Orleans LA

August
01 Nashville TN
03 Minneapolis MN
04 Racine WI
05 Grand Rapids MI
06 Pontiac MI

07 Cleveland OH
08 Columbus OH
09 Pittsburgh PA
10 Buffalo NY
12 Toronto Canada
13 Ottawa Canada
14 Montreal Canada
15 Providence RI
17 Richmond VA
18 Philadelphia PA
19 Baltimore MD
20 New York NY
21 Asbury Park NJ
22 Trenton NJ
23 Trenton NJ
28 London England
29 Reading England

September

11 Brisbane Australia
12 Burleigh Heads Australia
13 Sydney Australia
15 Canberra Australia
17 Melbourne Australia
18 Melbourne Australia
19 Melbourne Australia
20 Hobart Australia
21 Adelaide Australia
22 Perth Australia
25 Sydney Australia
26 Manly Australia
29 Singapore

October

02 Nagoya Japan
03 Osaka Japan
04 Tokyo Japan
05 Tokyo Japan
09 Honolulu HI
10 Honolulu HI
25 Tucson AZ

26 Albuquerque NM
29 Dayton OH
30 Kalamazoo MI
31 Indianapolis IN

November

01 Chicago IL
02 Toronto Canada
03 Montreal Canada
04 Durham NH
05 Boston MA
06 New York NY
07 New York NY
08 New Brunswick NJ
10 Raleigh NC
11 Atlanta GA
13 Orlando FL
14 Miami FL
15 Tampa FL
16 Jacksonville FL
18 New Orleans LA
19 Dallas TX
20 Houston TX
21 San Antonio TX
23 San Diego CA
24 Los Angeles CA
25 San Francisco CA

SPOKEN DATES

January

17 Sydney Australia
18 Sydney Australia
19 Melbourne Australia
20 Melbourne Australia
21 Adelaide Australia
24 Brisbane Australia
26 Sydney Australia
Jan. 23 & 25 sang with Australian band The Hardons in Sydney

March
06 Dublin Ireland
09 Glasgow Scotland
12 London UK

May
04 Eau Claire WI
05 Chicago IL
06 Cleveland OH
08 Denver CO
09 Salt Lake City UT
28 Los Angeles CA

August
26 London UK

December
23 Los Angeles CA